Postborder City:
Cultural Spaces of Bajalta California

Postborder City:
Cultural Spaces of Bajalta California

Edited by
Michael Dear and Gustavo Leclerc

With contributions by
Jo-Anne Berelowitz
Néstor García Canclini
Lawrence A. Herzog
Selma Holo
Norma Iglesias
Phoebe S. Kropp
Héctor Manuel Lucero
Carlos Monsiváis
David Palumbo-Liu
Richard Cándida Smith

Published in association with
the Southern California Studies Center
of the University of Southern California.

ROUTLEDGE
NEW YORK AND LONDON

Published in 2003 by
Routledge
29 West 35th Street
New York, NY 10001
www.routledge-ny.com

Published in Great Britain by
Routledge
11 New Fetter Lane
London EC4P 4EE
www.routledge.co.uk

Copyright © 2003 by Taylor and Francis Books, Inc.

Routledge is an imprint of the Taylor and Francis Group.

Printed in the United Stated of America on acid-free paper.

10 9 8 7 6 5 4 3 2 1

Library of Congress Cataloging-in-Publication Data

Postborder city : cultural spaces of Bajalta California / Michael Dear & Gustavo Leclerc (editors) ; with contributions by Jo-Anne Berelowitz . . . [et al.].
    p. cm.
Includes bibliographical references and index.
    ISBN 0-415-94419-8 (HB : alk. paper) — ISBN 0-415-94420-1 (PB : alk. paper)
    1. California, Southern—Intellectual life. 2. Baja California (Mexico : State)—Intellectual life. 3. Arts and society—California, Southern. 4. Arts and society—Mexico—Baja California (State) 5. California, Southern—Relations—Baja California (Mexico : State) 6. Baja California (Mexico : State)—Relations—California, Southern. 7. Cities and towns—California, Southern. 8. Cities and towns—Mexico—Baja California (State) 9. Social change—California, Southern. 10. Social change—Mexico—Baja California (State) I. Dear, M. J. (Michael J.) II. Leclerc, Gustavo. III. Berelowitz, Jo-Anne.
    F867.P74 2003
    303.48'272207949—dc21

                                                     2003001961

Contents

Part I: Regional Groundedness

Part II: Regional Imaginations

Part III: Regional Hybridities

List of Illustrations: Mixed Feelings

Preface

Social change often profoundly transforms the way art is made. But just as importantly, art can transcend its social situatedness, and thereby alter the way we know ourselves; in this sense, art can change the future. This book examines the nexus between art and social change in one of the world's most dynamic urban places—the border region between the U.S. State of California and Mexico's Baja California—and reveals how a new kind of international city is producing a transnational, post-border art that is harbinger of an emerging social order.

The United States–Mexico border is a region in continuous flux. It is a borderspace in which cultural *hybridities* are formed, where people from different ethnicities and classes, cultural and geographic backgrounds come together daily to remake their lives. The border, the locus of transnational crossings, is part of the present monumental migrations bridging notions of past and present, home and abroad, global and local, and modernity and postmodernity. In these in-between (or liminal) spaces, elements of different worlds simultaneously coexist and mutate; this process is what we refer to as the *postborder condition*. It is transforming urban centers on both sides of the border, creating a blurred macrofrontier—a transcultural borderland—from northern Baja California to Southern California, and beyond.

The border region is not solely the concern of those two nations still struggling with the legacy of the 1848 Treaty of Guadalupe Hidalgo, which brought the United States–Mexico war to a formal conclusion. Today, Southern California (which used to be part of Mexico's *Alta California*) is a major destination for international immigration and trade, making it one of the largest, most diverse city-regions in the nation. A key feature of Southern California's urbanism is minoritization, the process by which no racial or ethnic category becomes large enough to command a majority in public dialogue, elections, etc. For its part, Baja California is itself a target of international attention—including migrants from all over Central America, and multinational corporations anxious to add to the maze of *maquiladora* developments at Mexico's northern border. As a consequence, Baja's principal cities, Tijuana and Mexicali, are among the fastest growing cities in Mexico.

In many senses, Southern California and Baja California—what may be called "Bajalta California," consisting of the Los Angeles/San Diego and Tijuana/Mexicali metropolitan regions—no longer represent *separate* growth poles within each nation. Instead, they have coalesced to become a single city-region, or regional city, that just happens to be bisected by an international border. This integrated city-region is as much in tune with international forces as with anything that happens on the domestic scene. Bajalta California is by now one of the planet's most important *world cities*.

Artists and critics, academic and curators, have long been involved in an attempt to understand the relationship between economic, social, and political life and the forms of cultural production characteristic of an urbanized, industrial society. In this post-Cold War era, national boundaries are eroding, and the global is evermore manifesting itself in the local. In what some people call a "postmodern" era, cultural production is less and less a parochial, peripheral, or subordinate function, but is increasingly understood as a primary expression of social upheaval as well as a force for change in its own right. The future of art and culture, of criticism and self-understanding, will depend on our ability to develop conceptual and analytical tools more in tune with the precepts of a postmodern society. The development of such tools is the major goal of this collection of essays, as realized through a focused examination of the prototypical postmodern border metropolis of Bajalta California.

This book's central focus is on the importance of place in the production of artistic and cultural hybrids. The exact meaning of the term "postborder condition" is explored by Michael Dear and Gustavo Leclerc, who establish a framework for understanding the relationship between place and cultural production, especially as viewed through the recent work of cross-border artists (Introduction).

In Part I of the book, "Regional Groundedness," contributors outline a conceptual and historical framework for understanding the postborder condition in Bajalta California. In Chapter 1, Carlos Monsiváis paints a vivid picture of the place of the border in every Mexican mind, taking the form of a constant awareness of the potential for crossing. From Tijuana to Matamoros, from Monterey to Mérida, popular consciousness of what Monsiváis terms the "portable border" is everywhere creating hybrids—in architecture, telenovelas, and so on. Monsiváis' lyric sketches of the dreams and dangers confronting border-dwellers (on both sides of *la línea*) provide an essential opening for our investigations. His notion of a portable border is essential to understanding the future of Mexico as a whole, and (by extension) its northern neighbor.

Then, in the next two chapters, abbreviated accounts of the region's urban history are presented. In Chapter 2, Phoebe Kropp and Michael Dear record the phenomenal rise of Los Angeles and Southern California to become America's second city. In Chapter 3, Héctor Manuel Lucero tells the equivalent story for Baja California's border cities, focusing especially on Tijuana and Mexicali. In both narratives, our emphasis is on demographic change and diversity, both past and present.

Part II of the collection, "Regional Imaginations," explores how demographic diversity finds expression in border art. Lawrence Herzog takes to the streets to read the landscapes of Tijuana. He reveals how the forces of globalization and free trade are transforming the architecture and built environment of Baja (Chapter 4). Next, Jo-Anne Berelowitz looks at the past forty years of art in the San Diego/Tijuana region, and explains the shift from the first belligerent assertions of Chicano identity in the 1960s to today's efflorescence of transitional cultural hybridities (Chapter 5). Norma Iglesias switches focus to frontier cinema and independent video to invoke the dynamic and conflicted identities wrapped up in film representations of the border (Chapter 6).

The first two parts of this book examine the urban context for border art, and the kind of art that is being produced in this place. In Part III, "Regional Hybridities," contributors consider the emergent future of art and culture in a postborder Bajalta California. Richard Cándida Smith explores the persistent national rootedness of two border artists, one in Los Angeles and the other in Mexicali, to tease out the personal ambiguities and stimulus comprising a postborder condition (Chapter 7). David Palumbo-Liu next takes an important step away from the specificities of the United States–Mexico border (Chapter 8). He examines evidence that the postborder condition is, in fact, a global phenomenon that is related to changes in how nation-states operate, as well as heightened personal awareness of worldwide hybridization. This provocative extension of the border condition (beyond *la línea*) finds further support and elaboration in Néstor García Canclini's concluding reflections on the postborder condition as it pervades the field of cultural studies (Chapter 9).

The many illustrations throughout this book are much more than decoration. They serve as concrete manifestations of hybridity and postmodernity. They are parallel texts that represent the transcendence of gender, generation, race and ethnicity, national origin, and sexual orientation (even as they are necessarily composed of fragments of these elements). Such art is not a simple consequence of geographic adjacency, nor even of mixing; instead it involves the manufacture of something new. The true cultural hybrid represents a cosmopolitanism without precedence. In these images, we observe the tangible imaginings of something original, a postborder condition indicative of an emerging world order.

(Photo Credit for Preface Illustrations: Eunice Miranda)

Acknowledgments

We are most indebted to the writers and artists who collaborated to produce this book. Over a period of three years, they have come together in a spirit of curiosity, excitement, and experimentation to produce an original vision of art and culture in a postborder world.

At the University of Southern California's Southern California Studies Center, Héctor Lucero played a large role in organizing meetings, tracking contributions, and assembling the final manuscript, as well as contributing his own essay to the volume. Additional support was provided by Richard Parks, assistant director of the Southern California Studies Center, as well as Django Sibley, Dallas Dishman, Ana Uribe, Charisse Smith, Kristy Amorn-kul, and Syuzi Tadevosyan.

Richard Cándida Smith was instrumental in the project's inception, and acted as an intellectual sounding-board as the project developed. Richard met Michael Dear in 1995–1996, when they were both fellows at Stanford's Center for Advanced Study in the Behavioral Sciences. In many ways, this volume is a tribute to the long-lasting friendships and collaborations that the Center makes possible. Another Stanford 1995–1996 fellow was Jennifer Wolch, who also provided critical insight into the project.

Selma Holo, director of USC's Fisher Gallery, has been a strong champion of this project since its inception. This book would not have been possible without her support, intellectual insight, and energy. The staff of the Fisher Gallery, including Kay Allen, Matt Driggs, Jennifer Jaskowiak, Jeanette La-Vere, Ariadni Liokatis, and Kevin Parker, helped immeasurably toward the realization of this project. In its earliest stages, Suzana Bautista was responsible for a prodigious amount of research on contemporary art and artists in

Baja California. John Lodge took most of the photographs in the artists' portfolio following Chapter 1, which are reproduced with the kind permission of the Fisher Gallery and the artists.

Translations from the Spanish were by Sofía Ruiz-Alfaro (Chapter 1) and Chelo Alvarez (Chapter 9).

We were much encouraged in our explorations by Luis Ituarte and Tomás Ybarra-Frausto, both of whom have a wealth of knowledge and experience in artistic and cultural matters.

Thanks to all the individuals and agencies who granted permission to use the images that adorn this volume. Charles Merewether and Tyson Gaskill of the Getty Research Institute were especially generous with their time and expertise. Michele Urton, archivist at LA's Center for the Study of Political Graphics, made special efforts to guide us through the Center's wonderful collections.

At Routledge, David McBride offered continuing support and invaluable criticism. Comments by Claire Fox and one other anonymous reviewer significantly improved the original manuscript. It was a pleasure to work with the Routledge team, especially editorial assistant Angela Chnapko and production editor Brandy Mui.

Financial support for the artists and writers engaged in this project was provided by the following:

The James Irvine Foundation
Mexico–U.S. Fideicomiso/Fund for Culture
The Rockefeller Foundation
U.S. National Endowment for the Arts
USC Arts Initiative
USC Fisher Gallery
USC Southern California Studies Center
USC Zumberge Faculty Innovation Award
The Warhol Foundation.

USC's President Steven B. Sample, Provost Lloyd Armstrong Jr., and college dean Joseph Aoun deserve special mention for their material and moral support of the Southern California Studies Center at USC.

We are sincerely grateful to all these artists and writers, agencies and individuals who helped bring this project to completion.

Foreword

Some years ago, Michael Dear and I began a conversation on the relationship between art and place. At the time, I was just completing a manuscript (*Beyond the Prado*) that examined the role of museums in democratic Spain after Franco; and Michael and Gustavo Leclerc were about to publish a book on popular culture in Latino Los Angeles (*Urban Latino Cultures: la vida latina en L.A.*). We became intrigued with contemporary transformations in Mexican society as reflected in its art, artists, critics, collectors, museums, and galleries. One result of our collaboration is this book, edited by Michael and Gustavo, which examines the place of art in the border regions connecting Southern California and Baja California.

Needless to say, the notion that *place* is important in artistic and cultural production is not original to our work. All art is a regional process. The groundedness of cultural production has by now been demonstrated for a variety of times, places, and media. For instance, Richard Cándida Smith's *Utopia and Dissent* (1995) explained the relationship between California's artistic culture and American social thought. The collection of essays edited by Paul Karlstrom makes a similar case for California's modernist art (*On the Edge of America*, 1996), as does Peter Plagens' *Sunshine Muse: Art on the West Coast* (1974). Other international examples of this point include Carl Schorske's classic *Fin-de-Siècle Vienna: Politics and Culture* (1980) and Stephanie Barron's *Degenerate Art* (1991), which explored the fate of the artistic avant-garde in Nazi Germany.

Despite the manifest significance of the topic, books about cultural production in borderlands are rare; scarcer still are studies that simultaneously engage cultural production on both sides of a border. In the year 2000, Gustavo, Michael, and myself formally initiated a collaborative enterprise involving artists and cultural scholars from both sides of the United States–Mexico border. The project had two distinct but closely related components: an exhibition and a critical monograph. The purpose of the exhibition was to produce new art collaboratively, on both sides of the border, that was indicative of postborder cultural production. (See the portfolio of artists' work from the "Mixed Feelings" show that follows the Introduction of this volume.) The purpose of the book was to critically situate the genesis and potential of postborder art. Despite the strong interdependencies between the exhibition and book, each was conceived and executed as an independent project.

In search of collaborators, we deliberately transgressed boundaries of gender, race/ethnicity, generation, and national origin. Artists in the exhibition predominantly hail from Los Angeles and Tijuana, but in origin, they are Anglo-American, Mexican, Mexican-American, Chicano, African-American, and Asian-American. The book's contributors come from the University of Southern California, the University of California at Berkeley, San Diego State University, El Colegio de la Frontera Norte in Tijuana, the Universidad Autónoma Metropolitana—Izataplapa—in Mexico City, Stanford University, and the University of Pennsylvania. The essayists are architects and urbanists, geographers and historians, critics, and film and cultural studies scholars.

Since the project's inception, collaborating artists and writers met many times for work sessions that extended over several days, in Mexicali, Tijuana, and Los Angeles. The sessions were remarkable because artists were producing their work and essayists were developing their critiques simultaneously, within the synergistic context of the meetings. Smaller groups of participants also met informally outside the schedule to pursue their individual projects. This very special, even unique way of producing art and criticism has resulted in a book of striking originality. Given the volume and pace of change in the Southern California/ Baja California city-region, there can be few more important or more timely projects than this.

I am personally very excited by this artistic and scholarly project for two special reasons. First, because of its focus on identity in a postborder era, it convincingly examines how global and local events intersect, and become manifest in the work of the individual artists. Second, the project looks resolutely toward the future. Even though many of these essays trace the genealogy of a postborder art, they are not historical essays in a conventional sense. Instead, they persistently invite us to understand contemporary society through the lens of art, and force us to confront what art is saying about our collective futures.

Selma Holo
Director
Fisher Gallery
University of Southern California

The Postborder Condition
Art and Urbanism in Bajalta California

MICHAEL DEAR AND GUSTAVO LECLERC

Place matters. In the creation of artistic and cultural works, where you are, and at what time period, will have a constitutive effect on the kind of work you produce. Think of impressionist Paris, for example, or New York modernism, or fin-de-siècle Vienna. Especially during times of turmoil in social, economic, or political life, there are opportunities for a radically altered art. Such art is both a reflection of changing contexts but also an act of re-creation: it is an interpretive strategy and an opportunity to reimagine, even transcend, the future.

This book examines the link between the production of art and the altered conditions of the *borderlands* in the U.S. State of California and the Mexican State of Baja California. How are the profound social, political, and economic shifts in this international region being reflected in the region's cultural and artistic production? Are artists on both sides of the border engaged in creating new mental and material cartographies that proclaim our collective futures? To what extent do their projects reflect a *common* project constitutive of a "postborder" condition? And if so, is this project homogeneous, fractured, or something else?

In 1848, the Treaty of Guadalupe Hidalgo brought an end to the hostilities between Mexico and the United States of America. Under its terms, Mexico ceded to the United States approximately one-third of its territory,

1

including the land called Alta (or Upper) California. Baja (or Lower) California remained under Mexican sovereignty, while Alta California entered the Union as the State of California. Before the ink had dried on the Treaty, gold was discovered near Sutter's Fort, and California was plunged into its unstoppable, helter-skelter transition to global prominence. Baja California, in contrast, became part of Mexico's neglected periphery, its major urban centers (Tijuana and Mexicali) becoming more linked to the fortunes of California than those of their own nation.

By the year 2000, Los Angeles was the second most populous urban region in the United States. The five-county metropolitan area (including Los Angeles, Orange, Riverside, San Bernardino, and Ventura counties) had over 16 million inhabitants. The San Diego region had 1.5 million people. Tijuana and Mexicali (with about 2 million and 1 million people, respectively) were among the fastest growing cities in Mexico—powered largely by the growth of the maquiladora economy—and a hotbed of political experimentation and change. The Los Angeles–San Diego–Tijuana–Mexicali metropolis should now be regarded as a single, integrated urban system of global significance. This emerging world city is dominated by an important demographic trend: the "Latinization" of Southern California. As the population of Latino origin swells (primarily as a result of natural increase, as well as migration from Mexico), we may be witnessing the de facto reunification of Alta and Baja California, in the global metropolis we refer to as "Bajalta" California.

In practical terms, Bajalta California has never before been a truly integrated region. During pre-Columbian times the western coastlands of Northern and Central America were home to a wide variety of indigenous peoples who for the most part lived independently from one another. The Spanish conquest forcibly imposed colonial practices of permanent settlements, town-building, agriculture, religion, and so on. But the Spanish foothold on the region was as precarious and fragile as the far-flung missions and garrisons they established in the region. After Mexico gained independence in 1821, Alta and Baja California become integrated into the Mexican empire, even though they were neglected and peripheral to the concerns of a turbulent emerging nation. Soon the belligerent claims of Mexico's northern neighbor became more pressing, and were not to be satisfied until the Treaty of 1848, when Baja and Alta California were once again split—this time by an international border.

Since 1848, the State of California and the State of Baja California have been on distinct yet convergent historical trajectories. San Francisco, and later Los Angeles, grew rapidly to national and international prominence. Tijuana and the other cities of Baja developed more slowly. As we shall see in Chapters 2 and 3, growth in Southern California often acted as a spur to development south of the border. And as the twentieth century evolved, Baja California and the State of California became increasingly integrated, most prominently through the migration of farm laborers and their families from Mexico into the United States. By the end of the century, many cities in the U.S. southwest were approaching Mexican/Latino majorities, and the international border was being trodden by the footprints of millions of people regularly crossing it to pursue their lives. The livelihoods of border dwellers have obviously altered significantly since 1848, but it remains to be seen how much the "postborder" region is still characterized by coercion and disenfranchisement of its inhabitants.

This new place, this single metropolis that just happens to be bisected by an international boundary, is the focus of our study. It is huge, densely populated, and complicated; it is multicentered, multicultural, and multilingual. It is a world city of increasing national and international significance. (California alone has the fifth largest economy in the world, ahead of France and Italy.) In this volume, we are seeking to understand the interdependent relationships among place, art, and culture. Unfortunately, there are few signs guiding us in this inquiry. In her far-sighted examination of culture and politics at the United States/Mexico borderlands, Claire Fox points out that the border as a place has received only passing attention in cultural studies, which have tended to favor the border as an abstract metaphor for transnational studies.[1] Such works are rarely site specific, instead they regard borders as markers of "hybrid or liminal subjectivities."[2] Hence, although the relationship between place and culture is readily conceded, there are few mental or material maps of border cultures. Our cartographies will perforce be something new.[3]

Place and Culture

Many artists and cultural workers recognize the significance of *place* in their work. In interviews with artists, Barbara Isenberg uncovered the many dimensions of California as an inspirational milieu. For instance, Robert Irwin was born in Long Beach and lived in Los Angeles (L.A.) before moving to San Diego in 1988. He expressed his delight in the playful experimentation that California made possible:

> Artists in California have a sense of humor, a little levity about what we do. . . . Growing up in California was a footloose and fancy-free sort of thing. You're an incredible optimist, even to the point of being Pollyannaish. . . .[4]

Southern California allowed Irwin a valuable freedom:

> The beauty of growing up in California . . . is that you have very little dead weight. All the things that New Yorkers would say to me was wrong with Califor-

nia—the lack of culture, place, sense of city and all that—is exactly why I was here. It was very possible to entertain the future here.[5]

Irwin makes clear that Californians approach the world differently,[6] a point also made by theater/opera/film director Peter Sellars:

> This is the place where people have come to try new things. It's the newest edge of America, whatever that's going to be. New York and Chicago remind you of what America was. In California, the question is, what will America be?[7] . . . If you're interested in the future of this country, you have to deal with L.A.[8]

Needless to say, the same places have different meanings for individuals. Amalia Mesa-Bains, a Chicana scholar and artist, who was born in Santa Clara, CA, speaks movingly of California seen through different eyes:

> I think it's hard for people to understand that all the time California has been California, it's always been Mexico. There is a Mexico within the memory, the practices, the politics, the economy, the spirituality of California. It's invisible to everyone but Mexicans. We've known it, we see it, we live it, but Californians don't know it.[9]

Writers, too, take their inspiration from place. Novelist/ teacher Carolyn See reveals an appreciation for the abstract qualities of *space*, as well as the paradoxically generic qualities consequent upon the specific groundedness in her fictional writing:

> When I talk to my students about writing, I talk about characters and plot, space and time, but, most important, geography. Place has always been where you start. The more specific you can get about a particular place, the better chance you have of making it be universal and of really grounding it.[10]

The artistic inspiration provided by place is, then, a rich and delicate well-spring. It permits freedom and inspiration; it invites the future. Yet it also furnishes an essential groundedness that possesses deep archeologies of memory, as well as providing a frame of reference that enables us to make sense of a work.

The voices of artists begin to hint at the complexities of "regional groundedness," i.e., the significance of the place from which they operate. But how does place *work*? Manifestly, it operates at many different levels: as an abstract "container" for artistic production and diffusion, and as a crucible nurturing creative processes of all kinds; as a subject of, and inspiration for the work itself; and as a spark or dynamic that goes beyond the individual artist to catalyze regional, national, even international movements or schools of thought, both within the realms of art and the broader civic culture. Let's examine some of these notions in more detail.

On a most general level, place has an abstract quality as *container* for human behaviors. In this essay, we shall use the term *space* to identify this abstraction, and distinguish it from *place*, which is what humans make of space once they occupy it. Thus, humans may be said to manufacture place out of space, an idea that owes much to Henri Lefebvre.[11] Places, especially cities, represent sociocultural milieus on a large scale, comprising a concatenation of events that combine to manufacture a particular *zeitgeist*. Perhaps the most famous example of *city as crucible of innovation* is fin-de-siècle Vienna. In his widely admired study, Carl Schorske argued that Vienna, "with its acutely felt tremors of social and political disintegration," proved to be a fertile breeding ground for radical shifts in painting, music, philosophy, psychoanalysis, economics, architecture, and urban planning — even though the protagonists in each field "scarcely knew each other."[12]

Place acts too as an *inspiration* for art. In his landmark study of visual arts and poetry in California from 1925 to 1975, Richard Cándida Smith accords great weight on the State's relative *isolation* as a stimulus to creativity, linking this to an anticipation that artists were on the threshold of a renaissance, of bringing a "new culture into the world."[13] As Smith emphasizes, it was not that California artists desired isolation, but that the *tabula rasa* represented by California offered the opportunity to strike out against the primacy of New York and Europe.[14] Similar sentiments are expressed in Paul Karlstrom's study of California Modernist art during the period 1900–1950. According to Karlstrom, during this period California artists were stimulated by "distance," and the consequent need to "reinvent traditions for a new landscape and society."[15] The specifics of place also become the *subject* of art. For instance, Scott and Rutkoff revealed how early twentieth-century realists embraced New York City, "making its variety and life their subject."[16] Most notably, photographer Alfred Steiglitz saw New York as "a great modern machine, which, if carefully observed and recorded, offered artists a unique opportunity to comprehend the modern."[17] Early twentieth-century landscape painting in California may be regarded as an analogous gesture toward the artistic subject.[18]

Cities, and other places, can be transformed into a broad locus of dynamic artistic and social change through the activities and synergies of an *ensemble of cultural producers* that gather together in a particular place and time. The process of art, and its diffusion beyond the immediate locale in which it is produced, depends on what Sharon Zukin has called an "artistic mode of production."[19] In this, cultural production and consumption are combined via a set of market practices, which often link the culture industry with exogenous urban processes, such as heritage conservation and urban renewal. It is no coincidence that the past 30 years have seen the birth of more than 600 art museums in the United States alone, with equal proliferation in Europe.[20] These projects have often been undertaken as regeneration schemes for older neighborhoods, or (as in the case of the Bilbao Guggenheim) to resurrect a national/regional culture. Harvey Molotch,[21] in a pathbreaking study of how art works in a regional economy, demonstrates the design synergies among L.A.'s industrial/cultural producers, including movie-making, tourism, food, architecture, furniture, and automobiles. He underscores how much of the ferment in any artistic mode of production is actually stimulated by forces beyond the established institutions of exhibition, sale, etc.—a point also made by Scott and Rutkoff in the rise of New York modernism.[22]

Making Material and Mental Geographies

Art and culture are not solely about the materiality of place; they also reflect the perceptual cartographies of its inhabitants. So we must make an important distinction between the "hard" and "soft" city, between the structures of the built environment and the interpretive, perceptual constructs present in the mind of every urban dweller. The relationship between the material and the mental is complex, even indeterminate. As Jonathan Raban recounts, the newcomer to a city initially confronts the hard city, but soon

> the city goes soft; it awaits the imprint of an identity. For better or worse, it invites you to remake it, to consolidate it into a shape you can live in. . . . Decide who you are, and the city will again assume a fixed form around you. Decide what it is, and your own identity will be revealed.[23]

So, how you live and who you are depends upon how your mental map of the city relates to its physical form. An individual's curious, sometimes cautious perambulations through an urban setting depend upon a myriad factors, guided by the imprints of race/ethnicity, class, and gender, as well as access to resource-rich or resource-poor environments. Hence, our account of a postborder condition must also, of necessity, deal with the material physicality of border landscapes as well as the mental maps of its inhabitants. Our investigation must confront the hard edges of the fence between countries, as well as dreams of crossing the line.

Hard Borders

The built environments of the postborder megalopolis—the *maquiladoras*, fortified border crossings, *colonias*, and the like—are being created by a multitude of forces operating at global, national, and local scales. In general terms, the principal dynamics on both sides of the United States/Mexico border presently include the following:

- *globalization*, which we understand as the tendency toward a worldwide market economy (facilitated by the institutional frameworks of the World Trade Organization and NAFTA), and dominated by transnational corporations and transnational criminal organizations;

- *network society*, an associated global economic restructuring based on telecommunications and the information revolution—manifest in Mexico by the *maquiladora* industries, and in the United States as the rise of the service economy;
- *hybridization*, understood as a cultural and racial/ethnic mixing brought about by a new world geopolitical order (especially since the end of the Cold War), and the subsequent massive international migrations; and
- *privatization*, a reordering of claims and obligations in society that presently favors private civil society over the public realm; together with the other dynamics already noted, this trend is creating and exacerbating an unequal world, in which the gap between rich and poor is widening.

Needless to say, these tendencies reveal themselves in different ways in different settings. For instance, the rise of a network society is more advanced and has penetrated more deeply in the relatively affluent United States; and although privatization has taken the form of governments' shedding their assets and responsibilities in both countries, the impact of the retreat from a formal welfare state has been much more keenly felt in the United States. In truth, people and institutions on both sides of the border are experiencing the simultaneous overlay of these macrotrends on their everyday lives and activities. Every place is being obliged to absorb the material consequences of globalization, the information revolution, hybridization, and socioeconomic polarization. All four tendencies operate together to manufacture new urban landscapes, including the burgeoning world city, cybercity, hybrid city, and dual city. They also drastically modify existing cities, as Larry Herzog shows for the case of Tijuana in Chapter 4.

The challenges and opportunities confronting cities on both sides of the border as a consequence of these developments are often manifest as joint international issues. They include the urgent search for practical solutions to cross-border waste disposal problems around the San Diego–Tijuana region, and the pollution problems associated with extensive agricultural operations on both sides of the border in the Imperial Valley. International solutions are also being negotiated with respect to sharing the waters of the Colorado River, and the proposed development of an international airport to serve both countries simultaneously at the San Diego–Tijuana border. Of course, the constant backdrop to all these developments is the increasingly militarized international border—*la línea*—with its high-tech armaments and border patrol. It slices literally through the lives of people who must cross daily for work, is an unforgiving gauntlet for those who seek to cross without papers, and is a ubiquitous, ever-present shadow for everyone else facing the prospect of crossing or not crossing.

Soft Borders

The physicality of the hard metropolis matters only as much as the soft city of its inhabitants. The soft city measures ways in which residents construct mental maps to perceive, interpret, and interact with the built environment. In this thin veneer-like zone where the soft and hard cities converge, the process of creativity begins.

Along the Mexico–United States border there is now an unprecedented mixing, producing many new cultural and aesthetic forms. For instance, there are more Chinese restaurants in Tijuana than any other city in Mexico, and the desert region outside Mexicali is home to many people of Middle-Eastern origin. Nearby, on the U.S. side of the border (and in Tijuana on the weekends) there are military and surfing cultures. The booming Mexican *corrido* industry is headquartered in Los Angeles.[24] Tijuanenses and San Diegans can watch television channels that are broadcast from either side of the border in many languages. Mexican movies become box-office hits in the United States, including for instance *Amores Perros* (2000, "Love's a Bitch," Alejandro Gonzalez Iñarritú) and *Y Tu Mama También* (2000, Alfonso Cuarón). As Norma Iglesias demonstrates (in Chapter 6), these cultural interactions have the power to transform the perceptions of residents on both sides of the border. Indeed, since the election of President Vicente Fox, Mexico's drive toward a cultural diplomacy with the United States has reached new peaks.[25]

This process of knowing and/or seeing people from around the world instills a cosmopolitan demeanor into many border residents. Without having to travel far, they become international simply by crossing the nearby border for school, shopping, or social events. Changes in U.S. immigration and trade laws during recent decades helped generate large streams of diverse people and goods in motion. These human streams run in both directions, with the potential for repeated contact, including indigenous people selling their wares on Tijuana streets as well as middle-class Chilangos (natives of Mexico City) living in newly fabricated homes in Las Vegas. These connecting streams create interesting, though sometimes contentious mixes out of previously segregated cultural forms. Transnational flows across the border and through adjacent cities create a cultural heat, the friction from a metaphoric and literal rubbing together that releases tremendous creative energy. For artists, this cultural heat is a source of aesthetic inspiration, as they juggle the soft and hard cities, mixing the form of built environment with the mental and emotional overlays of Bajalta California.

The Rise of Cosmopolitanism and Cultural Hybridities

Some years ago, on a cool afternoon in Santa Monica, a group of Mexican señoras were standing on the sidewalk, gathered around an old brown

Chevy. Inside the faded car with its open trunk were many lumpy packages of food wrapped carefully in newspaper. They contained items such as snowy-white *queso fresco,* Mexican *chocolate,* and spicy red *chorizo.* The women began picking up their orders while a no-nonsense *jefe* spoke (in Zapotecan) their new orders into his cell phone. He was acting like a smooth-talking, cell-phone-distracted Hollywood producer making momentous movie deals. This curbside entrepreneur explained that he was originally from Oaxaca but was now based in nearby Culver City. He had a regular car route selling Oaxacan goods throughout L.A.'s Westside, and offered a business card, inviting us to call if we ever needed anything.

Such scenes allow a brief glimpse into the many small changes occurring throughout the Californias. These changes, primarily a result of the region's (re)latinization or (re)mexicanization process, accumulate to create a quiet revolution of hidden informal businesses, innovative social networks, appropriated technology, and rapid communication and mobility. Such changes are layered and infinitely repeated across the landscape. They are slowly congealing to create a new *cosmopolitanism,* the lost cousin of globalization and a childhood friend of postcolonialism. Initially understood as referring to the fundamental interests of humanity as a whole, free from nation-state affiliations, "cosmopolitanism" now encompasses many varieties of transnational experience.[26] No longer universal and privileged, cosmopolitanisms are now "plural and particular."[27] They are occurring from the bottom up, consisting of strategies through which people adjust, survive, and even thrive in this new world. Cosmopolitanism is neither European based nor class conscious, but instead is primarily grounded in an immigrant, diasporic experience of transnational crossings. The transformation from colonial subjugation to independence and the development of a globally connected economy have enormously complicated notions of identity and affiliation, and altered the meaning of citizenship. (These critically important points are at the heart of our understanding of the postborder condition, and are more fully examined in Part III of this book.) Cosmopolitanism's postmodern geographies do not uphold historic structures of power and knowledge, but daily reinvent new pathways for living, for personal and collective visions, and for sharing knowledge.

Ironically, the improvisations and contingencies of cosmopolitanism often remain invisible to much of Southern California's population. Prejudice blinds many people to the cultural shifts happening around them. Although the denial of emerging cultural diversity was more pronounced in the early 1990s, some people remain reluctant to admit that there are other valid experiences alongside their own. However, for many contemporary artists in Southern and Baja California, the cosmopolitan fusions (of here/there, present/past, and high/low) that are the by-products of rapid and chaotic changes in the region represent the tangible raw materials that they utilize to create a vibrant new aesthetic vocabulary. This invented, mutant language provides an important text for reading the altered society around us. Yet it remains to be seen if border artists have the collective power to serve as navigators in this uncharted journey.

Art and culture in contemporary Bajalta California are products of the tension between the twin poles of the United States and Mexico, or more precisely, between metropolitan Los Angeles–San Diego and the Tijuana–Mexicali urban agglomeration. According to Néstor García Canclini,[28] two tendencies fuel the consequent hybridization: the dislocation and deterritorialization of peoples and activites. The former is linked to migration, the latter to globalization. Each contributes to that emblematic border phenomenon: *hybrid cultures*—which emerge when something original is created in a new place, combining cultural and material forms from multiple origins (see his discussion in Chapter 9 of this volume). For Canclini, Tijuana is one of the major laboratories of postmodernity; it is Homi Bhaba's[29] "third space," the liminal place between cultures. For Guillermo Gómez-Peña,[30] the Tijuana–San Diego border is "the gap between two worlds," a space that allows for literal crossing, spiritual passage, struggle, and transgression. The border space holds a permanent potential for crossing or not crossing; it forms a pervasive presence in border-dwellers' lives. It is where alternative mental cartographies must continuously be recast and contested.

Our belief is that cosmopolitanism and hybridity are the constitutive elements of the postborder condition. If society is understood as a "time-space fabric" upon which the processes of human life are embroidered, then cosmopolitanism and hybridity can be imagined as stretching the dimensions of this fabric into hitherto unforeseen dimensions. Fredric Jameson[31] calls the consequent geography a "postmodern hyperspace," whose time–space coordinates we can so far only dimly perceive. But an effective reading of this hyperspace and its coordinates—especially as manifest in postborder spaces—is at the core of our problematic. It requires a theorizing of chronological contemporaneity and geographic adjacency, i.e., of the simultaneity of objects in time and space. More succinctly, it requires a theory of periodization and of regionalization. Obviously, the mere coexistence of two objects in space or time is no guarantee of their interrelatedness; and yet, coexistence can rarely be totally random, even if connectedness between objects may be tangential and difficult to articulate. Equally important, for our present purposes, is what happens when two previously separate objects are brought together in spatiotemporal juxtaposition. What does coerced or accidental adjacency and contemporaneity do to them?

Another piece of our puzzle is the problem of reading "culture." David Palumbo-Liu[32] emphasizes the cluttered nature of the concept:

> On the one hand, [culture] may designate a set of values, beliefs, and practices specific to a particular group; on the other, the production of art and media ob-

jects that variously mediate the representation of values, beliefs, and practices. Within our understanding of culture we include the set of material practices and apparatuses that are involved in the production, enacting, and reproduction of culture.

For now, we are content to understand culture as referring to beliefs, material representations, and institutional apparatuses; in short, culture concerns us, our stuff, and how we use it to define who we are. In a globalizing world, identity, cultural representations, and their attendant institutions are being radically altered. Although some insist that economic and political spheres remain resolutely bound to local and national places, the cultural sphere may be becoming increasingly uncoupled from such stable geographic points of reference (which is *not* to say that geography is becoming obsolete). According to Palumbo-Liu,[33] "the cultural realm is *the* most globalized arena," since "most of our lives' meaning-producing activities and transactions take place in that sphere," a position that he develops in Chapter 8 of this volume.

There can be little doubt that the political, economic, and sociocultural spheres are today being massively complicated by global interaction. Arjun Appardurai described contemporary "glocal" cultural flows as producing five landscapes: ethnoscapes, mediascapes, technoscapes, finanscapes, and ideoscapes. These are the consequences of (respectively) demographic change, the influence of the media, technological change, capital flows, and ideological diversification. As these spheres overlap, merge, and divide, the consequent hybrid cultures are generated contingently and nonpermanently; they are unevenly distributed through time and space. Like air or water masses of different temperatures, cultures can flow swiftly together, creating new currents charged with the potential for disruption and conflict, as well as interaction and fusion. The metaphors of flow and fire, of *el flujo* and *el fuego*, capture the fluidity, energy, and synergies involved in the production of cultural hybrids. Unexpected adjacencies and synchronicities in cultures release energy and heat; previously separate traditions flow together, sometimes retaining their separate textures (at least for a while), but at other times merging swiftly into a single flow. Once you step into the rivers of culture, the waters are forever altered; the river adjusts, but the flow continues with new energy.

The Place of Art in California

In twentieth-century California, nonrigidities in cultural norms and practices allowed for greater artistic and political experimentation. Such experiments simultaneously involved breaking apart traditional modalities and setting down new roots. In California (as in fin-de-siècle Vienna), artists participated in the "place-making" process, and in forming a new identity from the spaces around them. Among the many examples we could cite, the birth of the counterculture, the rise of women artists, and the Chicano movement in the second half of the twentieth century are especially persuasive.

The manufacture and diffusion of artistic innovation are questions that permeate Cándida Smith's examination of visual arts and poetry in mid-twentieth-century California. As we have seen, California's isolation heightened the sense of experimentation. Only later, after World War II, did the State's counterculture explode into national consciousness, involving the anti-Vietnam war movement, sexual liberation, a drug culture, and generic antiauthoritarianism. By the 1960s, Californian artists were regarded nationally (even internationally) as both authors and representative examples of shifts towards "(1) greater frankness in public expression about varieties of individual behavior, particularly as related to sexuality; (2) distrust of public life as a persistent threat to the primacy of personal experience; [and] (3) fracturing of a unified American identity based on shared myths of a common natural history."[34]

Important in the emergence of the art of the counterculture was the proliferation of California art schools during the latter half of the twentieth century. These experimental pressure-cookers became a mecca for students who were also attracted by a wealth of nonprofit exhibition spaces that provided the opportunity for exhibition free from commercial pressures. The relatively undeveloped California art market meant that artists' explorations experiments were not hampered by commodifying forces. These characteristics were also significant in the rise of women artists in the period 1950–2000.[35] The universal impact of their art was accounted for by Daniela Salvioni in this way:

> In the second half of the twentieth century, California became a supportive environment for artists. California's culture of experimentation, its proximity to centers of technology and media, its role as gateway for a myriad of immigrants, its history of social activism and alternative institutions—all contributed to a climate of unprecedented openness in which sizable numbers of women from diverse cultural groups found ways to establish new aesthetic practices of their own. In multifaceted ways, individual strands of autobiographical discovery have been recast as part of the identity of an entire culture.[36]

Salvioni adds that the "theme of space—physical, corporeal, spiritual, and virtual—reverberates throughout the art produced in California in the later half of the twentieth century."[37]

A similar shift in national consciousness was achieved by communities of Chicano artists in Southern California during the 1960s. They were among the first to theorize about the "Bajalta" connection, using mythical and aesthetic forms. Their work was inspired by the Texan scholar, Americo Paredes, who in the 1930s proposed new ways of understanding transnational identities and a future condition of decolonialization. Many Chicanos have since talked about the United States/Mexico–North/South relationship in terms of "Aztlan," the mythical homeland of the Aztecs. Though there are many opinions, most consider the original Aztec homeland to have been in the southwestern part of the United States. There, a powerful Aztec prophet saw a vivid vision of an eagle and a serpent on a placid blue lake, prompting him to lead his people on a long exhausting journey to Tenochtitlan. The relationship between North and South, Chicanos and Mexicans, Aztlan and Aztecs, was explored in the exhibition, *Aztlan*, at the Los Angeles County Museum of Art in 2001.[38] It chronicled the exchanges between Mesoamerica and the U.S. southwest—of populations, material culture, agricultural innovations, and belief systems—over many millennia to the present day. Against a backdrop of 1960s labor unrest led by Cesar Chavez and Dolores Huerta, plus important cultural movements such as *El Teatro Campesino*, Chicano artists and activists expanded the idea of Aztlan to include themselves as a separately identifiable, though connected generation. They thus created a place-based identity and history, distinguishable from Anglo-American iconography and roots in Europe.[39] The idea of Aztlan began as a local, place-based cultural and artistic philosophy, but later became the catalyst for a nationwide political movement for social change. It continues to have a lasting impact on the production of art in the Californias, as Jo-Anne Berelowitz explores in Chapter 5.

But what is the place of the Californias in the current world? What is the place of the postborder? In 1974, in one of the earliest sustained assessments of West Coast art, Peter Plagens agreed that geography mattered in what artists created and in what happened to their work. However, in a 1999 postscript to the reissue of his study, Plagens opines: "The influence of regional geography has declined precipitously since 1974, partly because artists have simply willed it to be less influential."[40] By this he means that artists have by now shrugged off their provincialism; they now possess goals that extend beyond "newly embodying a regional aesthetic."[41] Add to this the proliferation of museum outlets and the peripatetic nature of contemporary artists and you have a situation in which "geography is a much less significant factor in . . . West Coast art than it was a quarter-century ago."[42] In his general overview of twentieth-century art, Peter Conrad concurs: by the century's end, "The world I describe has effectively made both time and place redundant."[43] Though some will concur with the notion that the millennial globalization, the advent of cyberspace, etc., have resulted in time–space compression (implying an homogenization of capitalist connectivity and process on a global scale), we dispute the notion that time and place have lost their purchase on social life, including the processes of cultural production. For our purposes, the spaces of the borderlands are among the most important *places* in the world today. Not only are they the *genius loci* of radical shifts in demographics, economics, politics, and society, they are also pivotal moments in an evolving artistic mode of production.

Art in Postborder Bajalta California

To survive the Borderlands
You must live *sin fronteras*
Be a crossroads.[44]

The use of the term "border art" is contentious and problematic. Semantically, it tends (initially, at least) to marginalize all art so designated, implying a peripheral location separate from (and ignored by) the core. In this sense, all Mexican and U.S. art becomes subordinate to the projects and judgments of Mexico City and New York City! Further, the term leads to intense disputes over *whose* art is border art. Is Bajalta art defined by (say) Mexican, California, or Chicano artists? Or axiomatically by them all? Moreover, no matter how powerful the analytical import of a cultural label, too often it can be quickly coopted as a marketing device, or a political convenience, and thereby lose its cultural purchase.[45]

Nevertheless, borders have been an inescapable part of the global geopolitical life of the twentieth century. They present real barriers between nation-states, which jealously (and all too often, lethally) protect the traditions engendered within them. Such protectionism may often be the inspiration for art, as in the work of Mexicali artist Ramón Tamayo (discussed in Chapter 8). It is also true that nation-state boundaries have become increasingly permeable since the Berlin Wall fell in 1989, followed by large-scale migrations in many parts of the world. Curator Howard N. Fox describes California, for instance, as "a clamorous gathering of peoples in diaspora,"[46] and he approvingly quotes cultural historian José David Saldívar's "anti-geopolitical" sensibilities:

> Cultural forms can no longer be exclusively located within the border-patrolled boundaries of the nation-state.[47]

In this essay, we propose the notion of "postborder art," understood as *a new cultural aesthetic being created in the in-between spaces, and manufactured from the archeologies of past and emerging identities.* Or, to put it another way, postborder art is *a representational aesthetic concerned with the production of hybridities in the liminal/interstitial boundaries between political ideologies.*

We make no claims to define a completed historical moment, measured by specific times and spaces, nor will we attempt to fully specify the directions of a postborder art. For the moment, we simply take our lead from a demonstrable convergence in, and self-awareness regarding, a distinctly postborder sensibility; from a new assertiveness concerning the significance of border art, artists, and markets; and from a rapid internationalizing of border artists, who are increasingly by-passing the traditional gatekeepers in New York City and Mexico City. Another important piece in the contempo-

rary artistic mode of production is the question of who controls the exhibition (and sale) of border art. Karen Mary Davalos has emphasized that all
U.S. museums are "shaped by notions of difference, nationalism, and politics of identity."[48] And she links this with those institutions' "persistent refusal to collect and exhibit objects from cultures beyond the mythical idea of
the [U.S] nation."[49] A very different exhibition practice becomes possible
when Mexicans and Mexican-Americans put themselves in charge of the
collection, display, and interpretation of art. Until such time as representational autonomy is acquired, however, the representational practices of people of color (according to Davalos) remain fragmented, occurring only at
"the cracks and fissures of structural and ideological power."[50]

At the heart of our inquiry is the question of *convergence* in cultural practices at the Bajalta border. The merging of flows (*el flujo*) into a distinctive,
powerful stream provides the dynamic for a postborder art. We end this in-
troductory chapter by sketching the principal styles of convergence evident
in the new work of some contemporary Bajalta artists.[51]

Identity: The Subject/Site of Convergence

The question of identity has been central to the art of the twentieth
century.[52] Claire Fox characterizes the border as a "contact zone" where the
terms of self-identification are "extremely relative," and where centuries of
complex histories and migrations have produced a "multilayered" social system.[53] Personal consciousness is formed from origins in remembered or
chimerical places. One's body is the primary (and ultimate) site of being and
engagement, of compliance and resistance. As they encounter the transforming effects of everyday life, bodies become sensuous yet critical, assim-
ilative yet assertive, displaced yet rooted. In both old and new places, the
body's performative actions are bound to perceptions and representations
of self, as well as the peculiarities of specific time and spaces.

L.A.-based artist Daniel Joseph Martínez probes questions of power,
multilayered social systems, and individual body and consciousness in his
piece entitled "Nallekaghnituten: Man Who Throws Rocks (An Event for an
a-Moralist as Parrhesias)" (2002). Referencing the form and motivation of
classical sculpture, Martínez has created a small (18-inch) figure that is a
near replica of himself, standing on a three-foot high, white pedestal (Plate
1). The figure is dressed in a worker's blue uniform, holding one rock close
to his side, another high over his head, seemingly posed for imminent release. Yet the missile is never launched. Instead the figure, rocks still in hand,
draws back precariously, in slow motion, almost to ground level. At the end
of the motion, the artist's loud laughter rings out, from a speaker in the
pedestal's base. In this pose, like a character from the movie *Matrix* (perhaps
even "The One"), the figure evades an imaginary stream of bullets. As in another recent movie, *Crouching Tiger, Hidden Dragon*, power over material

reality begins in the mind. Yet the figure's clothing and hand-held rocks recall real struggles against occupation (in Los Angeles, Belfast, or the West Bank), and the precarious place of bodies that resist. In an ironic gesture Martínez positions himself as hero, god, or icon, getting the last laugh. (More on Martínez's work is to be found in Chapter 8 of this volume.)

If confrontation is a consistent foundation in Martínez's work, then humor and trepidation are what springs to mind in the unexpected iconic unions in the art of Rubén Ortiz Torres. Originally from Mexico City but now resident in L.A., Ortiz is deeply engrossed in the stuff of everyday life, using wry humor in a sometimes fantastical reworking of the stereotypes in Mexican and Chicano cultures. Victor Zamudio-Taylor particularly noted the profusion of sources (film, comic books, music, etc.) and of historical referents (including baseball and pre-Columbian cultures) used by Ortiz to produce a transcultural "hall of mirrors" that undermines stereotypes and their injuries.[54] Much of Ortiz's recent work employs ultrahybrid movable forms based in existing elements of popular culture. Building on the Chicano Low Rider tradition he has focused on the idea and process of *customizing*, taking functional mundane machinery (usually old cars) and altering it into something both aesthetically and functionally extraordinary. In his installation, "Alien Toyz" (1997), Ortiz manufactures a car that disintegrates, isolating the aesthetic elements of low-rider hydraulics, and giving his car the ability to dance (to split, move up and down, spin, etc.) in hugely exaggerated movements.

In "The Garden of Earthly Delights" (2002), Ortiz pursues the unexpected intersection of extremes, using glittering car paint, chrome, and gold to customize an ordinary tractor lawn mower (Plate 2). Equipped with hydraulic systems, the everyday tool becomes a break-dancer. It works in sync with an original composition based on the sounds of various gardening implements, including noisy leaf-blowers. This piece can cut two ways with very different readings. One is as the artist intended, picturing workers taking their trade to a higher level, customizing the tools of their trade in the highly stylized, low-rider tradition. Their use of this particular aesthetic proclaims a new ownership over craft and profession. Yet the type of lawn mower Oritz has chosen also evokes another deeply embedded vision. This is associated with middle-class suburban guys riding around on weekends in tee shirts and shorts, a beer in the drink holder, a tummy reined in by an elastic waistband, and old rock jams howling out from the radio. Now consider what it might mean to have a low-rider lawn mowing tractor traversing suburbia. Suddenly those who have fled the city are confronted with an urban aesthetic that makes no apology for "not fitting in." The radio is blaring oldies or norteños, and what has previously been rigorously homogenized and pasteurized reveals inroads of color. Suburbia is now not only claimed by the settlers of white flight, but also by Chicano and Mexican immigrants, as well as myriad others. Who can imagine the mixed aesthetics as a rainbow of races joins the ranks of weekend barbequers in the backyard by the pool, or squashing into early morning carpools, which meander through streets with names like Glenoaks Way and Greenvalley Place? What really happens when two distinct (and maybe hostile) iconic cultural forms, such as the urban low-rider and the suburban front lawn, make contact? Do they get along, even like each other, and plan a second date? Or do they brandish fists to challenge difference "at home"?

The specific dynamics of manufacturing hybridity is also an important theme in the work of Mark S. Bradford. In his art, he portrays detailed physical textures of the soft and hard city, and questions the particular lenses through which we represent and interpret them. In combination with traditional art materials, such as canvas, paint, and rectangular planes, Bradford mixes graphics and materials from his immediate environment. Bradford explores the spaces "where new trajectories of black popular culture are performed,"[55] deliberately blurring the lives between high and low culture, and the divisions of class and culture. As part of the Studio Museum in Harlem's "Freestyle" exhibition of contemporary African-American art (2001), Bradford created a pair of sensuous tapestries, entitled "Enter and Exit the New Negro." Close inspection revealed the "textile" to be composed of an endless number of endpapers used to wave hair, their incandescent hues derived from cellophane haircolors. Using ordinary stuff from the workaday world, Bradford creates a sublime geometric grid of gradually shifting monotone colors.

In a recent painting entitled "Nasty Ass Pigeons" (2002), Bradford's layout references a generic urban landscape as seen from "a bird's eye view." He has superimposed on this grid a line of black silhouetted birds, like pigeons perched on a telephone wire as the sun drops below the horizon. For the viewers, a disjoint occurs when trying to locate themselves in relation to this scene. On one hand, you are looking down on a placid city. On the other, you are looking up from street level to see the birds on the narrow wire above. This discontinuity in positioning and perception emphasizes the difficulty in locating oneself within the soft and hard cities. As a viewer, one needs to absorb multiple perspectives simultaneously, and identify with diverse locations. By rearranging this overlapping spatial order, Bradford poses important questions about what happens when material and social frameworks are unhinged and recombined, and the role artists have in renegotiating these spatial and social formats.

In his installation, "Jericho" (2002), Bradford cryptically assembles objects related to hair and nail salons, and evokes in the viewer a voyeuristic longing for beauty (Plate 3). All the objects in the installation are slightly wrong—the mirrors are small/smudged/squared/placed together, rendering the reflected objects fragmented and repeated. The salon chair is raised eight feet above ground level, so that it is unattainable, yet the void of possibility becomes one of the strongest presences in the piece. Repeatedly, each element reaffirms the distance between the viewer and its particular history. Many of the objects were found by the artist and seem to exude an unintelligible story about their past experiences. Framing a doorway are ten white ceramic praying hands. Each finger is crowned with a long, intricately painted false fingernail. The dusty store signs on the floor pulse with yellow lights, illuminating words that one can nearly make sense of, but which then slip away from comprehension. When Bradford speaks of the various materials in his work and their origins, he weaves a tale of people's lives that are intertwined and yet contentious, untrusting, and laced with forbidden desire.

Even as Mark Bradford rebuilds separateness within the matrix of uneven hybridity, Norman Yonemoto excavates more deeply into personal identity in a diverse world, and discovers isolation there. The complexities of place in an emerging Information Society are the focus of Yonemoto's interior "anti-geography." In "Self-Portrait" (2002), he explores the notion of "self" in cyberspace by disrupting normalized forms of individual and collective representation (Plate 4). Through an examination of the body in relation to the Internet and the generic space of an office cubicle, Yonemoto focuses on the (dys)functions of place, most especially the issues and contradictions surrounding mobility and containment/emplacement. The Internet constructs a borderless, physically disconnected zone through which the artist may represent himself in any way, free from the common descriptors of ethnicity, class, gender, age, or (dis)ability. Suggesting the possibility of transcending place and identity, Yonemoto's subject remains, however, a sedentary, solitary person sitting in front of a computer screen. Even as he soars through the net's vast virtual space and speed, with its seemingly infinite possibilities for human connection and mobility, the subject (the artist, and viewer seated in a wheelchair facing the computer screen) cannot defy the confines of hard boundaries.

In "Self-Portrait," as in earlier works completed with his brother Bruce Yonemoto, the looming presence of a screen cannot be escaped. Particularly, in "Golden" (2000), the brothers coated a portable film projection screen (commonly used in classrooms) with gold leaf, thereby creating a pun on the Hollywood "silver screen" of their American childhood, and the gilded screens of their Asian heritage.[56] In a crueler irony, the stark, real-world cubicle of "Self-Portrait" contrasts viscerally, even overwhelmingly, with the superlative, infinite riches of the computer's virtual world. The juxtaposition of cubicle and screen suggests the permeability of another kind of border, the physical limits of the human body. It recalls the choice made by Hiro Protagonist (in Neal Stephenson's novel *Snow Crash*[57]) who elected to live in poverty in the real world (renting space in an Inglewood storage facility!) so he could afford to rent a prime location on the main street in the virtual world of Metaverse.[58] Sherry Turkle,[59] in her *Life on the Screen*, further underscores the pivotal role of the screen in postmodern society. She observes that computing today is less about calculation and programmed rules, and more about simulation, navigation, and interaction. The aesthetics of the screen is making "cyborgs" of us all—so that postmodern identity becomes a mixture of biology, technology, and code. Wired, we seem increasingly able to transcend ourselves, even as our bodies remain resolutely in place. As the keyboard operator's finger touches the screen, Michelangelo-style, the boundaries between virtual and real dissolve, codes are broken and rearranged, and (for better or worse) cartographies of a new world emerge.

Space: The Place(s) of Convergence

Bodies are always emplaced. Individual performativities occur in *space*, and thereby create the *places* of human (as well as nonhuman) imprint. Space acts to contain, constrain, and mediate human behaviors. (Think respectively of, for example, the limited opportunities for the resource-based economic activities of mining and agriculture; the friction of distance on mobility; and the peculiarities of language and traditions in geographically isolated communities.) Limitations imposed by time and space act as a "prism" within which humans act to create places, and because resources are unevenly distributed, resource-rich and resource-poor environments ensue. In the latter case, the time–space prism may be said to reduce to a "prison" of limited opportunities for the individual.

An intricate dance of cultural production takes place at the prismatic intersection of hard and soft environments. Human agency – the voluntaristic action of individuals—interacts with deep-seated, long-lasting social structures and institutions that serve to shape individual actions. Such interactions occur at several different *scales*, from personal to family/domestic, from national to global. Such scalar dynamics rapidly become hugely complicated by global–local, hybrid, and cosmopolitan flows. Claire Fox calls these "multiple spatial registers."[60]

One of the most persuasive articulations of time–space relations in art is Amalia Mesa-Bains' project on "spiritual geographies." She writes:

> The visual production of Chicana/o artists has frequently been concerned with what is not told, what is not evident. In a sense the art has been committed to a transparency of memory. *The representations of spatiality can thus be seen as an intervention into a past that has been obscured from sight/site.*[61]

Mesa-Bains' work occurs at the intersection of geography, identity, and spirituality, creatively conflating a blizzard of personal and epic histories. According to Victor Zamudio-Taylor, her project reveals "the ability of the imaginative and aesthetic dimensions of art to represent a universe that is qualitatively different from the established reality."[62]

In her dialogues with the place-based philosophy of Aztlan, Mesa-Bains examines the relationship between individual identity and the specifics of place, with a focus on narrative. She conveys this through the use of memory, place-based signifiers, and personal artifacts. In "Reflections on a Transparent Migration" (2000), which she exhibited as part of the *Aztlan* exhibition on LACMA, she combines beautifully crafted glass maguey (agave) plants with an armoire covered with mirrors. Inside the armoire are various pieces of antique clothing. Etched into the mirrors are shadowy faces from old photographs. The piece palpably evokes the texture of life and home from some (distant?) past, yet the exact who, when, and where of the invocation are never revealed. Through shadowy portraits and carefully hung clothes, Mesa-Bains evokes a lost (or perhaps now-recovered) connection to a particular experience and identity. The translucent maguey, visible yet ethereal, gives the impression of an imminent vanishing, or a threat of fracturing—a promise that is fulfilled in the shattered glass fragments that surround the piece.

In "What the River Gave to Me" (2002)—the title is a play on Frida Kahlo's infamous "What the Water Gave to Me"—Mesa-Bains turns to the natural landscape (Plate 5). In this portrayal of a canyon etched deeply into a forbidding border landscape, she examines the paradox that separates the natural markers of division in the terrain plus the sense of spirit that resides there, from the subversions imposed by forced social separations because of human-induced boundaries. The arid yet beautiful landscape, evoking the harsh journeys facing those who cross the border without documents, is etched with the names of origins and destinations on both sides of the border. The terrain is dramatically bisected by the life-giving flow of a river—brilliantly illuminated, and studded by multicolored glass boulders bearing the names of immigrants past and present. As it flows, the river carries these glittering treasures to a place where dreams and the spirit may be fulfilled, thus transcending both natural and human-induced boundaries. Although they are inevitably *in place*, the glass dreams are borne forward by the river's flow, allowing the dreamer-travelers to reach back into the past, and forward to the future in order to guide their journey.

Joe Lewis is an African-American artist/educator who splits his time between Los Angeles and New York City. He is chameleon-like in his approach to artistic media and subject matter, yet he characterizes his *oeuvre* as consistently addressing transactions at/with borders. Lowery Stokes Sims captures the cosmopolitan nature of Lewis' work thus: He is "preoccupied with the realpolitik of the contemporary word . . . [which] attempts to relegate us all into convenient, definable categories."[63] Like Mesa-Bains, Lewis is deeply conscious of the power of place to commemorate what otherwise might fade from sight—for example, a place where murder occurred, but (hours, maybe days later) all traces of the horror have been erased. Lewis frequently operates at the scale of community and domestic life. His "no mire detrás: porqué?" ("don't look back: why?," 2002) creates a piece with three main elements. In front is a short, wide wall made of stacked, salt blocks (Plate 6). Carved across them is an image of the "running family," as seen on border highway signs in the United States. Behind is a wooden gate, propped up and draped with lace-like, military-like camouflage, which itself is coated with sliced limes pressed into red chile powder. The forms reference specific U.S. military artifacts—the fence, camouflage covering, and signs warning drivers of undocumented immigrants fleeing the border patrol. Yet the materials Lewis has chosen reflect a different frame of mind, founded in the textures of Mexican daily life. They effectively neutralize the forms they represent. In an apparent argument against technology used for domination, Lewis references materials that sustain life instead of destroying it.

Domestic and interior scales inevitably impact the manufacture of culture and identity. Barbara Jones is an L.A.-based artist who takes the matters of private fantasy and longing into the structure of urban/domestic spaces. In an excavation of the relationship between home and identity, she has for many years documented her family within the domestic environment. Through this process, her work captures the residual, in-between, or transitional moments of life. Her photographs focus on the intensity and movement that occur in casual encounters. Her children appear like action figures or characters from a science fiction movie, captured in mid-step. In "La Alianza" (2002) she uses these photographs, along with images of the nearby ocean and a 100-year-old family land deed and map from Mexico, to explore how people reimagine themselves out of past experiences and connection to place (Plate 7). By making scale unclear, and by selecting sometimes blurred or awkward-colored images she poses questions about the value of the seemingly ordinary or imperfect within society. Following in the tradition of mid-twentieth century modernist painters in California, she presents a personal and particular perspective as a counterbalance to what she perceives as the homogenization of American identity. Her images are placed in large, commercial light boxes and assembled like a modernist puzzle. In this piece, Jones explores the idea of situatedness, about how individuals are both formed and subject to the conditions of their environment, about how they transform those conditions through their actions and particular frame of mind. Although Jones' piece shows a detailed family orientation, its form resembles an architect's abstracted cityscape. Because the family history she portrays is in part an immigrant experience, she references the ways in which multiple locations can overlap in our minds (the distant places of our pasts and current places of our present). Through intimate details, she provokes questions about the interaction between transnational, place-based sensibilities, and the form of the city itself.

Political injustice at the level of the personal is a prominent theme in the work of Milena Muzquiz. Muzquiz is a binational artist who engages the overlap of contemporary popular cultural forms, from fairy tales to fashion, in both Tijuana and Los Angeles. In pieces such as her home-movie-style "Old School" (2000), she hybridizes images by crisscrossing contradictory styles and historic references. This, like much of her work, portrays spaces and social interactions as if they are coated in a metaphorical plastic wrap, where the contents of each package is partially masked, and yet each appears to hold the same, ironic value as the next. Yet there is always a tension in how she positions herself in relation to her subjects. She seems to be precariously poised just beyond the picture frame, teasing the viewer to guess what lies hidden under the mask.

In "Sunsplash" (2002), Muzquiz displays a minimalist wooden structure that gives a nod toward both a sparse Mondrian painting and, contradictorily, a home entertainment center. This somewhat fragile structure holds at its center a large livingroom style television set and VCR (Plate 8). The video that plays is in the style of a home movie of someone's "south of the border vacation." Yet soon it becomes uncomfortably voyeuristic, with close shots of women's bodies as they cruise around a Baja resort during spring break. The images also switch from women who are unaware that they are being observed to scenes of "special performances" for the camera by various scantily clad women. The video veers between a cheap vacation video and amateur soft porn. Muzquiz has appropriated and combined two versions of the male gaze, with their elaborate choreographies of desire and power. Tensions are thus established between inner desires and public expectations, between the stark, linear modernism of the home entertainment center and the raw, unfinished punk/neopostmodern representations of the body. Muzquiz seems to be warning us that the personal in a postborder world will still be subject to the imperatives of commerce, power, and exploitation. Places of transgression will persist.

The border is, by definition, a transnational as well as a personal/domestic place, extending far beyond a line on the map. Tijuana-based Marcos Ramirez ERRE recreates cultural symbols to reveal the contradictions inherent in uneven economic development at the borderlands. Utilizing the aesthetics of the local Tijuanese built environment, his artwork is resonant with the materials, sensibilities, and conflicts of his surroundings. In his installations, architectural forms speak directly to the human experience they contain. For InSITE94, Ramirez presented an installation called "Tijuana 21st Century," which consisted of an exact replica of a small house/shack, built in the border *rasquache* style of found and discarded materials, including parts of old tires, rebar, tar paper, and plywood. He attached this to the side of a structure on the grounds of the Centro Cultural de Tijuana, a monumental yet sparse modernist architectural complex, which includes a gigantic globular structure. The two architectural moments relayed a narrative about the paradoxical experiences of Mexican life, about official history and its relationship to individuals. In other projects, ERRE audaciously appropriates classic images of subversion to convey powerful political messages about borderlands. One of his most famous pieces, "Toy an Horse" (1997), depicts a massive two-headed Trojan Horse sitting astride the Tijuana/San Diego border crossing at San Ysidro. Gazing north and south simultaneously, ERRE's "fifth column" invited hundreds of thousands of border-crossers to imagine a postborder world (see Chapter 8).

In "Walls" (2002), ERRE deconstructs the international boundary to reveal the everyday lives adjacent to its emplacement (Plate 9). In a most direct sense, the piece is about the superimposition of the soft city (people's lives) on the hard city (the fence). The installation consists of two walls, one of wood, the other of brick, separated by mere inches. Both walls allow the viewer to see through to the other side. Each side of the wall displays a different video, projected onto a white, centered rectangle. Both portray building construction, but from either side of the border. On the U.S. side, house construction looks largely mechanized. On the Mexican side, construction workers build brick walls using labor-intensive, traditional trowel-and-mortar methods. The sounds of work are quiet—a scrape of the trowel against a brick, or a tap ensuring a brick is in place. On the U.S. side, the mostly Mexican workers use loud powertools at a breakneck speed. There is a repetitive bang of shooting nails into wood-framed structures and the continuous whirring of electric saws. At mealtimes, construction workers in Mexico put up a makeshift grill, then collectively cook and share food brought from home; in the United States, workers purchase individual prepared meals from truck vendors. In this piece, as in others, ERRE appropriates familiar symbols of national powers (walls, flags, etc.) and illuminates their interaction with the human scale. "Walls" also testifies that although the same people may work on both sides of the border, they must adapt to the different systems that govern the daily processes in each place.

Representation: The Aesthetics of Convergence

Our discussions of identity and place have already revealed much about the representational aesthetics of a postborder art. There is a preponderance of visualizations that employ a *screen* as a way of seeing (video, internet, television, film, photography, etc.). The topical foci of these postborder engagements have included the body and its performativity, as well as the emplaced (contextualized) nature of human behaviors over multiple spatial scales.

The subjects of postborder art are also becoming manifest, as the artists' representational obsessions congregate around matters relating to

- *Memory and dreams*, including coming to terms with past origins, and visions/longings for the future, both of which persistently mediate the claims of north and south on artists' allegiances;
- *Borders, hybridity, and resistance*, betraying a self-conscious prioritization of the liminal/in-between spaces of borderlands; their transformative capacity in the production of hybrids; and the potential for political resistance and localized autonomy (i.e., self-determination) through the appropriation of liminal spaces.

If there is a common denominator underlying these thematic concerns (and we realize that some may resist such a reductionist gesture!), then it may be the redefinition of *authenticity*. However, even when such issues are evident in the works, much of the artists' efforts are put into canceling the conventions of authenticity even as they are interrogating them.

In past collaborations, Rita Gonzalez and Jesse Lerner have included film and video programs that addressed Mexican and American identity and transnational cultural forms. Most notable among these is "Mexperimental," a widely shown program of avant-garde Mexican films and videos.[64] And in "Ruins" (2000), Lerner created what he called a "fake documentary," which examined the fabrication (even lies) that go into the production of cultural histories—in this case, the racist fantasies surrounding reconstructions of life in pre-Columbian Mexico. In "Border Slick" (2002), Gonzalez and Lerner create an installation that incorporates twin film presentations (Plate 10). The juxtaposed film programs simultaneously address contradictory representations of the border. The film on one screen shows a low-budget U.S.-made sexploitation movie, portraying the border as a place of license, corruption, and violence. In dialogue with these images are works by contemporary Mexican/Chicano film/video artists, emanating from a smaller, antiquated camera; these include, for example, Ana Machado's *Coca-Cola en las venas*, a personal portrayal of childhood (discussed by Norma Iglesias in Chapter 6). Situated between the film programs are two "zonkeys," replicas of the black- and white-striped, painted burros commonly seen along the touristic Calle Revolución in Tijuana. The zonkeys in Tijuana are props for tourists to pose alongside, providing an exotic, absurdist portrayal of border life. The fur-clad, life-size zonkeys in the Gonzalez/Lerner installation draw inspiration from Tijuana street life, declaring a new street-based authenticity, founded upon traditional contexts transposed to urban settings and mixed with technology and commerce. In the installation, the zonkeys appear to be lost in thought, oblivious to both representations.

The problem of authentication reaches entertaining, almost farce-like heights in the works of Jamex and Einar de la Torre, who are based in San

Diego, California, and Ensenada, Mexico. In a conscious criticism of the modernist aesthetic, the de la Torre brothers display a sensibility somewhat akin to cluttered suburban lawns. Each piece contains its own contradictions: from one perspective, it may resemble a multifaceted jewel; but from another, it almost seems that a magnet has been dragged through the streets of Tijuana and Los Angeles, attracting an array of objects and trinkets to its surface. These objects and surface detritus are then obsessively organized into careful, "more is more" arrangements. In pristine, vivid, blown or molded glass, the brothers combine elements of contemporary popular culture from both sides of the United States/Mexico border, and fuse them with a strong dose of Pre-Columbian iconography. In works such as "The Mexican Problem," art objects are imbued with a mix of Catholicism and sexuality, morphing them into an immodest, even perverse, proximity. The installations appear at times to be embryonic prototypes of a new species, loaded with an immanent consciousness and voices that speak about life in the postborder.

In "Colonial Atmosphere" (2002), the de la Torres have created a massive lunar module fashioned in the style of an Olmec head, accompanied by an astronaut that looks more like a pre-Columbian *tule* (statue figure) were it not for the spacesuit helmet atop its head and life-support system attached to the back (Plate 11). The colossal Olmec heads found in Mexico have African facial characteristics, and the brothers transcribe these onto the face of the lunar module. In so doing, they deliberately confound the question of origins—the United States was preceded in Bajalta California by Mexicans, who were preceded by the Spanish, who were preceded by indigenous peoples—by giving preeminence to Africa. And after humans have colonized new spaces, who can innocently speak of origins? The situation is complicated by the extraterrestrial references embedded in the work. So many unexplained features of our lives and world are accounted for by reference to the extraterrestrial, including gods, aliens, and spacecraft. In this piece, the brothers mock our need to know, and emphasize the impossibility of truly knowing.

Another significant dimension of Jamex and Einar's work is what we refer to as *overdetermination*. The lunar module is packed with everyday objects, often gaudily decorated: snakes and toy animals, busts of Jesús Malverde (the unofficial patron saint of the *narcotraficantes*), TV screens, etc. Similarly, the astronaut's life-support backpack contains not only a heart, but computer circuits, advertisements, and trash. There is simply too much stuff in these pieces! But this is why we speak of overdetermination. To create hybrids, a very small set (as few as two) is all that is necessary. Instead, in "Colonial Atmosphere," there is an excess of causal forces, making possible a kind of "hyperhybridity." In the de la Torres' vision, hybridity becomes an inevitable human state, and we can only laugh at our obsession with authenticity, origins, and racial purity.

The political aesthetic in postborder art becomes more explicit in the works of Mariana Botey. Botey, a Mexico City/L.A.-based artist addresses local/international juxtapositions by deliberately constructing binational identities. Her deep political convictions are expressed by disrupting the dichotomy between the contemporary and historical, creating a radical third space that collapses local experiences into international/global histories and archetypes. Her primary medium is film—experimental, disjointed spatial narratives and landscapes that combine specific locations (on both sides of the border) with mythic-historical personas and events relating to religious and political power.

With "The Motives of Cain/ *Los Motivos de Cain*" (2002), Botey creates an experimental film adaptation based on a short novel by Mexican author Jose Revueltas, which chronicles the personal story of Sergeant Jack Mendoza (Plate 12). The film presents three segments of the novel in the form of abstract narratives. Each scene reflects the metaphor of the novel: the other, the border, and the logic of war. Botey's multiple translation into image, cinema, and script brings a new critical reading to, and enhances the vocabulary of contemporary Mexican cultural history. Using Cain's symbol as a starting point, Botey shows how a radical, dialectical aesthetic can lead to a new decoding and recoding of earlier colonial ways of knowing. An exile such as Jack Mendoza emerges from the center of a collapsing narrative to an open landscape of contemporary fluid identity.

L.A./Orange County-based artist Laura Alvarez tackles a scrambled fusion of social, political, and material forms by creating the "Double Agent Sirvienta" as a point of departure for her artwork (which includes painting, video, and animation). Part of a larger rock-opera, Alvarez's latest episode in the saga of Double-Agent Sirvienta, entitled "*Sueños Intermedios*" ("In-between Dreams," 2002) features an undercover maid/nanny working in the homes of Santa Monica's affluent neighborhoods (Plate 13). She poaches high-tech equipment, including surveillance, computer, and communications systems. Like any good spy, the Double-Agent uses the everyday tools of her trade for this work: a vacuum cleaner detects hidden documents under floorboards; an earpiece helps her communicate with headquarters. These activities are for a greater purpose; they are hidden strategies that thwart the power of her employers. Alvarez's fictional narrative imagines an alternative representation of domestic workers by creating a character that is empowered, subversive, and organized. By putting previously disconnected social forms into adjacency and practical use, this "undercover maid" manipulates an oppressive system for her own goals. In loose plot-lines that resemble Hollywood and novelistic spy thrillers, Alvarez invokes an exuberant multilingual pastiche, full of humor and paradox. The espionage metaphor, realized primarily within a domestic setting, perfectly captures the intense two-way, cross-border gaze. The heavy hand of institutional surveillance is resisted by the personal/domestic activities of a wildly imagined postborder subversive.

Postborder Art in Bajalta California: A Preliminary Mapping

Postborder art exists and is flourishing in Bajalta California. We see this in the increasing numbers of artists and artworks engaged in the momentous subject matter of hybridity and cosmopolitanism, as well as a growing market for the works, which often by-pass traditional art centers.

In addition to enormous changes in the material world (globalization, the information revolution, etc.), postborder art is appearing at a time of fundamental ontological and epistemological shifts. These include, but are not limited to, "postmodernism," "postcolonialism," and "postnation" identity politics. Art, too, has been implicated in the rush to the "post"—witness the "Freestyle" exhibition by the Studio Museum in Harlem, which reputedly ushered in a "postblack" ethos.[65]

To this growing list we now add the concept of a "postborder" art, understood as a cultural aesthetic based in the reconstitution of identities toward new hybridities, composed in the liminal spaces between cultures.

To date, the demonstrable engagements of postborder art have included

- *Identity*, with a focus on body and performativity;
- *Space*, how it is translated into place through the interaction of structures, institutions, and agency operating at multiple scales; and
- A convergent representational *aesthetic*, emphasizing memory/vision and border crossing/hybridity/resistance.

Such aesthetics are characterized (though not universally) by an urban/quotidian emphasis; a transgressive/confrontational/subversive ethic; and inescapable wit, in multiple guises of satire, irony, paradox, farce, etc.; a flagrant embrace of pastiche and overdetermination; and a commitment to installation and screen. Postborder art is a distinct break from preceding traditions in border art, as represented most recently by the Border Art Workshop/ *Taller de Arte Fronterizo* (BAW/TAF), which is discussed more fully by Jo-Anne Berelowitz in Chapter 5.[66]

It is too soon to judge if all these tendencies add up to a distinctive "school," or "movement" of postborder art. In any event, we resist such a premature closure. The purpose of this book is to explore the existence and potential of a putative postborder cultural movement, by examining the regional groundedness of the contemporary Bajalta metropolis (Part I), the history of a distinctive border culture up to this point (Part II), and the promise of an emergent postborder aesthetic (Part III). By the end of this inquiry, we hope to show that postborder art in Bajalta California is a transcendental, transnational aesthetic that is reconstructing the way we see/ know ourselves.

Notes

1. Claire F. Fox, *The Fence and the River, Cultural Politics at the U.S.-Mexico Border* (Minneapolis: University of Minnesota Press, 1999), 1–2.
2. Fox, *The Fence and the River*, 119.
3. A good general overview of the recent trend toward the "Latinization" of U.S. cities is to be found in Mike Davis, *Magical Urbanism: Latinos Reinvent the Big US City* (New York: Verso, 2000). And for a general overview of popular culture in Mexico, see Sam Quinones, *True Tales from Another Mexico: The Lynch Mob, the Popsicle Kings, Chalino, and the Bronx* (Albuquerque: University of New Mexico Press, 2001); for popular Latino culture in Los Angeles, see Gustavo Leclerc, Raúl Villa, and Michael Dear (eds.), *Urban Latino Culture: la vida latina en LA* (Thousand Oaks: Sage Publications, 1999).
4. Robert Irwin, quoted in Barbara Isenberg, *State of the Arts* (New York: Morrow, 2000), 349–50.
5. Isenberg, *State of the Arts*, 350.
6. Isenberg, *State of the Arts*, 354.
7. Peter Sellars, quoted in Isenberg, *State of the Arts*, 151.
8. Isenberg, *State of the Arts*, 152.
9. Amalia Mesa-Bains, quoted in Isenberg, *State of the Arts*, 152.
10. Carolyn See, quoted in Isenberg, *State of the Arts*, 35.
11. Henri Lefebvre, *The Production of Space* (Oxford: Blackwell, 1991).
12. Carl E. Schorske, *Fin-de-Siècle Vienna: Politics and Culture* (New York: Knopf, 1979), xxvii.
13. Richard Cándida Smith, *Utopia and Dissent: Art, Poetry and Politics in California* (Berkeley: University of California Press, 1995), 5.
14. Smith, *Utopia and Dissent*, 9, 29.
15. Paul J. Karlstrom (ed.), *On the Edge of America: California Modernist Art, 1900–1950* (Berkeley: University of California Press, 1996), 4.
16. Scott Williams, and Peter M. Rutkoff, *New York Modern: The Arts and the City* (Baltimore: The Johns Hopkins University Press, 1999), 18.
17. Scott and Rutkoff, *New York Modern*, 50.
18. Stephanie Barron, Sheri Bernstein, and Ilene S. Fort, *Made in California: Arts, Image, Identity, 1900–2000* (Los Angeles: Los Angeles County Museum of Art, 2000).
19. S. Zukin, "How to Create a Culture Capital: Reflections on Urban Markets and Places," in I. Blazwick (ed.), *Century City: Art and Culture in the Modern Metropolis* (London: Tate Gallery, 2001), 260.
20. Victoria Newhouse, *Toward a New Museum* (New York: Monacelli Press, 1998).
21. Harvey Molotch, "L.A. as Design Product: How Art Works in a Regional Economy," in A.J. Scott and E.W. Soja (eds.), *The City: Los Angeles and Urban Theory or the End of the Twentieth Century* (Berkeley: University of California Press, 1996), 225–275.
22. Scott and Rutkoff, *New York Modern*, 43.
23. Jonathan Raban, *Soft City* (New York: Dutton, 1974), 11.
24. The best account (in English) of the history of *corridos* is to be found in Elijah Wald, *Narcorrido: A Journey into the Music of Drugs, Guns, and Guerrillas* (New York: Rayo/Harper Collins, 2001).
25. Stephen Kinzer, "Mexico's Cultural Diplomacy Aims to Win Hearts in US," *New York Times*, August 1, 2002, p. B1.
26. B. Robbins, "Actually Existing Cosmopolitanism," in P. Cheah and B. Robbins (eds.), *Cosmopolitics* (Minneapolis: University of Minnesota Press, 1998), 1.
27. Robbins, "Actually Existing Cosmopolitanism," 2.
28. Néstor Garciá Canclini, *Hybrid Cultures: Strategies for Entering and Leaving Modernity* (Minneapolis: University of Minnesota Press, 1996).
29. Homi Bhabha, *The Location of Culture* (New York: Routledge, 1994).

30. Guillermo Gomez-Peña, quoted by R. Rouse, "Mexican Migration and the Space of Postmodernism," in David G. Gutierrez (ed.), *Between Two Worlds: Mexican Migrants in the United States* (Wilmington: Jaguar Books, 1996), 248.

31. Fredric Jameson, "Postmodernism, or The Cultural Logic of Late Capitalism," *New Left Review*, 1985, 151, 83–4.

32. David Palumbo-Liu and Hans Ulrich Gumbrecht (eds.), *Streams of Cultural Capital: Transnational Cultural Studies* (Stanford: Stanford University Press, 1997), 3.

33. Palumbo-Liu, *Stream of Cultural Capital*, 15–16.

34. Smith, *Utopia and Dissent*, 446–7.

35. Diana Burgess Fuller and Daniela Salvioni, *Art/Women/California: Parallels and Intersections, 1950–2000* (Berkeley: University of California Press, and San Jose Museum of Art, 2002), 2.

36. Fuller and Salvioni, *Art/Women/California*, 13.

37. Fuller and Salvioni, *Art/Women/California*, 2.

38. Virginia Fields, and Victor Zamudio-Taylor, *The Road to Aztlan: Art from a Mythic Homeland* (Los Angeles: Los Angeles County Museum of Art, 2001).

39. Tomás Ybarra-Frausto (in conversation with Michael Dear), "El movimiento: The Chicano Cultural Project since the 1960s," in Gustavo Leclerc, Raúl Villa, and Michael Dear (eds.), *Urban Latino Cultures: la vida latina en L.A.* (Thousand Oaks: Sage Publications, 1999).

40. Peter Plagens, *Sunshine Muse: Art on the West Coast, 1945–1970* (Berkeley: University of California Press, 1999) (originally published 1974).

41. Plagens, *Sunshine Muse*, 7.

42. Plagens, *Sunshine Muse*, 7.

43. Peter Conrad, *Modern Times, Modern Places* (New York: Knopf, 1999), 9.

44. Gloria Anzaldúa (ed.), *Borderlands/La Frontera: The New Mestiza* (San Francisco: Aunt Lute Books, 1987), 195.

45. This point is made forcefully by Chon Noriega, "From Beats to Borders: An Alternative History of Chicano Art in California," in Stephanie Barron, Sheri Berstein, and Ilene Susan Fort (eds.), *Reading California: Art, Image, Identity 1900–2000* (Berkeley: University of California Press, and Los Angeles County Museum of Art, 2000), 367–8.

46. Howard N. Fox "Many Californias, 1980–2000," in Barron, Bernstein, and Fort, *Made in California*, 270.

47. Howard Fox, "Many Californias," 268.

48. Karen Mary Davalos, *Exhibiting Mestizaje: Mexican (American) Museums in the Diaspora* (Albuquerque: University of New Mexico Press, 2001), 8–9.

49. Davalos, *Exhibiting Mestizaje*, 8.

50. Davalos, *Exhibiting Mestizaje*, 7. Davalos goes on to make a very important point about the *inherent* hybridity of Mexican culture:

    > *Domination* is at the core of Mexican culture, which was invented out of the imagined and biological union between Spanish conquistadors and indigenous peasants. Thus Spanish colonial domination resulted in a cultural mixing, or *mestizaje*, which always situates Mexicans between cultures. At the same time, *diaspora* follows from colonial, imperialist, and capitalist domination. The border "crossed" people of Mexican descent in 1848, and people of Mexican descent cross the geopolitical border frequently. It is the combination of domination, diaspora, and cultural "betweeness" that shapes the form and experience of representational practices . . .

    Tenorio-Trillo examines Mexico's attempts at self-representation during the World's Fairs of 1880–1890, aiming for a "modernized image" of the country; see Mauricio Tenorio-Trillo, *Mexico at the World's Fairs: Crafting a Modern Nation* (Berkeley: University of California Press, 1996). For a broader examination of representational issues in the recent past of the United States, see Edward T. Linenthal and Tom Engelhardt (eds.), *History Wars: The "Enola Gay" and Other Battles for the American Past* (New York: Metropolitan Books, 1996).

51. The focus in our discussion is upon the projects that were included in the "Mixed Feelings" exhibition held at the Fisher Gallery of the University of Southern California during the fall of 2002. These projects are illustrated in the portfolio that follows this introduction. See also *Mixed Feelings: Art and Culture in the Postborder Metropolis/Sentimientos Contradictorios: arte y cultura en la metrópolis posfronteriza* (Fisher Art Gallery, University of Southern California, 2002).

52. This point has been made by many commentators, including (for example) Daniela Salvioni, in Fuller and Salvioni, *Art/Women/California*, 6.

53. Claire Fox, *The Fence and the River*, 13, 93.

54. Victor Zamudio-Taylor, "Inventing Tradition, Negotiating Modernism: Chicano/a Art and the Pre-Columbian Past," in Fields and Zamudio-Taylor, *The Road to Aztlan*, 354.
55. Quoted in The Studio Museum in Harlem, *Freestyle* (New York: The Studio Museum in Harlem, 2001), 26.
56. Howard Fox, "Many Californias," 262.
57. Neal Stephenson, *Snow Crash* (New York: Bantam Books, 1993), 24–6.
58. This is discussed more fully in Michael Dear, *The Postmodern Urban Condition* (Oxford: Blackwell, 2000), 210.
59. Sherry Turkle, *Life on the Screen: Identity in the Age of the Internet* (New York: Touchstone Books, 1997), 17.
60. Claire Fox, *The Fence and the River*, 13.
61. Amalia Mesa-Bains, "Spiritual Geographies," in Fields and Zamudio-Taylor, *The Road to Aztlan*, 336.
62. Victor Zamudio-Taylor, "Inventing Tradition, Negotiating Modernism," 354.
63. Lowery Stokes Sims, *Too Many Fish in the Sea*, 20–1
64. Rita Gonzalez and Jesse Lerner, *Cine Mexperimental Cinema: 60 años de medios de vanguardia en México/60 years of avant-garde media arts from Mexico* (Santa Monica: Smart Art Press, 1998).
65. The Studio Museum in Harlem, *Freestyle*. Curator Thelma Golden discusses the term "post-black" in an interview with Suzanne Muchnic, "Making the Case for the "Post-black" School of Art," in *The Los Angeles Times*, September 29, 2001, F1 passim. See also Christopher Knight "Cultural Evolution in 'Freestyle,' " *The Los Angeles Times*, October 2, 2001, F1 passim; and Holland Cotter, "Beyond Multiculturalism, a Way to a New Freedom in Art?" *The New York Times*, July 29, 2001, 2–1 passim.
66. A concise history of BAW/TAF is available in Claire Fox, *The Fence and the River*, Ch. 5.

Portfolio
The Art of Postborder Bajalta California

Plate 1   Daniel Joseph Martinez, *Nallekaghnituten: Man who throws rocks (An event for an A-Moralist as parrhesiates)*, Computer controlled mechanical sculpture with audio, 5 ft 7½ in. (height including base), 2002.

Plate 2   Rubén Ortiz Torres, *The Garden of Earthly Delights/El jardín de las delicias terrenales*, Modified lawn tractor, 4 × 6 × 3 ft., 2002.

Plate 3   Mark Bradford, Jericho, Mixed media installation, dimensions variable, 2002.

Plate 4   Norman Yonemoto, *"Self" Portrait*, Video installation, 6 × 6 × 6 ft., 2002.

Plate 5   Amalia Mesa-Bains, *What the River Gave to Me*, Styrofoam, glass, safety glass, Plexiglas, 3 × 14 × 7 ft. (variable), 2002.

Plate 6   Joe Lewis, *no mire detrás: ¿por qué?/don't look back: why?*, Carved salt blocks, wood, sliced limes, cloth mesh, chile powder, garlic powder, cumin, black pepper, 10 × 10 × 10 ft., 2002.

Plate 7   Barbara Jones, *The Alliance/La Alianza*, Duratrans, 8 lightboxes (2) 24" × 60", (1) 36" × 48", (5) 16" × 20", 2002.

Plate 8   Milena Muzquiz, *Sunsplash*, Dimensions variable, 2002

Plate 9   Marcos Ramirez ERRE, Walls/Muros, Brick, mortar, wood, metal, video, 8 × 12 × 1 ft., 2002.

Plate 10 Rita Gonzalez and Jesse Lerner, *The Tijuana Story: New Videos from the Border*, Media arts program and mixed media installation, dimensions variable, 2002.

Plate 11 Einar and Jamex de la Torre, *Colonial Atmosphere*, Mixed and multimedia installation, dimensions variable, 2002.

Plate 12 Mariana Botey, *The Motives of Cain/Los Motivos de Cain*, Multimedia installation, dimensions variable, 2002.

Plate 13 Laura Alvarez, *Sueños Intermedios*, Video installation, dimensions variable, 2002.

Plate 14 Gallery 1, 'Mixed Feelings' Exhibition.

Plate 15 Gallery 2, 'Mixed Feelings' Exhibition.

The installations portrayed in this portfolio were part of an exhibit entitled: *Mixed Feelings: Art and Culture in the Postborder Metropolis/ Sentimientos Contradictorios: Arte y Cultura en la Metrópolis Posfronteriza*, held at the Fisher Gallery of the University of Southern California, September 4–December 7, 2002. The exhibition design was by Ulises Diaz of ADOBE LA. All photographs (with the exception of Plates 2 and 8) were taken by John Lodge, and are reproduced with kind permission of the Fisher Gallery and the artists.

Plate 1   Daniel Joseph Martinez, *Nallekaghnituten: Man who throws rocks (An event for an A-Moralist as parrhesiates)*, 2002.

Plate 2 Rubén Ortiz Torres, *The Garden of Earthly Delights/El jardín de las delicias terrenales,* Modified lawn tractor, 4 × 6 × 3 ft., 2002.

Plate 3   Mark Bradford, *Jericho*, 2002.
(In background: *Colonial Atmosphere*, installation by Einar and Jamex de la Torre.)

Plate 4   Norman Yonemoto, *"Self" Portrait*, 2002.

Plate 5   Amalia Mesa-Bains, *What the River Gave to Me*, 2002.

Plate 6 Joe Lewis, *no mire detrás: ¿por qué?/don't look back: why?,*
2002.

Plate 7   Barbara Jones, *The Alliance/La Alianza*, 2002.

Plate 8   Milena Muzquiz, *Sunsplash*, 2002.

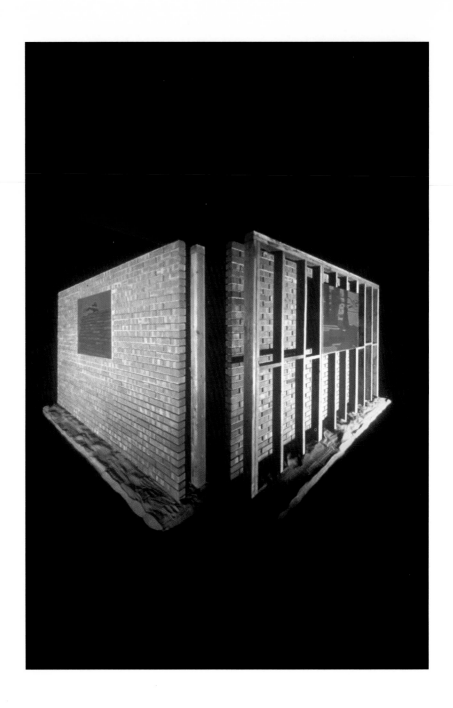

Plate 9   Marcos Ramirez ERRE, *Walls/Muros*, 2002.

Plate 10   Rita Gonzalez and Jesse Lerner, *The Tijuana Story: New Videos from the Border*, 2002.

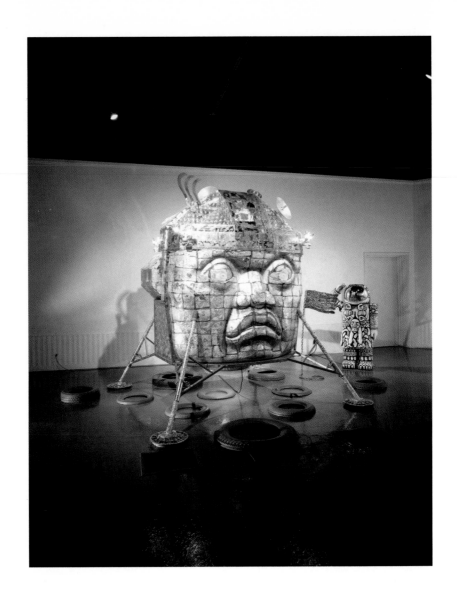

Plate 11 Einar and Jamex de la Torre, *Colonial Atmosphere*, 2002.

Plate 12   Mariana Botey, *The Motives of Cain/Los Motivos de Cain*, 2002.

Plate 13   Laura Alvarez, *Sueños Intermedios*, 2002.

Plate 14   Gallery 1, 'Mixed Feelings' Exhibition.

Plate 15   Gallery 2, 'Mixed Feelings' Exhibition.

Regional Groundedness

1
"Where Are You Going to Be Worthier?"
(The Border and the Postborder)

CARLOS MONSIVÁIS

Today, urban life is a gift: a daily negotiation that reconciles opposites, a contrast between genuine ugliness and prefabricated beauty, between a never-arriving prosperity and an ever-expanding poverty. In Latin America, urbanism is also a rejection of discipline, a miracle of order in spite of everything, an uncertain combination of strength and fragility, eating itself from its moment of birth, so that—almost without paradox—the present generation can take revenge on the indifference that will be professed by forthcoming generations ("They are going to forget us, so we bequeath to them these ruins").

Throughout the twentieth century and almost to the present, the cities of the Northern Border of Mexico have specialized in harmonizing improvisation. *This is where they're coming, this is where we came to....* Cities are assembled with patience and impatience by migrants with dreams and ambitions, by those who wanted to live in North America and those who have not yet achieved it, by establishing dynasties that take advantage of opportunities, by spreading throughout hills and organizing *colonias*, discovering how swapping gullibilities strengthens prestige ("I know you are a great physician, and you, better than anyone, appreciate what a great lawyer I am").

But above all, cities of the twenty-first century document the victory of space over time. There will always be time, space perhaps not. Although the metropolis sprawls, its typical inhabitants (the majority) are restricted to apartments and small houses, whereas others (the minority), the million-

33

aires and multimillionaires, live in confined or expensive spaces for security reasons, thus guaranteeing the ultimate certainty: the perfect solitude of a master requires a bedroom that would seem an infinite space to the twenty people squeezed into any room of the *colonias*. Fiercely chaotic, the cities of the Northern Border are governed by the insoluble contradiction of survival ("If we are going to stay here, let's try to leave as soon as possible"), and by the dazzle of its imperial neighbor, the United States of America.

"I Left Comala Because They Told Me That My Father Lived in Los Angeles, a Man Called Pedro Páramo"

If anything is common to border cities, it is the mobility of the great majority of their residents:

- from the ranch that is tedium redeemed by occasional sensations of significance to the city where anonymity is a synonym of secrecy,
- from the small town to the procurement of unknown freedoms,
- from the favorite dream of imagined utopias to the opportunities of mass production,
- from the joy of learning English to the memory of blue skies and clear places,
- from tribal family to nuclear family,
- from multiple descendants to a lineage that fits into an apartment,
- from intolerance to a tolerance that begins as resignation in the face of alien behavior that cannot be altered,
- from a gathering in a neighborhood patio to a hurried greeting in a condominium,
- from family evenings to television autism,
- from the violent protection of honor to the not-so-secret wish that adultery, by one or both parties, will revitalize a marriage,
- from idolatrous appreciation of the modern to the confused worship of the traditional, and
- from the desire of provoking envy to the fear of inciting the greed of strangers.

To inhabitants of the Northern Border, the time spent in the acts of waiting and hoping is their formative matrix. They wait in *la línea*, they wait in buses, they wait in line to obtain a North American visa, they hope for a steady job, for a place to live, for water, and transportation. And while they do this, they sometimes imagine how their houses and apartments will be; they are guided by a practical view, that everything and everybody will fit, that the furniture will not take a lot of space in case the relatives arrive, that the bed in the bedroom will be very wide, that the kids finally understand and settle down: crowding does not mean promiscuity.

Until recently, the idea and pleasures of the aesthetic had little or nothing to do with the Northern Border. The *beautiful* is a luxury of the second generation, a generation that distances itself from a peasant asceticism and ornaments of the Virgin of Guadalupe, and has, as the new center of its home, a television around which joy and despair revolve. As a general rule, the desire to obtain representations of the *beautiful* stems from television or newspapers, or from observation of tastes that permeate the city like a nomadic sensibility. And the *beautiful* is gaudy, a color that blinds, the repetition of religious themes, supermarket sales, and the never-ending sales.

"When I Arrived at the Border, I Brought with Me a Desire to Leave Soon"

The availability of physical space is declining because of the demographic explosion of people and poverty; in the social arena, the public and the private are merging and, despite everything, they intensify the geography of exclusion and inclusion. If there is a utopian sentiment, it is that of purchasing power; and if there is a valued sphere, it is that of a migratory urge to identify fallow lands, to settle them, and after twenty years exhibit them as "great urban development ." These days, this fact starts to define the Northern Border: that the city (as a totality, as a concept) is escaping from the traditional idea of a city and becomes instead an anxiety to populate city-space without the intention of staying.

Cities on the way, this is what Tijuana, Matamoros, Reynosa, Ciudad Juárez have become. Here, a fugitive from the provinces or the capital comes, and here an insecure fugitive stays, in tune with the provisional nature of his environment, with the public and private devaluing that drug trafficking creates (the work of many), and with the power of violence, which is the most tragic partner of urbanization. In past decades, extreme mobility around the Northern Border has modified it, and resulted in signs of permanence (institutions, personalities, recovered history, centers of higher education, the discovery of local prides).

Such changes were experienced in the twentieth century along routes from Mexico to Texas, California, New Mexico, Illinois, or the Northern Border: peasants fed up with living on the edge between tyranny and extreme poverty; political activists who flee to preserve their lives; youngsters who abandon their villages, unable to endure any longer a monotony without escape; families whose longing for opportunities becomes a catalyst for their legendary journey; adjustment to migration demographics (a good number of illegal immigrants, while escaping from the Border Patrol, write and rewrite their conference papers and doctoral dissertations); a decline in physical abuse due to the development of minor technological advances; racial harassment, insecurities, and surprises; an effort to understand, for just one instant, what is being assimilated throughout the years. In summary, the behaviors and attitudes that announce or denounce the thirst for change, the desperation, the grand illusions: "Let's go away from here, let's go any place except this, I am tired of looking at the *nopales*, the sheaves of *robavacas*, the thieves in the Credit Bank, the window that it is never open, the market, and the office. Let's go, the world is wide and maybe it is not that strange, this is over for us, let's go, *mano*, and hope that our families will reunite with us later."

The story is typical, a classic tale of migration from one place to any other place on the planet. To leave is to risk all; to stay is to accept that there will be no further opportunity to risk anything. Nomads aspire to a new sedentary life. Those living a sedentary life, as a compensatory strategy, used to imagine the place they never left. (This journey around my room is called "idealization" or "demonization" of the native land or city.) And the journey, even when executed alone, is still a matter of the tribe. Someone—from the town, the city, the *colonia*, from work, from the family—throws himself into it, and after him come the relatives, and sometimes after the relatives the entire community, which has already been abandoned to the anthropologists dedicated to researching customs and roots in the south of Oaxaca or the north of Jalisco. Exhortations become orders: "Come here, what are you doing over there? The season of the *pizca* is already coming, and the family that I work for assured me they will help you, you will live with us, I received your letter, *órale*, something will be done, don't stay in the hole." In this century, millions of nomadic Mexicans have departed from many more millions of sedentary Mexicans.

A web of emotional attachments and bonds attracts those eager for adventure and those anxious for survival. In their stories friends, relatives, and fellow countrymen idealize the region, city, or occupation that they have achieved, and the great dream of the outcasts is reconstituted, a dream that is not rooted in the open arms of the foreigner but in the solidarity of compatriots. (In foreign lands, no matter how one prefers to see it, the family is more family, the fellow countrymen more countrymen, the reconstruction of the familiar more devotional. This occurs even when the selfish and malicious side of human nature is not present, but even if it was, it would not break this norm.) And those who did not leave admire those who did; or, if they envy them, it becomes too late for them to talk about the "betrayal of the *pochos*," or even worse, of tourism without opportunities. Immigrants are constantly associated with a modernity that, once discerned, seduces or frightens, because since the end of the nineteenth century (not only, but not even centrally) it is geographic destiny that forces Mexicans to define the modern out of the concept of "North American." It is also the sense of anachronism that arises when comparing technological advance and knowledge about the world. Spoken or not, conscious or not, immigrants want to be modern; they want also to relocate themselves from one cultural condition to another, from one planetary existence to another. Does this mean that Mexico is an underdeveloped country? This implies, for the moment, a country in which the immigrant's anxiety becomes synonymous with *modernity* and the *opportunity for work*.

"Put This Portrait of My Mother in the Living Room/And Where Do I Put the Living Room?"

Aesthetics comes late to communities inspired by the rush and eagerness of settling down, right now, so that they can leave as soon as possible. In the years before the 1980s, the photographs and the few films about Tijuana, Ciudad Juárez, Mexicali, Matamoros, and Nogales, for example, give a sense of pragmatism taken to an extreme; of the efforts of efficient contractors and architects without imagination, experience, or models to go beyond the obligations of professional practice. Determinism dominates during most of the twentieth century, a fierce determinism that grants nothing to its users or victims. Nobody even thinks of the question: "Why don't I have the right to beauty?" And the few interesting or fearlessly kitsch buildings that exist usually are works by North American architects eager to give to the world the example of Los Angeles, California, or, more specifically, of Hollywood. (A noticeable example is the Casino of Aguas Calientes in Tijuana.)

Yet by the 1950s or 1960s, the cities of the border are a learning workshop. There, freedom, urban improvisation, and the metamorphosis of resignation to joy are being tested. The medieval proverb "City air makes us free" is combined with "Small town, big hell." The cities' downtowns arise through accumulation: from the lawyer's offices specializing in divorce; from doctors' offices where physicians adjust their specialization depending on their clients' illnesses; from engineers and architects pressured by contractors. This disdain for the aesthetic is contagious, and clerics and professors also lean toward the law of the minimum effort. The flow of new traditions slows down, turning architectural literacy into the worship of speed. *Hurry, hurry, hurry!* Let's put up a few more middle-class *colonias*, a few residences, schools, and some temples.

With the dissemination of construction and affirmation of the urban, the lack of aesthetic demands disappears as a defining characteristic of the border. But this does not happen before 1970 or 1980, still very recent times.

"We Are Escaping from Identifying Ourselves Everyday with Identity"

How are the basic ideas and mental habits of communities on both sides of the border formed and transformed? How are people far from the Center choosing Mexican traditions? What accumulated knowledge, frustrations, disillusionment, and hopes await those who have just arrived in North America? What knowledge do they borrow from other immigrants? How does the *conscience of the barrio* emerge (including its architecture), and how does a barrio differ from a ghetto? In what ways are the (merciless) rules of the game of Anglo society internalized by Mexicans who suffer them? How do immigrants know themselves, adapt, assimilate, and take advantage of social mobility?

In the case of people of Mexican origin, to be a "man or a woman of the border" in the United States is to live subject to prejudices against what is labeled "marginal," "newcomer," and "undesirable." But at what precise moment are Mexicans who recently arrived no longer considered "new"? Before the decade of 1990s, even if two or three generations had passed in a *Hispanic* family, its members were still regarded as part of the *Brown Tide*. The immigrants' descendents—even if they retain (or not) the denomination of Mexicans (in contrast to other ethnic minorities, excluding those from Latin America)—learn that they have also inherited, along with other habits and customs, the tradition of being exploited. *Another history*, further from the textbooks, shadows those of Mexican origin: the awareness of belonging to a people (until recently one would say "a race") forever identified as plunder subject to disposition by the powerful. As Claudio G. Vélez-Ibáñez states in *Visions of the Border. The Southeast Mexican Cultures of the United States:*

> After the Texas revolution, the war between Mexico and the Treaty of Mesilla of 1856, the basic strategy of the U.S. for acquiring property around the former missions, penitentiaries and large and small cities, was by using the taxation system, the control of borders, robbery, and by judicial means, for example, delaying the claims over land donations, in order to ensure [the U.S.] ownership of Mexican productive resources. The result was that a population already under a lot of pressure lost power and control over their land. In a very particular way, the majority of the people from Tucson, San Antonio, San Diego, Los Angeles, Santa Fe, and other rural areas, became subordinated not as a result of a cultural trait or practice, but of U.S. economic policy.

The fate of Mexicans in the United States has not depended on any "natural inferiority" or on any internal cultural barriers, but on a political and economical will that, because of racism, is used with a psychological ease and lack of scruples. Because of the cultural and moral underdevelopment of those who practice it, prejudice legitimates an appetite for the prey. The logic goes like this: "If I declare them as inferiors, I do not have to be responsible for my behavior, nor am I accountable to anyone. If I virulently deny the culture and spiritual resources of the *greasers,* I will gain the approval of those who are historically convinced of one thing: that nothing civilizes savages more than being the object of plunder. Among the poor in underdeveloped countries, only those who have been victims of pillage are capable of approaching civilization. What we are really doing is not pillage but fair appropriation."

The subjugation is carried out without the need for theories or special programs. It is enough that racist people are opposed to the fundamental rights of minorities: education, fair wages, health, opportunities for advancement, appointed positions, and participation in public debates. Once a system of rejection is enacted, it plans for exclusions. Since the nineteenth century, education has been a pivotal moment. As Vélez-Ibáñez says:

> Perceived solely as immigrants, Mexican children became foreign not only in their own land, but they also received a very clear message: their substantial poverty was caused by their own primitive culture and language. Therefore, the general educational strategy was to "Americanize" these children by eliminating their obvious "foreign" Spanish accents, forbidding the use of their language, and recommending imitation of "Anglo-Saxon models of work, morality, and government," thereby underscoring the inferiority of the Mexican practices.

The great advantage of knowing English is contrasted brutally with reminders of the disadvantages of a native language. Yet the process of Americanization is absorbed only in a difficult and defective manner. The ethnic minority's basic cultural tenets are forbidden, not even minimally motivated; and because of the contempt they experience, people are denied enjoyment of their native culture. To a great extent, this condition continues to the present day, with legislative measures that ignore the great advantages of bilingualism, that see in the Spanish language a basic obstacle to social mobility. And the devaluing of the Spanish language does not stem from books like Richard Rodríguez's *Hunger of Memory*, but from the racism that nourishes feelings of self-destruction and marginality among those who experience rejection. It is an efficient technique; those who speak English fluently feel conflicted if they use Spanish "outside the domestic domain of the household." So, another unexpected factor needs to be added to the oppressions that Mexicans suffer in the United States: a feeling of guilt for not speaking in English. And this deeply "intimate" condition of language may in fact explain the scarce consumption of books in Spanish on both sides of the border, as well as relegating the act of reading in Mexican tradition.

Thus, another convention is constructed, alongside language, family structure, religion, the Virgin of Guadalupe, regional cuisine and customs, and nationalistic nostalgia. This *other tradition*, a very pernicious one, defines an ethnic group as "cheap labor," inevitably bringing with it psychological, political, and social repercussions. As Vélez-Ibáñez explains:

> Regarding Mexican communities and culture, the idea exists that work defines a people. Allowing their bodies to weaken in mines, to wear out at construction sites, to be hunchbacked at age thirty-five through farm labor, to become

rheumatic through poorly-paid housework, and stigmatized because of accidents on the assembly line, Mexicans arrive prematurely at retirement.

However, as Vélez-Ibáñez clarifies, this ethos is part of the North American system, determined to enslave a minority via a cultural identity that it considers as devalued or depreciated merchandise, to be bought and sold. This distorts the human value of communities, and reduces cultural values to the numerical expression of its lowest salaries. Such a conversion, of a minority into a factor of production, is the extreme experience of Mexicans in the United States: when the word *Mexican* is no longer a positive or even a proud description, but usually as a result of cultural exchanges with others, with standards set from the outside, it becomes the beginning of a slow form of perverse incorporation into the *mainstream*.

The Common, the Particular in the Portable Border

If there is a phenomenon that marks the appearance of a new urban feeling in Latin America—tumultuous, carefree, shameless, measured by traditional values—it is the talk shows. Faced with the fortunes and misfortunes of its participants, the spectator dissolves into that interchangeable world where neighbors come and go, where the desire to leave immediately is a form of staying, where the dreadful "What Would They Say" is not scandalous but instead lacks any judgment. All is confusion on the verge of disintegration. This is the story line: The border, the bus, the traffic, the apartment that tries to accommodate the family of a brother who has just arrived from the village, and informal employment. From these cities in decay stems a self-confident vitality that articulates what was silenced and hidden: sexual orientation, the abyss of separating couples, and "psychopathologies." Plus a conservative spirit unnerved not by what it has seen and heard, but by the unfolding deluge of personal freedoms. Among the unlimited abuses heaped by the programs' hosts upon the participants, talk reality shows reveal the mentality of a city in chaotic flux, an outline of the architecture of the flood: we live so much with the multitude that "Only if I reveal my private life will I understand it."

The architecture of the border corresponds to talk shows and reality shows, to the end of privacy and intimacy. It is an architecture of mass production, of buildings that proliferate between psychological stereotypes that clash with the styles of youth subcultures (cholos, punks, *low-riders*), with superficial Americanization, with the conversion of youth culture in the City of Free Time—which for young people *is* the true Northern Border, completely modern and Americanized but not "gringo" (in the sense of community life) or aseptic. And already in the decade of the 1990s, it becomes an architecture that heralds a permanent change.

At the beginning of the twenty-first century, such changes are inescapable. If we look for an equivalent to Baron Haussman, the urbanist who rebuilt Paris in the nineteenth century, today we have the Internet, the reconstructor of electronic avenues, the creator of endless boulevards of communication. In everyday life, the story line is typical: the family is a defensive shell, institutions are the psychic forges, social life elevates intimacy, and the sensuality of footsteps announcing the dawn of the unexpected (the city as adventure) is replaced by computers, credit cards, taxes, e-mails, beepers, and cellular phones. Precise geographies are erased, and the ancient centers of cities, increasingly left to literature, are ignored by the rising social classes. The Mall replaces strolling and the Main Square, and television becomes the only conceivable urban culture, half consumption and half a construction of alien sensibilities. And daily life is invaded by fragmentation. If young people usually feel trapped by MTV video clips, adults rest uneasily between the television commercial and fear of being assaulted at a restaurant. The fragmentary is the mirror of cities.

The border city abandons any idea of being a locale free from the pressures of homelands, and recovers the ambiguities between collective and individual life. New species appear, very similar in each of the cities. They are cloned because of the urge to Americanize, to avoid becoming obsolete in the new age, encouraged by the distance from their parents' lives (the most precious victories of one generation always exist because of the sacrifice of earlier generations), divided between the anxiety of diversity and the fear of no longer being homogeneous.

In the final scene of the movie *Born in East L.A.*, a crowd symbolizes the explosive migrant rush from Tijuana to San Diego, California. And, with the force of an allegory, their movement reveals what seems irreversible: each year, in never-diminishing proportions, they hurl themselves at their obsessive goal (a modernity whose root is work, an opportunity that is always somewhere else). Hundreds of thousands of Mexicans, Salvadorans, Guatemalans, Nicaraguans, Dominicans, and Hondurans, challenge police brutality, the net of deceptions and fraud cast by those who guide the illegal immigrants (the *polleros*), the racism of their employers, and their own feelings of inadequacy (cultural, idiomatic, technological). In spite of all this, and the abandonment of their roots, the immigrants persist.

Since the 1970s, the Northern Border has been reconstructing itself, losing the character of a transitional place, going through "moral rehabilitation" and industrial development, an invasion and devastation caused by drug traffickers, is diversifying politically, opening its universities and cultural clubs, forgetting legends of minor corruption, facing up to crimes like "*the dead women of Ciudad Juárez*," and suffering, profiting, decaying, and damaging itself ecologically with the *maquiladoras*. It desires full employment, and full integration with the North American economy, yet some of its intellectuals argue about the preservation of national identity. The abuses of central-ism continue but, more importantly, the Northern Border lives with confu-sion: Is it the prelude to a migratory dream? Is it a space kidnapped by the drug lords? Is it a place with its own impetus for development?

One piece of border architecture seems inevitably at the margin of lessons taught by Frank Lloyd Wright, Le Corbusier, Mies van der Rohe, Philip John-son, I.M. Pei, Frank Gehry, and Luis Barragán. This is the dense peripheral zone around big cities, the homes and small shelters of migrants who dream of going to the other side; there they settle and support their children's ed-ucation, get involved in politics, or turn to crime. Finally they stay. A good example of this would be Tijuana's *colonia* Lomas Taurina, a city of demo-graphic desperation and furious urban settlement, where on March 23, 1994, Luis Donald Colosio, PRI presidential candidate, was assassinated.

"I Am a Frontier Person by Adoption. I Am a First-Generation *Fronterizo*; by Adoption Because I Arrived While I Was Planning My Exit to the States; and First Generation Because It Took Me Too Much Time to Accept I Was Not Going to Leave"

Some facts support the arguments of determinism: a border of 3000 km with the United States, Mexico's economic dependency (84% of its transac-tions are with North America), the strengths and weaknesses of the maquiladora industry, and the incessant migratory flow, mainly to Texas, California, and Chicago, but not only to these cities (there were already im-portant migrations to New York). In the past, to orient themselves to modernity, provincial people looked toward Mexico City; now, even as the country is unifying, people's attention—regulated by the media and the "traveler's fantasies" of immigration—is turning away from centralism.

In the catalogue of idealization, the city of Los Angeles wins by an over-whelming majority, being not only *the* place to live, but also an infinite mon-ster most generous in its opportunities, and already inhabited by millions of Mexicans. Los Angeles is a paradise of freeways, ghettos, and the fulfillment, according to the Polish writer Ryzsard Kapuscinsky, of the Cosmic Race's prophecy—the concept of a universal *mestizaje* that José Vasconcelos dis-cerned in 1925: "The different races of the world have the tendency to mix with one another, to the point of forming a new type of human being, con-sisting of a piece of each and every one of existing peoples."

In Los Angeles, Mexicans, Nicaraguans, Salvadorans, and Hondurans al-ready are *Hispanics*, members of a minority that will become the largest in the United States. There, they hope to gain employment denied them in their countries, as well as a house or apartment with all comforts and appli-ances, a school that will save their children from menial jobs, and the vi-brancy of the contemporary that is impossible to obtain in a town or *colonia* of the Northern Border. The experience of uprooting is brutal (the abandonment of unique identity, of knowing exactly the place they occupy in a community), and the migrants pay heavily for their uprooting, their new existence: the linguistic expansion, the first superficial contact with technology that will become their "second skin," and the transformation of their rural ethos into a highly modern medium.

Everything seems to be simultaneously available yet unattainable, everything seems to be reachable through work and the suspension of belief. "In Mexico nothing could be ours, but here it can be." The undocumented, the *wetback*, the illegal immigrant uses an unexpected tactic: he reveres the customs from which he distances himself, to more easily shake off those habits that make it difficult to belong in a hostile environment. This could be the immigrant's prayer:

> I thank you, Virgencita de Guadalupe, because you allow me to be myself, even though I don't know if you notice, Patron Saint, I am much more tolerant toward what I don't understand nor share; yet I am able to be loyal to you, the Nation, although I am now Pentecostal, Jehovah's Witness, Adventist, Baptist, or Mormon, I have decided not to change even though my outlook is so different. I listen to this enormous radio, a *ghetto blaster* is what I think they call it, a radio that plays melodies I never thought I liked. I swear to you, Virgencita, I am the same although I can't recognize myself in the mirror any more.

The peasant from Sinaloa looks for hours at the fence that separates him from the promised land. There, within reach of his cunning, there are the jobs, dollars, a prosperity inconceivable until now, and that which transcends everything: a world where everything is modern, like it was just made, new traditions on the brink of starting, and the powerful and extraordinary machines that save time (entire lives), and link their users to the future.

A bourgeois woman walks through a Tijuana *mall*, and she likes the simple idea of having escaped forever from the markets. That ordeal was her mother's, not hers. She orders everything by telephone, and shortly she will do it by Internet. It has come to an end, the hunt for vegetables, fruits, meat, brooms, soaps, the "popular scent," which is the way she refers to the resistance to deodorants. The *mall* is something else, it is a gringo invention, and that is why the atmosphere is *gringo* and the products are *gringos*, and if the clientele is not *gringo* it is midway between monolingual and bilingual. The *mall* fits into globalization, and it is for Mexicans one of the cathedrals of the border's new century.

The youngster is not sure of his knowledge of his country's history. He stays abreast with the minimum information possible, nothing extra. One need not cross the border with a burden of useless information. The day he needs to know about it, he will get some textbooks so he can recall the knowledge that his family passed on to him. In the meantime, he resigns himself. His "documentary" knowledge is not much, although he carries his cultural baggage of *boleros, rancheras,* and local pop groups. Plus his knowledge of sports is infinite. All these certainties and memories are impossible to leave behind at home. If he carries them with him, it is because crossing the border without these experiences is like leaving forever, to who knows where.

The *frontier*. Teenagers from poor *barrios* in Mexico City pass time dreaming of going to the border and from there to Los Angeles, Chicago, New York. Opportunities are always abroad, and they are enthusiastic, knowing they are ready for departure. They can leave tomorrow, in a month, or in a year, but in talking about preparations, everything they experience is *frontera*. Beyond their everyday life and their parents' existence (their parents never tired of doing the same thing), it is in work that *the other* starts, the unknown, that other about which adolescents are so enthusiastic, that they spend entire afternoons and nights talking about it. "Do you realize that in one day we could be at the border, it's like we were already there. I am so eager to leave, it is like I were already in Los Angeles. Have you ever noticed how everything you desire comes closer to you?"

And what does the young migrant carry of artistic culture, of visual heritage? Fragments, films (like those of Pedro Infantes), vague memories of Diego Rivera's murals, cards that slander Leonardo's *The Last Supper*, Michelangelo's *La Pietà*, and Dali's *Christ*, or popular crafts that defame the craftsmanship tradition; but not much more.

The ideal frontier is made out of dreams.

Mexico City is transforming itself architecturally to be close to the border. This is also known as Americanization, this search for resemblance to cities bordering the United States, with identical restaurants, malls that loom as bastions of abundance, movie theaters like those in San Diego or McAllen, *prêt-a-porter*, Blockbuster, McDonald's, Wal Mart, Sears Roebuck, Tower Records. Every day, the ideal frontier is crossed, and those "lacking roots" (the majority) realize that the roots of one's identity also defend against fads.

In this context, Mexico City is a frontier city par excellence. Industry, commerce, and entertainment closely resemble an urban monster of twenty million people with a *borderline* appearance. Of course it fails, but in some places they achieve it, at least an illusion of walking for a couple of minutes in another city of another country that vaguely recalls the scenes of certain North American movies with a Latin flavor. Part of the border visually congeals in Mexico, and in this way consumer society satisfies its desire for travel. Without passports or dangers, Mexicans are already crossing the Río Bravo.

Do not overstate the fantasy. The Border exists, with force, cruelty, and rejection. But the real, as important as it is, does not interfere with travelers' fantasies, of those desiring illusions of the contemporary, or those trying to match what exists with what they dream. If a computerized life and the Internet erase borders, if contemporary architecture tries to duplicate the forms of the urban edge, to "deterritorialize" and force Mexicans to cross the border virtually, then we should accept the *frontier* condition as already existing in wide sectors of the nation. To be *fronterizo* is to be willing to leave immediately, to come and go from one country to another in reality or the imagination, to identify the typical and traditional as repositories of nostalgia but not of reality.

The border is also, contrary to all evidence of racism and police brutality, a state of mind. When it is said that Mexico is becoming Chicano, it is like using this state of mind as a calling card for the modern era.

For most of the Mexican century, the border (with the United States, of course) marked a limit of hope and a peak of anachronism for those living on the other side. This has changed in an extraordinary way. The border is an allegory of a cultural, psychic, and custom exchange; and the idea of Mexico, as a nation of border-dwellers, has a remarkable weight. This does not imply an end to nationalism or (still less) a deterioration of the national conscience. To be from the border is to advance an era of binational integration, to accept globalization with a traveler's state of mind, and to make use of all the passports that the imagination allows.

The Acquisition of Pride

Between urban pride and border cities, there are hostile relations. For a while, Tijuana was marked as a place where everything happens quickly: fast divorces, casinos for Hollywood stars, a city of prostitution and *vicio* (any other word would lack the necessary resonance). Matamoros has been damaged by the drug trafficking, so has Ciudad Juárez, which in addition suffers a plague of *serial-killers* specializing in young *maquiladora* women (the number of victims, between 200 and 400, is undetermined, due to the inefficiency of the investigations). But how do we respond to this? For a long period of time, architecture did not matter, and a sense of the provisional was translated into housing construction. Such constructions generally lacked any aesthetic component, or they turned to kitsch, to the display of bad taste and gaudy colors. At that time, to talk about "border architecture" was almost a plea to the future. Why make an effort to build something that lasts, if one intends to leave as soon as one can? Or if it does not matter that someone stays, because they will not stir themselves to the contemplation of beauty or to enthusiasm for the aesthetic.

This situation has not yet disappeared; in some cases it is still in force. But it is not the norm, and the influence of contemporary world architecture is already being felt, especially, and for obvious reasons, from California. On the other hand, what type of architecture is being abandoned? In the majority of the cases, it's a very precarious one, without visual rewards or proud traditions, with a determinism that excludes aesthetics. But already there are more and more exceptions. Therefore, future architectural and aesthetic harmony will no longer be the product of resignation or happenstance.

Translated by Sofía Ruiz-Alfaro

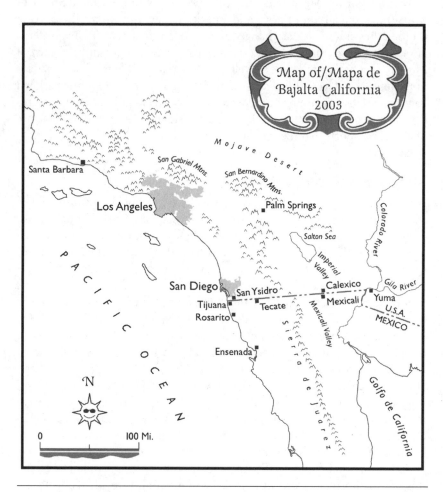

Map of/Mapa de
Bajalta California
2003

Artwork by Jane Sinclair

2
Peopling Alta California

PHOEBE S. KROPP AND MICHAEL DEAR

When Carey McWilliams wrote his seminal *Southern California Country* over half a century ago, he was among the first to discuss the area "south of the Tehachapi" as one contiguous region. And yet, McWilliams saw the region not as a unified whole, but rather as an "archipelago" of isolated communities.[1] Southern Californians developed their expansive and expanding network of suburban villages against the American urban models of Chicago and New York, self-consciously imagining cities that might hold a metropolitan allure while retaining semirural amenities. This regional consciousness, coming to the fore in the early twentieth century, rested on leisure, sunshine, and a distinctly antiurban impulse. As suburban paradises retreated further into the hills, residents might have continued to identify with an urban center, but likely did not visit it regularly.

Suburbs began to back up into each other, and today only the Marines' Camp Pendleton breaks the continuous line of development along the coast from Tijuana to Ventura. As these formerly spread-out, now-neighboring communities draw even closer via economic links, transportation networks, and residents' criss-crossing social ties, it becomes difficult to distinguish where one leaves off and another begins. If the nearly 19 million people who reside within the region's limits are not unified in sentiment or social conditions, they do live in an interconnected urban matrix. The 2000 annual report of the Southern California Association of Governments applies the label "the Southern California Metropolis"—one unit.[2] Despite the intentions of many residents, Southern California has become a complex, integrated, and incontrovertibly urban place.

Southern California's sprawl results from over a century of relentless growth. A constant imperative to grow lent the region its antiurban paradox—residents and developers crave growth but shun its consequences. In San Diego, the focus on attracting new residents, tourists, and business consistently wins out over local needs. Los Angeles emerged as the region's city center even as it formed a "fragmented metropolis," according to one of its biographers, Robert Fogelson. Other Southern California cities came to rely upon Los Angeles' urban infrastructure while they eschewed association with its urban image. A recent political candidate in San Diego ran on a platform of "Prevent Los Angelization Now." Moreover, the region's white population has been reluctant to accept Southern California's long-standing but increasingly nonwhite population, a situation in part generated by the region's appetite for a vast pool of cheap labor and by its proximity to the United States–Mexico border. Something white Southern Californians tend to see as the outer boundary of the region, the border also defines the region, something that connects rather than separates. Growth, after all, is largely measured in population—the flow of people, many kinds of people, pulled by conscious appeals and tacit needs, into the region. The history of Southern California, its urban and regional character, is largely the ongoing history of its peopling.

Missions and Pueblos, 1750–1850

The eighteenth- and early-nineteenth-century populations of Southern California did not prophesy the region's broad urban future. Indian village, Spanish mission, and Mexican rancho settlements alike remained rural, isolated, and small. Yet, successive waves of foreign interest in an already-peopled Southern California lent the region an immediate transnational context. While in Spain or in Massachusetts, people moved from one county to the next, Southern California's new residents arrived from far-flung nations. This early period also established two population growth vectors that would persist over the decades—north from Mexico and west from the United States.

Native Californians remain the region's longest-standing residents. Their evolving civilizations operated on the Southern California landscape for millennia, and their collective sense of the region as place belies the assumption that Californians always hail from somewhere else. On the eve of Spanish colonization, native peoples of Southern California, including the Kumeyaay/Diegueño, Luiseño, Cupeño, Cahuilla, Kumi'vit/Gabrieleño, and Chumash tribal groups, were settled throughout the coastal valleys in small villages. Their social, cultural, and political organizations were complex and differentiated, a fact that later immigrants to the region failed to recognize. They practiced a sophisticated hunting, fishing, and food-gathering economy based on a shared ecological knowledge base. Approximately 35,000–

40,000 Indians lived in the southern region prior to European colonization, about 12% of the total Indian population then living in what is now the State of California.[3]

On the far northern frontier of its holdings, Spaniards found California inaccessible and poor compared to the wealth of Mexico. Imperial rivalry, however, spurred Spain to begin a major push into California. To forestall Russian, English, and French designs on the territory, Spain sent missionaries and soldiers up from Baja California to coopt native populations and establish governance in the region. They located the first mission and *presidio* (garrison) at San Diego in 1769 and laid out one of the first *pueblos* (towns) at Los Angeles in 1781. With frontier life unappealing to many, Spanish governors had to lure colonists to these towns with promises of cash subsidies, stock and farmland, town lots, and tax exemptions. Still, the pueblos grew slowly—in its first twenty years Los Angeles gained only 500 residents.[4]

The missions were another story. Led by Junípero Serra, the Franciscan Order began to establish mission communities along the coast, among abundant Indian settlements. By 1792, there were six missions in the southern portion of California—San Diego, San Luis Rey, San Juan Capistrano, San Gabriel, San Fernando, and San Buenaventura. They included those with the greatest population and wealth of any in the chain, which eventually numbered 21 and stretched north to Sonoma. Missionaries' plans called for converting Indians into Christians and skilled laborers for the colony. Yet both Indians' consistent resistance and colonial disputes never allowed the Spanish to gain complete control over the native populations of California.[5]

Disease in part accomplished what no amount of Spanish persuasion or coercion could. Between 1769 and 1846, California Indian populations declined to about one-third of their precontact levels. As elsewhere in the New World, the havoc European-borne diseases wreaked on native political leadership, familial networks, village life, and religious traditions proved to be the most disruptive element of colonization. Though reduced in number, those that withstood the onslaught found ways to adapt their cultures to the Spanish system. Indians, indeed, formed the primary agricultural and artisanal labor force for Spanish California, without whom the colony might not have survived.[6] Mission construction also offered outlets for native artistic expression, an aesthetic that survived multiple whitewashings to inform the region's cultural landscape.

By 1820, despite half a century of colonization, Southern California remained sparsely settled. Capital and trade grew slowly. A newly independent Mexico inherited these difficulties. Attempts to encourage economic growth through liberal distribution of land grants did little to encourage migration, as the great ranchos supported many cattle but few residents. Mexico decided to secularize the mission properties to generate revenue. Though freeing Indians from Franciscan control, this action provided them few alternatives but to continue on the lowest rungs of the labor market. Secu-

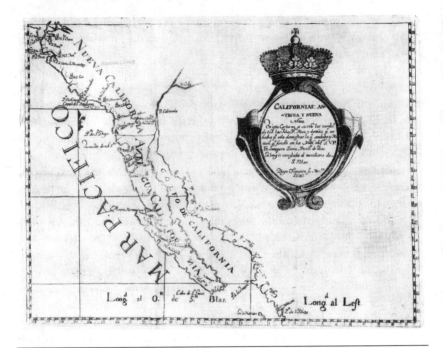

Figure 2.1 Map published in Francisco Palou's biography of Junípero Serra in 1787, the first to show any boundary between the two Californias. The line divided the mission territory of the Franciscans from that of the Dominicans. (Courtesy of the Bancroft Library, University of California, Berkeley.)

larization put mission lands and stock up for sale, throwing into disarray what had been the most efficient agricultural operations in the territory. These lands fell to a small group of ranchero families, the Californios (or California-born). Closely intermarried, this oligarchy became the de facto political power in the region.[7]

By the 1830s, Anglo-Americans began to arrive in Southern California in larger numbers. Traders and ambitious young men came to California, married into Californio families, and gained a measure of control over ranchos, politics, and the economy. These family alliances initially proved beneficial to both sides. When Alfred Robinson, Massachusetts native and agent for the powerful Bryant, Sturgis and Company, married Doña Anita de la Guerra in the 1830s, Robinson rose to the level of California gentry and the de la Guerras gained competitive advantages in the trade of their hides and tallow.[8] Though many Yankees converted to Catholicism, became Mexican citizens, and adapted their personal habits to Mexican custom, they also believed California held untold riches that neither Spain nor Mexico had yet fully tapped. Colonial disorganization and a perceived underdevelopment led many Americans to adopt a negative view of Mexican society, government, and people, and thus to a presumption that California was destined to be a State. Visitor Richard Henry Dana captured this sentiment in 1843 when he wrote of California, "In the hands of an enterprising people, what a country this might be!"

Many in the eastern United States agreed with Dana, believing that America had a Manifest Destiny to expand its territory westward all the way to the Pacific Coast. Under expansion-minded President James Polk, this belief became a military goal. Although the American conquest of California's territory itself was relatively swift and bloodless, Californios, particularly in the southern region, did offer some resistance and fought one pitched battle in the San Diego area before surrendering. The Treaty of Guadalupe Hidalgo officially ended the Mexican/American War in February 1848, ceding California and a large portion of the Southwest to the United States. Scarcely one month later, an American found gold in the Sierra Nevada foothills, the opening salvo in what would become a more feverish battle for California—the struggle to pull all the gold out of its hills.

The great rush of people into California changed its social dynamics and world economic significance overnight. In the north, Anglo-Americans overwhelmed the existing population; most of the 100,000 to 200,000 new people that arrived in California by 1852 landed in San Francisco. Nearly all the new inhabitants were men, and their points of origin could be found nearly as often in Europe, South America, Mexico, and China as in New York, Massachusetts, or Ohio. Although a few years earlier all immigrants would have been foreigners, the recent acquisition of California by the United States made American goldseekers into citizens.

The gold rush affected Southern California but did not inundate it in quite the same way. Though quickly reduced to a small minority of the state's population, Californios witnessed a more gradual waning of their demographic power in the southern portion and maintained a pivotal bloc at the state's Constitutional Convention in 1850. Californios cast crucial swing votes on issues such as borders, suffrage requirements, and division of the state into North and South. Although Californios believed this last move might permit them to forestall the transformation the North had already experienced, they came to realize that identification as a Southern state might inadvertently throw their lot in with slave states. They chose the devil they knew, and cast their votes for the Northerners. They must have understood it was the beginning of the end.[9]

Business Blocks, 1850–1884

Though Southern California developed more slowly following the gold rush than did the north, it underwent a sea-change in regional economy, city building, and demography. The first sign, the ranch economy, began to give way to commercial agriculture. This process reflected both the steady migration of Anglos to the region and the loss of land by Californios. Rancheros' immense land holdings became major tax burdens at the same time as their titles became less sure. By and large unsuccessfully, Californios were forced to defend their ownership to the U.S. government, selling off parcels to pay taxes and legal fees. Their problems were compounded by the fact that a gold-rush-sponsored windfall in the cattle market petered out and in the 1860s, several years of drought effectively killed the rancho system.[10]

Anglo-American capitalists acquired rancho lands by claim or purchase, cut them into smaller plots, and converted them to agricultural uses. The number of these "improved" acres in Los Angeles and San Diego counties increased tenfold in each of the first three decades of statehood—from 2,500 in 1850, to about 25,000 in 1860, and to 250,000 by 1870. The availability of agricultural land encouraged yet more migrants from the East. In their tow came tradesmen, artisans, and manufacturers to supply their farms and transport their goods, as well as lawyers and bankers to manipulate their capital. The comparatively dense settlement of this new economy stimulated the growth of Southern California's towns and cities. Although still dwarfed by San Francisco, Los Angeles began to grow at a fast rate. With only 1,610 inhabitants in 1850, Los Angeles almost tripled in size by 1860. By 1880 it reached over 11,000, still small next to the northern city's 200,000 plus, but compared to its earlier self, a metamorphosis. Cities north and south shared a high percentage of foreign-born inhabitants and growth due not to natural increase, but to net migration, both international and domestic.[11]

As the first transcontinental train arrived in Oakland in 1869, Southern Californians were busy expanding their urban horizons. Confused by the leftover pueblo system of local government, private Anglo forces undertook municipal improvements along Eastern expectations. Speculative investments in water supply, street railways, public utilities, downtown buildings, and real estate began to lay down an urban infrastructure. Although northern Baja California shared the environmental challenges, this period saw a divergence in the rate of growth, as both capital and people flowed primarily north of the newly created border.[12]

This burst of building generated a rivalry between upstart towns that would define Southern California's development for decades. Many localities vied for business and capital, but the preeminent competition was between Los Angeles and San Diego. Only in hindsight does the victory of Los Angeles look inevitable, as both cities were supplicants to the Southern Pacific (SP). San Diego had not kept pace with Los Angeles in the wake of the gold rush, but could claim the foremost natural harbor south of San Francisco Bay. For this reason, prior to the 1880s, San Diego was widely assumed to be the eventual victor. Ironically, the railroad chose Los Angeles because its poor harbor offered less of a potential rival to SP's shipping monopoly in the north.[13]

The Southern Pacific exerted a great degree of control over Southern California's development, an issue that would fester for half a century. Resentment against the railroad extended in California to the Chinese workers it hired to complete its rail network. The backlash against Chinese immigrants in the 1860s and 1870s is one early example of Californians desiring growth but disliking what it entailed. In this case, they desperately wanted a railroad, quickly and cheaply, but abhorred the SP's attendant dominion. They directed the lion's share of their frustration toward the laborers themselves, blaming the Chinese for being willing to work for low wages, and more generally blaming them for being Chinese. Although typically associated with San Francisco's Workingmen's Party, anti-Chinese sentiment took hold in Southern California as well. In fact, the worst outbreak of violence occurred in Los Angeles in 1871. After a white man was killed in a dispute between two Chinese companies, a mob nearly 1,000 strong looted and burned the small Chinatown, killing eighteen people and leaving their bodies on display in improvised gallows—hanging off wagons, awnings, and gates. Only six offenders received sentences.[14] Already, Southern Californians had established a precedent that the region belonged only to a portion of its residents.

Booster Times, 1885–1915

In the thirty years surrounding the turn of the twentieth century the population of California rose to nearly three million. During this time, Southern California made a bid to compete with San Francisco for population and prominence. The redirection of migrants was no accident. Turn-of-the-century Southern California was a booster's paradise. Known derisively throughout the West as self-interested town promoters, boosters both rose (or sank) to new levels of audacity in Southern California. Capricious speculation, carnival-style enticements, and exaggerated claims, as well as some well-documented swindles, earned boosters dubious reputations. Yet the more shrewd among Southern California promoters came to understand that they might build a sustained regional appeal based on climate, growth opportunities, and unique urban landscape. Over the course of this period, the region's leading capitalists, developers, and writers mounted an open-ended, nationwide booster campaign that extolled the virtues of Southern California, enticing tens of thousands of Americans to pull up stakes. Together, boosters and migrants put Southern California on a fast track to growth.

The first indication of a southward shift of California migrants came in 1885, when the Santa Fe Railway finally broke the Southern Pacific's stranglehold and opened a direct rail line from the east to Southern California in 1887. The ensuing rate war reached absurd proportions; a one-way fare from Kansas City to Los Angeles fell from $125 to $1. Real estate speculation matched the wild climate and hundreds of new towns were planned and advertised.[15] Though the boom collapsed in 1889, it left thousands of new residents and valuable new publicity tools.

The boom offered San Diego a measure of national prominence and a chance for surpassing Los Angeles. But when the boom went bust, San Diego suffered more than its rival and was slower in recouping its losses. San Diegans continued to talk big, but by 1900, its fate was sealed—it would play a supporting role to Los Angeles' star. After the turn of the twentieth century, the only place the rivalry really flourished was in the minds of San Diego leaders. Los Angeles had come to occupy the enviable position of ignoring local pretenders and competing with cities on a wider scale, within the West and beyond.

Though the ensuing years repeated the cycle of boom and bust, Southern California cities accomplished steady growth in population, infrastructure, and economy. Los Angeles agressively sought to become the region's manufacturing center. Once the city gained the direct railway route, its leaders decided to go after a premier commercial harbor. Los Angelenos managed to convince the federal government to spend $4 million to build a breakwater at San Pedro and help them create the Port of Los Angeles. Commercial traffic through the Port increased along with an industrial expansion begun in the 1890s. The city hosted 750 manufacturing enterprises and 21,000 workers in 1890; by 1909 it had grown to 1,325 enterprises employing 147,000 workers. These included lumber mills, publishing firms, machine shops, and branch plants of rubber producers and auto manufacturers. Though lagging behind smaller midwestern cities, Los Angeles surpassed contenders around Southern California and the West.

San Diego and Los Angeles grew nearly tenfold between 1890 and 1915, to approximately 50,000 and 400,000, respectively; smaller urban settlements in the region rose with this tide. The population that swelled Southern California cities contained a diverse mix of origins and ambitions. On the one hand, the rapid development drew a continuing stream of job seekers: southern African-Americans, encouraged by W. E. B. DuBois; Japanese immigrants looking for new opportunities; and Mexicans pushed off their peasant lands and toward the border by Porfirio Diaz's modernization policies and development of northern rail connections. Although these migrants often found factory work closed to them and were relegated to agricultural labor and domestic service, their ethnic-community businesses thrived. On the other hand, between 1890 and 1915, many native-born whites arrived, often with funds, skills, and professions. Indeed, they dominated the migrant flow. These newcomers came not in search of factory work but a new kind of urban home life. They put a conservative, Protestant, Republican stamp on the region. One commentator deemed Los Angeles, "Iowa with palm trees" and boosters began to promote it as a "city of homes."[16]

One of the mechanisms through which institutions like the Chambers of Commerce and the Boards of Trade attracted these "homeseekers" was tourism. As early as the 1870s Southern California had gained a small fol-

Figure 2.2 *Americans in El Paso Watching Mexican Insurectos From Across the Rio Grande.* (Andreas Brown Postcard Collection, The Getty Research Institute, circa 1914–1916.)

lowing as a health retreat, and hoteliers established resorts to cater to Pullman-car tourists. The Arlington in Santa Barbara (1876), the Raymond in Pasadena (1886), the Hotel del Coronado in San Diego (1888), and the Mission Inn in Riverside (1890) were only the most famous of the lavish tourist resorts. While visiting, these potential new residents attended Pasadena's Tournament of Roses first held in 1890, viewed Abbot Kinney's reconstruction of Venice complete with canals opened in 1905, and saw craftsman bungalows dotting the Southland in versions both grand and humble.[17]

A major tourist draw came to center on a fanciful image of the state's Spanish history. Helen Hunt Jackson's 1884 melodramatic novel *Ramona* bathed the Spanish era in a romantic light. Intended as a protest novel to call attention to the plight of California Indians, Jackson's readers responded instead to the narrative's lush descriptions of an idyllic rancho life. More than a few came to California in search of *Ramona's* homeland; alert residents promoted hallmarks of this past to cater to them. A popular initiative was to rehabilitate and publicize the local Spanish missions. This search for Spanish romance would consume several decades and come to mark regional identity for many white residents.[18]

Local writers elaborated on this and other regional themes. In fact, much literary production during this era concentrated on local promotion. Charles Fletcher Lummis edited a widely read magazine, first *Land of Sunshine,* later *Out West,* that promoted Southern California, its mission myth, transplanted writers, and himself. Lummis and his colleagues championed the regenerative qualities of the region's "Mediterranean climate" and Spanish heritage for the Anglo race. Moreover, he pointed out the possibilities for profit that lay in the marketing of these qualities. He elaborated on the sentiment expressed by a Los Angeles Chamber of Commerce president in 1916: "We realize today," he later wrote, "that the Old Missions are worth more than money, are a greater asset to southern California than our oil, our oranges, even our climate!"[19] Lummis' writings instructed Southern Californians in marketing the missions and all things Spanish. Both tourists and residents were sold, and they began to make the region over in Spanish style.

Orange stocks were on the rise after the turn of the century with the arrival of the Santa Fe and the advent of the refrigerated car. By 1900 over seven million orange and lemon trees stood in Southern California's citrus belt. Growers publicized their produce across the nation through their 1893-founded marketing cooperative, the California Fruit Growers' Exchange (Sunkist). They sent special winter trains loaded with oranges to the midwest and packaged their fruit in colorful crate labels with slogans like "Oranges for Health, California for Wealth." The citrus industry thus added to the alluring image of the region and enticed midwesterners to become citrus growers themselves, so-called "gentlemen farmers" who owned the groves but did little of the planting and picking. The citrus industry relied upon a labor force drawn from disenfranchised, nonwhite immigrants (first Chinese, and later Japanese and Mexican) whose absolute population numbers continued to rise despite a proportional decline.[20]

Whether they came for Spanish romance, orange groves, bungalow homes, or jobs, new residents demanded that Southern California's cities accommodate them, ushering in large-scale planning for urban amenities, transportation access, and land and resource usage. Private developers built up public infrastructure as part of the promotion of their own growth enterprises. Henry E. Huntington sponsored the laying of 900 miles of street railway lines between 1901 and 1911, which stimulated the subdivision of his holdings in places like San Gabriel, Sierra Madre, and Redondo Beach.[21] In San Diego, Ed Fletcher used his savvy at developing water resources, building dams and flumes around the county to enhance his subdivisions at Grossmont, El Cajon, Del Mar, and Solana Beach.

Water proved to be crucial. The very Mediterranean climate that travel brochures so extolled did not provide water in enough supply to meet the needs of Southern California's growing population, at least not in the ways Americans were becoming accustomed. Building reservoirs and aqueducts to service the burgeoning cities and farms was fairly haphazard before the Wright Irrigation Act. This seemingly mundane 1887 legislation allowed for the speculative development of water resources through irrigation districts, providing a major stimulus for local agriculture and sustaining the high rate of urban development.[22]

Although San Diego and the smaller counties were able to draw enough water for the time being from the surrounding mountains, Los Angeles' ranges could not meet the city's thirst. Local leaders looked to the liquid potential of the Sierra snowpack. Again, private profit and public works collaborated to bring water 233 miles from the Owens Valley in 1913. A story of urban ambition sensationalized in the 1974 movie *Chinatown*, the Los Angeles Aqueduct still stirs suspicions of conspiracy and corruption. Yet the connection of speculative real estate investment and municipal works was common to the region's development and less sinister than its reputation suggests. Suburban developers and city leaders shared the same booster logic and banked on Southern California's growth in many forms.[23]

Boosters and businessmen followed up this unrelenting commitment to growth with a conservative approach to government and labor, in contrast to San Francisco. In Los Angeles, capitalists established a near-iron-clad open shop. Led by the publishers of the *Los Angeles Times,*and the capitalist club known as the Merchants' and Manufacturers' Association (MMA), local employers waged war on unions. In a unique turnabout, the MMA undertook a boycott against employers who negotiated with unions. Its member corporations withheld bank loans and pulled orders, crushing labor organizing to a degree unheard of in most American cities. In 1910, following a series of divisive strikes, the *Los Angeles Times* building was dynamited, an act to which union activists John J. and James B. McNamara confessed. The conviction of the McNamaras at trial allowed conservative leaders to use fear of radicalism as a tool against reform and to keep the open shop in Los Angeles for another thirty years.[24]

Despite this conservative firewall, Southern California offered major support and many candidates to the state's Progressive movement. This loose coalition of middle-of-the-road, middle-class reformers targeted the Southern Pacific as a common enemy. Southern Californians had different reasons for resenting the railroad than their counterparts in the north—control over development being a more salient regional issue than corruption, the bugbear in San Francisco—yet they joined in hopes of ousting the railroad from its perceived dominant position in state politics, something assumed to be accomplished with the 1911 election of Hiram Johnson. Along with initiative, referendum, and recall, public regulation of railroads and utilities, and the direct primary, the issues Southern California Progressives concerned themselves most about were temperance, female suffrage, and immigration.[25]

That campaigns of racial exclusion that accompanied progressive-minded reform in Southern California is less ironic than it initially appears.

While working to improve the Southern California way of life, these reformers never questioned that it included only white Americans, in fact it needed protection from the incursions of nonwhite, non-Americans. Anglo Californians, who led the Progressive movement at large, resented the competition of often successful Japanese farmers. Assumptions of white supremacy as well as fears of a "yellow peril" drove California voters, Progressive or no, to pass an Alien Land Law in 1913, which forbade noncitizens from owning real property in the state. Directed primarily at Japanese farmers who cultivated Southern California soil, this measure had effects less economic than political, symbolic of a Progressive and Californian ascription of citizenship along racial lines.

Houses on a Thousand Hills, 1915–1929

In 1915, San Diego staged the Panama-California Exposition to celebrate the opening of the Panama Canal, drawing more than three million visitors and national attention to the region. This fair signaled the opening of a new era in Southern California. Despite the fact that San Francisco hosted the official World's Fair that year and thus held onto its formal status as the state's urban leader, Southern California's smaller fair broadcast the region's future in bold terms. It foretold the sophisticated booster apparatus, suburban development strategy, and population flood that would tilt state power southward in the pivotal decade of the 1920s. Of the three million new migrants who came to California in the 1920s, two-thirds went to Southern California, making for a region of three million by 1930.[26] If San Francisco was the capital of California's nineteenth century, Los Angles was already emerging as the capital of its twentieth century.

The Panama-California Exposition offered an explicit display of *Southern* California, the culmination of a nascent regional identity boosted for thirty years. It gave the region a spacious and lavish architectural vision of the Spanish Colonial, a style that influences home builders and buyers still. It pictured the region's future in ambitious expectations for agricultural, commercial, and urban development. Its most futuristic show staged a "War of the Worlds," a multimedia extravaganza in which New York and Chicago are overrun by African and Asian armies in the year 2000. In one piece, this feature expressed hostility toward nonwhite races and separated the region from the supposed urban polyglots of eastern cities.[27] The carefully nurtured Southern California self-image exhibited at the Panama-California helped to draw the hoped-for millions.

San Diego's urban ambitions and growth anxiety had spurred it to attempt the Exposition as a grand civic advertisement. And though by 1915 it could not hope to compete with Los Angeles, a city ten times its size, San Diego remained obsessed with growth. Having lost the railroad, population, industry, and ship-

Figure 2.3 Palace of Transportation in the Corinthian Collonade. Panama-Pacific International Exposition, San Francisco, 1915. (San Francisco looks to Classical Greece for inspiration.)

ping stakes to Los Angeles, San Diego took aim at federal investment and lobbied for the U.S. Navy, offering port facilities and coastal lands for military uses. This placed San Diego on a different path, as the city set its economic sights on mercantile, tourist, and retirement incomes rather than industrial development. While Los Angeles manufacturing was expanding to over 4,900 plants and 581,000 workers by 1929, San Diegans developed a kind of ambivalent antipathy about industry. Leaders wanted the economic and political power that came with industrial might, but preferred to think of their city as prettier and quieter. City leaders held out hope that San Diego might escape Los Angeles' considerable shadow in qualitatative if not quantitative terms.[28]

Figure 2.4 Fine Arts Building, Plaza de California. Panama-California International Exposition, San Diego, 1915. (San Diego looks to the mission for inspiration.)

Numbers told an interesting story, however, as the great influx of migrants in the 1920s amplified previous population trends but altered them in subtle ways. Although white midwestern states continued to send its sons and daughters to Southern California, immigrants began to make inroads. Percentages of those classified "foreign-born white" remained markedly below those of Eastern industrial cities, but numbers and proportions of nonwhite migrants and immigrants were on the rise. African-Americans, for example, responded in sizable numbers to the booster notices, drawn by the possibility of owning their own homes and businesses. The black population of Los Angeles more than doubled in the 1920s to 38,000. Employers still preferred the labor of noncitizens and vigorously recruited the services of new immigrants, often sending agents into Mexico to entice workers north. Counter to the wider immigration restriction movement of the 1920s, Southern California land owners lobbied the federal government to exempt Mexicans from proposed quotas, as they formed the key agricultural labor force for the region. Mexican immigrants also established an urban presence in Southern California, 100,000 strong in Los Angeles by 1930.[29]

The booster message was getting to the people, as an expanding publicity network advertised California on a mass scale. Spearheading this new promotional campaign was the fledgling motion picture industry that had recently converged on Hollywood. Production companies found Southern California's varied climate and terrain to their liking, and by 1914, seventy had established themselves in the area. Movie popularity exploded in the 1920s, with recognizable stars and the addition of sound, along with the corporatization of the industry. By the end of the decade, a few studios emerged to control the movies from filming to viewing. From Hollywood's association with glamour and stars' life styles to the region's scenery appearing as a constant backdrop, the movies boosted Southern California.[30]

Americans found movie stars' suburban life styles captivating. During this era, both tours and magazine spreads of stars' homes got started. Starlets' stylish homes seemed to represent the region's ideal, and the Universal City neighborhood exemplified the connection of Hollywood and suburban dreams. Built in the hills of the San Fernando valley by theater owner Carl Laemmle in 1913, the town contained homes, studios, and administration buildings in the ascendant Spanish Colonial style—white stucco, recessed windows, red tile. Laemmle pointed not to the loftiness of its star-residents, but to their similarity with other Los Angelenos. Universal City was, he claimed, a "melting pot," where ordinary people had climbed the ladder of success and claimed the American dream.[31]

The desire for this ideal pushed suburban development and home construction to a frenzied pace. The value of Los Angeles building permits in 1919 stood at $28 million; the year 1923 brought in $200 million worth of new building. Developers began to construct complete communities prior to sale, rather than just selling empty lots. One might move into a ready-made neighborhood, with paved streets, complete utilities, parks, and an architectural theme. The all-Spanish architecture of Rancho Santa Fe and Palos Verdes during this era offered definitive examples of the planned community, but less affluent areas followed their lead and packaged homes and neighborhoods along remarkably similar lines.[32]

Migrants, residents, and real estate developers alike deliberately decentralized Southern California cities. Desiring a certain rustic quality to home life, Anglo midwesterners came in search of suburbs that were, according to Fogelson, "spacious, affluent, clean, decent, permanent, predictable and homogeneous." These criteria dictated "single family houses, located on large lots, surrounded by landscaped lawns, and isolated from business activities." Southern California urban planners were among the first to suggest zoning ordinances, furthering the separation of home and work, and residents established homeowners' associations to protect their neighborhoods from encroachment.[33]

The consequences of this need for "protection" meant that the "American Dream" in Southern California was doled out along racial lines. Whatever the increasing numbers of non-Anglo residents, the boom of the 1920s was fed primarily by middle-class, midwestern white migrants and they dictated the terms of the housing market. Developers and homeseekers alike promoted a racially and residentially segregated vision of homogeneity through restricted title deeds. These prohibited owners from selling property to any one not of the white race, although allowing nonwhites to reside in domestic service capacities. Such deeds provided legal underpinnings for a long-standing pattern of racial segregation in Southern California and pushed nonwhites into ghettoes and barrios that still exist today. Rapid population growth in the face of fewer residential options made the black districts of Los Angeles, for example, much more dense than the white suburbs. By 1940 nearly 70% of African-Americans in Los Angeles resided in an area known as South-Central.[34]

Southern Californians adopted the automobile as an accomplice in spreading out the city. Southern California had been a haven for motor car enthusiasts since early in the century. With the introduction of the inexpensive Model T, automobile ownership increased throughout the country and skyrocketed in Los Angeles. During the 1920s, as the population of the city was merely doubling, the number of registered automobiles quintupled to over 800,000; by 1925, Los Angeles had one auto for every three people, more than twice the national average.[35] The drivers of these many motor cars began to transform the region's landscape, lobbying for paved highways, good roads, and parking lots.

Literally fueling this mass motorization were the abundant oil supplies in the region, which made gasoline cheap and easily available. Though oil had been discovered in the Los Angeles basin in 1892, in the 1920s, phenomenal strikes coincided with high levels of demand to make California the nation's largest oil-producing state for a time. Three tremendous discoveries defined this boom—Standard Oil found the first field at Huntington Beach in 1920; Union Oil struck at Santa Fe Springs in 1921; and, the same year, Shell discovered the rich Signal Hill, barrels per acre, the most productive oil field ever tapped. California oil produced more than $2.5 billion during the decade, a half-billion more than all the gold ever mined in the state. This financial bonanza inspired Southern California homeowners to dig up their back yards in hopes of hitting a strike themselves—and a few even did. Yet by the end of the decade, the oil industry consolidated into a few corporate entities that controlled the product from well to pump.[36]

Culturally, Southern California in the 1920s was a puzzle. It produced racy Hollywood movies like *The It Girl* and *Why Change Your Wife?* but it also contained a significant following of the Ku Klux Klan and the Better America Federation. Suburbanites followed flamboyant evangelists like Aimee Semple McPherson, but also harbored pronounced tendencies toward conservatism and prohibition. Los Angeles began to acquire its reputation for bizarre movements and unorthodox ideas, yet residents also flocked to "State Societies," where former neighbors from Iowa, Indiana, or Kansas gathered to swap stories over roast chicken and picnic blankets. It was a land of "single-family" homes and yet saw the growth of corporate conglomerates in oil, film, and agriculture. Southern California widely advertised an emergent vision of the suburban good life, but sold it with racially restrictive title deeds. These paradoxes would prove difficult to shake.

Pushing and Pulling, 1929–1945

The decades of Depression and World War in California saw the desperate want of poverty followed by a voracious need for labor. Such U-turns in fortune exacerbated regional paradoxes built around growth. Whereas the crush of wartime migrants transformed the region's population, urban character, and industrial might and set a new tone for the second half of the century, the dilemmas of the 1930s crystallized competing images of Southern California that would endure. The Great Depression inaugurated a lasting imaginative struggle in the region between, as Mike Davis aptly reckoned it, sunshine and noir.

From afar, the Depression appeared to have dealt Southern California a gentle blow. Busby Berkeley, Shirley Temple, and Fred and Ginger offered Hollywood fantasies unharmed by bleak conditions. A jet set of wealthy rode out hard times in well-heeled splendor in places like Palm Springs, Malibu, and Newport Beach. Their barbecues, swimming pools, and resort vacations in part represented the good life people wanted to climb out of the Depression to attain.[37] However, arguably the most compelling image of the Depression, one that Americans seized upon to represent all that had gone wrong, was a California image as well—Dorothea Lange's *Migrant Mother*. Lange's photograph of a destitute woman at a pea-picker's camp in Nipomo seemed to express Depression in elemental symbol and to expose California's boasted plenty as a cruel joke. The literary and film genre of noir built upon the bitterness of the Depression to offer an alternative vision of Southern California as a place of falsity and artifice, a brilliant illusion with a seamy underbelly. It was the Los Angeles streets that Raymond Chandler's Phillip Marlowe prowled and made the city famous for its purported display of such perfect ironies. Though the Marlowe and *Migrant Mother* iconography may be no more "real" than that of Hollywood fantasy, the establishment of this polar tendency in Southern California image-making—booster/cynic, sunshine/noir—marked the Depression/War era.[38]

The powerful pull of the Southern California paradise image remained strong in the early 1930s, as local boosters kept up the charm offensive. Yet many who arrived to collect on the region's promise found disappointment and hostility, for the assumption that the Depression had skipped Southern California was a myth. Major regional industries such as tourism and film were vulnerable to plummeting incomes across the nation. Rural areas and citrus groves were hard hit; state farm revenues fell to half their pre-Depression level by 1932. Overproduction of oil and overspeculation in real estate and finance wiped out jobs and savings for thousands in Southern California, especially with its high number of white-collar professionals and the highest percentage in the nation of retirees. Relief agencies were overwhelmed. In 1931, Los Angeles county welfare rolls rose from 3,500 individuals to 35,000 families. Two years later, at the Depression's nadir, 126,000 families, or up to 600,000 individuals, subsisted on public relief.[39]

Anglo Southern Californians, unaccustomed to poverty in what was supposed to be paradise, invented a series of scapegoats. The first place they looked was the Mexican immigrant population. Newspapers printed wild exaggerations of both the number and percentage of Mexicans on relief, though these incendiary reports failed to mention that although each Anglo family on relief received thirty dollars per month, Mexican families received only twenty. In 1930 many Anglo residents and leaders in Southern California began to push for the "repatriation" of Mexican nationals residing in the region. With their rail fare and meals paid courtesy of city and county agencies, about 35,000 people from Los Angeles (approximately one-third of the city's Mexican population) and up to 75,000 people total were returned to Mexico in the supposedly voluntary program. However, surprise police raids on Mexican neighborhoods, one in Los Angeles' historic Plaza, more than hinted at the use of coercion.[40]

Offering a note of reproach for this repressive racial atmosphere was a group of Mexican muralists who left a lasting artistic impression upon Southern California in the 1930s—David Siqueiros, Jose Clemente Orozco, and Diego Rivera. Painting a number of significant public works in California, these artists offered a regional imagery that undermined booster myths and protested the discrimination of Mexican people. Siqueiros, for example, painted a mural sharply critical of U.S. imperialism on a wall on Olvera Street, a Mexican-themed tourist attraction in downtown Los Angeles. Although some fearful leaders had the offending statement whitewashed, an undercurrent of support for this political style of art developed. According to Sarah Schrank, "American supporters of the WPA art projects saw Mexican muralism as a type of pubic art that could represent a radical, democratic vision for the United States, as well as put people to work using their particular talents and skills." Despite the booster anxiety about tarnishing the region's myth, Mexican and other WPA artists lent Southern California an alternate regional imagery.[41]

The Mexican population, repatriation, and the Depression had a complex effect on the region's agribusiness concerns and their farm labor. The Imperial Valley provides a case in point, as it was the model for the corporate method of mass farming. Its massive and amazingly productive tracts of melons, lettuce, and other thirsty vegetables planted in desert lands required huge irrigation works and armies of seasonal workers. Irrigation, mechanization, and cheap labor made these "factories in the field" possible. Agricultural concerns were inclined to dislike repatriation—ethnic Mexicans

Figure 2.5   The Wonder City of Los Angeles. E.O. Withers, 1931. California
State Library. (Cover of souvenir program celebrating opening of L.A. City Hall.)

provided much of their field and packing labor, and reducing the labor pool
was likely to create a labor scarcity that might force higher wages and foster
unionization. In the 1930–1935 period, in fact, California experienced widespread farm strikes. The Communist organized and multiethnic Cannery
and Agricultural Workers Industrial Union provided leadership for a num-

ber of strikes, particularly one by several thousand vegetable pickers in 1934. Grower reaction was swift and violent, using tear gas, mass arrests, evictions, and arson to break the action. In the end, however, one of the most effective weapons they found to clamp down on union activity was repatriation. Union leaders and followers were easily and repeatedly deported upon any suspected agitation or organization.[42]

Labor confrontations in the fields in the first half of the 1930s became scarce as the decade wore on, primarily due to the migration of 150,000 poverty-stricken midwestern farmers who gutted the labor market. These migrants, arriving in Southern California and dispersing throughout the central valley, came largely between 1935 and 1939 from the Dust Bowl regions of the southern plains and quickly acquired the derogatory moniker of "Okies." They had little choice but to accept low wages, as they arrived with precious few resources and remained ineligible for relief for one year. Their need allowed growers to hold the line against the increasingly unionized Mexican labor force, which was briefly displaced in farm labor.[43]

Okies eventually created other problems. The sudden swell of the labor pool pulled wages down and reduced camps to appalling squalor. The fact that these workers were white, Anglo-Saxon, American citizens made their shocking living conditions and abject poverty more visible to a wider audience than Mexican laborers had been. Activists such as photographer Dorothea Lange, economist Paul Taylor, journalist Carey McWilliams, and novelist John Steinbeck publicized the Okies' plight and exposed California's exploitative agricultural system to the nation. Though Okies proved reluctant to join union efforts, they created vocal demands on the communities in which they lived. Growers could not deport these new workers, though they did try to stop them from coming. Led once again by the City of Los Angeles, the 1935 "bum blockade" posted policemen at major points of entry into California, along the Arizona and Nevada border. Their orders were to turn back indigent transients who could not prove prior California residence. Though this blockade lasted only a few months, it highlighted the near-Fascist lengths to which Southern Californians could go to control the region's population.[44] Nevertheless, the Okies, speaking in part through the fictional voice of Tom Joad and the mute stare of Migrant Mother, sounded a rare warning that the California dream was not everything its boosters had promised.

Such scapegoating efforts, however, did not solve the state's economic difficulties. Southern California residents and politicians began to propose some radical solutions. A multitude of utopian and pension schemes appeared in rapid succession.[45] The radical movement that came the closest to garnering elective power was the unique race for Governor run by muckraker and former Socialist Upton Sinclair in 1934. Running as a Democrat but far more eloquent about the Depression's effect on poor people than state party leaders, Sinclair captured thousands of followers with his dramatic, simply worded plan to End Poverty in California (EPIC). His proposals included a repeal of the sales tax and the controversial idea of "production for use," where the state would purchase idle farms and factories and allow the unemployed to use them in cooperatives. Los Angeles County was an EPIC stronghold; its unemployed, lower-middle-class, white-collar workers found Sinclair's proposals and grassroots tactics appealing. Sinclair managed to defeat his Democratic rival in the primary, but lost the support of the state and national party machinery during the general election, and thus lost the governor's office to a Republican who spent over $10 million to look moderate in comparison.[46]

In the end, federal funds funneled through New Deal projects made the most significant impact upon Southern California's Depression economy. Along with the WPA, PWA, and CCC, which provided employment for thousands of workers, artists, and young people, several public works projects stepped up the region's public investment in infrastructure. The Colorado River Project, including the Hoover Dam and the All-American Canal, supplied more than jobs and water for Southern California; it offered an opportunity for reinvestment and new capital.[47]

Federal funds on a much larger scale during World War II not only pulled the region out of the Depression but also transformed its economy. Nearly 10% of all government war spending found its way into California, sparking a high rate of industrial expansion. The aircraft industry in Southern California advanced rapidly. Companies that had established a foothold in Los Angeles, Orange, and San Diego counties in the 1920s and 1930s grew to employ more than a quarter million workers by 1944.[48] Having repatriated, restricted, and refused new migrants to the region in the 1930s, Southern California employers now found themselves in dire need of labor. Ordered to produce tens of thousands of planes and their armaments, these industries almost single-handedly reignited the region's population growth with a wide-open invitation for workers. War-related industries attracted potential employees from across the nation. African-Americans in particular came in large numbers; the black community of Los Angeles in 1940 numbered some 60,000. It would add almost 200,000 new members in the next five years.[49]

The rapid pace of migration—San Diego rose from 203,000 to 362,000 between 1940 and 1945—created social difficulties: where were all these new residents going to live? Overcrowding and makeshift housing were the result of a slowed housing industry, retooled on the fly in the context of a shortage of materials and labor. As the war continued, developers introduced war workers to a modified suburbia, one that included familiar elements of homogeneity, single-family homes, and lawns, but where low-cost, fast construction, and proximity to defense plants won out over isolation and theme architecture.[50]

Wartime suburbs were less stratified along class lines, as executives and engineers often moved next door to their semiskilled factory employees. Nevertheless, racial discrimination in housing remained prevalent and the wartime crunch solidified racial segregation. Restrictive deeds and covenants abounded in newly planned communities as well as in federal, state, and local policy. Though these legal instruments were struck down in 1948, whites responded to black home buyers with extralegal tactics. In the Allied Gardens subdivision in Compton, white residents threw rotten fruit at their black neighbors' houses, defaced them with paint, ripped out rose bushes, cut electric wires, flooded floors with garden hoses, and burned crosses.[51]

Another manifestation of this urban racial tension brought to the surface by the war was the misnamed Zoot Suit Riots in Los Angeles. Many Mexican youths had adopted a flamboyant style of dress as a marker of a distinctive youthful and cross-cultural identity, but many Anglo-Americans interpreted it as disloyal. In the Summer of 1943, hundreds of white servicemen attacked the zoot suiters, stripped them of their clothes, and beat them, while the police arrested the victims for disturbing the peace. Local newspapers and police officials, blaming "marauding Latin gangs," "roving wolf packs," and a "pachuco menace" for the violence, painted Mexican-Americans as a threat to the Southern California community and, indeed, the American way.[52]

Both local Anglo prejudice and American national security paranoia were at work when the federal government, at President Roosevelt's hand, decided to "relocate" over 100,000 people of Japanese descent to detention camps for fear of sabotage and treason. Beginning in mid-1942, these Japanese-Americans were forced to sell their shops and farms at tremendous losses, leave their homes and possessions, and live for the duration of the war in guarded camps in isolated and unforgiving areas of the West—the Mojave desert, southern Utah, and the eastern Sierras. Two-thirds of those detained were American citizens, and a large percentage of them were Southern Californians. They faced a difficult postwar task of rebuilding their communities among great residual prejudice. The abrogation of civil rights, tremendous economic losses, and an unrecoverable human cost experienced by Southern California's Japanese citizens were as much part of the legacy of World War II in the region as was postwar prosperity.[53]

Full Speed Ahead, 1945–1970

A notable postwar symbol of Southern California was the highway cloverleaf. Reproduced in aerial views on postcards and magazines, the cloverleaf guided highway travelers through major crossroads and garnered praise for the elegant efficiency of its engineering design. Southern California came to rely upon these marvels to handle the millions of new drivers that arrived in the region in the quarter-century following World War II. With 3.5 million living south of the Tehachapis in 1940, Southern California was a major metropolitan area. When that number swelled to 5.5 million by 1950 and 9 million by 1960 (57% of the state's population), it was a region of nearly unprecedented size in America. These new migrants came for old reasons—climate and homes—as well as the new jobs and training provided by the emergent technology industries and GI Bill funds.[54] By the 1960s, with a maturing baby boom youth culture, continued in-migration, and increasing racial diversity and tensions, the Southern California cloverleaf started to bog down in traffic. Shifting directions became slow and painful as residents for the first time in a century looked to put the brakes on growth.

Sustaining war-induced population growth was a long economic boom. The Cold War underwrote the continuation of federal defense spending at a high level and sponsored the development of research and technology-oriented industries. Producing jet aircraft, missiles, satellites, and modern weaponry, defense and space contractors came to dominate Southern California. By 1960, for example, 70% of San Diego's manufacturing workers and 60% of their counterparts in Los Angeles and Orange County were employed in these industries. Additional thousands of military personnel were stationed in the region's numerous bases, particularly in San Diego. Other job sectors grew along with the population, including construction, electronics, chemicals, and garments. Yet the continued reliance on the federal defense budgets made the region's economy vulnerable to future cutbacks.[55]

The housing industry, freed from wartime shortages, exploded to meet the rising demand for suburban homes. Developers came up with new methods to quicken the pace of construction and sales through prefabrication and generous federally underwritten mortgage terms. The California ranch-style house, a rambling one-story structure with outdoor patio, swimming pool, and two-car garage, became the tract-home of choice. Automobile-sponsored, leisure-oriented suburbs devoured farmland and foothills. Rural communities ballooned; Garden Grove in Orange County grew from an outlying town of 4,000 to a city of 100,000 in five years.[56]

The federal government supported the suburban sprawl with its tremendous commitment to building infrastructure. Private and local municipal developers could no longer meet the demand for essential services—water, gas, electric, and sewage. Federally sponsored interstate highway systems and elaborate flood control channels poured thousands of tons of concrete onto the region's urban landscape in the postwar decades. These highways completed the demise of urban railways in Los Angeles and San Diego, as miles of track were pulled up and paved over. In Southern California as across the nation, cultural costs and benefits ran along ethnic lines—highways facilitated access to far-flung affluent suburbs but cut through the heart of ethnic and working-class urban communities.[57]

Southern California received a significant amount of state funds as well, as leaders in Sacramento doled out much of the treasury's surplus on education. It transformed some of the region's colleges to campuses of the University of California. Most of the new UC campuses added or expanded during this era were in Southern California—Los Angeles, Santa Barbara, Riverside, Irvine, and San Diego. UCLA in particular would come to rival the parent institution at Berkeley in funding, student body, and research stature. Private institutions such as the University of Southern California and the California Institute of Technology kept research expertise and baby boom students in the region. The growth of education in Southern California in the 1950s and 1960s profoundly influenced the region's culture for decades to come.[58]

The pursuit of an imagined California suburban dream concentrated on leisure, consumer goods, and the traditional family structure. These all found idealized expression in the 1955 opening of Disneyland in the Orange County suburb of Anaheim. In its first year, more than four million people visited, more than a few of them Californians themselves. Disneyland took theme entertainment to a new level. On the one hand it displayed "Tomorrowland," complete with the latest conveniences for the modern home, and on the other, "Main Street America," a recreation of an ideal of small-town life and a celebration of traditional values, homogeneity, and capitalism. All were neatly encapsulated in a safe container for family-oriented leisure.

Prosperity, however, was not evenly distributed. A key example of this was the extension of the 1942 Emergency Farm Labor Program. This "bracero" program addressed the shortage of farm labor in California and the West by inviting Mexican immigration along prescribed lines. In an agreement negotiated with the Mexican government in possession of some wartime leverage, these braceros were to be extended contracts that guaranteed sufficient wages, adequate housing, health care, and nondiscrimination. Kept in operation until 1964, the bracero program never lived up to these ideals in practice, at least partially because the continuing need for farm labor encouraged extralegal migrants as well as official braceros. Growers could thus exploit the former to undercut the assurances to the latter. When the United States undertook Operation Wetback in 1952 to stall unauthorized entries from Mexico, the California border hosted an ironic situation in which one government agency was recruiting Mexican workers and another was turning them away. This simultaneous encouragement and criminalization of Mexican immigration persists today.[59]

Continued prosperity brought the region in the early part of the 1960s to the apex of its continuous growth. Yet the yawning gap between rich and poor, white and nonwhite, right and left widened. On the right, the John Birch Society offered a parody of conservative ideologies, impugning the United Nations, the graduated income tax, racial desegregation, and fluori-

Figure 2.6 Huelga! Andrew Zermeño, 1965. Offset, 24 × 18.5 in. (Collection of the Center for the Study of Political Graphics.)

dated water as communist plots. The center of its national strength radiated from Southern California's postwar, blue-collar suburbs. On the left, anti-war protesters saw different threats. Although the student movement and hippie culture did not permeate the region to the degree it did in the San Francisco Bay area, the mounting critique of the suburban life style transformed the image of Southern California if not its stratified suburbs themselves. For it was from these suburbs that the New Right rose to stem the tide of radicalism, with two of its spokespersons reaching national power, Richard Nixon and Ronald Reagan.

The Watts Riots of 1965 offered perhaps the most telling example of the poor distribution of California's prosperity. In 1964, largely white California voters approved Proposition 14, which aimed to roll back housing desegregation. Though declared unconstitutional several years later, the passage of this ballot measure by more than a two-to-one margin proved to be the proverbial last straw for many African-Americans in Los Angeles. For them the tragic riots in the Watts ghetto represented a measure of protest against

Figure 2.7   Libertad para Angela, Felix Beltrán, 1971. Offset, 23 × 15 in. (Collection of the Center for the Study of Political Graphics.)

the state's legacy of discrimination and their everyday experiences of inferior housing, inadequate schools, and persistent high unemployment or underemployment. Following arrests and rumors of police brutality, six days of violence left thirty-four people dead, all but three black, and nearly 4,000 in the city jail. The riots involved 10,000 people, damaged over $40 million worth of property, and prompted California officials to call out the National Guard. That their cities might contain the same kind of racial discontent as industrial cities of the northeast shocked many white residents who had assumed that their region's "palm-tree" ghettoes were the exception to the national rule. The riots, however, energized local communities, both black and white. It was following the riots that institutions such as the Inter-City Cultural Center and the Watts Festival got their start.[60]

The great upward trend of population growth in Southern California, which had survived the Great Depression, came to a halt at the end of the 1960s. Though the total population reached approximately 13 million by

1970, the increase that year was less than 1%, by far the lowest rate on record. At the same time, the population was diversifying, as Mexicans now counted for 12% and African-Americans numbered 8% of Southern California residents. These numbers rose both in absolute terms—by natural increase and in-migration–and relative to the slowed pace of white arrivals. Though a national recession in 1969 contributed to it, this slowdown had roots in the deteriorating image of the California dream. The postwar era, despite prolonged prosperity, had replaced images of sunshine, leisure, and opportunity with reports of campus and racial unrest, nagging unemployment, pollution, traffic, and crowds. The region's ability to accommodate a population the size of several small nations appeared to be approaching its limit.

Multiplication and Division, 1970–1990

For the first time, Southern Californians had to deal with the limits of their sun-drenched land. Only in the region's proliferating theme parks—Knott's Berry Farm, Universal Studios, Magic Mountain, Sea World, and the San Diego Zoo and Wild Animal Park—did Southern California appear as rosy as booster legend. As the region's population pushed toward 20 million, the pressure built on local governments, tax structures, the environment, ethnic relations, and the economy. A series of events made plain the lack of consensus.

Though reaching across the West, the Chicano Movement of the late 1960s and early 1970s drew strength from Southern California Mexican-American youth. In a newly bold political stance, Chicanos asserted their citizenship, even rightful ownership to the Southwest as their mythical homeland of Aztlan. In Los Angeles in 1968, nearly 10,000 Chicano students walked out of their high schools, hoping this action would force public attention on the poor quality of their schools, racist curriculum, and alarming drop-out rate. Two years later, Chicano activism centered on protesting the Vietnam war in part because of the high number of Chicano draftees. A rally in East Los Angeles in August 1970, spearheaded by the antiwar Chicano Moratorium, drew between 20,000 and 30,000 supporters. As the peaceful march ended with a celebration in Laguna Park, Los Angeles police, reacting to a minor shoplifting incident at a nearby store, converged on the park, spraying tear gas and mace into the crowd, injuring hundreds and killing one boy. The years following witnessed an increased militancy in the Chicano Movement as well as a flowering of cultural expression and community organization. The San Diego neighborhood of Barrio Logan, for example, took possession of the dead space underneath a highway interchange and turned it into Chicano Park, filling the pillars with murals that depicted their history, heroes, and culture. (Jo-Anne Berelowitz discusses this example in Chapter 5.)

As much a grassroots movement as the Chicano Movement, the taxpayer revolt of 1978 reached far and wide into Southern California's suburban populations who were fed up with the convergence of several economic factors. Inflation had driven up the cost of living in California by 79% since 1968. Still, property taxes were beating the inflation rate twice over and consuming greater and greater shares of personal income. The problem with the current tax system, according to the sponsors of Proposition 13, Howard Jarvis and Paul Gann, was that by the end of the 1970s property values were rising by about 2% per month. When several years passed between assessments of property value, it was not uncommon for homeowners to be hit with tax increases of 50% or more. The high tax burden made home ownership increasingly difficult and taxpayers increasingly angry, especially in the context of a growing state revenue surplus of nearly $3.5 billion by 1978. The Jarvis–Gann initiative rolled back property assessments, allowed reassessments only upon sale or improvement, capped taxes at 1% of property value, and limited the increase to 2% per year. Proposition 13 passed with 65% of the vote, the lion's share of its support coming from Southern California.

The full impact of Proposition 13 would not be felt for years, as the surplus temporarily offset declining revenues. As Chief Justice Rose Bird predicted, it eventually created a skewed tax world in which great disparities in property taxes emerged among properties of similar value. New home buyers with freshly assessed properties found their tax rate higher than neighbors' whose properties had not been assessed in years. Moreover, as the surplus dwindled to nothing by 1981 and economic contractions forced state budget cutbacks, the state began to lose its ability to provide public services such as school buses and museums or to maintain infrastructure such as roads, bridges, and water mains.

Throughout the 1970s and 1980s, Southern Californians explored several ways of putting the brakes on the growth of the region in order to preserve its promises. The environmental movement offered a new directive. Sparked in part by the late-1970s energy crisis and drought, environmentalists' message was that the region's land, water, and air had been deteriorating for decades and would continue to do so. Disturbing sights, like the blanket of smog that had increasingly enshrouded Los Angeles and the polluted coastal beaches, suggested that the physical basis for Southern California's outdoor life was eroding. Environmentalists recruited supporters among slow-growth advocates and incurred reaction among leading industries—oil, real estate, construction, and technology—whose financial interests rested upon continued growth. Environmentalism put such concerns at the forefront of political debates, even if solutions were not always pursued with the vigor activists insisted upon.

The 1980 and 1990 censuses indicated that the changing ethnic diversity of Southern California would reinvent the region as much as tax reform or environmental issues. Mexican- and Asian-Americans in particular began to exert demographic power. Mexicans, whether American citizens or not, had been a significant part of Southern California's population throughout the century, but their numbers rose significantly after 1970, reaching 19% by the end of the decade, and nearly 30% by 1990, an addition of over 2 million people each decade. Their sheer numbers as well as historic and continuous presence foretold an increasing level of influence within regional politics, culture, and society. Nevertheless, the Hispanic population was far from singular; although Mexicans continued to form the largest bloc of Spanish-speaking Southern Californians, Salvadorans, Guatemalans, and other Central Americans have established distinct and sizable communities in the region.[61]

The largest new ethnic group during this period came from Asia. The 1965 Immigration Act repealed quotas and lifted restrictions on immigrants from third-world countries. As a result, the number of foreign-born residents doubled in Los Angeles between 1970 and 1980, largely due to Asian arrivals. This reform led not only to a reopening of Chinese and Japanese immigration, officially closed for nearly a century, but also to a marked increase in immigrants from Hong Kong, South Korea, the Philippines, and (with the end of the Vietnam War) Southeast Asia. Asian populations were ten times more numerous in 1990 than in 1960, and composed nearly 10% of the state's population. A significant majority of this population either resided in Southern California or used it as a point of entry.[62]

One statistic that made heavy rounds in local media and caught the perilous eye of many a white resident was the decline in the relative and absolute numbers of white people in Southern California. In Los Angeles County, between 1960 and 1990, the percentage of whites dropped from over 80 to near 40, and in real numbers fell by 25%. In part this reflected the continued flight to ever-more isolated suburbs in adjacent counties (San Bernardino, Riverside, San Diego). The percentage of whites region-wide also fell below majority level, to approximately 47%. More telling perhaps was the constant repetition of these statistics; the frequency bespoke an anxiety on the part of many white residents who feared they were losing the Southern California good life to various sorts of invasions—immigrants, smog, crime, crowding, and poverty.[63]

A Millennium in the Making, 1990–2000

In the 1980s and 1990s, urban renewal became the watchword. Los Angeles began to build upward as much as outward for the first time, sending skyscrapers to ever more dizzying heights. Developers built stylish downtown lofts in hopes of enticing more affluent city residents. Sports and entertainment complexes got snazzy new locales in the heart of cities, as the Staples

Center moved the Lakers in from Inglewood and a contested new ballpark will likely pull the Padres toward the downtown waterfront in San Diego. Places such as Universal City Walk, the Getty Center, the Ontario Mills Mall, the Gaslamp Quarter, and many others reconstructed the city as a network of spectacular spaces. In them appears an idealized version of the city, without racial strife, homelessness, or poverty.[64] Whatever the booster rhetoric about reinvestment in the city, these efforts reclaim certain spaces from poverty only to push the poor out to other places. Downtown is prettier but is the region any different? The economy, housing trends, urban planning, and race relations have all forged new patterns but remain part of the legacy of more than a century of growth in Southern California.

The end of the Cold War led to downsizing in Southern California's space and defense industries, pulling the region into a sharp recession in the early 1990s. Chickens finally came home to roost in the shrunken financial basis for public services. As the state budget was slashed, educational institutions, social agencies, and city governments found they had little to work with. Southern California's economy, however, began to bounce back quickly. Conversion from defense contracts led to an emergence of a wide array of high-tech industries in the wake of the computer revolution. Though Silicon Valley had led the development of this technology in the 1980s, other locations, in San Diego for example, pioneered biotechnology research and promoted the establishment of a number of major high-tech firms. The gains of this economy for the highly educated, upwardly mobile segments of the Southern California population, however, have been mirrored in the rise of low-wage, low-skill jobs, especially in the service industries.

The high-technology sector also contributed to the decentralization of Southern California's cities. Firms rarely set up shop in downtowns or traditional industrial districts, preferring to locate in amenity-rich semirural campuses, closer to their employees in suburban peripheries. This process accelerates what had been an ongoing phenomenon since the 1960s at least—white flight. This term encompasses a host of reasons why many affluent white residents leave the inner city, or even older suburbs, for increasingly distant, newer communities. Fleeing mixed-race, high-crime, depressed-market areas, white Southern Californians in particular, plus an increasing number of relatively affluent residents of various races, continue to relocate to newly constructed neighborhoods dozens of miles from city centers. Orange County, the Inland Empire, and eastern San Diego county experienced tremendous growth rates in the 1990s. The fastest growing towns in the region between 1980 and 1999 are all located on the former peripheries of urban settlements—Palmdale (879%), Adelanto (589%), Lake Elsinore (390%), Perris (362%), and Victorville (342%). Despite the sprawl, housing costs in the region spiked, making home ownership a much less attainable goal in the 1990s than it was in the 1920s or the 1950s, at least for whites. Home prices in the region, equal to the national average in 1974, rose to 55% above it by 1985, and have continued to spiral upward. Los Angeles County's rate of home ownership fell to 48% in 1998, 18% below the national average.[65]

This suburban exodus fed inner city decline for decades, as it eroded the tax base available for schools and other services in metropolitan neighborhoods. In line with national economic trends, forces that created the high-tech sector led to a loss of manufacturing jobs overseas and their replacement by service-related jobs, many of which do not pay a living wage. A lack of new construction in low-cost and even mid-range housing has led both to its shortage and its dilapidated condition. As rents became less and less affordable, a variety of nontraditional housing forms have proliferated—garages, cars, vans, campers, trailers, tool sheds, and motels. At both federal and local levels, cutbacks in welfare, public health, and mental health services disproportionately affected poor urban areas and left many to fall through the cracks and onto the streets.

So it was that in the 1980s Los Angeles became the homeless capital of the nation. By 1990–1991 an estimated 125,000 to 200,000 homeless people lived in the county. Their population, like the rest of the region, has become dispersed, with high concentrations in Pomona as well as South Central. Though the homeless are often held up as reminders that Southern California has been backsliding from the dream of an abundant good life for all, few coordinated efforts to address the problem have appeared. Actions often appear more concerned with the visibility of the homeless rather than how they got that way; tubular antihomeless bus benches went up around Los Angeles in the early 1990s and localized law enforcement sweeps moved homeless from one district to another and back again.

Many of the same economic forces that led to the homeless crisis contributed to the largest urban conflagration the region had ever seen. In April of 1992, four white police officers were found innocent of any wrongdoing in their beating of a young black man, Rodney King, an act that had been videotaped and since broadcast throughout the world. The trial took place in Simi Valley, a predominately white suburb, while the African-American citizens who awaited their verdict in South Central were outraged. For three days, thousands of people raged against the city, looting stores, beating bystanders, and destroying property. Police returned fire, and the Rodney King riots left 52 people dead, nearly $1 billion in property damage, and 16,000 people arrested (45% Latino, 41% African-American, and 11% white). Clearly, the trial provided a catalyst for the unloading of decades of frustration. In 1990, in South Central, the per capita income was just $7,023 as opposed to $16,149 for Los Angeles County; half its residents were unemployed; and the poverty rate was 30%, 3% worse than it had been in 1965.

Figure 2.8 Operation Gatekeeper: The fence at Tijuana. (Photo: Michael Dear.)

As residents pondered the riots and their aftermath, however, they discovered that the problems ran deeper, were more complex than they had been in the 1965 Watts riots. It was more than just blacks angry at whites. The roots of the 1992 violence were different, part of a new dynamic of immigration. Although Korean shop owners construed the riots as a narrow attack on their success and blacks understood their "rebellion" as a protest against economic inequality and racism, most whites believed the riots represented the "destruction of civil society" itself. White communities blamed the rioters for this breakdown of order; rioters laid the responsibility for the collapse at the feet of the suburbanizing white community and its unwillingness to tackle urban problems. For however brief a moment, the riots evoked regional realization that naive lip-service to multiculturalism as a solution for deep, structural problems of racism and poverty was folly. As two analysts of the riots noted, "the myths of multiculturalism only disguise the sad reality of a society still 'separate and unequal.'"[66] Such willful blindness produced the utter frustration of the rioters and the genuine shock of the region and nation at large.

The barbed rhetoric about illegal immigrants and the militarization of the border further sharpened ethnic tensions. Operation Gatekeeper began in 1993 at San Diego's busy border crossings, with the mass hiring and show of force by Border Patrol agents. (This program is discussed in more detail in Chapters 3 and 4.) Though for a time, numbers of illegal immigrants seemed to decline, Southern California employers continued to rely on them, with few sanctions. In fact, when the North American Free Trade Agreement (NAFTA) went into effect at nearly the same time, the governmental tug-of-war created by the simultaneous operation of the Bracero Program and Operation Wetback reappeared. NAFTA is supposed to encourage a greater integration of the regional economy across the border, yet the border itself becomes more clearly and lethally defined. How can we have a borderless economy with a barricaded border?[67]

When California voters in successive years passed Proposition 187, which would have denied essential services to illegal immigrants, Proposition 209 outlawing affirmative action, and Proposition 227, an English-only initiative that proposed to end bilingual education, the backlash against Mexicans and nonwhites intensified. The various arguments offered—that illegal immigrants were taking valuable tax dollars away from citizens, that nonwhites were taking job and college opportunities away from more qualified white applicants, and that Spanish speakers were taking away the region's American identity—give eerie reminders of the many scapegoats Southern Californians have invoked over the years.

In fact, much of California's "government-by-initiative" has used scapegoats of varying types in lieu of policy by analysis, the major one being government itself. As Peter Schrag pointed out, the conservative neopopulism born out of Proposition 13 maintained a semipermanent revolt against government. Antitax, term limit, and voter-approval-required measures have made it more and more difficult to govern the state just as it becomes a more and more complex place. These trends all contributed to Orange County's bankruptcy in 1994. County revenues declined as a consequence of underfunding following voter measures distrustful of government spending; state fiscal austerity after Proposition 13 that left localities to fend for themselves; an increasingly diverse county with a greater need for public services; and a politically fragmented leadership with bad investment strategies. Yet Orange County is but one instance of the continual retreat from optimism that can be dated almost precisely to 1978. As Peter Schrag characterized it: "the passage of Proposition 13 serves as a convenient way of dividing the post-World War II era in California between that postwar period of optimism, with its huge investment in public infrastructure and its strong commitment to public services, and a generation of declining confidence and shrinking public services." This burden has come to rest more heavily on those who have diversified the region's demography, and particularly, he noted, on children, whose educational opportunities have declined.[68] Yet the divide tells of more than a shift in eras. It echoes the consistent Southern California tendency to operate at cross-purposes: to welcome a burgeoning population but close the doors to part of it; to desire progress but be willing for only part of the population to participate; and to claim success but blame failures on the most convenient scapegoats of the time.

Much attention has been focused on Los Angeles as the portent of our urban future. We are told to pay attention to Southern California because what happens here will eventually come to cities across the nation—it happened with racial pluralities, suburban sprawl, traffic, smog, and urban riots. If this is true, it is then equally important to pay attention to its past, to its peopling. Southern California's residential growth has been assisted by a great investment of public money that subsidized suburbia with both infrastructural and financial incentives. Such assistance goes unrecognized by the Not-In-My-Back-Yard folks who barricade themselves in gated communities and balk at the bill for social services for other parts of the population. The region's economy has been continually undergirded by immigrant labor, people who take great risks to work in Southern California's fields and factories only to be made scapegoats for cultural, urban, and economic problems. The region's population has risen to new levels of racial and ethnic diversity because its businesses reach into global markets and send their booster messages all over the world. Southern California remains a place of paradox amid palm trees.

Notes

1. Carey McWilliams, *Southern California Country: An Island on the Land* (New York: Duell, Sloan & Pearce, 1946), ch. 15. We take our definition from McWilliams as well, including in Southern California the region "south of the Tehachapi," the cities, suburbs, and hinterlands of the following seven counties: Ventura, Los Angeles, San Bernardino, Riverside, Orange, San Diego, and Imperial.
2. Southern California Association of Governments, *The State of the Region, 2000: The Region at the Dawn of the 21st Century* (Los Angeles: SCAG, 2000), p. 21.
3. George Harwood Phillips, *Chiefs and Challengers: Indian Resistance and Cooperation in Southern California* (Berkeley and Los Angeles: University of California Press, 1975), 6–19; Sherburne F. Cook, *The Population of the California Indians, 1769–1970* (Berkeley and Los Angeles: University of California Press, 1976), 34–43. The 12% figure is interesting in light of the fact that nearly 50% of California Indians now reside in Southern California.
4. Robert M. Fogelson, *The Fragmented Metropolis: Los Angeles, 1850–1930* (Berkeley: University of California Press, 1993 [1967]), pp. 6–7; Richard B. Rice, William A. Bullough, and Richard J. Orsi, *The Elusive Eden: A New History of California* (New York: Alfred A. Knopf, 1988), 84–5.
5. Albert L. Hurtado, *Indian Survival on the California Frontier* (New Haven: Yale University Press, 1988), 10–13; Phillips, *Chiefs and Challengers*, 5, 22–34.
6. Hurtado, *Indian Survival*, 10–13; Rice, Bullough, and Orsi, *Elusive Eden*, 84–7, 89–94.
7. Fogelson, *Fragmented Metropolis*, chapter 1; Rice, Bullough, and Orsi, *Elusive Eden*, 95, 115–23; Walton Bean and James J. Rawls, *California: An Interpretive History*, 5th ed. (New York: McGraw-Hill, Inc., 1988), 44–55.
8. Albert L. Hurtado, *Intimate Frontiers: Sex, Gender, and Culture in Old California* (Albuquerque: University of New Mexico Press, 1999), ch. 2.
9. Robert Glass Cleland, *The Cattle on a Thousand Hills: Southern California 1850–1870* (San Marino: The Huntington Library, 1941); Fogelson, *Fragmented Metropolis*, 15; Bean and Rawls, *California*, 96–100.
10. Cleland, *Cattle on a Thousand Hills*; Fogelson, *Fragmented Metropolis*, 15–20.
11. Fogelson, *Fragmented Metropolis*, 18–23; Elias Lopez, "Major Demographic Shifts Occurring in California," *California Research Bureau Note*, vol. 6, no. 5 (October 1999).

12. Fogelson, *Fragmented Metropolis*, ch. 2.
13. Fogelson, *Fragmented Metropolis*, ch. 3.
14. Bean and Rawls, *California*, 178; McWilliams, *Southern California Country*, 91.
15. Rice, Bullough, and Orsi, *Elusive Eden*, 315–16.
16. Fogelson, *Fragmented Metropolis*, ch. 4, 110–23.
17. McWilliams, *Southern California Country*, 143–50; Kevin Starr, *Inventing the Dream: California through the Progressive Era* (New York: Oxford University Press, 1985), 101–5.
18. Phoebe Kropp, "'All Our Yesterdays': The Spanish Fantasy Past and the Politics of Public Memory in Southern California, 1884–1939" (Ph.D. dissertation, University of California, San Diego, 1999), Introduction.
19. Starr, *Inventing the Dream*, 75–87.
20. Bean and Rawls, *California*, 188–92; McWilliams, *Southern California Country*, 205–17.
21. Fogelson, *Fragmented Metropolis*, 89–93.
22. Rice, Bullough, and Orsi, *Elusive Eden*, 271.
23. Bean and Rawls, *California*, 295–98.
24. Bean and Rawls, *California*, 230–34; McWilliams, *Southern California Country*, 287–89.
25. Bean and Rawls, *California*, ch. 22.
26. Fogelson, *Fragmented Metropolis*, 78; Rice, Bullough, and Orsi, *Elusive Eden*, 376.
27. Kropp, "All Our Yesterdays," chs. 2–3; Robert Rydell, *All the World's a Fair: Visions of Empire at American International Exposition, 1876–1916* (Chicago: University of Chicago Press, 1984).
28. Kropp, "All Our Yesterdays," chs. 2–3; Abraham Shragge, "Boosters and Bluejackets: The Culture of Civic Militarism in San Diego, California, 1900–1945" (Ph.D. dissertation, University of California, San Diego, 1999).
29. Causal factors in Mexico of this emigration included Mexico's continuing industrialization; the sudden political shifts of the Mexican Revolution; and the established links between Mexicans south and north of the border. Fogelson, *Fragmented Metropolis*, 76; George Sánchez, *Becoming Mexican American: Ethnicity, Culture, and Identity in Chicano Los Angeles, 1900–1945* (New York: Oxford University Press, 1993); David G. Gutiérrez, *Walls and Mirrors: Mexican Americans, Mexican Immigration, and the Politics of Ethnicity* (Berkeley: University of California Press, 1995).
30. Lary May, *Screening Out the Past: The Birth of Mass Culture and the Motion Picture Industry* (Oxford: Oxford University Press, 1980).
31. May, *Screening Out the Past*.
32. Rice, Bullough, and Orsi, *Elusive Eden*, 376–77; Fogelson, *Fragmented Metropolis*; Kropp, "All Our Yesterdays," chs. 5–6.
33. Fogelson, *Fragmented Metropolis*, 144–45.
34. Bunch, in Norman M. Klein and Martin J. Schiesel, *20th-Century Los Angeles: Power, Promotion, and Social Conflict* (Claremont, CA: Regina Books, 1990); Edward T. Chang and Jeannette Diaz-Veizades, *Ethnic Peace in the American City: Building Community in Los Angeles and Beyond* (New York: New York University Press, 1999), 14; Fogelson, *Fragmented Metropolis*, 137–63.
35. Rice, Bullough, and Orsi, *Elusive Eden*, 377–78; Bean and Rawls, *California*, 282–85.
36. Bean and Rawls, *California*, 278–82.
37. Kevin Starr, *Endangered Dreams: The Great Depression in California* (New York: Oxford University Press, 1996), chs. 1 and 9.
38. William A. McClung, *Landscapes of Desire: Anglo Mythologies of Los Angeles* (Berkeley: University of California Press, 2001).
39. Rice, Bullough, and Orsi, *Elusive Eden*, 396–400; Francisco E. Balderrama and Raymond Rodríguez, *Decade of Betrayal: Mexican Repatriation in the 1930s* (Albuquerque: University of New Mexico Press, 1995), 12.
40. Balderrama and Rodríguez, *Decade of Betrayal*, ch. 1; Rice, Bullough, and Orsi, *Elusive Eden*, 412.
41. Sarah Schrank, "Art and the City: The Politics of Civic Identity and the Visual Arts in Los Angeles" (Ph.D. Dissertation, University of California, San Diego, forthcoming), ch. 2; Kropp, "All Our Yesterdays," ch. 8.
42. Rice, Bullough, and Orsi, *Elusive Eden*, 412–13; Balderrama and Rodríguez, *Decade of Betrayal*.
43. Rice, Bullough, and Orsi, *Elusive Eden*, 413–15.
44. Rice, Bullough, and Orsi, *Elusive Eden*, 413–16; Starr, *Endangered Dreams*, 176–77.
45. For example, in 1932 the short-lived Technocracy movement advocated replacing the current monetary system with an energy system. In 1933, the first public meeting of the secretive, essentially planless Utopian Society drew 25,000 people to the Hollywood Bowl. A doctor from Long Beach, Francis Townsend, proposed a plan for old age pensions in 1934 that drew many

followers among the region's senior citizens. These economic cults had little political salience, and in a way occupied the same social niche as the popular religious cults that had flourished in the 1920s. More practical were the many self-help cooperatives that acquired, grew, and shared surplus produce that flourished in Southern California. McWilliams, *Southern California Country*, 294–96, 301–3; Rice, Bullough, and Orsi, *Elusive Eden*, 407.

46. McWilliams, *Southern California Country*, 294–99; Rice, Bullough, and Orsi, *Elusive Eden*, 404–6.
47. Rice, Bullough, and Orsi, *Elusive Eden*, 401–2.
48. Rice, Bullough, and Orsi, *Elusive Eden*, 444–45.
49. Greg Hise, *Magnetic Los Angeles: Planning the Twentieth-Century Metropolis* (Baltimore: The Johns Hopkins University Press, 1997), 129–30; Bunch, 115–17.
50. Hise, *Magnetic Los Angeles*, 114–52.
51. Hise, *Magnetic Los Angeles*, 7, 146–47; James P. Allen and Eugene Turner, *The Ethnic Quilt: Population Diversity in Southern California* (Northridge, CA: Center for Geography Studies, California State University, Northridge, 1997), 77–9.
52. Gutiérrez, *Walls and Mirrors*, 121–27.
53. Rice, Bullough, and Orsi, *Elusive Eden*, 449–51; Allen and Turner, *Ethnic Quilt*, 123–27.
54. Rice, Bullough, and Orsi, *Elusive Eden*, 459–60.
55. Rice, Bullough, and Orsi, *Elusive Eden*, 467–68.
56. Rice, Bullough, and Orsi, *Elusive Eden*, 460–63; Hise, *Magnetic Los Angeles*.
57. Rice, Bullough, and Orsi, *Elusive Eden*, 462–63, 560–65.
58. Rice, Bullough, and Orsi, *Elusive Eden*, 465–66.
59. Gutiérrez, *Walls and Mirrors*.
60. Davis, *City of Quartz*, 67–78.
61. Allen and Turner, *Ethnic Quilt*, 34–40.
62. Allen and Turner, *Ethnic Quilt*, 34–40.
63. Allen and Turner, *Ethnic Quilt*, 34–40.
64. Michael Sorkin, ed., *Variations on a Theme Park: The New American City and the End of Public Space* (New York: The Noonday Press, 1992).
65. SCAG, *State of the Region, 2000*, 17, 110.
66. Edward T. Chang and Jeannette Diaz-Veizades, *Ethnic Peace in the American City: Building Community in Los Angeles and Beyond* (New York: New York University Press, 1999), 4–5, 9–10, 16.
67. Peter Andreas, "Borderless Economy, Barricaded Border," *NACLA Report on the Americas*, vol. 33., no. 3 (November 1999). An excellent overview of the history and consequences of Operation Gatekeeper is provided by Joseph Nevins, *Operation Gatekeeper: The Rise of the "Illegal Alien" and the Making of the U.S.-Mexico Boundary* (New York: Routledge, 1998). See also Belinda I. Reyes, Hans P. Johnson, and Richard van Swearingen, *Holding the Line? The Effect of the Recent Border Build-up on Unauthorized Immigration* (San Francisco: Public Policy Institute of California, 2002).
68. Peter Schrag, *Paradise Lost: California's Experience, America's Future* (New York: The New Press, 1998); Mark Baldassare, *When Government Fails: The Orange County Bankruptcy* (Berkeley: University of California Press, 1998).

3
Peopling Baja California

HÉCTOR MANUEL LUCERO

The Farthest Corner of Mexico

The Baja California Peninsula was discovered in 1532, as a result of Hernán Cortés's interest in exploring what we know today as the Pacific Ocean. The news of the existence of a "great island to the west" (which turned out to be a peninsula) motivated Cortés to venture there in 1535. Although his visit to the peninsula was brief, it marked the time when Europeans arrived at the Californias. For thousands of years before then, people had lived in the peninsula and the land to its north, which today is California. These indigenous peoples were dispersed throughout the territory, forming different groups that are commonly identified and classified by their linguistic roots. Although most of the groups were hunter–gatherers, several practiced agriculture, including the Cucapa Indians, the original settlers of the lower Colorado River.

The 150 years following the peninsula's discovery witnessed several modest attempts at colonization. All of them ultimately failed. The arid conditions of the peninsula as well as its complicated topography made it difficult for these initial colonizing attempts to prosper. It was not until the establishment of the first Jesuit Mission in Loreto in the year 1697, on the eastern coast of the present-day state of Baja California Sur, that the first permanent settlement existed in the Californias. Even if they did not succeed in colonization, many of the previous expeditions were valuable in that they recorded information about the peninsula coastline and its islands. One of the best examples of these explorations was the 1602–1603 expedition under the command of Sebastian Vizcaino. Its main objective was the exploration and demarcation of the California coastline to the northernmost point possible. The expedition reached just north of what is today San Francisco Bay. Upon his return in 1603, Vizcaino presented diaries and plans to the viceroy in Mexico City, recommending the colonization of the ports of Monterey and San Diego. Even though many years passed before the plans for colonization were realized, Vizcaino's expedition established a lasting toponymy of the coast, and the cartography produced from it was used for the following 200 years.[1]

With the arrival of the Jesuit Father Eusebio Francisco Kino at the peninsula in 1683, at La Paz, the legendary missionary task of the Californias began. Even though the actual responsibility of establishing the first mission in the peninsula (at Loreto) fell upon Father Juan Maria Salvatierra, Father Kino played a key role in obtaining the viceroy's approval for its foundation. Afterward, from across the gulf in Sonora, he offered support for the development of many other missions in the peninsula. Father Kino was one of the first to establish that California was not an island, but a peninsula. This realization was based upon his many trips to Arizona and along the Colorado River, in an endless search to find a route by which the missions of the peninsula could be supplied by land from Sonora. From the founding of the Loreto Mission to the expulsion of the Jesuits from all territory under Spanish rule in 1767, the Jesuits established 17 missions, began one more, and abandoned four. In a report sent to the Spanish King in 1745, Cristobal De Escobar y Llamas described the condition of the existing missions in California, which according to him had a collective population of 6,000.

With the departure of the Jesuits from the peninsula, the viceroy decided to place the Californian missions under the care of the Franciscan congregation. On April 1, 1768, Father Junípero Serra arrived in Loreto, heading a group of friars that was to take charge of the existing missions. Shortly after the arrival of the Franciscans, the King of Spain ordered the prompt colonization of Upper California. Father Serra thus began the Alta California missionary system, which ultimately totaled twenty-one missions. Nine of these missions were founded during the lifetime of Father Serra, and twelve following his death.

In 1771 the Dominican Congregation obtained permission from the Spanish Crown to share the missionary work of the Californias with the Franciscans. This event was important in that it led to the first significant territorial division between the Baja California peninsula and Alta California. Realizing that the operation of two different congregations in the same area was inconvenient, the Franciscans proposed handing over the missions of the peninsula to the Dominicans so that they could concentrate solely on Alta California. In 1772 the Franciscan and Dominican friars signed an agreement in which they divided the area of influence of each group and established a boundary (see Figure 2.1). The agreement between the congregations became a political boundary in 1804 when the Viceroy, Jose de Iturrigaray, declared Baja and Alta California independent provinces.[2] The location of the dividing line between both provinces was very important. The division took place some miles south of the present international border between Mexico and California. Since then, the northern Baja California region has been closely linked with the history of Alta California. Even after the border was moved north to its present location as a consequence of the Treaty of Guadalupe Hidalgo in 1848 (justified, because without this shift, Mexico would not have access to the peninsula by land), Baja California's social and economic development continued to be linked strongly to what happened in Alta California.

In 1821 Mexico became an independent nation, after eleven years of a bloody and debilitating struggle against Spain. The role of Baja California in the conflict was marginal. So distant and isolated from the Mexican Central Plateau, where the struggle for independence was principally fought, the Californias were content to join in with the proclamation of independence in 1822. The effect of the war was, however, clearly felt in the Californias. Begun in 1810, the war diminished what little economic help the Californias had received from central Mexico prior to the armed conflict. With the emergence of Mexico as an independent nation, the situation did not improve much, mainly because the new governments found themselves bankrupt after ten years of internal strife. Such events encouraged an increase in legal and illegal commerce with foreign ships (particularly American, British, and Russian) present in California ports at this time. It was during this period that the Californias consolidated their clear economic and political independence from Central Mexico, a condition that would persist well into the twentieth Century for Baja California. The political instability that Mexico experienced during its first years as an independent nation, the indifference and incompetence that characterized the government's dealings with the Californias, and the region's isolation from the rest of the country set the stage for the United States to turn an acquisitive gaze toward Baja California and (for that matter) all of northern Mexico.

Although the population of Alta California began gradually to increase around the turn of the nineteenth century, Baja California's population declined. In a census conducted by order of the Viceroy in 1793, a population of 12,666 was recorded for both Californias. By 1805, Baja California by itself had 9,000 inhabitants, although by 1842 some sources point to a total of only 3,766 inhabitants. Even though this figure seems somewhat low, it appears to confirm the fact that the peninsula's population was declining during the early nineteenth century. According to a census provided by Miguel

Martinez in 1836, Baja California had a population of 6,488, which included only *gente de razón*, that is to say "people of reason." This figure did not include Indians living in the region. By 1857, Ulises Urbano Lassepas estimated a population of 12,585 in Baja California, of which 9,713 were located in the southern half of the peninsula and 2,872 in the northern region known as *La Frontera*. Of the northern residents, 375 were *gente de razón* and 2,500 were Indians.[3] Thus, even though it is difficult to know with certainty the precise demographics of Baja California during the first half of the nineteenth century, it is possible to establish the general trends during this period. The majority of the already-diminished Indian population lived in the north of the peninsula. The Indian population of the south had practically disappeared, attributable mainly to contagious diseases introduced by Europeans. Conversely, the overwhelming majority of white people was concentrated in the south; the north generally had few whites.

During the period from Mexican Independence to the outbreak of war with the United States in 1846, a series of events took place that would profoundly affect the future of what is today the northern portion of Baja California. The region around present-day Tijuana, Tecate, and Rosarito participated in the accelerated growth of cattle ranches that occured in Alta California during this period. This was a prosperous time for those few people who were able to obtain land grants. Some of the principal factors behind the explosive growth of cattle ranches at the time were the secularization of the missions and the distribution of their land into private hands, as well as new colonization laws formulated by the Mexican government that among other things allowed foreigners to obtain property and guaranteed security with respect to land ownership. It was during this time that Santiago Arguello received a land grant that was part of the territory of the *Rancheria de Tia Juana*, where the city of Tijuana is located today, and that had previously been part of the territory administered by the San Diego Mission.[4] At this same period, Juan Bandini received the land grant that gave origin to the *Rancho de Tecate*, where the border city of Tecate sits today.[5]

While this was happening in the northwest corner of Baja California, to the northeast, along the delta region of the Colorado River, multiple expeditions were launched to establish communication routes between the coastal plains of the Pacific and the Colorado and Sonora regions. Levels of activity along the Colorado River gradually increased. As time progressed and the region was explored further, great resources were discovered that had previously remained unnoticed or had been inaccessible due to the extreme climate and hostile environment. During the 1890s and the beginning of the 1900s, plans that had been envisioned for the region by land speculators since the middle of the nineteenth century began to be realized. Even though the Mexicali Valley experienced few significant physical or demographic changes during the nineteenth century, many people who visited the Lower Colorado had the opportunity to learn about the region and its potential.

The end of the Mexican-American War, and the signing of the Treaty of Guadalupe Hidalgo in 1848, established a new political boundary between both countries. As a result, Mexico lost almost half its territory. During the negotiations regarding the demarcation of the new border, the United States clearly stated its intention of including the Baja California peninsula as part of the territory that would be ceded to the United States. It was at this point, after conceding much of the northern half of the country, that the Mexican representatives became intransigent, arguing that although the peninsula was of little use to the United States, it was very valuable to Mexico, given its location in front of the coastline of Sonora. The United States ultimately agreed and Mexico kept the peninsula. Going one step further, the Mexican negotiators requested that a portion of southern Alta California should be kept by Mexico, arguing that if this was not permitted, Mexicans would have no access to the peninsula by land. As a result, the boundary between California and Baja California was set where it stands today, thus setting the scene for the cities of Tijuana, Mexicali, and Tecate to flourish in part of the territory that once had belonged to Alta California.[6]

The bitter experience of losing such a vast amount of territory to the United States created a sense of urgency within Mexican governmental officials to protect what had been retained. The sparsely populated and unprotected northern states of Mexico became a constant source of concern to the central Mexican government after 1848. What may be viewed as Mexican paranoia after their great territorial loss was actually a well-founded worry. Even after the signing of the treaty that established the new boundary, many Americans kept a close eye on desirable Mexican territory, particularly Baja California. There is probably no better evidence of this than the invasion of the Baja California peninsula by William Walker in 1853. Walker, son of a Scottish banker who immigrated to the United States in 1820, was allegedly attempting to create an independent nation that would include the state of Sonora and would be called *República de Sonora.* Walker's attempt failed after a group of courageous Mexican patriots, led by Antonio Melendrez, fought the invaders and forced them out of Baja California into San Diego in 1854.[7]

Facing the threat of further foreign invasions, the Mexican government introduced a colonization law in 1857, mainly targeted at limiting the amount of land owned by foreigners in the unsettled territories of northern Mexico. This new law ushered in an era of on-going, contradictory legislative reform regarding colonization and land ownership that continued throughout the second half of the nineteenth century.[8] The incompetence of local and national officials in enforcing the laws and their subsequent reforms, as well as flaws within the laws themselves, often produced an effect opposite to what was intended. By the end of the century, the Baja California

Figure 3.1 Original boundary monument between the United States and Mexico in the Pacific Coast. (Museo Universitario—UABC.)

peninsula had become a major center for land speculation by foreigners. Mexico's economic and foreign policy had greatly altered since the late 1850s and 1860s. During the extended presidential term of Porfirio Díaz, which began in 1876 and ended in 1910, foreign investment was encouraged and the government opted to open colonization (*colonización*) to private hands, both domestic and foreign.

Although all these developments were taking place in Mexico during the second half of the nineteenth century, Gold Rush California was experiencing an impressive economic and demographic growth (see Chapter 2). The energy and prosperity that had been building up in California for fifty years were ready to pour south by the turn of the century. Yet, even as late as the 1880s, the northern border of Baja California showed few signs of becoming a major center for population growth and economic prosperity. Tijuana was a small village with a customs building and a few shacks around it, Ensenada a tiny port of about 200 people (1883), Tecate a small agricultural colony, and Mexicali was completely nonexistent.

Founding Times (1880s–1910)

Although the histories of Tijuana and Mexicali, the two major urban centers of Baja California where 80% of the state's population is presently concentrated, have many similarities and were affected by many related events at the larger scale, initially they developed quite separately from each other. The regions in which Tijuana and Mexicali developed during the twentieth century had historically belonged to different, though not totally unrelated, corridors of travel and trade that ran parallel but only rarely intersected. The region in which Tijuana flourished, located just north of the dividing line between Lower and Upper California, had for a couple of centuries belonged within the context of the Pacific Coast mission corridor. On the other hand, the Mexicali and Imperial Valleys lay within the corridor of the Gulf of California and the Colorado River, on the opposite side of the Baja California peninsula.

The mountain ranges and deserts that bisected the peninsula and the State of California made east–west movement of people and goods difficult, and created a strong barrier between the coastal and inland corridors. Before railroads were introduced to the region in the last quarter of the nineteenth century, steam boats would depart from San Francisco and head south along the California coast, turn back up north into the Gulf of California, and head up the Colorado River to supply goods to the Yuma fort, located at the confluence of the Gila and Colorado rivers. The enormous logistics required to supply the isolated fort by sea illustrates the difficulty of land-based travel across the peninsula.

The differences between Tijuana's and Mexicali's local histories narrowed as the twentieth century progressed, largely due to the Mexicanization process in Baja California and the development of infrastructure that promoted greater communication. Still, throughout the twentieth century, both cities evinced a distinct personality and particular growth dynamics.

The first significant manifestation of settlement and the urban future of the Tijuana Valley was the establishment of a customs house on the Mexican side of the border in 1874. Before this, Tijuana and its surroundings had been a cattle ranching region whose only notable settlements were the *Rancho Tia Juana* (a ranch house) and a scattering of tiny rural settlements. The Arguello family were the owners of most of the land in the region, under a land grant to Santiago Arguello in 1829 by then governor of the Californias, Jose Maria Echeandia.

The establishment of a customs house was the Mexican government's response to the continuous demand from local inhabitants to control the unregulated traffic of American goods, mail, military supplies, and, occasionally, armed troops through Mexican territory. Mainly for topographic reasons, Americans found it easier to make their way to the Colorado River and Yuma Fort in Arizona via the Mexican side of the border. The customs house was considered a good way to control the transit of foreigners through Mexican territory, and to produce much-needed revenue through the taxation of goods in transit. Ultimately, because of atrocious management and corruption, the customs house never served its purpose and became practically obsolete when the railroad was introduced. Soon after the establishment of the customs house, a number of modest wooden houses and shacks began to cluster nearby. Around 1879, an elementary school was established to tend to the children of the small settlement and surrounding rural communities. Not long after, the customs house, school, and homes had to be abandoned due to recurring floods on the Tijuana River.

During the second half of the 1880s, northern Baja California, particulary its western edge, joined in the explosive land and property speculation boom affecting Southern California. The idea of subdividing lots and putting them up for sale spread south of the border. In Ensenada, The International Company of Mexico (based in Hartford, Connecticut) was developing an ambitious plan to lay out the Carlos Pacheco Colony, which comprised three cities by the bay.[9] In Tijuana, members of the Arguello family, who by this time were living on the American side of the border mainly in San Diego, and who were very much in tune with the dynamics of Southern California, decided to set aside a portion of the *Tia Juana* ranch that lay close to the border, so that it could be subdivided and sold. The family commissioned an engineer named Ricardo Orozco to come up with a plan for the new town. In 1889, a long legal dispute regarding this portion of land came to an end in favor of the Arguellos, and the plan created by Orozco was added to the agreement that ended the dispute. Local historians consider this year (1889) as Tijuana's founding date.[10]

The initial success of the Arguello plans for their subdivided parcels was limited. The land boom in Southern California suddenly collapsed in 1889, and sales did not match expectations. The town grew slowly but steadily, and the Orozco plan of 1889 provided the framework for growth (part of the plan's rectangular grid persists to this day in Tijuana's *Zona Central*). The small town began to grow mainly along Olvera Street (today's *Avenida Rev-*

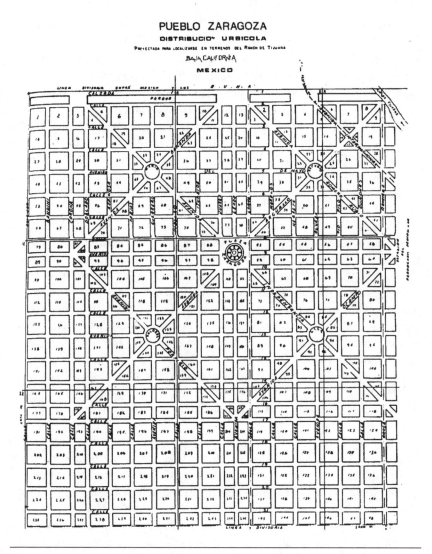

PUEBLO ZARAGOZA

Figure 3.2 Tijuana's first urban plan of 1889, developed by Ricardo Orozco. (Instituto de Investigaciones Históricas—UABC.)

olución, Tijuana's biggest and most famous tourist attraction). Homes and commercial establishments, such as restaurants, bars, and hotels, began to shape the landscape of Tijuana, which by 1900 had an estimated population of 242 residents. The increasing importance of San Diego as a commercial and military port at the turn of the century affected Tijuana's growth by constantly raising the number of tourists who crossed the border to visit Mexico during their stay in San Diego.

Meanwhile, as turn-of-the-century Tijuana was experiencing growing pains, to the east, the vast desert plain known as the Colorado Desert, was being introduced to modernization. Throughout the second half of the nineteenth century, the enormous agricultural potential of this region drew the attention of land speculators and entrepreneurs from places as far away as Europe. The presence of abundant water resources in the region, mostly due to the Colorado River, inspired more than one visionary to suggest that with the implementation of an appropriate irrigation system, the valley could become an agricultural empire. At the turn of the century this vision was to become a reality. The great desert, divided politically by the Treaty of Guadalupe Hidalgo in 1848, came to be called the Mexicali Valley to the south of the border, and the Imperial Valley to the north.

During the last quarter of the nineteenth century, the Mexicali Valley was subject to a series of confusing and irregular land speculation activities and transactions, involving mostly foreign companies and capital, from as far away as Hartford, Connecticut and England. But by the turn of the century, an ambitious Mexican businessman by the name of Guillermo Andrade, whose main business partners were from the United States, had managed to acquire the colonization rights (*derechos de colonización*) and thereby control of practically the entire Mexicali Valley and its resources. Andrade's business decisions, at the end of the 1890s and the first years of the 1900s, would shape the early rise and development of Mexicali.

Meanwhile, since the mid-1890s, a group of U.S. businessmen had come together to develop an ambitious plan to irrigate, settle, and urbanize the extensive desert plain west of the Colorado, on the U.S. side of the border. At the turn of the century, this region was identified as Imperial Valley by its promoters. A man named Charles R. Rockwood was the biggest advocate and promoter of an irrigation system derived from the waters of the Colorado. Rockwood's project became a reality when he was able to persuade a Canadian businessman, George Chaffey, to invest in the endeavor in 1900. Chaffey, a wealthy man with experience in developing and promoting irrigation systems, would ultimately take full control of the operation for the next two years.

The main obstacle to the irrigation network was a natural physical barrier west of the Colorado River. A series of sand dunes basically parallel to the river made it difficult, if not impossible, to carry water from the river to the desired destinations. The solution to this problem became the catalyst for the rise of Mexicali. The only option was to have the principal canal, which would begin at the Colorado River, traverse Mexican territory, where there were no obstacles to its flow, and then cross back into the United States at some point further west. This solution had several advantages. The topography of the desert naturally descended from the point where the water would be taken from the Colorado River, offering the possibility that water could move by simple gravity. Another advantage was that a natural ditch, known as the Alamo Canal, already existed. The Alamo for many years had channeled, through Mexican territory, excess waters from the Colorado into U.S. territory. Guillermo Andrade owned the land through which the water would flow while on Mexican soil. For that reason, Rockwood approached Andrade to establish an agreement that would favor both men, and make the irrigation dream a reality. On June 29, 1898, Andrade and Rockwood's California Development Company, with Andrade as a partner, signed a contract to form a new company by the name of *Sociedad de Irrigación y Terrenos de Baja California*, based in Mexico. It would be responsible for the construction and operation of the irrigation network on the Mexican side.

News traveled fast in Baja California about the construction, on the Mexican side of the border, of a portion of what would come to be known as the Imperial Canal System. Soon, workers from different places, along with their families, began to arrive in a region that, other than the tiny *Los Algodones* ranch, was devoid of permanent settlement. However, between 1900 and 1902, a small group of humble rustic dwellings appeared around the floodgate where the water brought along the Alamo Canal was introduced into the United States and rerouted into Mexican territory. The floodgate was located a few miles east of where Mexicali lies today. Far from being a formal settlement, this group of temporary dwellings was nevertheless the first manifestation of the urban center that would begin to develop shortly thereafter. Due to the extreme susceptibility of the area to floods, this first incipient settlement was relocated further west in 1902, to a safer location where Mexicali's downtown and Calexico are located today. The new relocated *caserío*, or small group of houses, was by this time beginning to be called Mexicali.

At this time, on the U.S. side, the Imperial Valley was undergoing a process of rapid transformation. Towns were being planned and laid out, land was being sold and cultivated, and irrigation networks were continuing to expand. Since 1901, with the opening of the Alamo canal and the floodgate located at the border, water had gushed into the Imperial Valley, which was vigorously promoted across the United States by land companies that operated in the region. One ad put out by the Imperial Land Company claimed: "It is founded on the largest and most fertile tract of irrigable land to be found in arid America. The Imperial Canal System is what its name indicates—the most abundant supply of water that can be used for irrigation purposes in America. Not only is the water abundant, but it is cheap." The same ad promoted the creation of three new cities called Imperial, Paringa (Heber), and Calexico, stating: "One of these towns will become a large city. All of them will become cities."[11] The ad proved to be half right: one town within the Imperial Valley project would become a large city, but it would turn out to be Mexicali, the first formal urban plan for which was designed simultaneously with that of Calexico.

In October 1902 Antonio H. Heber, who that year had replaced George Chaffey as the president of both the California Development Company and the Imperial Land Company, bought from Guillermo Andrade a portion of land on Mexican soil, roughly 187 hectares. This piece of land was located adjacent to the international boundary, directly south of the new town of Calexico, California, which, since the fall of 1901, was being laid out by the Imperial Land Company on a 160-acre plot of land donated by Chaffey. As soon as Heber had secured the property, he commissioned Charles Rockwood to come up with a plan for what would become the new town of Mexicali. To this day, it is uncertain if the plan for Mexicali was an extension of the grid of the Calexico plan, which supposedly had been drawn up a year earlier, probably by the same team of engineers, or if both cities had been conceived simultaneously. In any event, by the beginning of 1903, Calexico and Mexicali had been designed basically as a single urban system, in which the north–south grids of both town plans were integrated in a perfect alignment.[12]

Since its conception in the late 1890s, a major component of the overall development project for the region was the introduction of a railroad. By February 1903, a branch of the Southern Pacific Railroad was completed from Los Angeles to the town of Imperial, and by the middle of 1904, the line reached the border at Calexico. In May, the Southern Pacific Railroad obtained a permit from the Mexican government to extend the construction and administration of the railroad into the Mexicali Valley. Before the end of the year, hundreds of men were laying down tracks, on Mexican soil, of what would be called the Intercalifornia Railroad. The railroad stations at Mexicali and Calexico were built simultaneously. The connection of Mexicali to the California railroad system consolidated its ties to the economy and life of California, especially because it took forty-four more years for the city to be connected to the Mexican railroad system.

By the end of 1904, the small, scattered settlement known as Mexicali had for the most part been relocated to the site where the new town was being laid out. During this year, the first registered lot sales, as marked on the 1902 plan, took place. Several lots were also given away to some of the early settlers who had been living in the area, under the condition that they build permanent structures on the parcel they had just obtained. According to a census that took place in November 1904, the town was composed of a single street, fronted by simple adobe and wood buildings. The population was 397, consisting of about sixty families.[13]

As the town of Mexicali was emerging, a series of major land transactions involving most of the land in the Mexicali Valley also occured. Since 1902,

Guillermo Andrade had been in talks with a group of investors, for the most part from Los Angeles, who were interested in acquiring land in the Mexicali Valley. Between 1904 and 1905, the Colorado River Land Company (CRLC),[14] led by Harrison Gray Otis, owner and editor of the *Los Angeles Times*, and his son-in-law Harry Chandler, acquired the colonization rights for most of the irrigable land in the Mexicali Valley through a number of major transactions, mostly with Andrade and his land companies. Among the few properties that were not involved in the transactions of this period was the 187-hectare plot of land purchased by Antonio Heber to establish the town of Mexicali. Yet through these deals, "*La Colorado*," as it came to be known, achieved almost complete control of the region. For the next thirty years, the Colorado River Land Company played a major role in Mexicali's history.

Mexicali's first settlement almost completely disappeared as a result of the devastating floods of 1905–1906, which greatly affected both valleys and were caused by unexpectedly high water levels along the Colorado River.[15] More than half of the city blocks, subdivided according to the 1902 plan, were washed away and destroyed. Only a small portion of the northeast end of town, a handful of buildings, was saved. By 1907, when the waters had returned to normal, the reconstruction and realignment of the town began. Former settlers and newcomers began occupying lots under the authorization and supervision of municipal officials. New city blocks were planned, expanding the Rockwood plan, which remained the basis for the new development.[16] The newly reestablished city began to grow mainly eastward along the border.

American Influence and Tourism's Golden Age (1910–1930)

By 1910, when the Mexican Revolution erupted in the rest of the country, Tijuana had established itself as a small town with a population of 733, surrounded by small ranches and rural communities. Mexicali, with around 500 inhabitants, was quickly acquiring importance as the commercial center for an incipient but growing agricultural community. Mexicali's activities were affected more by what was happening in the Imperial Valley, which had developed earlier and faster. Tijuana and Mexicali's role in the Mexican Revolution, like that of all the Northern District of Baja California, was limited to a series of events that took place during the first half of 1911 mainly in Mexicali. From January to June of 1911, Mexicali fell under the control of a small and unorganized revolutionary army of the movement led by Ricardo Flores Magón and his Liberal Mexican Party, which since 1909 had been based in Los Angeles, and was one of several revolutionary groups looking to bring down the thirty-year dictatorship of Porfirio Díaz.[17] Flores Magón's movement never caught on with Baja California residents, who were against it, and by mid-1911, the already weak armed movement was suppressed in Baja California.

In the next two decades there was an overwhelming series of events that would transform Baja California forever. The moralist movement that swept across the United States in the beginning of the twentieth century had strong political roots in California. In Southern California, the Republican-led Lincoln-Roosevelt League endorsed the eradication of gambling and vice in all its forms. Northern Baja California, but especially Tijuana, became an ideal place for American promoters of the now-prohibited activities. During the first years of the 1910s, an increasing number of liquor shops, night clubs, and *cantinas* appeared in the small border towns, mostly owned and frequented by Americans. In the space of a couple of years, Tijuana's character shifted from a quiet cattle and agricultural town to a thriving tourist center.

The opening of the Panama-California Exposition in San Diego's Balboa Park in 1915 (discussed in Chapter 2) inspired Antonio Elozua to organize and promote a fair in Tijuana that would attract visitors to the San Diego exposition. The Tijuana fair was very successful, having as its main attraction all those activities that were prohibited in California, such as boxing matches, cock fights, bullfights, and gambling in all its varieties. The fair also included a night club based on ideas brought from San Francisco.[18] Around the same time, an American boxing promoter from San Francisco, James Wood Coffroth, arrived in Baja California. On January 1, 1916, he opened Tijuana's first horse racetrack, which was operated by the Lower California Jockey Club, and whose president was Coffroth himself. The racetrack was an instant success. Thousands of tourists would make their way from California every week, among them Hollywood stars, to enjoy the atmosphere that reigned at the track and in Tijuana in general. Both the Tijuana Fair and the racetrack brought Tijuana's tourist fame to a new level.[19] The rise of tourism had a temporary setback in 1917 when the United States announced war on Germany, and Mexico declared itself neutral in regard to the conflict. The border was closed temporarily, a difficult blow for the growing tourist industry. But soon after the end of World War I, Tijuana's leisure activities began to recover, and even intensified as prohibition began in the United States, opening the way to what has been called Tijuana's "Golden Age of Tourism," the 1920s.

From 1915 to 1920, Colonel Esteban Cantú served as governor of the Baja California district. Cantú's presence on the political scene of Baja California was crucial for the development of tourism. Mayor Cantú, who would shortly receive the title of Colonel, arrived in Baja California in June 1911, as part of a contingent of federal troops sent to this remote district to suppress

4793. Tijuana Fair, Tijuana, Mexico.

Figure 3.3   Postcard of the entrance to the Tijuana Fair, 1916. (Archivo Histórico de Tijuana—IMAC.)

the Flores Magón-inspired revolt. Upon his arrival, he was appointed commander of the Mexicali garrison. For about four years, Cantú held this position in Mexicali, becoming a popular figure among local residents and throughout the district. In 1914, taking advantage of both his strong position in Mexicali and the state of anarchy in revolutionary Mexico, Cantú refused to recognize the governor of the district appointed by one of the many transitory federal governments of the time, claiming that Colonel Enrique Anaya did not have the appropriate credentials. Shortly after, Cantú became the de facto governor, with the support of the people; there was little that central Mexico could do to prevent it. During his rule, Baja California experienced prosperous and peaceful times, relative to the rest of the country. Because of its isolation, Cantú was able to maintain a government free from the vicious revolutionary struggle that was taking place in every corner of Mexico, creating what was, effectively, an autonomous and independent nation. He even went so far as to declare himself neutral when the United States occupied the port of Veracruz during this period, and during Pershing's incursion into Mexico in pursuit of Pancho Villa.

The deserts, mountains, and the Gulf of California served as protection for the new governor and his district, offering a relatively peaceful haven for a tourism boom to take place. Cantú promoted a diversity of economic activities that brought great revenue through taxation, including agricultural exports, especially cotton; but most importantly, he encouraged activities that made the region a paradise for tourists—gambling, prostitution, alcohol production, and sales. The district in general, and Mexicali in particular, benefited from the infrastructure investments of the Cantú government. (These would have probably been even greater if Cantú had not spent such an enormous amount of resources in sustaining a very well-equipped and properly paid army, which was crucial to his autonomy.) For instance, during his administration, the first elementary school in Mexicali was built, many streets were paved, and construction for a government palace begun. Cantú moved the capital of the Northern District of Baja California from Ensenada to Mexicali early in his administration, making it his center of operations, and giving the booming agricultural region a new status that would endure throughout the century.[20]

Another important feature of Cantú's rule was the immigration of thousands of foreign workers, mostly Chinese, to the agricultural fields of the region. At one point, Chinese immigrants heavily outnumbered Mexicans in the Mexicali Valley. The Chinese, who had slowly been arriving since the first decade of the 1900s, were a perfect fit for Cantú, who found it easier to control and exploit the hard-working and obedient Chinese farm workers. During the 1910s, especially toward the end of the decade, a strong anti-Chinese movement, with roots in the states of Sonora and Sinaloa, arose in the region. It would exist well into the 1930s, despite promises by Cantú that he would control Chinese migration and promote Mexican colonization. In 1920, the political climate became complicated for Cantú, who for five years had defied the Mexican federal government, practically ignoring its existence. That year, Cantú, despite his extraordinary political abilities, was unable to maintain his leadership and was forced to resign the rule of Baja California, at a time when the Mexican federal government became more stable as a result of the triumph of the Sonora Faction (led by Alvaro Obregón and Plutarco Elias Calles), which would come to rule Mexico throughout the 1920s.[21]

The implementation of the Volstead Law in January 1920 in the United States outlawed the production and sale of alcohol, thereby opening the floodgates of tourism in Baja California. The fame of Tijuana, and to a lesser degree Mexicali, reached New York, Chicago, and even Europe. Bars and liquor stores proliferated. Wineries and breweries flourished, producing immense amounts of alcohol for local consumption and for contraband into the United States. Thirsty Americans would make their way across the border every day, especially on the weekends, consuming alcohol, but also choosing from an array of other leisure activities. Gambling (which was formally legalized in the Baja California District in 1908) proliferated, and became more sophisticated with the appearance of many new upscale casinos, culminating in the opening of the *Agua Caliente* casino in 1928 in Tijuana.

Figure 3.4 Chinese colony parade in Mexicali. (Archivo Histórico del Municipio de Mexicali.)

The racetrack, which had opened in Tijuana in 1916, was very successful throughout this period; it was one of the main attractions of the city, and prize money rose every racing season. The largest enterprises were owned and operated by Americans, who took their profits back to the United States. So, despite Tijuana's growth, the local government still had to confront economic hardship. Nevertheless, the high taxes set by the Baja California District government resulted in important infrastructure works that benefited the region.

The peak of the golden age of tourism in Tijuana came in 1927, when the *Compañia de Agua Caliente* was founded to operate what became the *Agua Caliente* tourist complex. *Agua Caliente,* which literally translates as "hot water," was the site of natural hot springs in the Tijuana Valley that for hundreds of years had been visited by locals and foreign visitors seeking a cure for different illnesses, ranging from rheumatism to tuberculosis. In 1926, Abelardo L. Rodríguez, governor of the Baja California District at the time, bought a fraction of land of the Tia Juana ranch from Alberto Arguello, including the Agua Caliente springs. Rodríguez obtained permission from the federal government to develop the springs, and joined Baron Long, a horse-racing promoter from Los Angeles, and two other U.S. business men (Wirt G. Bowman and James N. Crofton), to form the *Compañia de Agua Caliente* and build a tourist complex of the same name. The Agua Caliente complex opened on June 23, 1928, with a hotel, casino, restaurant, spa, and a greyhound race-track. A golf course, Olympic-size swimming pool, and airstrip were soon added. A new horse-racing track was constructed by the company and inaugurated in 1929. Thirty-three bungalows were built when the number of hotel rooms became insufficient to host the increasing number of tourists. At one point the complex also included a print shop, an elementary school, and a radio station. Because it was located outside the town to the southeast, a paved road was built to make the journey by car more comfortable.[22]

At its peak, Agua Caliente was one of the best and most famous casino and resort complexes of its kind in the world. Aristocrats, Hollywood stars, and gangsters were among the main clients of Agua Caliente, especially attracted by gambling. It was also common for European nobility to visit the resort. The complex's popularity among Hollywood stars increased its appeal to other tourists. Clark Gable, Charles Chaplin, Bing Crosby, and Al Capone were only a few of the famous names to have reportedly visited Agua Caliente. Elena de la Paz de Barrón, a former employee of Agua Caliente, who was in charge of the check room, would remember (fifty years later) her unforgettable encounter with Al Capone: "After spending some time in the casino, when time came to give him back his hat, POW! As a tip he gave me a fifty dollar bill. Consider: fifty dollars at that time! A new car was worth nine hundred!"[23]

Like all the other successful tourist enterprises of the 1920s in Tijuana, Agua Caliente was created by U.S. dollars for American consumers. Accord-

Figure 3.5 Postcard of the Spa at *Agua Caliente*. (Archivo Histórico de Tijuana—IMAC.)

ing to testimony from another Agua Caliente worker, at one time more than 90% of all employees were Americans from all over California. Mexican workers were limited to janitorial jobs; they were rarely permitted to have a higher-paid job, and only if they could speak fluent English.[24] As time went by, unions pushed for better working conditions for Mexicans in Agua Caliente and generally in all Tijuana. Agua Caliente continued to operate successfully throughout the first half of the 1930s, surviving the Great Depression and the end of prohibition in the United States. It was not until President Lázaro Cárdenas outlawed all types of gambling in Mexico that Agua Caliente faced its decline.

Despite Tijuana's fame and wealth, the settlement remained for the most part a small dusty town of scattered single-story buildings. The only exceptions were found in a few city blocks of bars, night clubs, casinos, and hotels, basically around what today is Revolution Avenue. The other exception was the majestic palace of Agua Caliente on the outskirts of the city. As Lawrence Herzog noted: "Tijuana allowed itself to be molded in the image of a giant carnival; the small village near downtown where the workers lived was just that—a village, outside the main path of urban life."[25] By 1930, Tijuana had a population of 8,400.

For Mexicali, the dynamics of Baja California's "Golden Age of Tourism" were an important, but not dominant factor during this period. The implementation of prohibition in 1920 had a strong impact on the town itself, but this did not extend elsewhere in the valley. A tourist-driven affluence developed diverse commercial activities and restaurants, especially those serving Chinese food, within the busy commercial center of an increasingly important agricultural region. The 1920s were a transitional period for Mexicali, serving as a foundation for the Mexicanization process that would shortly take place. World War I inspired the Colorado River Land Company to develop the cultivation of cotton in the valley, consolidating the area's agricultural preeminence. In a few years, a series of small settlements appeared along the railroad line that ran through the valley, forming a system of rural communities whose activities revolved around the main urban nucleus of Mexicali. Despite high agricultural production, the economy of the region was characterized by continuous fluctuations throughout this period, which had its roots in the fluctuating prices of cotton on the world market. Mexicali consolidated its position as the most important economic center of the district, and warranted the presence of the governor in the valley on a regular basis. This hampered attempts of several political groups to move the Baja capital back to Ensenada during the early 1920s.

The presence and activities of Japanese, Hindu, and Chinese immigrants and workers decreased in importance during the 1920s. At the beginning of that decade, the Chinese community was the largest ethnic group in the

Mexicali Valley, with a population of about 8,000. It occupied a large commercial and residential district within the eastern portion of the town's core. (To this day, the district is known as "*La Chinesca*," Mexicali's Chinatown.) As the decade progressed, the presence of Mexican farm workers began to increase gradually, because the demand for *braceros* increased in the highly productive cotton fields of the Mexicali Valley. Since the late 1910s, both local and national governments had prohibited Chinese migration in order to promote colonization by Mexicans. Under such circumstances, the Colorado River Land Company, which along with Esteban Cantú's government had promoted the migration of Chinese farm workers, was forced to bring Mexican workers from other regions of the country to work in the valley. As the number of Mexican workers grew, a series of political, labor, and agrarian movements began to challenge the presence and control of American money and interests.

For many years, the Colorado River Land Company had feared that the increasing number of Mexicans in the region would be detrimental to their interests, which is why the company had promoted Chinese and Japanese immigration during previous decades. By 1924, the governor of the district was forced to urge local businesses and ranch owners to have at least half of their workers be of Mexican origin. By the end of the 1920s, the Mexican community had increased significantly, and a strong agrarian movement was pushing the government to acknowledge that the productive lands of the valley should be owned by Mexicans. Many "radical" leaders in the movement were beginning to demand expropriation of the valley's agricultural lands from the Colorado River Land Company, and their distribution among Mexicans. It took several more years before political and economic conditions would make this idea a reality, but the movement set the basis for what would later be accomplished during the presidency of Lázaro Cárdenas. By 1930, the valley had a population of 29,985, of which 15,143 were living in rural areas, and 14,842 in the town of Mexicali, making it the most populated region in the Baja California district. As a whole, the Northern District of Baja California[26] had a population of 48,327, of which 2,982 people were of Chinese origin, 958 Japanese, 576 American, 473 Russian, and 159 Spanish.

Mexicanization (1930–1950)

The coming of the Great Depression in the United States had a crucial impact on Baja California. The hardship and high unemployment produced by the depression triggered the repatriation of many Mexicans who had been living and working north of the border. A significant number of returning Mexicans settled in Tijuana and Mexicali.

Figure 3.6 Postcard of the old Mexicali–Calexico border crossing, around the 1930s. (Archivo Histórico del Municipio de Mexicali.)

At first, the repercussions of the depression were felt in Tijuana only to a slight degree, because the casino clientele of Tijuana, especially Agua Caliente's, were not as severely affected by the depression. In fact, Agua Caliente prospered, stealing clientele from other casinos that could not compete with the giant. In addition, prohibition was still in effect at the time. When the repeal of prohibition came in 1933, Tijuana entered a period of major economic crisis. Wineries and breweries shut down almost immediately, and more than half of the town bars and liquor stores suffered the same fate. The large casinos kept operating with relative success, because their main business was gambling not liquor.

The end of Tijuana's golden age came suddenly in 1935, when Lázaro Cárdenas, by presidential decree, abolished and shut down all gambling activities in Mexico. President Cárdenas' decision, among many he took favoring Baja California's future development during his presidential term (1934–1940), was received negatively at first. But it offered the opportunity for a new Tijuana to develop on a solid economic foundation based in commercial activity and a new type of tourist industry (despite a brief revival of the old Tijuana-style of tourism, based mainly on vice during World War II).[27]

In the Mexicali Valley, the economic crisis, which had begun in 1928 with the sudden crash of cotton prices, forced thousands of Chinese workers to leave the region. They had, by this time, become the target of attacks by

Mexican workers who were increasingly displacing them in the region's economy. From March to August of 1931, a total of 2,000 Asians reportedly left the territory and headed mostly to the United States. However, their presence would persist in the commercial development of the region for years to come. The depression had a devastating effect on Mexicali's economy. Hundreds of farm owners declared bankruptcy and unemployment reached a record high. To make matters worse, the constant flow of Mexicans repatriated from the United States was adding to unemployment. Addressing the level of misery in which many families were living during this period became a priority for local governments. The repeal of prohibition in 1933 made the situation even worse, as Mexicali residents witnessed a further slump in tourism. Fortunately, the price of cotton rose unexpectedly at the end of 1932 and once again during early 1933, somewhat alleviating the region's distress.

The decade of the 1930s was a difficult time for Mexicali, causing major headaches for both local and federal governments. A 1929 study conducted by a Mexican federal official had suggested that the monopoly of the Colorado River Land Company over productive lands in the Mexicali Valley should be dismantled as soon as possible. The company had failed to comply with the agreement by which it had acquired the land, and not colonizing it with Mexicans in a short period of time. In 1936, thirty years after the concession had been granted to the company, it still owned or controlled close to 95% of the land. The idea of expropriating the land from the company gained many supporters at the federal level during the early 1930s. However, action on the idea was postponed due to the lack of resources in the federal government, which was experiencing its own economic problems.

The agrarian movement in the Mexicali Valley became stronger as the decade progressed, its members demanding the expulsion of all American interests, and that land be distributed among Mexicans farmers. Meanwhile, CRLC investors were becoming increasingly worried as expropriation rumors intensified. Onto this stage marched General Lázaro Cárdenas, a nationalist of strong socialist ideals, who began his presidential administration in 1934. In 1938, Cárdenas expropriated the petroleum industry from foreign companies, ignoring the threat of serious international conflict. He had already signed, in 1936, an agreement that basically forced the CRLC to complete colonization in less than twenty years, under the close supervision of the Secretariat of Agriculture. Ten years later, by the beginning of 1946, more than half of the land owned by the company had either been sold and distributed or expropriated by the federal government for the creation of *ejidos*, a centuries-old Spanish concept that in the Mexicali Valley took the form of a "communal farm," consisting basically of a large territory surrounding an existing rural settlement, granted to that settlement for its specific use. Over forty-four *ejidos* had been established by 1946, outlining the urban structure of the Valley that persists to this day, although over time, many of these *ejidos* and their urban nuclei have been absorbed into the city of Mexicali. That same year the federal government purchased the land that remained in the CRLC's possession, which amounted to roughly one-third of the original grant.

The new structure of land ownership permanently transformed the region. Waves of Mexicans arrived, hoping to benefit from the extensive distribution of land that was taking place. Since the early 1930s, the Mexicanization process had been fueled by the constant arrival of *braceros* from elsewhere in Mexico to work in the Mexicali cotton fields, and by the thousands of repatriated Mexican farm workers who found a permanent home in the region. The migration produced by the agrarian reform had by the mid-1940s consolidated the Mexicanization process of the valley. The number of localities in the valley exploded from 57 in 1930 to 163 in 1940.

The growth patterns in Baja California during the 1940s set the tone for the rest of the twentieth century. Tijuana's population more than tripled, from 16,400 in 1940 to 59,954 in 1950; and the town of Mexicali went from 18,775 in 1940 to over 65,000 in 1950, making it the second largest Mexican border city behind Ciudad Juárez. Since then, Baja California cities have continued to experience some of the highest population growth rates in all of Mexico.

The economic and demographic expansion of California during and after World War II provided further impetus to growth in Baja California. The implementation of the well known *bracero* program in 1942, by both the Mexican and U.S. governments, in order to cover the high demand for labor in the U.S. production centers of the war economy, especially the agricultural fields, brought even more Mexican workers to the border states of Mexico. Baja California received thousands of farm workers who were looking to be hired as *braceros* in the United States during this period. Many of those who arrived never crossed the border but stayed in Tijuana and Mexicali, and many border towns. In other instances, many *braceros* did become part of the U.S. work force, but their families stayed on the Mexican side of the border.

In twenty years, the social and cultural face of Baja California had undergone a remarkable change, from a region that was scarcely populated and controlled by U.S. money and interests, to a series of densely populated urban centers that were increasingly integrated into the life and dynamics of mainstream Mexico. The demographic explosion of the 1930s and 1940s had finally solved the Baja California "problem": the region was finally populated, and, most importantly, populated by Mexicans!

Although the migration waves of Mexican *braceros* to Baja California were probably the most important Californian legacy of World War II to its southern neighbor, other developments at that time had enduring impacts. Wartime Tijuana once again became a major center for entertainment and vice, its main clientele coming from the San Diego Naval Base. Cantinas and night clubs prospered, even as the growing population of Tijuana was becoming increasingly uncomfortable with their city's role as a playground for Americans. Even before the war ended, residents and government officials took steps to control tourism and reckless behavior. The economic prosperity of Tijuana also extended beyond the vice-oriented industries, producing a boom in other sectors, including the commercial.

In the Mexicali Valley, the impacts of World War II and Mexicanization triggered an era of prosperity described by Herrera as "the most spectacular growth of population and wealth that has been seen in Mexico, during our independent life."[28] Population growth ignited a commercial and industrial transformation that complemented the strong agricultural economy. By 1950, the Mexicali Valley was the third largest cotton-producing region in Mexico, and occupied fifth place as a source of exports in the country. The 1948 opening of the Sonora-Baja California Railroad, as well as the *Carretera Nacional* (National Highway) during the same period, consolidated the integration of Baja California with the rest of Mexico. As was the case in Tijuana, the region began to consolidate its ties with other places in the country, links that already flourished because of Baja California's high rates of immigration from all over Mexico. (In 1950, almost two-thirds of the population of the valley had been born outside Baja California.) Even though the full integration of the region into Mexican national life was still incomplete by the middle of the twentieth century, Baja California had finally established an identity and dynamic closer to Mexico than the United States.

Integration and Industrialization (1950–1980)

The second half of the twentieth century was marked by strong demographic and economic expansion in Baja California, as well as its full integration to the economic, political, and social life of Mexico. In 1952, Baja California ceased to be a territory and became the twenty-ninth state of the Mexican Republic.[29] Even though the Mexican government at this time was extremely centralized, Baja California's new autonomy gave the state the ability to control its own destiny. One of the earliest examples of this autonomy was the state's creation of the *Universidad Autónoma de Baja California* (UABC) in 1957. Throughout the next forty-five years, UABC would develop into the most important center of education and culture in the state and northwestern Mexico in general, becoming one of the top public education institutions in the country. Baja California's new-found autonomy also provided the opportunity for the region to develop a political life that began to challenge political norms in the country. The isolation and neglect historically experienced by Baja Californian society had laid the groundwork for a more free-thinking, less hierarchical, and more democratic society. In 1953, Baja California elected Aurora Jiménez de Palacios as the first woman to serve in the Mexican national congress. By the end of the twentieth century, Baja California had become the avant-garde of Mexican politics.

The ongoing integration of the state with the rest of Mexico was one of the main narratives in Baja California during the 1950s and 1960s. The continuing migration of Mexicans from every corner of the country to this region during this period, bringing with them their own type of *mexicanidad*, gave way to new and diverse cultures. In 1960, 65% of Tijuana's and 63% of Mexicali's population had been born outside Baja California.[30] The new transportation infrastructure also meant greater and faster communication with the rest of the country, and made Mexican products more readily available. In addition, this period was characterized by the arrival of important national institutions that had previously eluded Baja California. The *Instituto Mexicano del Seguro Social*, by far Mexico's largest social security agency, began operating in the region in 1958. PEMEX and CFE, the government-owned petroleum and power companies, located in the state in 1960 and 1963, respectively.[31] Prior to this, the region had bought gasoline and energy from the United States, mainly California.

Mexican immigrants continued being attracted to the region by the high demand for labor in California's prosperous postwar economy, throughout the Korea and Vietnam conflicts. The *bracero* program was kept in operation until 1964, and thousands of official *braceros* and unofficial migrants crossed the border every year during this period. Even if workers never did cross the border to the United States, or were deported (under the U.S.-sponsored Operation Wetback), border cities in general, especially Tijuana, had much higher standards of living and higher minimum wages than the rest of Mexico, thus many migrants elected to make border cities their final destination. The results were an extremely high demand for housing and explosive urban growth. The impressive amount of planned and unregulated *colonias* that appeared in Tijuana during this period began to produce serious problems for local and state governments, whose capacity to provide services and infrastructure for these new settlements was quickly surpassed by the fast-paced growth. An adequate supply and distribution of water, a pressing issue across the region, became the central problem. The expansion of Tijuana across a complicated mountain topography complicated efforts to supply water. In 1960, Tijuana had a population of around 152,000, which by 1970 had almost doubled to about 300,000. It was during this decade that Tijuana surpassed Mexicali as the largest city in the state, for the first time since the early part of the twentieth century.

And yet, Mexicali's urban expansion during the 1950s and 1960s was impressive, and much more manageable for authorities and planners. The flat topography of the valley has made it relatively easy for the city to expand. Efforts to provide water and to develop a sewage network have given the city a most comprehensive infrastructure network. The transformation and growth of the Mexicali Valley during this period can be characterized as a process in which settlements shift from a predominantly rural to an increasingly urban base, reflecting the growing importance of industrial and commercial sectors and a decline in agriculture. By the 1950s, half the population of the Valley was located within the urban center of Mexicali, with the rest distributed among another 166 settlements. By 1970, the city of Mexicali was home to 66% of the region's population, and by 1990, this figure had risen to 73%. Mexicali was now capital of the State of Baja California, and from 1950 to 1960, the population of the city almost tripled from 65,000 to 179,000. By now, the entire state of Baja California was experiencing some of the highest growth rates in all of urban Mexico.

Fast growth made it impossible for some facets of the region's life to develop at the same pace. Even with the creation of UABC in 1957, during the 1960s (as in previous eras) many young men and women chose to leave Baja California and pursue university studies in other parts of the country, such as Guadalajara, Monterrey, and mainly Mexico City. Young artists and writers followed a similar path, because staying in Baja California meant almost certain anonymity or exclusion from the high circles of Mexican art and culture. Such was the case of the accomplished Tijuana writer and journalist Federico Campbell, who left the region as a young man, because to stay would have caused "creative frustration and personal discouragement," according to another Baja California writer.[32] Things would soon change, however, and by the late 1970s and 1980s, aspiring college students would begin to stay home and attend UABC, or private universities such as CETYS in Mexicali, and the *Universidad Iberoamericana* campus in Tijuana. Artists and writers also found new audiences and spaces for their work, and were no longer obliged to appeal to the traditional centers of cultural power, mainly in Mexico City. (The important role of UABC in independent filmmaking in Baja is discussed by Norma Iglesias in Chapter 6.)

During the 1960s, the Mexican federal government implemented a series of programs designed to address the long-term economic, social, and cultural isolation of Mexican border cities, perhaps in a belated recognition of one of the fastest-growing markets and most dynamic demographic centers in the country. The first and best-known program was the PRONAF (*Programa Nacional Fronterizo*), begun in 1961. Officially, the main goal of the agency was to elevate the economic, urban, functional, and cultural levels of towns and cities on both the northern and southern borders of Mexico. Although enjoying only limited success, the program did result in important works of infrastructure that had a direct impact on the tourism industry, as well as aiding the expansion of the border economy.

Another federal program, established in 1965, was known as the Border Industrialization Program (BIP). The BIP formally established the conditions for one of the most crucial developments of the Mexican border during the second half of the century: the *maquiladora* industry (assembly plants). Tijuana established itself early as the leader of the *maquiladora* industry among Mexican border cities. Only Ciudad Juárez and Mexicali have challenged Tijuana's preeminence. By 1992, Tijuana had 515 of the 775 *maquiladoras* in the state of Baja California, employing 68,960 workers.[33] According to a report of the National Council of the Maquiladora Industry in Mexico, the number of *maquiladoras* in Tijuana was up to 794 by the year 2000, representing 22% of the 3,611 establishments in Mexico. Baja California as a whole was home to 1,228 *maquiladoras*, or 34% of the national total. Although the *maquiladora* is a key sector in Tijuana's economy, the city's commercial and tourist activities remain the cornerstone of its economy.

The *maquiladora* made its first appearance in Mexicali as the region's prosperous agriculture began its decline. The first plant was established in Mexicali in 1962. As in other border towns, the BIP created favorable conditions for the *maquiladora* industry to prosper and grow. At first growing steadily, Mexicali's *maquiladora* industry boomed in the 1980s, growing from 54 establishments in 1982, to 135 in 1988, and 196 by the year 2000.

Yet, for all the impressive numbers of the *maquila* industry in Tijuana and Mexicali, the smaller border town of Tecate probably best exemplifies the powerful effects of the industry in Baja California during the last quarter of the twentieth century. In 1980, Tecate had twenty-two *maquiladora* establishments. By the end of the 1990s, more than half the jobs in the Tecate municipality were in 138 *maquiladora* establishments. This number represented about 70% of Mexicali's total at the time, even though Mexicali's population was ten times greater than that of Tecate's.[34]

During the late 1960s and early 1970s, major infrastructure projects became more typical in Baja California's expanding urban centers. The first industrial parks began to appear in the landscape. Boulevards and commercial strips were planned and built. In Mexicali, a new government center was constructed to house the executive, judicial, and legislative powers of the state government in a new civic center. Construction of the UABC main campus began, and a new sports complex with a baseball stadium was unveiled. Meanwhile, in 1972, Tijuana began what is arguably the largest and most ambitious urban redevelopment project in Mexico's modern history. The project focused on urbanizing a total of 400 hectares in the bed of the Tijuana River, in the heart of the city.[35] Today, the modern *Zona Rió*, designed and built for the automobile, is the heart of Tijuana's commercial, social, civic, cultural, and financial life. It has become a symbol of Tijuana's emergence as a major metropolis, and has contributed to the popular view of Tijuana as a "*México Chiquito*," or "little Mexico City."

Political Transition and the Mature Metropolis (1980–2000)

The late 1970s and 1980s were times of economic and political crisis in Mexico. Baja California continued its integration into Mexican life. Large Mexican commercial chains, especially supermarkets, arrived in the region. Up to the early 1980s, most Baja California residents still did their shopping on a regular basis in the United States. As the large chains began to establish themselves, products of high quality at competitive prices became accessible to the general public.

During this period, few new upscale or middle-class housing developments were built. The recurring economic crisis, peso devaluations, and soaring interest rates slowed the economy of Baja California, which experienced some of its smallest population growth rates of the second half of the twentieth century, especially Mexicali. Still, Baja California seemed to weather the crisis. The flow of foreign investment into the *maquiladora* industry, and its multiplier effect in the service economy, deflected the worst effects of the national crisis.

During the 1980s and 1990s, Tijuana consolidated its position as the most important city of Baja California. Its role in Baja politics was formative and crucial during this period. In 1989, Baja California became the first state to elect a governor who was not from the long-lasting ruling party, PRI.[36] Ernesto Ruffo of PAN[37] won the election in the summer of that year, handing the PRI its first major defeat in a state or federal election in sixty years. Ruffo had previously served as mayor of Ensenada, but Tijuana voters were the most important force in Ruffo's victory. In that same election, Carlos Montejo Fabela, also from PAN, became the first non-PRI mayor in Tijuana's history. PAN subsequently captured the following four mayoral elections in Tijuana. Mexicali, as state capital and headquarters of both major parties, has traditionally been where Baja California's politics are shaped. But Tijuana, with the largest base of voters in the state, has become the determining factor in election results. The city has become a national symbol of "*Panismo*," which some people suggest was the reason it was chosen as the place to assassinate Luis Donaldo Colosio, PRI's presidential candidate in 1994.

Ernesto Ruffo's triumph in the 1989 election legitimized the intense political struggle PAN had fought in Baja California for decades. PAN had fallen victim to well-known electoral frauds in 1968 mayoral elections in Tijuana and Mexicali. The election was annulled, reportedly due to the many irregularities. In 1983, a similar episode took place in the election for mayor of Mexicali, when Eugenio Elorduy apparently received the majority of the votes, but where victory was handed to the PRI candidate. By 1995, a major change had taken place: PAN simultaneously had control of the governor's office, the cities of Mexicali and Tijuana, and a majority in the state legislature. PAN's rise as the state's major political force was consolidated in the year 2000, when Vicente Fox obtained 50% of the vote in Baja California during the national presidential election;[38] and again in 2001, when PAN retained the governor's seat for six more years, and won four of out five mayoral elections throughout the state, including those in Tijuana and Mexicali.[39]

During the 1990s, businesses, corporations, media, politicians, and the country as a whole began to acknowledge Tijuana´s importance. Although much of the attention was a result of economic and demographic growth, much attention was also due to less positive developments. The assassination of Colosio in 1994 was only one of a depressing sequence of high-profile criminal acts. The Tijuana Drug Cartel, headed by the Arrellano Felix Brothers, became one of the most powerful and sought-after criminal organizations in the world. The Mexican national media began to identify Tijuana, along with a couple of other places in Mexico, as a prime example of how violence and organized crime had taken over the country. The assassinations of the director of Municipal Public Safety of Tijuana, José Federico Benitez in 1994, and Tijuana's Police Chief Alfredo de la Torre Márquez in 2000, along with high-profile kidnappings (of, for instance, Mamoru Konno, a Japanese businessman of the SANYO corporation) brought international attention to Tijuana.

Despite the negative attention, Tijuana and Baja California remained attractive to investors and migrants. In 1996, Hollywood formalized its century-old relationship with Baja California as an on-and-off shooting location by establishing the Fox Studios Baja, south of Tijuana near the beach resort of Rosarito. The blockbuster film *Titanic* became the studio's first production. Electronic giants such as Sony and Mitsubishi, among others, made multimillion-dollar investments in plants and technology in Tijuana and Mexicali during the 1990s. And in June 2002, Toyota began construction of a major production plant in Tijuana (note: not an assembly plant, but an auto *production* center). According to the 2000 census, Tijuana's population grew from 742,686 in 1990 to 1.25 million in 2000. Unofficial estimates put that number at over 1.5 million. Baja California as a whole became the fifteenth most populous state (out of 32) in Mexico, with the second highest growth rate in the 1990s, just behind the state of Quintana Roo.[40]

Although Tijuana has taken the title of largest urban and economic center of the state of Baja California, Mexicali´s role within state, national, and international contexts has become increasingly important. By 2000, Mexicali was the third largest Mexican border city, and one of Mexico's fourteen

Figure 3.7 Mexicali, Baja California, looking north toward the U.S. Border, clearly demarcated by the switch to agricultural land uses. (Photo: Carlos Cesena.)

largest urban centers, with an official population of 764,602.[41] (Unofficial estimates put the total at about 900,000.) Mexicali has successfully connected its economy to the global dynamics of the Pacific Rim, with extremely close ties to Korea and Japan that for the most part are a result of the growing *maquiladora* industry. Mexicali's role in state and national politics has also raised its profile.

The spectacular growth trends experienced by Tijuana and Mexicali have been shared by the other, smaller cities of Baja California. By 2000, the municipality of Ensenada reached a population of 370,730, while Tecate, during the 1990s, had the highest growth rate of all four principal cities in the state. Its population soared from 57,000 in 1990 to 77,000 in 2000.[42]

In 1951, Fernando Jordán, a young Mexican anthropologist and journalist from Mexico City published a wonderful and now classic book, *El Otro México* (The Other Mexico).[43] His 7,000-km trip to Baja California in the middle of the twentieth century was the subject of the first work to firmly focus the attention of the rest of Mexico on Baja California. In the introduction to the book, Jordán explains its title. Standing atop of a scarp, looking out over the Bay of Ensenada, Jordán was asked by a companion: "What do you think of our land?" Immediately he responded: "*Pienso . . . , pienso que es un otro México.*" (I think . . . , I think that it is another Mexico.)[44]

Although the integration of Baja California with the rest of Mexico may be considered complete, Jordan's words still stand today. Despite its "mexicanization" experience, Baja California's links with Southern California have become stronger than ever. There has never been a time when Baja California was more integrated into Southern California than today; at the same time, Baja California is more Mexican than it has ever been. Contradictory? Perhaps, but no more contradictory than pursuing an almost military-like campaign to deter border crossings at the same moment as plans for a binational airport for Tijuana/San Diego are advancing.[45]

Notes

1. Instituto de Cultura de Baja California, *Diccionario Enciclopedico de Baja California* (Compañia Editora de Enciclopedias de Mexico, SA de CV, Mexico City, 1989), 61–2.
2. David Piñera Ramirez, *Historia de Tijuana* (Universidad Autónoma de Baja California, Tijuana, 1985), 23–5.
3. Jorge Martinez Zepeda and Lourdes Romero Navarrette, *Mexicali: Una Historia* (Universidad Autónoma de Baja California, Mexicali, 1991), Vol. I, 85.
4. David Piñera Ramirez, *Historia de Tijuana*, 30–5.
5. Adalberto Walther Meade, *Tecate Cuarto Municipio* (Universidad Autónoma de Baja California, Mexicali, 1993), 11–15.
6. David Piñera Ramirez, *Historia de Tijuana*, 37–40.
7. Jorge Martinez Zepeda and Lourdes Romero Navarrette, *Mexicali: Una Historia*, Vol. I, 105–11.
8. Jorge Martinez Zepeda and Lourdes Romero Navarrette, *Mexicali: Una Historia*, Vol. I, 149–68.
9. For more on Ensenada's urban life in the late 1800s, see David Piñera Ramirez, *"Las Compañias Colonizadoras en Ensenada, 1886–1910,"* in *Ensenada: Nuevas Aportaciones Para Su Historia* (Universidad Autónoma de Baja California, Mexicali, 1999), 165–223; Antonio Padilla Corona, *"Influencias Urbanas en la Región,"* in *Ensenada: Nuevas Aportaciones Para Su Historia* (Universidad Autónoma de Baja California, 1999), 225–64.
10. David Piñera Ramirez, *Historia de Tijuana*, 62–4.
11. Adalberto Walther Meade, *Origen de Mexicali*, 37.
12. Jorge Martinez Zepeda and Lourdes Romero Navarrette, *Mexicali: Una Historia*, Vol. I, 182–85; Adalberto Walther Meade, *Origen de Mexicali*, Mexicali (Universidad Autónoma de Baja California, 1983) 50–1.
13. Adalberto Walther Meade, *Origen de Mexicali*, 65–93; Jorge Martinez Zepeda and Lourdes Romero Navarrette, *Mexicali: Una Historia*, Vol. I, 189–90.
14. For more on the Colorado River Land Company and its impact on the Mexicali Valley see Dorothy P. Kerig, *El Valle de Mexicali y la Colorado River Land Company, 1902–1946* (Universidad Autónoma de Baja California, Mexicali, 2001). This book is based on a doctoral dissertation presented in 1988 by Dorothy P. Kerig at the University of California, Irvine.

15. Adalberto Walther Meade, *Origen de Mexicali*, 94–101; Jorge Martinez Zepeda and Lourdes Romero Navarrette, *Mexicali: Una Historia*, Vol. I, 191–95.

16. Jorge Martinez Zepeda and Lourdes Romero Navarrette, *Mexicali: Una Historia*, Vol. I, 195–96.

17. Jorge Martinez Zepeda and Lourdes Romero Navarrette, *Mexicali: Una Historia*, Vol. I, 203–52; David Piñera Ramirez, *Historia de Tijuana*, 70–84.

18. David Piñera Ramirez, *Historia de Tijuana*, 96.

19. David Piñera Ramirez, *Historia de Tijuana*, 96–8.

20. Jorge Martinez Zepeda and Lourdes Romero Navarrette, *Mexicali: Una Historia*, Vol. I, 253–75; Adalberto Walther Meade, *Origen de Mexicali* (Universidad Autónoma de Baja California, 1983), 102–14.

21. In broad terms, the most critical time of the Mexican Revolution was from 1910 to 1920, when most of the armed conflict took place. In 1920, General Alvaro Obregón, supported by other military leaders from Sonora, was elected president. Once in office, his main goal would be to establish institutional stability to end the decade-long tradition of presidential successions decided through military coups and assassinations. From 1920 onward, military revolts and sporadic acts of violence would continue, but the government and presidency were never seriously threatened. Obregón's administration began the transition of Mexico's political system from one of violence to one of institutional order.

22. David Piñera Ramirez, *Historia de Tijuana*, 114–17.

23. David Piñera Ramirez, *Historia de Tijuana*, 128.

24. David Piñera Ramirez, *Historia de Tijuana*, 123–24.

25. Lawrence A. Herzog, *From Aztec to High Tech* (Baltimore: Johns Hopkins University Press, 1999), 76.

26. In 1930, Baja California's category and title changed from *Distrito Norte de Baja California* to *Territorio de Baja California*.

27. David Piñera Ramirez, *Historia de Tijuana*, 134.

28. Celso Aguirre Bernal, *Compendio Historico-Biográfico de Mexicali* (Mexicali, 1966), 351.

29. Adalberto Walther Meade, *Origen de Mexicali*, 196–200; Jorge Martinez Zepeda and Lourdes Romero Navarrette, *Mexicali: Una Historia*, Vol. II, 124–25.

30. David Piñera Ramirez, *Historia de Tijuana*, 203; Jorge Martinez Zepeda and Lourdes Romero Navarrette, *Mexicali: Una Historia*, Vol. II, 139.

31. David Piñera Ramirez, *Historia de Tijuana*, 170–71.

32. The quote is attributed to Luis Humberto Crosthwaite by Gabriel Trujillo Muñoz in Gabriel Trujillo Muñoz, *Literatura Bajacaliforniana Siglo XX* (Editorial Larva, 1997).

33. Secretaria de Desarrollo Económico, *La Economía de Baja California en Cifras, 1998* (Gobierno del Estado de Baja California, Mexicali, 1998), 37.

34. The early history of Tecate is broadly similar to that of both Tijuana and Mexicali—cattle ranching during the late-nineteenth century (plus some mineral exploration), early railroad connections with the United States only, municipal establishment in 1917, followed by a steady expansion in commercial enterprises (including flour, whiskey, oil, and, most notably, beer). See Paul Ganster, Felipe Cuamea Velázquez, José Luis Castro Ruiz, and Angélica Villegas (eds.). *Tecate, Baja California: Realities and Challenges in a Mexican Border Community/Tecate, Baja California: Realidades y Desafíos de una Commidad Mexicana Fronteriza* (San Diego: Institute for Regional Studies of the Californias, 2002), especially 67–73.

35. David Piñera Ramirez, *Historia de Tijuana*, 192–93.

36. The *Partido Revolucionario Institucional* (PRI; Institutional Revolutionary Party) was founded in 1929 under the name *Partido Nacional Revolucionario* (PNR); in 1938 the PNR was retitled the *Partido de la Revolución Mexicana* (PRM), and in 1946 the party changed its name and registration once more to the one it holds today. Since its initial founding in 1929, and until the election of Ernesto Ruffo in Baja California in 1989, the PRI had won every federal election for president as well as all elections for governor of every state in Mexico. In addition, throughout this entire period, PRI held a majority in both houses of the federal congress.

37. The *Partido Acción Nacional* (PAN; National Action Party) was founded in 1939 and has usually been associated with the Mexican right wing political class. During the second half of the twentieth century, PAN represented the only significant opposition to the PRI.

38. Instituto Federal Electoral, *Sistema de Consulta de la Estadistica de las Elecciones Federales de Mexico City, 2000*.

39. Instituto Estatal Electoral de Baja California, *Resultados de las Elecciones, Mexicali, 2001*.

40. Instituto Nacional de Estadistica, Geografia e Informatica (INEGI), *XII Censo General de Población y Vivienda 2000: Sintesis de Resultados* (Mexico, 2000).

41. INEGI, *XII Censo General de Poblacion y Vivienda 2000: Resultados Preliminares* (Mexico, 2000).

42. Especially interesting are Tecate's recent attempts to confront its own rapid growth, as well as the threat of sprawl from nearby Tijuana. See, for instance, Paul Ganster et al., *Tecate, Baja California*. It is also noteworthy that Mexicali and (later) Tecate followed Tijuana with proposals for their own Zona Río developments; but, in a sign of the times, Tecate's project is more concerned with the creation of a river parkland and other kinds of sustainable development. Tecate's plans are outlined in Suzanne M. Michel and Carlos Graisbord, *Urban Rivers in Tecate and Tijuana: Strategies for Sustainable Cities/Los Ríos Urbanos de Tecate y Tijuana: Estrategias para cuidades sustenables* (San Diego: Institute for Regional Studies of the Californias, 2002).

43. The first edition of *El Otro México: Biografia de Baja California* was published in 1951 by Biografías Gandesa, México. The book was republished in 1993 by the Universidad Autónoma de Baja California in association with Consejo Nacional Para La Cultura y las Artes (CONACULTA) and the Instituto Sudcaliforniano de Cultura, as part of the collection: *Baja California: Nuestra Historia*.

44. Fernando Jordán, *El Otro México: Biografia de Baja California* (Universidad Autónoma de Baja California, Mexicali, 2001), 63.

45. As part of the U.S. Immigration and Naturalization Services's (INS) "Operation Gatekeeper," launched in 1994, a new fence constructed from metal landing mats recycled from the Gulf War was built in urban areas of the Baja California-California Border. In many instances, the new obstacle replaced a chain-link fence that for decades had permitted visibility from one side of the border to the other (see Figure 2.8).

PART **II**

Regional Imaginations

4

Global Tijuana

The Seven Ecologies of the Border

LAWRENCE A. HERZOG

Nearly a century ago, the United States–Mexico border zone was a vast swath of uninhabited desert, canyon lands, and mountain chains, interrupted by occasional bursts of agriculture. It was fittingly labeled the "land of sunshine, adobe and silence."[1] But in the short span of the past half-century, the region absorbed millions of newcomers. Today, it is blanketed with burgeoning cities and vast global industrial complexes, one of the fastest growing economic corridors in the Americas. Along the southern edge, the Mexican cities grow spontaneously, frequently with minimal planning. They borrow from the language and culture of their counterparts north of the boundary. In this part of the world, urbanization marches to the beat of the global economy; its landscapes are driven by the triple engines of global assembly, free trade, and the international division of labor.

Globalization discourse has either misrepresented or failed to take notice of this important transnational region. "Global cities" are typically associated with the headquarters of multinational corporations (New York, London, Tokyo, etc.) or with megacenters of the third world (São Paulo, Shanghai, Mexico City). International border regions have generally been dismissed as marginal places. At the Mexican border, observers imagine "global" intertwined with drug smuggling, illegal immigration, or violence.

But the global ecology of the twenty-first century border goes far beyond such misconceived stereotypes. Indeed, border ecologies are far more central to our understanding of world city formations than might seem at first

119

glance. The Tijuana/California border zone offers an ideal laboratory for understanding how globalization is shaping a new kind of urbanism.

This new borderland urbanism springs from a simple principle: processes once thought to define urban form are no longer geographically restricted within the boundaries of the nation-state. Globalization means that a set of exogenous forces (foreign investors, transnational workers, etc.) is now brought to bear on the local and regional construction of urban form. What happens when those forces, and the ecologies they create, operate within a floating physical space that literally transcends international boundaries? Here lies the magic of border cities—not only are they defined by distant global processes, but their global character is imprinted in real geographic space. They literally transcend the physical limits of nation-states. Border cities are tangible living spaces that cross national political boundaries. We can call this new global prototype a "transfrontier metropolis."[2]

If we are to craft an ecology for a transfrontier metropolis, we must confront the conditions under which the global economy collides with social space in a bicultural, first-world–third-world, high-density, rapidly urbanizing international boundary region. We must go beyond the traditional measures of urban ecology, into a world of postmodern ecology. Tijuana challenges our notions of urban form, just as Los Angeles did some thirty years ago. Los Angeles was originally seen as the antithesis of good urban form, a new age, postindustrial sprawling, confused mass of formless ecologies. It took an outsider, a visiting British architect (Reyner Banham), to jolt urbanists into seeing the possibilities of Los Angeles' innovative ecology. Los Angeles offered a novel mixing of physical form and social behavior. The automobile and the freeway provided for a rich ecology of individual expression and optimism imbedded in private, low-density, single-family residential ecologies (in foothills and lowlands), and in the spiritual luxury of vast open spaces, beach life styles, and health consciousness.[3]

Perhaps Los Angeles and the shift toward postmodernity also teach us that urban ecologies are physical and material, yet also conceptual and cognitive[4] (a point emphasized by Dear and Leclerc in the Introduction). In a world of global marketing, high technology, instantaneous communication, and rapid-fire cross-border movements, ecologies are not measured merely by physically bounded space, but by the behaviors and perceptions of local and regional actors, responding to the new global reality.

This brings us to Tijuana, a metropolis pulled between the forces of globalization and those of traditional Mexico. Tijuana is a Mexican city, born to a culture whose urbanism is anchored in the indigenous cosmologies of sacred space and nature as well as Spanish grid designs of colonial royal power and urban Catholic order. These foundations have been modified by Latin modernity, fused with twentieth-century nationalism, and managed under a highly centralized political system in which the federal government dictates the form and function of its cities (cf. Chapter 3). Yet Tijuana's ecology is also being mediated by many new global and transcultural forces; the city is a conduit and homeland to international migrants, a staging area for the new global factory, and the site for experiments in expanded free trade and cross-border consumerism. Taken together these divergent forces have produced one of the great global examples of an urban work-in-progress, a metropolis literally caught between paradigms—modernity and postmodernity, North and South, local and global—a place on the verge of being catapulted beyond, to a new level of innovation, or what has been termed hybridity.[5]

With this in mind, this chapter begins to unravel the landscape of Tijuana's emerging global ecologies. Seven new ecologies form the superstructure of this bustling metropolis of nearly two million people. They include spaces formed by global economic actors (global factory zones, transnational consumer spaces, and global tourism districts) and spaces that represent regional and local responses to globalizing forces [post-North American Free Trade Agreements (NAFTA) neighborhoods, transnational community places, spaces of conflict, and invented connections].

- *Global factory zones* consist of vast, sprawling industrial parks with foreign-owned assembly plants in which color television sets, video players, and other consumer goods are manufactured in cheap labor enclaves, then shipped to markets in the United States and other developed nations.
- *Transnational consumer spaces* include new shopping malls, strip developed corridors, and commercial zones with international chain stores. Their landscapes are homogenized and carefully controlled as part of a global marketing strategy.
- *Global tourism districts* are spaces being invented for international tourism, in which the dominant built environment strategy is to craft homogeneous, easily recognized cultural landscapes—luxury resorts or formal tourism districts.
- *Post-NAFTA neighborhoods* include a variety of living spaces directly or indirectly created by the global economy. Transnational elite residential zones, or gated communities, are being designed either for U.S. and other foreign residents, or wealthy Mexican nationals. New elite suburbs are decentralized residential spaces built along the lines of U.S. suburban developments, and immigrant barrios *(colonias)* are the spaces for new migrants to the border region, generally characterized by spontaneously constructed self-help

housing and locally engineered community infrastructure needed for survival in a globalizing system.

- *Transnational community places* include nodes and public gathering spaces that transform the international boundary line from a militarized, protected space into a part of the community. They are made possible by the gradual evolution of a more porous border where trade and exchange are valued above defense and security.
- *Spaces of conflict* are symptomatic of the condition of unresolved tension embedded in settlements on the boundary. The national debate—security vs. open borders—remains embedded in the visual landscape and geography of the immediate boundary zone.
- *Invented connections* are opportunistic forms of urbanism imagined (and built) by entrepreneurs and planners who seek to find profit from the emerging transnational phenomenon.

Global Factory Zones

The "global factory" is one of the great inventions of late twentieth-century world capitalism. As labor costs impinged on profits among multinational firms in the 1950s and 1960s, the idea of global cheap labor enclaves emerged. Firms discovered they could simply move the factory floor to a less-developed nation. Third-world countries suddenly loomed as the new industrial labor pools for global industrial giants. Thus was born the global factory.

Mexico quickly became a key player, through the so called "twin plant" or *maquiladora* (assembly plant) project. In the 1960s, Mexico's government hatched a new federal office to promote border economic expansion—it was known as PRONAF, the National Frontier Program. The biggest plank in the PRONAF development strategy was reduction of unemployment through industrial growth. In 1965, the Border Industrial Program (BIP) was introduced. It built on the emerging "off shore" production concepts that U.S. manufacturers had already started in places such as Hong Kong or Taiwan. The BIP project envisioned foreign-owned (mainly American) factories relocating their labor-intensive assembly operations to the Mexican border.

And relocate they did. The BIP forever changed the Mexican borderlands. In 1970, there were 160 *maquiladoras* in Mexico, employing around 20,000 workers. Some twenty-five years later, there were an estimated 2,400 assembly plants in Mexico, employing nearly three-quarter million workers, with a value-added estimated at roughly three billion dollars. All of these plants are foreign owned; the majority come from the United States, Japan, South Korea, Canada, and Germany.

Maquiladoras brought a dramatic global shift to the Mexican border. They single-handedly legitimated the border region as a place for foreign in-

Figure 4.1 The arrival of hundreds of global factories form the core of a dramatic late twentieth-century transformation in Tijuana's ecology. Panasonic/Matsushita *maquila* assembly plant façade, Mesa de Otay, Tijuana. (Photo: L. Herzog.)

vestment. Asian, European, and U.S. investors facilitated the border's rise onto the radar screen of the global economic community. The construction of assembly plant complexes served to anchor the real estate and development boom of the late twentieth century, bringing road, sewerage, and other infrastructure to outer lying areas of the cities. *Maquilas* created an alternative labor source for millions of Mexican immigrants heading north. Their multiplier effects in generating linked employment clusters in services further expanded urban growth. The sheer numbers of workers amplified pressure on cities such as Tijuana to find ways to absorb new migrants.

The factories themselves descend upon the landscape of Tijuana, consolidating around an ecology of the modern industrial park, not unlike the counterpart U.S. suburban industrial parks to the north. As in the United States, the dominant feature is the use of uniform lot sizes and street setbacks, as well as controlled landscaping. There are also sophisticated systems of screening and security, as well as large-scale parking facilities. The *Ciudad Industrial* (Industrial City) on the eastern Mesa de Otay is Tijuana's principal global factory zone. Because this *maquila* zone lies on the outskirts of Tijuana, it resembles a kind of suburban *hacienda* compound, an insular space in which workers provide labor to the "*patron*" (the industrial giant) in return for a modest salary. However unlike industrial parks in San Diego, Tijuana's *maquila* parks are surrounded by poor *colonias*, low-income settlements that typically house many of the assembly workers.

Transnational Consumer Spaces

One of the guiding principles of global capitalism has been the "culture-ideology of consumerism." Global corporations use advertising and transnational media not merely to sell their products across the globe, but to promote a style of consumption that becomes part of a standardized global culture.[6] Examples of consumption that has been globalized include soft drinks (Coca-Cola, etc.) and fast food. Part of the success in marketing these commodities globally can be traced to corporate strategies to homogenize consumer tastes. By constructing globally uniform consumer behavior (through advertising and construction of recognizable images) multinational corporations can better control the marketing of their products.

This global homogenization of consumer taste arguably exists not only in food products, clothing, or automobiles, but in the built environment as well. The design of shopping malls, fast food restaurants, hotels, resorts, and other urban spaces has become globalized. There are no longer vast differences between shopping mall designs in China, Ireland, Peru, or Mexico. Malls have a standardized site plan and design concept—including the use of anchor stores, public areas for walking and sitting, food courts, movie theaters, and restaurants. Further, there is a growing trend in renting space to global chain stores that sell clothing, electronics, and other consumer goods in shopping malls around the world. Hotels and resorts often use standardized designs as well. Indeed, many corporate hotel chains believe that travelers like the predictable, familiar designs of hotel chains in the United States and Western Europe, and thus seek to replicate those designs in other cultural settings. Their marketing departments will tell you that consumers prefer the familiar images of their hotel, over the less familiar components of local cultures.

These designs are not merely limited to buildings. The new public spaces of the twenty-first century will be privatized streets, festival marketplaces, or giant mall complexes. Increasingly, these consumer spaces seek to replace the traditional downtown as the primary pedestrian-scale gathering place for postmodern city dwellers. The quintessential privatized street is "City Walk," on the west side of Los Angeles. The architects successfully recreated the scale and the feel of a pedestrian street; for example, each store is visually presented as a separate façade, giving the impression of a street lined with individual buildings. City Walk promotes itself as a series of city streets on

Figure 4.2 Homogeneous consumer images bombard the automobile traveler in Tijuana's sleek new River Zone commercial district. Blockbuster and Carl's Jr. signs, Tijuana. (Photo: L. Herzog.)

which people can walk and interact. In fact, it is a large private shopping center disguised as a small village of pedestrian spaces, lined with restaurants, clothing boutiques, specialty stores, and movie theaters.

Mexico has embraced the commodified landscape in the NAFTA era. Four decades ago, nationalist and proud Mexico rejected most U.S. commercial enterprises within its borders—there were virtually no McDonalds or Burger Kings, and no U.S. clothing enterprises anywhere in Mexico as late as the 1980s. But since the signing of NAFTA, Mexico has opened its doors to U.S. and foreign business. Today, hundreds of U.S. chain stores and hotels have swept across the Mexican landscape—from Blockbuster Video, Office Depot, and Sears to Direct TV, Costco, and Wal-Mart. Most of the global hotel chains—including Hilton, Hyatt, and Sheraton—have also exploded onto the Mexican scene.

Along the international border, the dominance of the U.S. culture-ideology of consumerism has been particularly intense. In the early 1990s, the invasion of fast food outlets in border cities such as Tijuana occurred virtually overnight. In the span of one or two years, every major food outlet—McDonald's, Carl's Jr., Burger King, Domino's Pizza, etc.—burst onto the urban landscape. Around the same time, small, medium, and large shopping centers began appearing along commercial boulevards and high-ways. In Tijuana, these minimalls served to interrupt the pedestrian scale of the downtown, as buildings were set back from the sidewalk, while parking lots stood in front. U.S.-style mega-shopping malls also sprouted along the border—Tijuana has two regional-sized shopping malls. U.S. and foreign cor-porate interests have little trouble selling consumption to Tijuana and other border city residents. Most Mexican border city dwellers can use satellite tele-vision to receive programming from Southern California. An enormous, cap-tive Mexican audience can therefore be reached by advertisers on California channels. Mexican consumers learn how to consume, partly by watching American television. As a result, Mexicans living along the border have proven to be highly motivated customers on the U. S. side. Studies in California, have shown, for example, that Mexican consumers have similar, if not better infor-mation and a slightly better understanding than California residents of loca-tions and qualities of stores and products in the San Diego region.[7]

Global Tourism Districts

Tourism development adheres strongly to the principles of the culture-ideol-ogy of consumerism. A central premise of tourism design is the manipula-tion of visitors' experience of place to maximize profit. Global tourism investors and corporate decision makers tend to view regions as stage sets for generating profit, rather than as genuine places whose identity should be protected. Because global developers generally view investments from distant world headquarter cities such as New York, Chicago, or San Francisco, they often lose touch with the places their investments are transforming. The main strategy of tourism development is to enhance marketability and client interest through the production of landscapes that satisfy the needs of pro-jected users.[8] Studies have shown that tourists prefer comfort, reliability, and pleasure, especially in foreign settings. The architecture designed to accom-modate visitors, which one writer calls the "tourism gaze," is, in effect, a land-scape socially constructed for a targeted population. It has been compared to Foucault's "medical gaze," a strategy of controlled design aimed at a different economic interest group—consumers of medical services and facilities.[9]

Tourism developers seek to create homogeneous, readily distinguished, easily consumed built environment experiences for their client populations. Controlled resort structures with recognizable designs (oceanfront board-walks, small clustered, shopping and restaurant complexes, hotels, fast food outlets, global boutiques) have become the central pillars of tourism land-scape design. The value of tourist space is measured by its marketability for short-term tourism visits, rather than by its cultural uniqueness or environ-mental purity.

Global tourism reveals the dangers of commodification—the transformation of tourism spaces into generic commodities for sale in the world market. As with product marketing, global companies want to standardize the tourism experience. Large-scale tourism resort developments, based on uniform design criteria, are not crafted with the local environment in mind, which is why they are often not sustainable.[10] The tourism industry, controlled from international command centers in wealthy nations, tends to promote distorted images of third-world nations such as Mexico, the main destinations of their clients. Global tourism firms have little interest in portraying nations as they really are. For example, it is almost always the case that poverty is minimized or ignored, as are many local customs and practices.

The distinct marketing strategies of the international tourism industry lead to the production of placeless landscapes, devoid or destructive of culture and nature. If tourism is more profitable in built landscapes that are homogeneous, then what incentive can there be for tourism developers to preserve the original landscapes of the places in which they invest? Even in ecologically sensitive zones (jungles, mountains, etc.) or culturally preserved spaces (colonial downtowns), the demand for cosmopolitan infrastructure by tourists—luxury hotels, swimming pools, and plush shopping spaces—has the effect of diminishing the original cultural landscapes, which become overwhelmed by structures designed for consumption.

In Tijuana, the main commercial street in the old downtown tourism district—Revolution Avenue—is a striking example of a manipulated, commodified space. Revolution Avenue is to Tijuana what Main Street, U.S.A. is to Disneyland—an artificial promenade that sets the mood for a carefully choreographed experience. In Disneyland, visitors park their cars and walk across the parking lot, through the entrance gates, and onto Main Street, a theatrical stage set, built at 4/5 scale, and lined with costumed characters, from Mickey Mouse to a Barbershop Quartet. In Tijuana, tourists park their cars in vast lots just north of the border, cross the pedestrian entrance into Mexico, and move along a path that leads them to Revolution Avenue.

Revolution Avenue is a mini-theme park—a clever stage set of outrageous color and grotesque facades. Buildings resemble zebras or Moorish castles. Flags and colorful blimps fly overhead. Music blares, whistles blow, barkers shout along its nearly one mile length. The setting is a classic "other directed space," a vacation-land and consumer haven created for outsiders.[11] "Revolution Avenue is theater," states one Mexican architect. "You see a life-sized yellow school bus on the exterior of a building—it is oriented toward the market of high school age Americans who come to drink. The architecture is fun. It says 'Now come on your school bus and you can drink.' It's all an exercise in border craftsmanship."[12]

This argument comes full circle. Disneyland is the quintessential "other-directed" landscape, "a world without violence, confrontation, ideological or racial clashes, without politics . . . a world that is white, Anglo Saxon, and Puritan-Protestant, often redneck, void of ethnic cast."[13] One could argue that Revolution Avenue was designed to be an idealized "Mexico-land," a fantasy exotica of what Americans imagine Mexico to be. Ironically, Tijuana entrepreneurs tried to build a Mexican version of Disneyland—called Mexitlan, a theme park that celebrated Mexico's architectural history. By the late 1990s, the border theme park was a ghost town that had gone out of business. Its demise points to an apparent marketing error made by Mexitlan designers. Along the border, American tourists prefer a landscape of the exotic and the fantastic. For them, the border's magnetism lies in the world of the unknown, the imagined. Mexitlan gave tourists beautifully designed glimpses into Mexico's real architectural history. If Mexitlan tried to be a Mexican Disneyland, it was, in the end, not playful enough; it was more minimuseum than theme park, as it celebrated something close to the heart of Mexicans—architecture. This kind of serious tourism experience works in central Mexico but not along the border.[14]

Tourism breeds "enclavism," the creation of isolated zones for visitors, buffered from the everyday city, to allow the outsider's fantasy of the place to remain distinct from its reality, which is usually less exotic. Enclavism leads to the creation of artificial tourism districts that become segregated from the city itself. In Tijuana, globalized enclaves include Revolution Avenue, the aforementioned Mexitlan, commercial/entertainment complexes in the River Zone, and beachfront tourism zones.

Along the beachfront, just south of the city proper lies an excellent example of an enclave—the village of Puerto Popotla, near the town of Rosarito. Popotla was once a small fishing village of less than 100 residents. The Hollywood film company Twentieth Century Fox leased land adjacent to the village to build a major studio—Fox Baja Studios—for film production in the mid-1990s The first film was *Titanic*; its enormous global success has had ripple effects on this zone of Baja California. The Titanic facilities consisted of imposing, massive, ugly gray metal warehouses, and a giant concrete wall surrounding the site, which townspeople have dubbed "the Berlin wall." The film production facilities completely dwarf the fishing village, and evoke the feeling of a prison: security around the site is extremely tight, with high walls and a guardhouse. Here "enclavism" takes an interesting form—a "movie maquiladora," or an assembly plant for film making."[15]

More recently, Fox Studios Baja built and opened a new theme park adjacent to its Baja Film studio site. It is called "Foxploration" and is devoted to the art of moviemaking. The park includes exhibits of the original *Titanic* set, technology of filmmaking, and the craft of props and accessories.

This enclave has already brought environmental degradation to the Tijuana/Baja coastline. During construction, underwater explosives may have

Figure 4.3 Mexican tourism entrepreneurs' attempt at a hybrid tourism theme park fails to capture the U.S. market. Mexitlan sign, downtown Tijuana. (Photo: L. Herzog.)

been used to grade the beach area and build several giant pools for the *Titanic* filming, causing destruction of marine life for kilometers around the site. Further, according to some observers, during filming the company dumped chlorine into the pool, and emptied its tanks in the ocean, allowing the chlorine to seep into the kelp beds and nearby ecology. Privately owned, protected, commodified spaces tend to remain closed off from government code enforcers and housing inspectors.

The irony, as one explores the landscape of Popotla, is that the very company (Fox) that specializes in making spectacular, finely crafted images for movies, houses its activities on the edge of the Pacific Ocean in ugly gray warehouses surrounded by concrete walls and barbed wire fences. The design of the film compound, apparently rushed through without a serious environmental impact study or planning analysis, dwarfs the nearby village of lobster fishermen, modest wooden shacks, and restaurants for workers. Fox Studios Baja would never be approved in California because it violates the Coastal Act. It is one of many examples along the border of U.S. companies relocating to Baja, and not conforming to environmental/land use standards back in their homeland.

Post-NAFTA Neighborhoods

The traditional social geography of Mexican border towns reveals an inverse model of the U.S. pattern. In Mexico, wealthy residents cluster in older established neighborhoods adjacent to downtown, or along a commercial corridor leading out of the central business district. Middle class, working class, and poor neighborhoods are arrayed concentrically around the core, with the poorest residents living farthest from the center.

Globalization exacerbates this social geography; at the same time, it adds new twists to it. The biggest changes are the addition of new residential enclaves for transnational investors and visitors. In Tijuana, the valuable coastline just beyond the city offers comparatively inexpensive real estate for U.S. residents, either in the form of second homes, or permanent dwellings for retirees. Some 25,000 Americans reside in the coastal corridor between Tijuana and Ensenada, and that number will grow.[16] Global real estate projects are aiming to create golf resorts, beachfront condo complexes, and luxury marina housing enclaves for foreign residents. These high paying land users routinely outbid Mexicans for coastal properties; the result is that the social ecology of the coastal strip is global—it is dominated by foreign residents.

Meanwhile, U.S.-style condominiums and suburban housing developments for Mexicans have accelerated across Tijuana. Mexican consumers are familiar with U.S. housing, both from crossing the border, or through the print and visual media. Global advertising has altered their taste in housing. Wealthy consumers want condominiums with jacuzzis, sunken bathtubs, and satellite television. Even poor migrants aspire to U.S.-type houses. A former border architect speaks of his frustration with people who, despite incredibly limited incomes, refuse to live in houses that could be technically designed to fit their budgets. "My clients don't want to live in a house designed with recycled metal or junk parts, even if it is excellently constructed. They want a California tract house, with a picture window and a garage. A lot of people can't afford to buy a house in the United States, but they buy the magazines, and then they find a photograph of a house they like. They bring it to the architect in Tijuana, and they say "I want a house like this." But they forget that in Mexico our lot sizes are smaller and narrower. We don't have the space to design with ideal lighting and ventilation. To meet their needs, we end up designing caricatures of American-style houses in miniature".[17]

As mentioned earlier, worker housing has been dispersed around the *maquila* zones. Migrants to Tijuana live on the edges of the city, near or beyond the zone of *maquila* workers, in squatter communities of substandard housing, also known locally as *colonias populares*. This class of marginal, disenfranchised urban poor may not ultimately benefit greatly from globalization, but they respond to its seductive pull. The struggle of the urban poor to survive in booming, globalizing cities constitutes a key debate underlying the globalization protest movements around the globe.

Colonias are pockets of haphazardly constructed houses, built by the poor themselves, usually on the worst possible sites in the city—flood-prone canyons, steep sloping hillsides, airports, major highways, or land far removed from the city proper. Many of these settlements were created by illegal land invasions, because the poor do not have liquid capital to pay the cost of a home purchase or even rent. This means that *colonia* residents live in a precarious state—burdened by the dual limitations of inadequate house materials for construction (cardboard, tar paper, scrap wood, scrap metal) and questionable legal ownership. Further, these *colonias* often lack basic services such as running water, sewage disposal, paved roads, or street lighting. Most of the households use pirated electricity, stolen from illegal lines connected to nearby electricity grids.

As NAFTA's grip strengthens along the border, more global economic activities—factories, commercial developments, tourism enterprises—create a higher demand for low paying jobs. This in turn attracts even more migrants from the interior of Mexico. Globalization has exacerbated an already burgeoning migration stream headed north, thus spreading the landscape of squalid shanties across the hills and canyons on the outskirts of Tijuana. In the midst of increasing wealth in certain privileged areas (coastline, downtown, River zone), there is increasing deprivation scattered through the squatter communities in the region.

Transnational Community Places

Although nations continue to militarize borders in some regions of the world, a parallel universe of relatively stable border regions has evolved. On these borders new kinds of transnational community spaces are forming. The creation of community spaces and places near international borders runs counter to nearly two centuries of history, where cities were organized

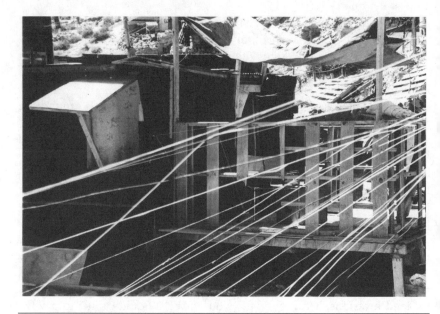

Figure 4.4 One of the principal post-NAFTA neighborhood ecologies is the formation of ex-urban squatter communities in which many assembly plant workers live: pirated electric lines enter *Colonia Pegaso*, eastern Tijuana. (Photo: L. Herzog.)

as physical entities that lie territorially within the boundaries of one sovereign nation. This is no longer the case today. In a number of global boundary zones, most notably Western Europe and North America, we find community spaces that sprawl across international boundaries.[18]

The development of a transnational urban ecology is an overlooked dimension of globalization. A century ago, territorial politics dictated that nations meticulously guard their international boundaries. This "shelter function" mentality[19] fostered a common pattern of national settlement: the largest concentrations of urban population tended to locate away from the physical edge of the nation-state. In fact, before 1950, boundary regions were mainly viewed as buffer zones that served to defend the larger nation from land-based invasions. Under these conditions, few significant community spaces evolved on or near national boundaries. Indeed important urban settlements did not appear near borders. A quick glance at a map of Western Europe corroborates this point: the great cities of Paris, Madrid, Rome, Vienna, and Frankfurt all lie in the borderless interior of their national settings. Across the Atlantic ocean in the Americas, a similar pattern emerges: Mexico City, Lima (Peru), São Paulo (Brazil), and Santiago (Chile) are all positioned at a considerable distance from the nearest international boundary.

Yet today, globalization is opening up border territories to new community formations. Citizens on either side of the United States–Mexico boundary are increasingly drawn together; old differences are set aside as urban neighbors become part of a common transnational living and working space. The building blocks of these new transnational communities lie in the social and physical linkages that connect settlements across the boundary. Such linkages in Tijuana–San Diego include the existence of international commuters, transnational consumers, global factories, cross-border land and housing markets, and transnational architecture.

Nearly 300,000 workers legally travel across the border, from the Mexican to the U.S. side of a transfrontier metropolis, to work in the United States on a daily or weekly basis. Countless thousands of others cross illegally with a border resident card (which permits Mexican border residents to cross into the United States for nonwork purposes, but which is frequently used illegally to get to work). Billions of dollars in cross-border commercial transactions take place annually. Several hundred million border crossings also occur each year, primarily between the partners that form the transnational metropolis. Consumers constitute the most active group of legal border crossers, and are perhaps the primary population that ties together the two sides of the Mexico–U.S. transfrontier metropolis. Collectively they form a complex regional network of flows north and south across the border. The existence of this volume of flows is leading to the emergence of what we might term "transnational citizens," people who exist on both sides of the border.

The evolution of a community of transnational citizens that has a presence north and south of the border is expressed in the social ecology of the region. Urban dwellers do not merely consume goods, they consume the built environment itself—by purchasing land and housing on both sides of the line. NAFTA has opened the door for purchase or lease of land by global investors along the border, particularly in the Baja California region, where plans for international resorts, hotel complexes, commercial development, and luxury housing are abundant. Baja California already has the second largest enclave of expatriate American homeowners (the largest lies in the Guadalajara region), with some 15,000–20,000 Americans residing in homes along the Baja coast. Meanwhile, increasing numbers of Mexican immigrants, as they legitimize their work and immigration status, are purchasing homes on the U.S. side of the border. Some members of a family may live on the U.S. side, whereas others remain on the Mexican side. The hard edge of political demarcation—the physical boundary line—begins to blur. The larger transfrontier region becomes the true urban life space of the border dweller, a more precise spatial construct for defining the experience of binational urban families.

The border has never really separated the cultural construction of the built environment, but today we are seeing an acceleration in the diffusion of global influences on Tijuana's built environment, and in Mexican influences north of the border. In Tijuana, evidence of U.S. influence on the landscape abounds. Why else would one find a Tudor revival home in an upper-class neighborhood of Tijuana, suburban tract homes and condominiums, U.S.-style shopping malls, and fast food outlets sprouting everywhere? U.S. influence even appears in the squatter communities, or *colonias*, in the form of recycled materials purchased in the United States—such as rubber tires, used lumber, or scrap metal highway signs, an important element in the vernacular architecture of Mexican border cities. In sum, what we are seeing are sets of everyday landscapes—shopping centers, freeways, outdoor markets, commuter lanes—that begin to behave as if the international boundary were invisible.

One of the more vivid examples of transborder community place-making is visible in the strategies employed by border residents in taking back the boundary zone itself. The wall, legally managed by the State, is being physically reincorporated back into the adjacent communities by users, be they local residents, border crossers, artists, or community political groups. Rather than let the boundary zone continue to be a space of liability, a no-man's-land, a zone of insecurity, potential crime, and international bureaucracy, local citizens are choosing to humanize the border. Monuments to people who died crossing the boundary have been erected on the border fence itself. The fence is transformed into a public space that can be visited by local residents, a sacred place that commemorates the regional struggle at certain moments in history.

This grassroots place-making seeks to redefine the boundary space, turning a negative (smuggling, illegal immigration, border police forces) into a positive (works of art, monuments, and commemoratives that are part of the community). People who live near the fence use it to define their living space—gardens are planted, clothesline may connect to it, telephones are installed for use by the clandestine border crossers. The boundary zone becomes not only a part of the everyday neighborhood landscape, it is textured into the built landscape of migration, redesigned as a conduit to help those Mexicans who are desperate to cross the frontier and work in the United States. Why not let them make the phone calls to their families north of the border?

Spaces of Conflict

> "*Si el de Berlin cayó, el de Tijuana porqué no?*"
> *(If the one in Berlin fell, why not the one in Tijuana?).*
> —graffiti on the international boundary fence at Tijuana-San Diego.

For more than a century, Tijuana's existence was defined by its link to the physical boundary. Tijuana, like so many Mexican border cities, occupied a

Figure 4.5 Residents near the boundary are taking back the zones near the fence by creating public spaces that commemorate those who died trying to cross; crosses on border fence near Tijuana airport, eastern Tijuana. (Photo: L. Herzog.)

schizophrenic world, dancing between the reality of its economic ties to the United States and its nationalist link to Mexico. The physical boundary—the wall, the fence—stood as a constant reminder of this double identity.

Today, globalization along the border evokes a critical debate: does the region's future lie with perpetuation of the wall and all that it symbolizes (national security, sovereignty, defense, and militarization), or does it reside in the propagation of a world of transparent boundaries and transfrontier cities? This theme shapes an underlying tension embedded in the built environment of border cities, a tension that is manifest by the conflicted landscapes of the immediate boundary zone where the two nations meet.

The popular global icon of militarized boundaries is the Berlin wall—a landscape of bleak, gray images of barbed wire, concrete barriers, soldiers in watchtowers peering through binoculars, and bodies of failed border-crossers draped across the no-man's-land between East and West. The German wall, before its destruction, ran sixty-six miles in twelve-foot high concrete block and thirty-five miles in wire and mesh fencing. It had over 200 watchtowers, and blinding yellow night lights mounted on tall poles.

The Tijuana–San Diego "wall" is forty-seven miles long, and built from corrugated metal landing mats recycled from the Persian Gulf War. Migrants have punched it full of holes, so a second parallel wall is under

Figure 4.6 The border fence continues to embody a landscape of conflict along the line; the fence at Playas de Tijuana enters the Pacific Ocean at the border's western terminus. (Photo: L. Herzog.)

construction a few hundred feet north. The new wall includes eighteen-foot-high concrete "bollard" pilings topped with tilted metal mesh screens, and an experimental cantilevered wire mesh-style fence being developed by Sandia Labs. The fence/wall runs toward the Pacific Ocean, where it becomes a ziggurat of eight-, six-, and four-foot-high metal tube fence knifing into the sea. It is buttressed by six miles of stadium nightlights, 1200 seismic sensors, and numerous infrared sensors used to detect the movement of people after dark.

Like the Berlin wall, landscapes along the Tijuana boundary explode with messages of danger and conflict. These images tend to reduce the border to a cliché, a war zone, a place controlled by national governments and their police forces. Signage on fences and along the line reinforces an underlying theme—that only the governments can decide who enters and who crosses. The U.S. government's "Operation Gatekeeper," a strategic 1994 plan launched by the U.S. Immigration and Naturalization Services, is perhaps the most blatant example of a national policy determined to "Berlinize" the California–Mexico border. Indeed, one official claimed that the goals of the operation were to "restore the rule of law to the California–Baja California border."[20] This general theme of "militarization" along the border has remained as part of the landscape, always threatening to move to the forefront each time a crisis looms. The September 11, 2001 terrorist events in the United States had the immediate effect of resurrecting the policing, enforcement-oriented functions of the international border.

But this landscape cannot hold. It bumps up against the resounding voice of a great global acronym—NAFTA. Mexican and U.S. presidents publicly celebrate globalization, and the goal of a less restrictive boundary. But stand among the hordes of migrants who have just arrived at the border's great immigrant reception hall, the *Central Camionera*, Tijuana's main bus station. Workers from central and southern Mexico arrive here by the thousands each month, and most are still trying to sneak across this border illegally. They crowd onto city buses for the short ride up the plateau through one of the border's largest and booming global factory districts— Mesa de Otay—finally arriving at the international boundary line. There, they await darkness, and a *coyote* (smuggler) to guide them across the heavily guarded frontier. The barriers they face remain decidedly Berlinesque. The multibillion dollar U.S. border security system in place here is a product of over a century of U.S.–Mexican immigration and drug smuggling policy. Meanwhile the governments on either side of this line speak glowingly of NAFTA, and the billions of dollars it will bring. The two nations can't move fast enough to build more freeways, ports, airports, rail systems, and improved border gates—launchpads for the free trade future.

In San Diego–Tijuana, five million inhabitants share an economy with six billion dollars of annual exports and eight billion dollars in cross-border trade. Tourism is booming. Billions will be invested in megaresorts, luxury marinas, and vacation homes along the coast of nearby Baja California. Some 1,000 international assembly plants employing a quarter million workers will be here by 2010. This could be the next Hong Kong. Yet, to poor immigrants huddling at the taco stands along the boundary fence, these dreams lie thousands of miles away in the national capitals. Here on the edge of Mexico, every night as the sun sets, Border Patrol helicopters emerge, like mosquitoes, buzzing the skies above and beaming laser spotlights down into the canyons and migrant footpaths. The wall lives.

Invented Connections

The image of the border as a place of violence and chaos has, for many decades, acted as a built-in form of redlining. Border uncertainty and risk depressed the value of land around the line for most investors. As a result, many boundary zones attract only low-rent land uses, such as warehouse storage facilities, parking lots, or currency exchange houses. Properties frequently remain vacant or abandoned, while landowners wait to see what governments have planned for the future. This risk traditionally created a vacuum for investors; yet it also opened the window for those willing to gamble that NAFTA might ultimately transform the boundary zone into a place to do business.

Such is the case along the Tijuana boundary where it bumps up against the town of San Ysidro, California. Tijuana–San Ysidro is the most heavily traveled border crossing in the western hemisphere; its adjacent border crossing space has languished as an underutilized subarea. It is complicated by the security precautions of the U.S. government, and the problems of smuggling and illegal Mexican migration that cause the border to be preserved as a kind of buffer zone between the two nations.

The San Ysidro–Tijuana port of entry/border zone is the single largest binational connector along the United States-Mexico border. Thirty-four million vehicles and over seven million pedestrians cross through this gate each year. But the port of entry and surrounding zone on both sides of the border are fragmented by a variety of land use and design problems—from traffic congestion, poor circulation routes, and disorganized land uses, to crime, public safety concerns, and unresolved land development plans. This vital physical space, the anchor for the region's cross-border economic development, needs to be carefully planned and redeveloped in the next decade.

In a globalizing world, the border zone may no longer be able to function purely as a "pass-through" space. It is becoming a connector for the regional economy, and even an important destination in its own right. Thousands of transnational citizens utilize this space each day. Trade and tourism flourish here. The border town of San Ysidro has a population of some 20,000 inhabitants, about 90% of whom are of Mexican origin. Downtown Tijuana lies a few hundred yards further south of the line, and houses over 100,000 inhabitants within a radius of one mile of the border.

If there is one single characteristic of the Tijuana–San Ysidro crossing zone today it might be termed a crisis of image. Speaking of this border crossing, one San Diego city council member stated: "Few would disagree that its iron bars, concrete walls and blighted surroundings are an unsightly disgrace to our regional dignity."[21] A member of the Planning Commission in the late 1990s commented, "The border entrance is a very seedy kind of place. There is no elegance to it. When you cross the border into Mexico, you feel like you are going into a second rate place. And it really shouldn't be."[22]

This zone is ripe for an "invented connection," a new ecological space created when global investors or entrepreneurs seek to alter the built environment. Large-scale privately funded development projects at boundary crossings are in various stages of completion along the entire 2,000-mile boundary. These projects envision a number of different types of developments, mostly mixed use, and medium density. A prominent feature is that they are mainly privatized spaces, with partnerships maintained with relevant public border-monitoring agencies.

Figure 4.7 The border's ecology continues to be refined by "invented connections." The creation of a border village at San Ysidro will provide the first direct pedestrian link into downtown Tijuana, enhancing business along Revolution Avenue. FX Club disco, Revolution Avenue, Tijuana. (Photo: L. Herzog.)

On the San Diego–Tijuana border, adjacent to the San Ysidro crossing, a private firm purchased large tracts of land, and with the Redevelopment Authority of the City of San Diego government, put together a new, large-scale project called "Las Americas." Their initial idea was to create a complex of mixed uses, a public plaza, a landmark pedestrian bridged linked to a new pedestrian crossing, a World Trade Center, a market facility, and links to the existing trolley, as well as across the border to Revolution Avenue.[23] The investment plan imagines a new future for Mexico's boundary—an integration of pedestrian walkways, gardens, and plazas with private retail, entertainment, hotel, and office buildings. What is novel about this vision is its recognition of the boundary itself as a space of community life, rather than a space of instability, conflict, and smuggling. Of course, it also signals the discovery of the potential revenues to be gained by private sector interests in allowing the border to become a privatized place.

This "invented connection" would transform the zone at Tijuana–San Ysidro into a destination, where more tourists and local residents would simply come to the border, and not necessarily even cross it. To the north,

San Ysidro, and the surrounding "South Bay" region, would become a surrogate for a "Mexican"/border cultural experience, where consumers would feel comfortable coming to the border, without having to deal with the perceived inconveniences of crossing into Tijuana. If pedestrian bridges and other new infrastructure make it easier to cross back and forth into Tijuana, the invented "border urban village" would benefit the economies of both sides.

Phase One of the Las Americas project—a pedestrian-oriented outdoor shopping mall, was inaugurated in December 2001. The mall is designed as a network of walkable streets. The larger vision is to build a pedestrian bridge from the mall across the border and into downtown Tijuana's lower Revolution Avenue sector. This would establish permanent flows of pedestrians from Mexico crossing lower Revolution to shop in San Diego, and from U.S. tourists and citizens moving from the shopping mall into downtown Tijuana.

Conclusion

The spatial form of global Tijuana is that of an urban region that sprawls across an international boundary. Within this "transfrontier metropolis," a new global landscape is taking shape. It can be disaggregated into seven ecologies, each one a reflection of the many global processes that are redefining the Mexico–United States, and the cities that reside along it.

Global actors—investors, developers, real estate corporations, business interests, local governments—all seek to remake Tijuana, to prepare it for the global economy of the future. Hundreds of millions of dollars are being spent to build cross-border infrastructure (ports, highways, mass transit, border crossings) to better connect Tijuana to the economy north of the border. Global employment centers—factories, shopping malls, tourism projects, housing developments, and commercial enterprises—are further reconfiguring Tijuana, Mexicali, and other border cities (as Lucero explains in Chapter 3).

The result of all this restructuring is the production of a new global cultural landscape. The new social ecology includes innovative building strategies and architectures, and new kinds of gathering zones, public spaces, community niches, and business districts. Perhaps most notable, there is evidence of enormous contradiction in this landscape: a conflicted transition zone at the boundary line, as opposed to the optimism of the transfrontier NAFTA community; chaos at the Tijuana–San Ysidro border gate, juxtaposed against the promise of a new Las Americas cross-border commercial project; a pedestrian scale in the old downtown vs. suburban, car-oriented shopping centers; American-style condo complexes and wealthy suburban enclaves, as against the tar paper shacks and dusty streetscapes of the poor *colonias*. In the end, the global landscape is one of contrast and contradiction—between rich and poor, investment and disinvestment, labor and capital, modernity and postmodernity, planning and spontaneity. What lies ahead? At least two contrasting futures face Tijuana. On one side, the momentum of NAFTA endures—and will be buttressed by the establishment of more democratic elections in Mexico, and more global interest in the economic opportunities native to the Mexico–U.S. cross-border region. On the other hand, global security concerns in the aftermath of 9/11 will continue to shape formal policies of enforcement at the boundary. This seeming contradiction between cross-border economic integration and strict border enforcement is a thorny knot that will continue to tear at the fabric of border urban ecology.

Global equity must also be addressed as a long-term problem for this region. NAFTA participants must learn how to resolve the contradictions manifest by the unequal social landscape of border cities, such as Tijuana. The equity component of the NAFTA must be brought out in the open and addressed. If this can be done, the cultural landscape of border towns such as Tijuana might be saved. If not, the old stereotypes of the border will live on in a new form—"the global badlands."

Notes

1. Charles Lummis, *Land of Poco Tiempo* (New York: Charles Scribner & Sons, 1925).
2. This concept is developed in two of my prior books: Lawrence A. Herzog, *From Aztec to High Tech: Architecture and Landscape Across the Mexico-United States Border* (Baltimore: Johns Hopkins University Press, 1999), and Lawrence A. Herzog, *Where North Meets South: Cities, Space and Politics On the U.S.-Mexico Border* (Austin: University of Texas Press/CMAS, 1990).
3. Reyner Banham, *Los Angeles: The Architecture of Four Ecologies* (London: Penguin, 1971).
4. Jonathan Raban, *Soft City* (New York, E.P. Dutton, 1974).
5. See, for example, discussions of hybridity in Gustavo Leclerc, Raúl Villa, and Michael J. Dear, *Urban Latino Cultures* (Thousand Oaks, CA: Sage, 1999); and also in Michael Dear, *The Postmodern Urban Condition* (Oxford: Blackwell, 2001), 166–75.
6. Leslie Sklair, *Sociology of the Global System* (Baltimore: Johns Hopkins University Press, 1991).
7. See Lawrence Herzog, *From Aztec to High Tech.*
8. Ibid.
9. John Urry, *The Tourist Gaze* (London: Sage, 1990).
10. Proponents of sustainable development point out that "bioregionalism"—the relationship between settlement formation and nature—must be one of the anchors of economic growth. See, for example, Devon Pena, *The Terror of the Machine* (Austin: Center for Mexican American Studies, 1997).
11. J.B. Jackson, "Other Directed Houses," in Ervin Zube (ed.), *Landscapes: The Selected Writings of J.B. Jackson* (Amherst: University of Massachusetts Press, 1970).
12. Arq. Jorge Ozorno, cited in Lawrence Herzog, *From Aztec to High Tech*, 208.
13. Edward Relph, *Place and Placelessness* (London: Pion, 1976), 95.
14. See Lawrence Herzog, *From Aztec to High Tech*, 163–64.
15. This idea is explored in the documentary "Factory of Dreams," produced by Paul Espinosa, KPBS- TV, San Diego, 1999.
16. Mexican property law does not allow foreigners to own land; however post-NAFTA legislation makes it possible for foreigners to lease land through a trust or *fideicomiso* arrangement for up to sixty years.
17. Jorge Ozorno, cited in Lawrence Herzog, *From Aztec to High Tech*, 206.

18. Important European transfrontier urban agglomerations, with populations ranging between 300,000 and one million inhabitants, include Basel–Mulhouse–Freiburg (Swiss–French–German border), Maastricht–Aachen–Liège (Dutch–German–Belgian border), the Geneva metropolitan area (Swiss–French border), and the Strasbourg metropolitan area (French–German border). In North America, one finds transfrontier urban regions housing between 250,000 and four million people along the Canadian–U.S. border at Vancouver–Victoria–Seattle, Detroit–Windsor, and Toronto–Hamilton–Buffalo, and on the Mexico–U.S. border at Tijuana–San Diego, Ciudad Juárez–El Paso, Mexicali–Calexico/El Centro, Nuevo Laredo–Laredo, Reynosa–McAllen, and Matamoros–Brownsville.

19. The notion of "shelter function" is defined in Jean Gottman, *The Significance of Territory* (Charlottesville: University of Virginia Press, 1973).

20. Alan D. Bersin, U.S. Attorney, San Diego, cited in Joseph Nevins, "The Law of the Land: Local-National Dialectic and the Making of the United States-Mexico Boundary in Southern California," *Historical Geography*, 2000, 28, 41–60.

21. Juan Vargas, "A Link, Not a Barrier, at the Border," *San Diego Union Tribune*, Opinion essay. January 10, 1999.

22. Mark Steele, cited in Lawrence Herzog, "A New Tijuana Needs a New Image," Opinion essay, *San Diego Union Tribune*, March 1, 1998, G-4.

23. Land Grant Development, *International Gateway of the Americas*, Project Proposal (San Diego, 1997).

5
Border Art Since 1965

JO-ANNE BERELOWITZ

In the 1980s the art world, ever eager to highlight a new trend, announced that border art was *it*. Critics in New York, Chicago, Los Angeles, and other art world centers adjusted their myopic focus to accommodate distance, periphery, and margin. Suddenly art produced along the United States–Mexico borderspace became hot, and critical discourse abounded with terms such as *cultural hybridity, liminality,* and *bicultural identity.* Particular attention was paid to the San Diego–Tijuana region where an artists' collective, the Border Art Workshop, staged a series of brilliant cultural interventions. But the group disbanded, and the art world's restless gaze, endogenously incapable of sustained focus, flickered and moved elsewhere. Border art entered the penumbra to which yesterday's fashions are assigned.

Yet vital forms of border art are still produced, and were produced before the art world paid attention. Indeed, both prior to and since the 1980s the San Diego–Tijuana border region has been a significant locus for the production of contemporary art—both participating in general trends and contributing to them. However, because of the region's geographic marginality, these engagements have been largely ignored by art historians and critics. It is my intention to address that oversight by connecting the "marginal" art of the border zone with "mainstream" art world concerns and tendencies. While mapping connections and highlighting contributions, I also trace the unfolding saga of approximately thirty-five years of art production on and about this border. Because this art engages the border both as a subject and as a site, it is often referred to as "border art," yet this term has, over this period, undergone very different inflections of meaning. Part of my project is to unpack those inflections and to demonstrate how the referents "border" and "border artist" have shifted from something specific, literal, and local in meaning to something more metaphoric and intangible, something that has more to do with consciousness and the movement of the artist's body through space than with political geography.

Over this thirty-five-year period, three distinct models of production and organization have emerged at the border and each corresponds with a major tendency not only in the art world but in the world at large. Each will be mapped in what follows.

First, in the art world at large, a period of "*identity politics*" extends from the late 1960s through the early 1980s when artists identified with and participated in political struggles by ethnic and gender minorities for parity in the nation's social fabric. Such artists deployed their art to affect political change, to rally members of their group, and to offer them positive self-images. To this end, they sought representational icons to articulate their group's identity. Recognizing that the mainstream stereotyped their group as "different," the icons they developed exaggerated their alterity and thereby entrenched them—transgressively—in difference. In the San Diego–Tijuana border region, this engagement was articulated by Chicano artists working within the Chicano Movement. A key moment was the struggle of Chicanos in San Diego to establish a park in Barrio Logan Heights and a Centro Cultural in Balboa Park. The aesthetic, iconography, and ideology of these facilities drew on cultures from both sides of the border. One of the most prominent participants in this movement was artist Salvador Torres, and this part of the discussion focuses on him.

Second, and developing out of identity politics, was the movement of *multiculturalism*—a particular set of concerns that rose to prominence in the middle 1980s and continued through the 1990s. Multiculturalism has been a much debated and controversial term, but for purposes of this essay I draw on two usages. The first—and most literal—recognizes diversity as a positive value, acknowledging that different cultures enrich and complement the overall culture. The second reads it as an examination of identity formations and acknowledges that identities are not pure but, rather, complexly hybridized—constructed across and from many registers. According to this model the essentialized sense of "difference" that marked the politics of identity is now superseded by a model whereby identity is seen to be fluid, multivalent, syncretic, and appropriative—a hybridized subjectivity constituted multiculturally. Having broken with the concept of an exclusionary collective identity, the multiculturalist artist often foregrounds his or her artistic self as a paradigmatic instance. The example I draw on in the San Diego–Tijuana arena is the Border Art Workshop/*Taller de Arte Fronterizo*

(BAW/TAF), an artist collective founded in 1984 and comprised of members from both sides of the border. Particular attention is paid to the collective's most prominent member, Guillermo Gómez-Peña.

The third model is marked by a culture of *globalization* and dominates the art world from the 1990s to the present. Now cultural production becomes increasingly subject to administration by powerful institutional agencies such as national and international biennials. These agencies fund and mobilize large amounts of capital that they deploy to commission internationally renowned artists from scattered points across the globe to converge upon well-publicized tourist "art destinations," there to exhibit their artwork. According to this model, the artist becomes "an international flâneur,"[1] a nomad, acutely sensitized to the cultural politics of different institutional sites. At the San Diego–Tijuana border this model makes its appearance in a binationally-administered organization known as InSITE, which sponsors a major art event every few years at strategic sites on both sides of the border. From among the many artists commissioned by InSITE, I focus most particularly on three, Francis Alÿs, Kryzstof Wodiczko, and Alfredo Jaar.

Period 1: Identity Politics
Chicano Identity: 1968–1980

Since the signing of the Treaty of Guadalupe Hidalgo, there has been a history in border towns of institutionalized racism and sanctioned violence against Mexican-Americans and Mexican immigrants—and a concomitant history of political activists seeking to establish rights for such citizens and would-be citizens. The most concerted of these activist endeavors was the Chicano Movement, which arose in 1965 to demand civil rights for Mexican-Americans. A form of counterhegemonic politics, the Chicano Movement was based on a praxis of resistance against the mainstream Anglo culture and an affirmation of Mexican and indigenous roots. Inscribing the binary logic of class struggle—labor against capital, proletariat against bourgeoisie, inside against outside—its goals (during the early years) were nationalistic—with "nationalism" serving as an umbrella concept that included the principles of separatist self-determination and the preservation of indigenous culture. With roots not only in Mexico but also in the pre-Hispanic American-Indian past, the movement was marked by a binational transcontinental consciousness that downplayed the political division of the international border. Artists working within the Movement became an important part of the struggle, for it was they who created poetic symbols that articulated a proud heritage with a sense of historical identity. Not coincidentally, the visual iconography these artists developed was also binational,

Figure 5.1 Pylon, Chicano Park, showing figures from different periods in Mexican and Chicano History.

mixing personalities from mythologies and histories that originated south of the border together with portraits of contemporary Mexican-Americans who worked to further *la causa*. Thus there might appear together with Aztec warrior heroes such as Cuauhtémoc and Quetzalcóatl, such contemporary Mexican-American heroes as César Chávez, Reies López Tijerina, and Rubén Salazar. Symbols of motifs other than the human figure also came from both sides of the border, for example, the frequently recurring pyramids of ancient Mexico together with the thunderbird emblem of the United Farm Workers Union. As with the Movement's governing ideology, its visual iconography thus reached across the borders of time and space. On the temporal plane, the approach was that of a nation needing to construct a history by connecting with an ancient autochthonous civilization, thereby establishing a foundational narrative that predated colonialism and anchored them in the land. On the spatial plane, it was the manifestation of a bicultural consciousness derived both from the physical experience of living in the geographic zone of the borderlands and from the psychological experience of living between two cultures in a diasporic third territory to which they gave the name Aztlan—which the Aztecs in their Nahuatl language had identified as their original homeland. To the activists who fought to regain this mythic homeland, they gave the name Chicano.[2]

Figure 5.2   Interstate 5 and Coronado Bridge.

Chicano Park, the Centro Cultural, and Salvador Torres

In San Diego a key episode in the struggle to reclaim territory and to develop a grounding iconography was focused on an area of land now known as Chicano People's Park. The Park's history is one of fierce antagonism between entrenched authority and a marginalized ethnic minority determined to make a space for itself in the local and national landscapes. The area that became the site of contention had long been part of Barrio Logan Heights, the second largest barrio on the West Coast. For many years, and to no avail, the community had petitioned the city to establish a park there. In the early 1960s, the city took action—not to establish a park, but to tear down a vast area of the barrio to make way for the intersection of the Interstate 5 freeway and the on-ramp for the Coronado Bridge. The eight-lane freeway bisected the community and displaced about 5000 residents who had lived there all their lives. By 1969 when the Coronado Bridge was completed, the area had become a desolate tract of massive concrete pillars. During the degradation, community residents petitioned the city for permission to establish a park in the wasteland under the pylons. Their petition was granted, but the city almost immediately went back on its word and began the unannounced clearing of land to construct a substation and parking lot for the Highway Patrol. On April 22, 1970, the community mobilized by occupying the land under the bridge and forming human chains to halt the bulldozers. Their

Figure 5.3 Occupation of Chicano Park.

occupation lasted twelve days during which they began the process of creating the park they had for so long dreamed of. Resolute in their unwillingness to compromise, they took a stand. In the words of one activist, "the only way to take that park away is to wade through our blood."[3] On a telephone pole they raised the Chicano flag, and using garden tools and their own labor, began to work the land, planting nopales and flowers. After extensive negotiations, the city agreed to purchase the site from the state for the establishment of a community park.

A key figure in the envisioning of a park from a wasteland was artist Salvador Torres, who had grown up and lived most of his life within the zone to which the city had laid claim for the construction of the bridge and freeway. As a resident with deep affective ties to Barrio Logan he was appalled by the daily devastation wreaked upon his community, but as an artist he was fascinated by what he saw—the digging of huge pits, the volumetric monuments that arose out of them, and the play of shadow, daylight, and nightlight that danced over and around their sculptural forms. Caught between fascination and despair, he made sketches of everything. As he came to accept the bridge as a reality within the heart of his community, he began to envision its transformation from a scar into a thing of beauty, something that might be used to enhance and draw together the residents of Barrio Logan—and even, perhaps, become a source of pride to the citizens of San Diego.

Figure 5.4   Mural in Chicano Park, Frida Kahlo.

Torres conceived the Chicano Park Monumental Public Mural Program in 1969 and since then he has worked tirelessly to enlist support from city and arts officials not only to extend the project, but also to preserve what has already been created. Today, to the extent that Chicano Park is recognized outside the barrio, it is known for the murals that adorn the pylons.[4] They are extensive, they have been created by many individuals and artist groups, and work on them has been an on-going endeavor since 1973 (when permission was first granted by the San Diego Coronado Bridge Authority). The range of imagery on the murals is vast and very much in accordance with the binational, bicultural consciousness of the Chicano Movement. The list of figures represented, which is too long to be given here in its entirety, includes Quetzalcóatl, Emiliano Zapata, Pancho Villa, Rubén Salazar, Reies López Tijerina, Ché Guevara, César Chávez, David Siquieros, Diego Rivera, José Orozco, Salvador Allende, a pachuco, an ancient Indian dancer, a migrant farmworker family, Coatlicue (Aztec Goddess of the Earth), the Virgin of Guadalupe, Father Hidalgo, Benito Juárez, Frida Kahlo, La Adelita, an undocumented worker, low-riders, Aztec warriors, and community residents occupying Chicano Park. Symbols include Mexican pyramids, the sacred heart, the huelga eagle, an image of Tamoanchan (an Aztec mythical place of origin and, supposedly, an ancient Mexican Eden or paradise), an image of the founding of Tenochtitlán/Mexico City, and pre-Columbian glyphs. Although Torres is credited as being the mastermind that conceived

Figure 5.5   Community Master Plan for Barrio Logan, circa 1971.

Chicano Park, very few of the murals are directly attributable to him. His role in the project has been not so much that of muralist, but, rather, conceptualizer, architect, activist, even gardener and janitor, for he has continued to work the land and to care for it and the murals.

The battle for Chicano Park was a struggle for territory, for representation, for the constitution of an expressive ideological-aesthetic language, for the recreation of a mythic homeland, for a space in which Chicano citizens of this border zone could articulate their experience and their self-understanding. In short, it was a manifestation of what social theorist Raúl Villa has termed "barriological practice"—the "re-creating and re-imagining [of] dominant urban *space* as community-enabling *place*" as a tactic to counteract external oppression of barrio residents.[5] However, the project as it is currently realized represents only a small part of what Torres envisioned. A glimmering of that dream can be gleaned from an examination of the Community "Master Plan" for Barrio Logan. This represents a plan developed by the Barrio Planning Committee (of which Torres was a key member) for extending the barrio to the Bay, by taking over the industrial structures that occupy the waterfront and establishing in their place a complex of Chicano-oriented facilities, centered on Chicano Park and designed according to motifs based on pre-Columbian architectural forms. These include a University of Aztlán, a Cosmic Ball Park, a mercado, a Chicano Free

Hospital, and a Chicano Free Port that would welcome people from Ecuador, Panama, and Argentina—refugees who would share with Mexican immigrants the dream of a better life in the Shangri-la of the United States, but who might have difficulty with ingress through regular U.S. channels. Extensive parkland (including community gardens) would connect these different amenities so that the whole would comprise a utopic space for the community's educational, recreational, shopping, health, and humanitarian needs. In positing a Chicano city beside the Anglo-dominated San Diego, the plan accorded with the Chicano ethos of establishing a distinct and separate identity. The pre-Columbian style of the proposed structures was part of the Movement's tendency toward nostalgic romanticism, a longing for an earlier, supposedly glorious age when a proud sovereign people determined its own destiny. A large version of the plan hangs in a bedroom in Torres's home—a fitting space for an image that embodies a dream.

This unrealized plan (about which he still talks with impassioned longing) indicates that for Torres the achievements of Chicano Park are bittersweet. The community does have its park—much beloved, much used, and a source of community pride. But for Torres and other members of the Planning Committee, the Park was to have been only the beginning of an ambitious project in which the Chicano community would have carved out for itself a Chicano urban space contiguous to and parallel with the city of San Diego. Chicano Park was to have been only the first step toward a reconquest of territory that was once, supposedly, part of the mythical land of Aztlán.

The Chicano Park Mural Project relates to larger art world concerns in two ways. First the iconography of the murals is clearly directed at articulating an identity politics. Second, in terms of the relationship of the murals to their supports and of the supports to the community, the project is site specific—a discursive space grounded in politico-socioeconomic relations. Although some of the murals were made in studios and attached to the abutments, they were designed *for* those abutments. Their meaning is intimately bound up with their site, and they cannot, without losing a fundamental part of that meaning, be transported elsewhere—to a gallery or museum, for example. In its site specificity, the murals in the Park share an ideology of sited art that prevailed in the mainstream art world from the 1960s to the early 1980s. This tendency was marked by (in the words of a noted critic) a "refusal of circulatory mobility."[6] A paradigmatic example of such work is Richard Serra's *Tilted Arc* of 1981 which, Serra argued, was conceived to have meaning only in relation to its siting in Federal Plaza, so much so that Serra chose destruction of the piece rather than its removal to another site when workers in the federal building won a legal battle to have their Plaza restored to its pre-Serra configuration. The following description by James Meyer of sited avant-garde art sums up its ethos:

> The premise of site specificity to locate the work in a single place, *and only there*, bespoke the 1960s call for Presence, the demand for the experience of 'being there.'. . . Presence became an aesthetic and ethical cri de coeur among the generation of artists and critics who emerged in the 1960s, suggesting an experience of actualness and authenticity.[7]

The earliest murals in Chicano Park were painted according to this ethos, for while teams of muralists (many of them residents of Barrio Logan) worked on the project, community residents came to see, witness, and interact. The work thus included an element of performance. Now, Torres laments, much of the work is first prepared in studios and then attached to the pylons. The performance element that demanded the viewer's and artist's simultaneous "presence" has been lost.

There is another sense in which the terms "presence," "actualness," and "authenticity" apply to border art produced during this moment of identity politics. Although neither Torres nor his colleagues would have articulated it at the time, an important component of this art was that it be made by people intimately associated with this border, people for whom the border was a "presence," an "actualness" of daily life and that made them, accordingly, "authentic" border residents. The only reason that these values would not then have been articulated as necessary qualities in the artist is because they would have been assumed—art that imaged a people's identity would, it stood to reason, be made by persons who shared that identity and who understood the experience of marginality and life in the border zone. Later, when Mexico City-born Gómez-Peña moved to this area, made art about the border experience, and was acclaimed by the art world, long-term border residents took issue, and debate ensued as to who has the right to make art about the border. Local artists argued that Gómez-Peña had no organic relationship to the border but had exploited it as a careerist strategy. Thus "authenticity" came, in retrospect, to be an important attribute not only of the work's relationship to the site, but also of the *artist* to the site.

Concurrent with the struggle to claim a park, the community was also engaged in a struggle to establish a cultural center, a Centro Cultural de la Raza. The struggle involved many of the same protagonists, among them Torres. In 1968 he began a search for studio space large enough to accommodate mural-scale works. He fixed on an abandoned facility, the Ford Building in Balboa Park, and late in the year was given permission by the San Diego Parks and Recreation Department to make use of it. Designed in 1935 as a display space for the Ford Motor Company's participation in the California-Pacific International Exposition, it was a large circular building on the outer periphery of Balboa Park where several of the city's cultural facilities are concentrated. Shortly after being granted the space, Torres invited other artists to share it. Access was then expanded to include other forms of the arts such as dancing and music. The arrangement developed into the idea of establishing a cultural center for all the arts within the Chicano community.

Shortly after the community began to use the facility, a group of key members got together to draw up a plan to convert the building into a Centro Cultural de la Raza.[8] The name under which they formally organized was Los Toltecas en Aztlán. The name was devised by Alurista, a poet and founding member of the Chicano Studies Program at San Diego State University. The Toltecas were a pre-Aztec Indian culture, supposedly of master craftsmen, that flourished in Central Mexico, and by adopting their name Alurista and his colleagues were establishing for themselves a venerable lineage that predated colonialism and was, moreover, binational and bicultural. Los Toltecas then petitioned the city for the use of the Ford Building as their Centro Cultural. Although barrio residents had by then used the facility for a couple of years and were now identifying it as their own, the city had plans to develop it into an aerospace museum. Conflict thus arose between the city and the Chicano community. Toward the end of 1970 the city asked the group to vacate the Ford Building and they refused. Viewing the situation as another occupation, they resolved to fight for their cultural facility.[9] They chained the doors and police were sent to evict them. They did not leave the building until the city agreed to designate another site in the park as a Centro. This was an abandoned concrete water tank, about ninety feet in diameter, built in 1914. It was in need of extensive renovation, but, under pressure, the city agreed to shoulder the renovation expenses.

The move to the new building occurred in 1971 and with it was realized the dream of a Centro Cultural de la Raza. Its founding principles were and are to support "the expressions of those people who are indigenous to the border region," to foster "an ongoing dialogue about the native cultures in the border region," and to produce, promote, and present "Chicano, Mexican and Native American arts, crafts, music, dance, literature and folklore." Additionally, it was predicated on the principle that "cultural self-determination [is] the only way to preserve and develop the ideologies and contributions of San Diego's native population."[10] Many of these ideas are articulated in visual form in a large mural on one of the curved interior walls inside the Centro. Designed and coordinated by local artist Guillermo Aranda, it is known as La Dualidad. Begun in 1971 and completed in 1983, the mural's symbolism is derived from Mayan, Toltec, and Aztec iconography, while also referencing the contemporary. It shows Cuauhtémoc, the last Aztec ruler, who was also a resistance fighter. He hangs in agony on a cross. The flames of modern industrial society threaten to engulf him as does a procession of hideous mechanical soldiers. The ancient cultures of Mexico are represented by a pyramid. A young woman is shown running from the military machine, toward the pyramid and other symbols of life and rebirth.[11]

Thus the ancient periods are seen as gloriously heroic, whereas the contemporary, by contrast, is portrayed as monstrous, destructive, pregnant with death, and something from which to flee. In so distinguishing the present from the past and valorizing the latter over the former, the artists participated in a tendency, frequent in Chicano art, to romantic nostalgia. The work's title, La Dualidad, points to a sense of the duality inherent in a binational, bicultural, transborder identity. Indeed, many Centro activities were designed to foster such an identity, for example, cultural exchanges with folkloric theater and dance groups in Mexico, and caravans to Indian reservations to express solidarity and identification with the plight of indigenous peoples. In short, there was a concerted effort to establish connections between Chicano culture and the indigenous precolonial cultures of Mexico and, indeed, of North America generally.

In summary, the efforts to establish a Chicano People's Park and a Centro Cultural brought the San Diego Chicano community into conflict with city authorities. The community had few, or no, advocates, and their struggles for voice, space, and representation were fierce and protracted, and pushed them into defying the law. Torres, for example, recounts that "a lot of the artists went to jail" and that he "went to jail about six times"[12]—arrests that he attributes to petty acts of harassment designed to intimidate and deter artists from militant participation in the Chicano cause—and Torres, like many artists within the Movement, was a member of the Brown Berets, the militant wing of the Chicano Movement. Making art about civil rights and a transborder identity was viewed, by some authorities, as a form of political confrontation that carried punitive consequences for its creators.

Period 2: Multiculturalism
Multicultural hybridity: 1984–1992

BAW/TAF began in June 1984, when a group of artists was brought together by David Avalos who was then artist-in-residence and gallery curator at the Centro Cultural de la Raza in San Diego. Younger by a generation than the Centro's founders, Avalos's roots lay within the Chicano Movment, for he viewed art as a social act involved with communication, community, and power. Invited to curate an exhibition on the theme of the border at the Galería de la Raza in San Francisco, he called on artists who shared his views of art-as-social-engagement. The artists whom he recruited (and who shortly thereafter constituted themselves as the Border Art Workshop) were Victor Ochoa, Michael Schnorr, Isaac Artenstein, Jude Eberhard, Guillermo Gómez-Peña, and Sara-Jo Berman. They were an eclectic, multicultural mix of Mexicans, North Americans, and Chicanos—all with family histories that mapped journeys of migration, displacement, and translation, and all having histories of art activism with a particular focus on the border. Indeed, it was engagement with border issues that constituted the criterion of membership, not identification within a particular ethnic group. Of their various approaches, the most unusual was that of Gómez-Peña—writer, poet, journalist, and performance artist, who had come to the United States from Mexico City in 1978. In 1982, together with Berman, he had founded Poyesis Genética, an experimental, culturally pluralistic performance troupe in which the protagonists underwent cross-cultural adventures and assumed hybrid cultural personas: Wrestler-Shaman, Multimedia Pachuco, Aztec princess/cabaret chanteuse, androgynous Maori warrior/opera singer. His concept of the hybrid (a cross-cultural liminal subject) would become key for the Border Art Workshop.

The two most literature- and theory-oriented members of the group were Gómez-Peña and Emily Hicks (who joined in 1986). Both were writers and, more than any other members of the collective, they were engaged by philosophy and cultural theory, specifically existentialism, semiotics, structuralism, and poststructuralism. In consequence, the "border" was, for them, a more mobile, elastic, and theorizable concept than for most other members, who tended to treat it as a site-specific geopolitical demarcation that was, secondarily, inflected with symbolic and psychological resonances. That Gómez-Peña and Hicks were more prolific as writers than makers of visual objects should also be considered in assessing their utilization of the term "border," for writing is a mobile medium, generated and disseminated by mobility. In the work of these two members, the border both belonged to and became disengaged from its signification as a geopolitical marker, and took on the ambiguity and indifference of a link in the chain of a mobile signifying system. Gómez-Peña's different orientation to the border led, at a later point in the group's history, to misunderstanding and rupture between him and some BAW/TAF members.

In 1988, the collective published a General Statement that serves, effectively, as a manifesto of their key concerns:

> BAW/TAF, the Border Art Workshop/ *Taller de Arte Fronterizo*, is a group of Mexican, American, and Chicano artists working . . . to discover and define the myriad levels of a border consciousness. Using the past history and present realities of the San Diego/Tijuana border region BAW/TAF members incorporate image, text, media analysis and performance to reveal the negative aspects of ethnocentricism and the new growing dynamics of borderland cultural multiplicity. BAW/TAF does not recognize cultural borders but is extremely concerned with the border between present and future. If the United States-Mexican border is to become a region of human cooperation and cultural consciousness then Mexicans and North Americans must establish a process of social dialogue to deal with the many problems now confronting them.[13]

This statement makes clear that BAW/TAF's agenda was both to examine the "realities of the San Diego/Tijuana border region" and, secondarily, "to discover and define" the more symbolic "myriad levels of a border conscious-ness"—thus inflecting site specificity with something that, because it ad-dressed "consciousness," opened up to mobility. As their Statement indicates, the San Diego–Tijuana border region would be their focus, they would make art that addressed its complex geospatial-cultural issues, and they would represent the border as a set of intricate relations between and among people.

Membership and participation were somewhat elastic, and the roster of members changed a great deal over BAW/TAF's history. Occasionally non-member artists were invited to collaborate on projects and, when they had proved their worth, they would be admitted to membership. Thus, in the fol-lowing three years, the founding members were joined by (among others) Marco Vinicio González, Emily Hicks, Robert Sanchez, Berta Jottar, Rocio Weiss, and Richard Lou. The swelling of the ranks by new members was bal-anced by the departure of others. However, by the end of 1990, all but one of the members listed here had resigned and most felt that BAW/TAF, having achieved some significant goals, had run its course and should be disbanded.

The base of BAW/TAF's operations, its institutional support umbrella, was the Centro Cultural de la Raza, which already had a prior history with most of the members, having sponsored individuals either as artists-in-residence, exhibitors, or staff. But members were careful to attribute to the Centro much more than mere sponsorship, for its aesthetic and ideological agendas were themselves productive factors in BAW/TAF's generation: mul-tidisciplinarity combined with a commitment to community, border issues, and civil rights. The Centro also made available to BAW/TAF the insti-tutional network and frame of the Chicano Movement. As one former member acknowledged: "Without the Centro, BAW/TAF would never have happened."[14]

Although the Border Art Workshop was, in many ways, "a natural out-growth"[15] of the philosophical goals of the Centro, it carried some of these ideas much further than any artists previously associated with the Centro. At a certain point, a difference in degree becomes a difference in kind. Let us take, as an example, the claim of "natural outgrowth" and consider the ques-tion of identity. When the Centro was established in 1970 its founders were keenly aware of the binational, bicultural, indigenist roots of the Chicano community, and many Centro activities were designed to foster and pro-mote these connections. BAW/TAF also sought to establish connections with Mexico and with Native American Indians, but these were of a very dif-ferent kind from those pursued by the Centro. For example, via Guillermo Gómez-Peña the collective had strong connections to Mexico City-based conceptual artists. Additionally, BAW/TAF members Marco Vinicio Gon-zález and Gómez-Peña were actively engaged in recruiting Mexican scholars and artists for Tijuana's experimental Casa de Cultura, and were intensely involved with cultural groups on both sides of the border. Further, the bilingual/experimental magazine, *The Broken Line/La Línea Quebrada*, published by BAW/TAF members,[16] included contributions (both text and artwork) from both sides of the border. Based on two Mexico City interdisciplinary experimental magazines, *El Corno Emplumado* and *La Regla Rota*, *The Broken Line* was a thread connecting cultural thinkers in Mexico City and San Diego. In terms of Native American contacts, Gómez-Peña collaborated with Luiseño tribal member James Luna in a conceptual performance piece.

The fundamental difference distinguishing the transborder activities of the Centro from those of BAW/TAF is that the former's contacts with Mexico and with Native Americans were ways of pursuing the past, reaching back to connect with a precolonial history when brown-skinned people were sovereign in their own land—hence the appropriation of pre-Columbian iconography. By contrast, the Border Art Workshop directed its energies to the present—to collaborations with conceptual artists engaged with contemporary art practices and issues. Additionally, they were also overtly focused on the future. For example, the General Statement not only specifically mentions the significance of "present realities" for the Workshop but also its "extreme concern . . . with the border between present and future." This is a distinctly different orientation from the Centro's (and the Chicano Movement's) tendency toward a nostalgic revisiting of the past.

The notion of the future comes up again and again in statements by BAW/TAF members, in their writings, and in the writings of their associates. Thus, for example, in a collectively produced five-year retrospective catalogue, there is an essay by Jeff Kelley that spells out BAW/TAF's philosophy, including its orientation toward the future. In it, Kelly mentions that BAW/TAF members view the border as a "paradigmatic place, a social microcosm of the *future* United Americas" and he goes on to claim that "BAW/TAF's members are *de-facto futurists*." He concludes the essay with the statement that BAW/TAF's "art is preparing the ground beneath the *future* America" (all emphases added). In the same catalogue, we are asked "to imagine a [future] world in which this international boundary has been erased," to become "part of the birth of a new way of seeing our world"; told that "our great challenge is to invent new languages capable of articulating our incredible circumstances [in the borderlands]"; and invited to "toast to a borderless future." Although such future-driven utopian sentiments are undoubtedly romantic, their romanticism is different from the nostalgia that characterized the Chicano Movement. Ultimately what saved BAW/ TAF's version of romanticism from free-floating idealism was its grounding *in place*—its imbrication in the specific contemporary dynamics of the San Diego–Tijuana border.

There are further differences. For example, artists within the Chicano Movement sought to establish their identity by selecting icons that foregrounded their alterity and thereby positioned them transgressively in difference. BAW/TAF members were also concerned with issues of identity, selfhood, otherness, separation, and connection, but they approached them from a different perspective. Instead of attempting to establish an *essential* "otherness," they operated on the premise that cultures and ethnicities exist in a dynamic dialectic, that subject positions—and identities—are always in a state of process, and that, accordingly, there is no fixed essence but, rather, a condition of multicultural hybridity. With most of its members younger by at least half a generation than the protagonists of 1960s and 1970s Chicanismo, many of the group had been schooled in the wake of Conceptualism's ascendance in the art world, and were thus familiar with theories of poststructuralism, which hold that social meaning—and subjectivity—is never fixed but is produced contingently from a multiplicity of representations. The issue of identity was thus never as cut and dried for BAW/TAF members as it had been for those within the nationalistically driven Chicano Movement. As with "identity," so too with the concept of "nationality," for BAW/TAF's agenda was to complicate monolithic, unitary notions of nation and statehood. For example, in place of the more traditional approach that maintained Anglo, Chicano, and Tijuanense as distinct and separate categories, they proposed, rather, a polymorphous, polyglot, hybrid, and binational *border subject*—a new type of subject, postmodern and postnational, a result of the confluence of the many different realities peculiar to this porous border zone. Where the Chicano Movement concentrated on Chicano and Mexican-American rights, BAW/TAF was interested, more generally, in *human* rights.

The term "border" operated as a key trope for the collective, because the word signified for them a material geographic reality, a set of relations between and among people, and a powerful visual symbol. It was, therefore, crucial in articulating a visually based radical critical discourse of a spatialized cultural politics. Their General Statement bears this out, for it claims the goal of "defin[ing] the myriad levels of a border consciousness . . . and the growing dynamics of borderland cultural multiplicity," and goes on to assert that "BAW/TAF does not recognize cultural borders but is extremely concerned with the *border between present and future*" [emphases added]. This last phrase is important, for it indicates that for BAW/TAF the border was not only a spatial and psychological, but also a temporal marker, one that opened a path to a better future. Whereas the Chicano Movement looked back to a time that predated the establishment of international borders, BAW/TAF looked forward to a *post*border world in which international barriers would be dissolved.

Thus BAW/TAF both evolved out of and went beyond the ideas of the Chicano Movement. Its divergences were such a natural outgrowth from those undergirding the Centro Cultural that there was no friction, or at least none that members (at my questioning) recalled. Moreover, by 1984 when BAW/TAF began, there was a younger generation of administrators at the helm of the Centro and they were open to and participated in BAW/TAF's contemporary engagement with a broader community beyond the Centro's constituency. They were also open to conceptual art, which is markedly different from the social realism (offshoot of the Mexican mural movement) that typified most Chicano art of the late 1960s and 1970s.

BAW/TAF's revolutionary dream of a borderless world of multi- and intercultural exchange, mutual respect, and peaceful cooperation was imbued with belief in the transformative power of art. To establish this vision, they would make art that challenged official notions of territoriality and illustrated that geography is not an innocent spatial vessel for social life but, rather, is inscribed with politics and ideology. According to their model, the artist is a social interventionist, a binational diplomat, a broker between communities and cultures, and a border crosser; at best, the artist is a visionary capable of transforming a space of restriction into one of radical openness, at least, a myth-maker capable of changing the stories told of contested spaces.[17] In short, they were visionaries who viewed the border as a highly complex zone in which tragedy might serve as a negative model from which to work for a better future.

As conceptual artists, their principal focus was to reframe the concept of the border. To attain this end they knew they would need to change the language in which the border was represented, for they realized that the media did not simply reflect the "reality" of the border but actively produced and reproduced its meaning(s) as a key strategy in creating and maintaining a particular power dynamic. As one member stated:

> We understood that language is power. We needed to understand how the media portrayed information about the border, how they edited it, how they put it out there. Could we effectively deal with them so as to subvert their reality effects?[18]

Accordingly, media analysis constituted a significant part of their agenda, and BAW/TAF meetings were heated forums for the discussion of articles on the border that had appeared in various publications. Indeed, for the group's first five years the thrust of their activity was as much debate, dialogue, and analysis as the implementation of art projects.

One of their concerns was to change the terminology in which the media referred to immigrant-laborers without papers. Prior to their interventions the media had referred to this group of people as "illegal aliens," thereby producing a category of human being coterminous with subjection, domination, and exploitation and defined by a quintessential "otherness." Subsequent to BAW/TAF's efforts, the terms "undocumented worker" and "undocumented immigrant," with their vastly different associations, became widespread. In the words of a former BAW/TAF member:

> The term "undocumented worker" really grew out of BAW/TAF. I'm not necessarily arguing that we coined the term, but we did emphasize and insist on its usage in all our interviews with the press, in articles that appeared on us, and in our own writings. As small as it might seem, it brought about a big perceptual change amongst readers.[19]

Additionally, they focused on the kinds of identities that the border posits, for example, the binary couplings of "legal tourist/illegal alien" or "anglo/cholo" in which the first term is always valorized and the second is vested with associations of criminality. The group worked to destabilize and denaturalize these terms by revealing how they produce and reproduce systematic patterns of inequality. One strategy of countervention was to propose a new concept that avoided the binaristic relation between hegemon and subaltern, and, instead, constituted a third term—"border citizen"—that also spatialized sociality, inflecting it with geohistorical resonance instead of the rigidities of hierarchical ordering. Another was to focus on the on-going human rights violations perpetrated against migrant Mexican workers by the Border Patrol, the San Diego Police, and right wing vigilantes. Yet a third was to deconstruct and challenge media representations of border issues on the premise that such representations foster divisiveness and promote a psychological climate that permits the contravention of human rights.

Fully cognizant of the power of the media as a prime disseminator of "reality," they realized that they needed to engage the media in order to change it. To achieve this goal BAW/TAF members knew they had to break down the traditional barrier that news writers and art critics interpose between themselves and their subjects, a barrier whose purpose is to maintain "objective distance." By training and experience, they were well equipped to produce a discourse that would run counter to that of the mainstream media. Gómez-Peña, for example, had worked as a journalist in Mexico City, and David Avalos had studied communications at UCSD with renowned media specialist Herb Schiller. Both were brilliant strategists and knew how to create events that the media would find irresistible. They were fortunate, too, in the serendipitous hiring in 1986 at the daily *San Diego Tribune* of a progressively minded editorial page editor, Joe Holley. Formerly of the *San Antonio Light*, Holley was brought to San Diego to open up a more liberal point of view for San Diego readers. A maverick at the paper, Holley's own agenda—to shift border coverage from the alienating "otherness" of horror-fraught sensationalism to more nuanced accounts of everyday life—was fundamentally sympathetic to that of BAW/TAF. The collective fascinated him. He spent time with Avalos and Gómez-Peña, learning about their ideas and the language they proposed to redefine the border, championing their cause with his more conservative editors, and even writing an editorial proposing that images and preconceived notions of the border were ripe for change and that "it is the artist among us who dares shift the kaleidoscope . . . forcing us to see our world in a different light."[20] His editorial went on to refer to the Border Art Workshop and quoted extensively from members Gómez-Peña, Avalos, and Schnorr, thereby disseminating BAW/TAF's ideas to hundreds of thousands of readers. Holley's presentation of the border as a place of generation and fluid exchange was unprecedented in a mainstream (conservative) newspaper. His thinking came directly out of the Border Art Workshop, and its inscription into the editorial page of the *Tribune* was a huge victory for the collective.[21]

Other journalists also became sympathetic and, in covering the collective's events, often quoted BAW/TAF members verbatim, with little editorial intervention, for BAW/TAF's articulate, provocative comments were news. Additionally, BAW/TAF members wrote letters to the editors of the *Tribune* and the *San Diego Union*, and the newspapers published them. Occasionally, as with Holley's piece, reports of their actions moved out of the Arts and Letters section to the editorial pages or to areas of hard news—largely because of friendships cultivated with sympathetic journalists or because of the collective's skill in making news. Essentially BAW/TAF was a conceptual project that involved not only the production of installations and performances, but the engagement and collaboration of the media to project their ideas beyond the confines of the art world to a broad and disparate public.

With backgrounds that included journalism, video, and film, BAW/TAF's work developed a strong textual component featuring publications, critique, poetry, faxes, and other multimedia. Their cultural forebears in these modalities were European and international. One example is the internationalist movement Fluxus.[22] BAW/TAF members understood their work to be within the Fluxus spirit, and described at least one of their projects as "a continuation of a Fluxus project within a trans-border context."[23] The Fluxus artist who most inspired them was Joseph Beuys, who combined art-making with writing, education, documentation, and the dissemination of information. Other influences included popular culture such as Mexican street art, comics, and the masked personas of Mexican wrestling. Thus the Border Art Workshop traversed the border not only in terms of ideals and composition of members, but also in terms of artistic sources and strategies, crossing the boundaries of nations, hemispheres, cultures, and media as well as the hierarchical divisions between high and low art.

BAW/TAF as an "Art of Place"

For BAW/TAF members the "border" was a complex term, one that signified a site-specific, dynamic, geopolitical demarcation inflected with symbolic and psychological resonances. Significantly, for almost all members, it was grounded in the specifics of the San Diego–Tijuana border region. Indeed, BAW/TAF's place specificity was unusual enough in contemporary art practice that critics often commented and tended to focus on it at the expense of eliding the collective's more metaphoric invocations. Thus local art critic Robert Pincus described BAW/TAF as evoking "the spirit of place"[24] and Jeff Kelley, in his BAW/TAF catalogue essay, focused on place as a key concern in the Workshop's practice. His essay, "Crossed Places," describes their work as "a place-particular theater of political spectacle," and points out that the place they represented in their work was also their home, for they are "artists who make art about, in, and of the place where they live."

Although BAW/TAF's artwork resonated powerfully with "a spirit of place," the work was not always site specific. Indeed, as the collective gained recognition in the art world and was invited to present work in locations far from the United States–Mexico border, many members experienced unease at the work's dislocation from the border and its attendant reframing in the aestheticizing environment of an art-institutional context, that is, its unmooring from the border. Here let me reference a useful distinction, made by James Meyer, between "two notions of site: a *literal* site and a *functional* site."[25] Meyer describes the literal site as being "in situ; it is an actual location, a singular place," and the site-oriented work as being dependent upon and inseparable from it. In contrast, the functional site has a far more tenuous relation to a singular physical place. Rather, "it is a process, an operation occurring between sites, a mapping of institutional and textual filiations and the bodies that move between them. . . . It . . . refuses the intransigence of literal site specificity"[26] becoming, rather, "a site within [the] network of sites"[27] that makes up the art world. Work by BAW/TAF artists falls into both these categories, with a gradual shift from the former to the latter. As the collective acquired notoriety in the art world and received invitations to showcase work at venues far from the literal site of its grounding, sites tended to become more functional than literal. Over time some members grew concerned at the dislocation of work from site and resigned.[28] Others, however, seized the opportunity to carry the ideas of BAW/TAF beyond its local base and were comfortable operating within the frame of the functional site. BAW/TAF thus stands at a threshold between a literal and a functional concept of "the border." Yet even when the work was made for a functional site, it carried a sense of being deeply rooted in the experience of the border, keenly attuned to its complex dynamics. It was this that set it apart from the later engagement of InSITE, in which "the border" became an "art site" that

Figure 5.6 Richard Lou, *Border Door.*

attracted artists who often lived far from any border and came from major metropolitan centers. To illustrate the rootedness of BAW/TAF's art, I present the following examples by Richard Lou and Robert Sanchez. The first example occurred at a literal site and the second at both literal and functional sites.

Richard Lou's Border Door

Lou created *The Border Door* in 1988 in response to an invitation by the Border Art Workshop to contribute to their annual art show at the Centro. He made it for a specific site—the border line one-quarter mile east of Tijuana's Rodríguez International Airport, seven feet from the main highway. Lou chose the site carefully, wanting it to be public enough that people would see what he was doing, but not so public as to provide a spectacle, and not so public that police might intercept and prevent him from completing his action. And so he chose a site that "was just public in terms of people driving by, passing by."[29] Although made in response to a BAW/TAF invitation, no member of the Workshop ever saw the piece *in situ*—although they did see photographs—for it was destroyed (presumably by the Border Patrol) within two days. It has nevertheless become an icon in the Workshop's history and is given a two-page spread in the BAW/TAF catalogue. Lou describes it thus:

> It was a freestanding door and it worked. . . . And there were 134 detachable keys
> on the south side. They're on nails on the door. It was an installation but it was
> also a performance piece, because in addition to installing it, the other aspect of
> the performance was going to the neighborhood where I grew up, the Colonia
> Roma, starting at the house where I grew up, walking to the other neighborhood
> where my wife grew up, where I handed out between 200 and 300 keys and in-
> vited people to use my border door, to open it with a key and cross the border
> with dignity. The keys on the door were for the people I couldn't encounter. . . .
> It really was a way to counter the image of the undocumented migrant running
> through the night, cutting through wire, being illegal. If you have the key to a
> door and you enter through it, then you're legal, you're walking into a place to
> which you have a right.[30]

The only invited "audience" were potential border-crossers—invited as
"users" rather than spectators. By effectively foreclosing the possibility of art
world spectacle, Lou safeguarded the privacy of the experience. Although
The Border Door is a powerful universal symbol for an alternative to shame-
ful crossing, it was deeply grounded in the life he had lived at the border
and, therefore, belonged there, at the literal site of the border where the
fence had already been trampled down by the passage of undocumented migrants. It was, as he explained to me "very much infused with the conflicts
that I had as a teen and as a young man embroiling myself emotionally, politically, and ideologically with this particular border. It was a pilgrimage."
"Pilgrimage" is an interesting word choice, suggesting that for Lou the site
carried a certain sacramental significance.

The intensely private and personal quality of *The Border Door* and its literal siting contrast with a later experience Lou had within the Workshop. In
1989 the Border Art Workshop was invited to participate in the prestigious
Venice Biennial—a functional site in Italy. Their installation was hugely successful and invitations poured in for other exhibition opportunities. At that
point Lou pulled back, uncomfortable with the idea of "traveling" and "exhibiting" the border. As he put it:

> For me it was always about the local community. I was emotionally and spiritu-
> ally invested in this community because I grew up here. I related it to my own ex-
> periences and those of my family. There was a danger in commodifying our
> work, of exploiting the iconography, for how does it serve our community to
> have a show in Italy other than to promote the careers of the artists? If you con-
> sider yourself a person of conscience there's a line that you have to draw.[31]

Although the functional site offered enormous career opportunities, Lou
turned away from it, preferring to return his art to the community and site
that had formed him. For him, the literal site was the mark of authenticity
and of the artist's contribution and commitment to the community from
whence he'd come.

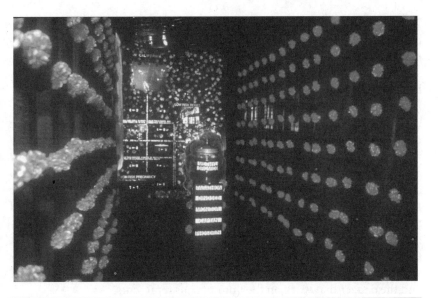

Figure 5.7 Robert Sanchez, *Encinitas Gardens.*

Robert Sanchez's Encinitas Gardens

Sanchez created *Encinitas Gardens* as part of a BAW/TAF exhibition at Artists Space in New York in January 1989. Located far from the United States/Mexico border, Artists Space was a functional site. Nonetheless, Sanchez's installation carried a deep sense of being rooted at the border. Although his installation bore its own title, the overarching rubric of the show was *Vidas Perdidas/Lost Lives.* Its theme was the cost—in lives—of current immigration policy toward those who make the hazardous journey to the United States, and then attempt to live and work illegally when their precarious status leaves them vulnerable to exploitation. For this, BAW/TAF artists focused on the consumerist economy and its need for cheap labor—factors that lure workers northward across the border. They wanted to pinpoint the irony of a situation in which there is both pervasive antiimmigrant hysteria and, at the same time, a heavy dependence on cheap, exploitable migrant labor. As part of their ongoing investigation of border issues, BAW/TAF members had begun doing projects in the community, making contact with border crossers, and having discussions and dialogues with them. The intention was that rather than researching and writing about the experiences of migrants, and making interventions on their behalf with the media, they would engage with workers directly so that their voices would be embedded in the art, thereby representing them in a more intimate way. The enterprise involved seeking out and talking with workers, explaining what the art was about, and asking workers whether they might be interested in having their ideas or experiences reproduced in visual form. For this piece, Sanchez had sought out undocumented laborers living in the canyons of San Diego's North County. His installation directly addressed and drew on their experiences of lives—and lives lost—in California's agricultural industry.

Encinitas Gardens is the name of a flower farm adjacent to the upscale coastal suburb of Encinitas, twenty miles north of San Diego. Its laborers are undocumented. Though the flowers bring delight to their purchasers, they are agents of death to those who tend them, for the fields where they grow are treated with heavy doses of lethal pesticides. Sanchez's installation set up a tension between visual beauty—red paper flowers (made by Tijuana paper flower artist Julian "Chiquilin" Ortega) against a black background—and the ugly reality that subtends the flower industry, for interspersed throughout the installation were large black bins of pesticides such as Azodrin, Chlorinil, and Sulfan, and pasted on the floor were newspaper clippings with data about their toxicity. A poster by Sanchez highlighted both the lure and the danger that work on the flower farms represents.

His installation was linked with that of BAW/TAF member Berta Jottar. Together, they had interviewed (the mainly female) workers in the flower fields, and the installation contained texts from those interviews—stories of miscarriages, high-risk pregnancies, birth defects, and other medical problems arising from exposure to chemicals used in cultivating sturdy flowers. In addressing the toxic poisoning of migrant laborers, the installation also pointed to a structural contradiction with which Mexican immigrants have to deal: the mainstream conception that Mexicans are carriers of contamination. To the contrary, it is conditions of labor in the United States that contaminate Mexican laborers.

As with almost all BAW/TAF's work, Sanchez's installation was grounded in place. Although initially exhibited in New York, far from the place it represented, it resonated with a sense of place. Significantly, Sanchez titled the work with a place name identifiable on a map—Encinitas—approximately fifty miles north of the border. His installation thus pointed away from Artist's Space to the place it denoted. After exhibiting the work in New York, he brought it home and showed it at the Centro—a site that although not physically at the border was inscribed with a deep consciousness of it, was known as the closest of all Centros to the United States–Mexico border, and was the Workshop's patron institution. Thus, although the work's first site at Artist's Space was functional, its second at the Centro returned it to the local community and its base of operations. Further, while showing at Artist's Space, the group collectively acknowledged the Centro as their foundation—thereby emphasizing that the work originated at and "belonged" to a place other than the functional exhibitionary site that was their temporary venue at Artist's Space. The work's appearance at this functional site, they seemed to say, was not part of their customary operations.

Like Lou, Sanchez was keenly aware of the inherent pitfalls in "aestheticizing a very dire social-political situation."[32] In an interview he explained why he felt that the collective had been successful in avoiding that danger:

> I think that living the reality of the border made the work strong—stronger than that of artists who were invited in from elsewhere to comment on the border. There was a certain rawness and freewheeling quality in our installations that had a very different feeling from installation art up to that point. We sincerely tried to avoid aestheticizing the issues and tried to be as real with the information as possible. Many of our shows were titled "Border Realities"—an interesting, potent title because it succinctly mapped out that this work was going to address 'reality.'[33]

Sensitive critics, attuned to the works' deliberate avoidance of aestheticizing finish, described it as marked by "ugliness, incompletion, disharmony, mixed modes and registers" and as "raw in execution."[34] Although such comments are usually negative, here they were positive, making the point that rawness in execution "empower[s] the viewer to analyze reality."[35] They praised the work for partaking of the grittiness of the realities it represented.

Gómez-Peña's "Mobilization" of the Border

Regardless of whether their installation sites were literal or functional, Lou's and Sanchez's work was marked by a specific sense of place and of attachment to that place. In this, their work was typical of members of the Border Art Workshop with one notable exception: Guillermo Gómez-Peña. For this artist, "the border" was not only a specific social-geography but also a deterritorialized form of subjectivity. This orientation marked Gómez-Peña's work from at least as early as 1981, when he co-founded Poyesis Genética as an experiment in dissolving borders between cultures, in exploring hybrid characters and liminal emotional states. From this early point in his career and continuing through and beyond his involvement with BAW/TAF, he has focused on the artist's ability to embody and project liminality, and to function as a kind of intercultural performative trope—an ambassador, a vanguard in the dismantling of monoculturalism, an embodiment of border subjectivity. His personal experience has always informed his work, and his interest in the theme of deterritorialized subjectivity grew out of the frequent crossings he made (starting in 1978) between Mexico and the United States, and the cultural relativism that biculturalism affects. It was deepened by his discovery, in 1979, of Chicano culture, which, by definition, is hybridic, both evoking and invoking border consciousness. Indeed, so much did the term Chicano seem to him to embody the hybridity of border consciousness that he assumed it as his own identity. With his appropriation, the term became unhinged—referring not so much to a specific history of struggle and oppression but, rather, becoming a metaphor or allegory for a condition of being in the world. During his association with BAW/TAF, he came to see the San Diego–Tijuana border as a paradigmatic instance of border culture from which he might extrapolate to speak of borders elsewhere and of borders that are not physical. Thus for Gómez-Peña (unlike his BAW/TAF colleagues who inflected the term "border" to carry secondary metaphoric resonances), the term was multiply resonant—both site specific and mobile, both moored and unmoored, both regional and internationalist.

As he increasingly traveled beyond the San Diego–Tijuana border region, taking the thematic of the border to audiences distant from it, so his direct connection with this specific border lessened, and his concept of the "border" became more markedly mobile, refusing "the intransigence of literal site-specificity."[36] More than any other artist, he shifted the meaning of "the border" from a geographic zone to a mode of consciousness, from something literal to something functional, from a meaning that was denotative with specific determinations to one that was connotative and overdetermined. It must, then, have seemed ironic to many when Gómez-Peña denounced mainstream art institutions as they began showcasing border art, arguing that such cooptation spelled "the death of border art." The key moment here was a 1991 article titled "Death on the Border: A Eulogy to Border Art,"[37] in which he set out his position. First, he gave a brief history of BAW/TAF, its struggles and successes. He noted that as the group gained notoriety, so border art suddenly "became grantable, presentable, fashionable," and BAW/TAF's utopian ideals were "processed, altered and presented as a new exotic fad." Then:

> In 1989 everyone went border. Our difficult experiment in collaboration between Anglos and Latinos was turned into an open invitation for major institutions and opportunistic artists with no track record whatsoever to jump on the Aztec-high-tech express. Border art left the trenches to become a specialized exercise in grant writing and institutional self-promotion. . . . Major institutions, whose previous histories and interests were almost exclusively Eurocentric, suddenly organized conferences, festivals, and blockbuster exhibits about border this and border that, without consulting or including the creators of the movement.

The target of his distress was the San Diego Museum of Contemporary Art, which in 1989 had written a proposal to the National Endowment for the Arts (NEA) to undertake an ambitious three-year binational project based in San Diego and Tijuana titled "*Dos Cuidades*/Two Cities." The project would be multifaceted, incorporating lectures, a film series, artist exchanges, and—most significantly—a major exhibition of artists from the border region to be titled *La Frontera/The Border*. Gómez-Peña and many members of the Border Art Workshop were angered not only because they—as pioneers in this territory—had not been consulted about the project, but because much of the language in the NEA proposal appeared to have been lifted without attribution from writing by Gómez-Peña and other BAW/TAF members. Gómez-Peña accused the Museum of having "gone border," of having appropriated an art phenomenon that was born of struggle but had become transmogrified by media attention into something trendy. He ended the article with the following:

> A movement that began as an attempt to dismantle Anglo-Saxon patriarchal authority ends up being appropriated, controlled, promoted and presented by Anglo-Saxon patriarchs. . . . The border as metaphor has become hollow. Border aesthetics have been gentrified and border culture as a utopian model for dialogue is temporarily bankrupt.

The article triggered intense response in San Diego. Hugh Davies, Director of the San Diego Museum of Contemporary Art, wrote an angry rebuttal arguing that the Museum "had long been interested in border art and that [a]rt about the border is not the exclusive property of one group or another, nor, more importantly, a single person's property to claim dead or alive."[38] It also upset many local artists who were committed to remaining in the region and to making art that continued the ideals of BAW/TAF regardless of whether they were affiliated with it.

The article marked a kind of watershed for Gómez-Peña and for the Border Art Workshop. Factions formed with former members either for or against the author of "Death on the Border." Indeed, some claimed that Gómez-Peña (not Hugh Davies) was the interloper, for he was not really *of* this region and had used "border art" to make himself famous, in his words "grantable, presentable, a new exotic fad." The article and the ensuing debate raised critical questions about representation and the Who has the "right" to the border as a subject? Is it the property of marginalized peoples in close proximity to contested national boundaries? Must practitioners of border art have suffered the indignities that are so often perpetrated on immigrants and would-be immigrants by border police and vigilantes of porous borders? Can immigrants of any class or color lay claim to it? How long must one have been an immigrant to have a claim? Do its practitioners need to have dislocated themselves by the traversing of national boundaries, and must these crossings have been made under conditions of hardship? Is everyone (as a subject in a postmodern world of displacements and disjunctions) an inhabitant of a marginal zone of liminality—and thereby eligible to claim this topic? Is the border a subject that anyone might engage with—third- or fourth-generation citizens of the nation-state as well as immigrants recently arrived? What is the claim of a white Anglo-Saxon Protestant such as Hugh Davies, who occupies a prestigious position at the helm of a mainstream cultural institution such as the Museum of Contemporary Art at the heart of an exclusive and conservative community such as La Jolla?

The Border Art Workshop reformed with a cadre of new members and issued a document denouncing Gómez-Peña. They—and he—continued to make art about the border. Border art was not dead, but it had changed, and Gómez-Peña, who had unhinged it from an earlier requirement of being grounded in a life lived at the border, was a key agent in that change.

The San Diego Museum of Contemporary Art and La Frontera

In 1993 the Museum of Contemporary Art hosted its exhibition on the theme of the border. Although it brought in artists from elsewhere, they came, for the most part, from towns along the United States–Mexico border. Thus the exhibition harkened back to a pre-Gómez-Peña concept of the border, taking it as a geographic reality, a literal site rather than a metaphor for a condition of deracinated postmodernity. Although the show was useful in offering viewers an overview of art produced along the length of the border, the work (with few exceptions) lacked the raw power of BAW/TAF's installations, giving the overall impression of a series of discrete aesthetic objects organized around an interesting theme. What most distinguished the show occurred not so much in the exhibitionary spaces as at an administrative level—the fact of its being a collaboration between a well-funded mainstream institution, the Museum of Contemporary Art, and an underfunded ethnically marginalized one, the Centro. Presented by the Museum and received by the art press as a unique model of cross-cultural process, it was a harbinger of a much more ambitious cross-cultural project that followed shortly thereafter: InSITE.

Period 3: Globalization
Mundo Sin Fronteras: 1992–Present

Established in 1992, InSITE has been an experiment in staging art at scattered sites on both sides of the San Diego-Tijuana border. Held initially at two, then at three-year intervals (1992, 1994, 1997, 2000/2001), the one constant in its developmental unfolding has been its transborder and bicultural orientation. In almost every other regard, InSITE has changed significantly each time it has been staged. Initially administered solely on the U.S. side of the border, governance has been marked by a growing collaboration—and now parity—with Mexican institutions, internationalization of the curatorial team, expansion of the concept of "art work" into the larger cultural field, and a willingness to risk losing established audiences by commissioning and positioning art in sites and for audiences usually quite remote from the art world. Manifesting many of the characteristics of international biennials (the commissioning of internationally renowned artists, an international curatorial team, advertisements in national and international journals di-

rected toward a global art audience), InSITE is conceived on a scale far more
ambitious than any of the region's earlier instantiations of border art.

A qualification and a caveat are immediately in order: InSITE's directors
have been careful to aver that InSITE is *not* a project *about* the border and
that the art it sponsors is not "border art"—a claim that initially discon-
certed me, for although there is no directive to InSITE's artists to make art
that addresses the border, most of them do. Certainly the most interesting
projects do. Moreover, InSITE's directors have carefully cultivated an extensive infrastructure of transborder connections that makes possible the staging of work at sensitive areas along the border—a site inherently intriguing
to participating artists. Nonetheless InSITE's directors avoid presenting In-
SITE as a project *about* the border, promoting it rather as being *about* other
issues, such as binational collaboration, the investigation of public space,[39]
or "the daily trafficking in goods and people."[40] On further reflection, however, the claim makes more sense. First, by not foregrounding the border as a
primary concern, InSITE's directors sidestep the delicate issue of who has
the right to make art about this border; second, they expand their artist base
beyond the local to others who might interestingly address the region's complex issues. Moreover (and perhaps more to the point), InSITE operates in a
world in which "the border" has already been unhinged from a literal connection to a site-specific border and unhinged, too, from requiring artists
who make work about the border to have been its long-term residents. This
uncoupling is part of a major shift over the past forty years in the relationships artists have to the local and global. InSITE is part of a *mundo sin fronteras*, a globalized art world in which sponsoring institutions fly in artists
from many different points around the globe, and from the many different
(but also similar) international biennials where they have installed their
work and established their reputations. *This* border thus becomes one more
site—another temporary stop—in the vectored movement of the artist as
nomad moving across borders and through countries in a perpetual peripa-
tus. Given the deracinated mobility of its artists, it makes sense that its directors would avoid fixing InSITE's engagements as being *about* the border.
Rather, InSITE is about the facilitation of opportunities for artists interested
in exploring possibilities offered by the richly resonant complexity *at* the
border. "The border" thereby becomes a catalyst for cultural projects that
address the tragedies inscribed across it.[41]

Because InSITE has itself been an ongoing experiment, an art event that
is always in the process of defining itself, a brief history of its origin and unfolding will assist the reader. It evolved out of a now-defunct nonprofit experimental visual arts organization in San Diego called Installation Gallery.
Founded in the early 1980s, Installation Gallery focused on installation
art—work made for and installed at a specific site to which it then presumably belonged—in this case, Installation Gallery. During its brief flourishing, Installation Gallery was on the cutting edge of contemporary art, even

attracting viewers from the art-rich world of Los Angeles. Part of Installation's mandate was multiculturalism, and it showed the work of artists from across the border. In the late 1980s, the art scene in San Diego (which had a brief moment of vibrancy in the late 1970s and early 1980s) expired, and Installation ran out of money and sponsors. At that point it was taken over by Mark Quint, a gallerist, and Michael Krichman, a former attorney who had a long-standing passion for art. Together they transformed Installation from a physical space (an operating gallery in the city) to a sponsoring organization. Under the governance of an Arts Advisory Board, Installation would stage an art event in the San Diego–Tijuana region, and they would call it InSITE. Sites included community colleges, public and private spaces, the Centro Cultural de la Raza in Balboa Park, the Centro Cultural in Tijuana, the Museum of Contemporary Art, coffee houses, theaters, and bookshops. For the first incarnation of InSITE, there was no centralized curatorial oversight, but each participating institution orchestrated its own show under the rubric of InSITE. In all, forty-nine artists showed work at twenty-two different venues. Although the exhibition spanned the border, the border was not the focus. Rather, the agenda was to encourage installation art in the region. The border was incidental rather than primary to the project, although several of the artworks did address it and the very necessity of crossing the border to view all the art works gave InSITE an unusual transborder aspect. When the event was over, in the winter of 1992, the Board decided to continue the project as a biennial.

InSITE94 was conceived on a much larger scale, for it had thirty-eight institutions across San Diego County and Tijuana curating seventy projects of more than one hundred artists at nearly forty sites. It extended geographically from Playas de Tijuana and the Centro Cultural Tijuana south of the border, to Escondido's California Center for the Arts near the northern edge of San Diego County. It thus traversed the border in a span that extended over eighty miles. Again, each institution selected its own artist or artists. Now, selected artists came not only from the United States, Mexico, and South America, but also from Europe and Japan—thereby introducing a kind of globalization to this border-based event. The full title of InSITE94—"A Binational Exhibition of Installation and Site-Specific Art"—emphasized the binational character of the project and a mode of contemporary art practice rather than the charged politics of the border. Likewise, the catalogue's Introduction (undersigned by InSITE's directors), did not feature the border as a theme but focused rather on the binational collaborativeness of the project, for now various cultural, educational, and political institutions from Baja California and Mexico City were involved at an organizational level. Central oversight was still, however, from San Diego's Installation office.

With InSITE97 this changed, for InSITE became a truly binational venture, with administration the joint responsibility of Installation and the Instituto Nacional de Bellas Artes (INBA), the foremost fine-arts institution in Mexico, working together with the city of Tijuana, the state of Baja California, and the Mexican Consulate of San Diego. The other new and significant feature was that participating artists now committed to two residencies in the region in order to enable them make work that would connect in some way to its dynamics. For this incarnation, the roster of (fifty-five) artists was restricted to the Americas and was selected by four curators, which lent the project more coherence. The geographic compass was also much narrower—and more manageable; the preponderance of San Diego sites was in the downtown area, but the Tijuana sites were distributed among four areas, all of which could be accessed in a day's viewing. There was, too, for the first time, an overt theme: Public Space in a Private Time. Open-ended enough to allow artists total freedom, the theme nonetheless served to offer a focus other than the border, which was, notably, elided in the title. The theme did, however, invite an examination and comparison of the different publics that comprise Tijuana and San Diego, and so it might be argued that the border was implied in the title.

InSITE2000/01 continued the positive innovations of '97: parity in binational governance, selection of artists by a team of four curators, extensive residencies for artists, and an overt theme and a title. Conceptually interrogative and open-ended, the guidebook addressed the public as "When Where What." The lack of diacritical markers for words that ordinarily require them rendered the title ambiguous. Simultaneously an interrogative and a declarative, the title elicited discomfort and uncertainty in the viewer—precisely the effects that InSITE set out to produce. In short, InSITE2000/01 was less about producing artworks for selected sites than about deploying art to destabilize and disrupt expectations about contemporary art and about the biennial/triennial experience. The most unusual feature was that it unfolded over five months as a series of events, spectacles, and performances; many were visible for only a day or a few days, whereas others existed only as documentation, the core work having been a process rooted in collaborations with neighborhoods or groups. Interested viewers/participants (there was not a lot to *see*, although a great deal to *think about*) experienced the events over a sequence of Exploration Weekends—concentrated moments with active schedules of events, conferences, and organized Expeditions to project venues. Thus viewers/participants were themselves propelled into motion, becoming part of the mobility of border traffic as they repeatedly crossed the border to engage events.

Given the huge diversity and numbers of artists' projects in InSITE's four incarnations, it is impossible to offer any meaningful summary of what the work encompassed. Instead I have selected a few examples that highlight distinctive aspects of InSITE. They are by Francis Alÿs, Krystof Wodiczko, and Alfredo Jaar.

Alÿs participated in InSITE97. His project emblemized the deracinated artist who travels from one international venue to another as an "international flâneur" hawking a grab-bag of conceptual art "goods." For InSITE his work addressed the border or, more accurately, *borders*. Titled "The Loop," it was a journey from Tijuana to San Diego without crossing the United States–Mexico border. To accomplish this he traveled around the globe to exotic destinations such as Shanghai and Hong Kong, eventually making his way back to San Diego. His project, in the words of one of the curators, was a

> 'non-effort' to cross the border the way the usual Mexican migrants do—jumping the fence, facing the Border Patrol and all that it implies. Instead of waiting for the right moment, of looking for the right crossing spot, he took the opposite path. His impatience resulted in a twenty-day roundtrip, almost without leaving aircrafts, airports, and airport hotels. His project was kind of cynical . . . the cynicism of an artist who is able because of his status as an artist to fulfill many people's dreams. . . . [It] was very much about the artist as a tourist.[42]

As a record of his travels, he exhibited boarding passes, hotel receipts, postcards, and e-mails in a file box at the Centro Cultural Tijuana. It was, indeed, a fascinating project in which "the border" figured as nonsite, as abstraction, signifier of placeless nomadism. Correlatively the artist was foregrounded as unhinged from place, a rootless traveler, collector of frequent flyer miles.[43] In effect Alÿs represented what social scientist Marc Augé calls "nonplaces"—signifiers of "the accelerated circulation of passengers and goods."[44] His project connected *this* border with the globalized movement of bodies across borders, and also drew attention to the different economic conditions that mark the passages—and experiences—of border crossings. It was a perspective marked by his nonorganic relation to this border, by his addressing it as one more stop in his artistic odyssey, by his *being a stranger*. It is projects such as this that lend credence to claims by its directors that InSITE is not about the border and does not produce "border art." In Alÿs's case, InSITE's sited-ness at the border offered an opportunity to comment on "sited-ness" and "borders" as abstractions and mobilizations—interruptions in an endless itinerary between phantom sites.

The second two examples are both performance events. Here my interest lies only partially in their moments of performance before an audience. What I want to address are the negotiations and processes that subtended them, the processes whereby they were brought to the public as art works. My argument here takes off from George Yudice's arresting claim that InSITE is "a work in its own right, produced by the actions of the directors, staff, curators, artists and often redirected by . . . co-investigators and collaborators . . . ;"[45] and that "the *organizational work* done by InSITE directors and staff . . . deserves at least as much attention as the most successful art projects in the program."[46] By focusing on aspects unseen by the general

Figure 5.8 Krystof Wodiczko, *Tijuana Projection.*

public, we learn about InSITE's modus operandi and about the creativity exercised by directors and staff in affecting interaction and intervention in the region. We learn, too, how artists with no organic relationship to this border are facilitated in making art about it, and in creating art that could arise, perhaps, only from the perspective of a stranger. Additionally, we come to view InSITE as an operation in the "real" arena of border politics that produces art experiences.

The two projects I have selected illustrate the different possibilities and connections provided by InSITE. The first, Krystof Wodiczko's *Tijuana Projection*, climaxed the extended schedule of InSITE2000/01. For this, Wodiczko, a Polish artist whose home base is New York and Cambridge, Massachusetts, projected the talking heads of women from Tijuana's *maquiladora* industry onto the sixty-foot diameter façade of the Centro Cultural Tijuana's Omnimax Theater, known to local residents as "La Bola." It was a live projection, for the women whose faces filled the huge expanse of the dome stood in front of it, recounting into microphones narratives of sexual abuse at the hands of family members. Wodiczko was already experienced with projecting images onto public monuments, but this was the first occasion on which he used live projection.

At an early point in his engagement with InSITE2000/01, Wodiczko decided to focus on women working in *maquiladoras*. But for a Polish artist to complete such a project—speaking no Spanish and living far from the site of his subject—required extensive assistance from InSITE's staff. The two who became most actively engaged were Cecilia Garza and Tobias Ostrander. Through InSITE's interventions, Wodiczko made contact with the director of a fifteen-year-old activist organization, Factor X, that fights for women's rights, including those of *maquila* workers. The director, Ana Enríques, was willing to help and arranged for a select group of women to attend a meeting where Wodiczko, accompanied by Garza, Ostrander, and cameraman Kenny Strickland, would explain his ideas. Described by both Garza and Enríques as exotically European in appearance with a "very beautiful white face and beautiful cold blue eyes," Wodiczko was clearly cognizant of the power of the stranger. He not only looked like a stranger, but he introduced himself as "the artista Pollacko"[47]—the foreigner, not a party to the harsh cruelties of this border zone and, therefore, somehow outside them. As with Alÿs, but in a very different way, his intervention –his very credibility—was predicated on his nonorganic relation to the border, to his clear assumption of the persona of the stranger.

At this first meeting, he showed videos of previous projections in Krakow and Boston in which participants spoke about deeply personal concerns, primarily about domestic violence. His goal here, he explained, was to give the women a voice and thereby "make the city hear what the city doesn't want to hear,"[48] and he asked them to consider what they would like to say to the people of Tijuana. Interested and curious, they agreed to meet again and to participate. Wodiczko met with them on four subsequent occasions to conduct video recordings in preparation for the February event. Initially he prompted them with questions but soon they gained confidence and spoke freely. At first they spoke about health concerns in the *maquilas*, but quickly the theme reoriented to domestic violence, to narratives of rape and abuse extending over generations. The subject thus shifted from the *maquilas*— the signifier of labor relations at the border—to narratives that were simultaneously both personal and universal, and that belonged within the same genre as those recounted by Wodiczko's other subjects in Krakow and Boston.

Wodiczko visited the region four or five times to work on the project, focusing intensely for twelve to fourteen hours each day that he was here. During that time Garza and Ostrander worked the long hours with him. Additionally, their task was to sustain the interest of the participants during the extended intervals when Wodiczko was absent. They also reviewed and edited the videos in preparation for his visits, made suggestions, and offered options. When asked how he viewed his engagement, Ostrander responded:

> Do I consider myself a collaborator on this project? This project would not have happened without the hard work of myself and Cecilia, Cecilia in many ways more than myself. We were both extremely involved in the decision processes, but only by facilitating Wodiczko's many requests and offering suggestions based on what we understood the goals of the project to be. The decisions were all

taken by Wodizcko and often they were not ones that we personally agreed with. In this sense the project was his and only his.

Both Garza and Ostrander commented on how emotionally involved they became with the women who so courageously revealed secrets they had hidden for years. Again, to cite Ostrander:

> We entered very much into each other's lives, these women, myself, Cecilia, and Kenny. Wodizcko in many ways kept a certain distance, but this is part of his personality, which is more comfortable with the intellectual than the emotional. At times I feel he missed out on the real meat of what happened and didn't fully try to *feel* what these women were saying. But he pushed it all to happen.

Although aloofness may be part of Wodiczko's character, it is also a mark of the stranger, as Kristeva notes in her *Strangers to Ourselves*, "Indifference," she writes, "is the foreigner's shield."[49] I am not suggesting that Wodizcko had no feelings for these women. I *am* suggesting that his detachment (remarked on also by Garza) is a corollary of his being from elsewhere, the exotic "other," "the artista Pollacko." I am also suggesting that his aloofness, his foreignness, was a necessary condition for this powerful art project, and that only a foreigner could have brought to fruition the monumental staging of the *ob-scene*, or what is normally off-stage.[50] As Kristeva comments: "the foreigner can utter all sorts of indecencies without being shaken by any repugnance or even excitement, since his unconscious shelters itself on the other side of the border."[51] Although Wodiczko did not "utter . . . indecencies," he staged their revelation by the *maquila* workers.[52]

Wodiczko appears to be sensitive to charges of "detachment," for in the introduction to his recent book he comments:

> One could look at my artistic biography and conclude that I am a nomad. Even were I to see myself this way, *I would emphasize that, contrary to popular opinion, nomads are not detached from their terrain,* but in fact try continuously to affix themselves to it and must know the characteristics of the terrain well in order to be able to do so. *In many instances, they know it better than native residents.* After saying this, I must admit that I may indeed be a nomad, since the meaning of each of my projects is strongly grounded in its specific terrain, which in each case I have attempted to approach with an attitude of usefulness, and to leave with a judgmental contribution. *This survival tactic is similar to the one used by all those who are displaced and who assume the tricky mission and function of magician, storyteller, critic, and soothsayer.*[53] (emphases added)

Even if we leave aside the issue of detachment, by his own account the effectivity of his projects is predicated on his being from elsewhere.

Where Wodiczko's project marked the finale of InSITE's sequence of Exploration Weekends, Alfredo Jaar's marked their opening. Titled *The Cloud*, it consisted of over 1,000 white balloons suspended and then released above the border, and was intended as an ephemeral monument to those who died trying to cross. The site that Jaar chose for the performance was Goat

Figure 5.9 Alfredo Jaar, *The Cloud*.

Canyon, on the Mexico side. It is a treacherous landscape and many have died there while waiting to cross. Like Wodiczko, Jaar is a foreigner to this region and relied on InSITE's administrators to realize his project. Although the project was slight in impact, the extensive research and negotiations that subtended it were impressive. They were conducted by Carmen Cuenca, In-SITE's Mexican director, and their recitation allows a fascinating behind-the-scenes look at InSITE's operations.

Land ownership in Baja California is very complicated. Goat Canyon appeared to be owned both by the federal government of Mexico and by a private party. After obtaining permission from a federal commission, Cuenca examined city files to track down the private owner, a process that took weeks. Once that was resolved, technicians were consulted about air and weather conditions. Additionally, InSITE had to inform Aero-Space Commissions at both the U.S. and Mexican airports because the balloons might interfere with the radar of airplanes. The canyon serves as a dump site for Tijuana residents as well as a squatter camp for would-be crossers, and so needed to be cleaned to serve as a stage from which to launch InSITE 2000/01. To that end, Cuenca contacted the mayor of Tijuana who agreed to provide local prisoners to remove the trash. Further, the permission of the Border Patrol had to be obtained, as vehicles with art tourists and balloon technicians would need easy access to and from the Canyon—a sensitive area carefully monitored by the Border Patrol. Because Jaar was addressing a subject that was the purview of other organizations working to safeguard migrant workers, their permission and cooperation also needed to be established. Jaar wanted live music to accompany the floating balloons and this, too, proved complicated to organize. All this Cuenca arranged.

That she was able to do so points both to her extraordinary skills at public relations and to the network of connections that InSITE's directors so carefully developed. Cuenca, who is from Mexico City and has a degree in art history, came to the border in 1989 and was shortly thereafter hired by Tijuana's Cecut (or Centro). In 1994, the director of the Cecut and the President of Bellas Artes appointed her as Baja California Coordinator of Activities for InSITE—a relationship that developed into the partnership that marked InSITE97. She was also appointed Cultural Attaché to the Mexican Consul General in San Diego, an appointment that permitted her to continue to work as the Mexican representative of InSITE . Her knowledge of Mexican cultural institutions and of the political infrastructure of Mexico has been invaluable for the evolution of InSITE.

Co-director Krichman has worked with equal dedication to develop InSITE as a binational and bicultural project. Indeed, if the directors were to be asked to pinpoint InSITE's principal accomplishments, they would focus not on the art that it sponsors, but on the extraordinary feat of crafting a binational cultural endeavor. As Yudice points out, "the public . . . private partnerships brokered by InSITE are unique, and together with the U.S.-Mexico Fund for Culture, inaugurated in 1991, are the only initiatives that have created long-lasting bi-national institutional unions in the cultural sphere."[54] Although InSITE's directors deflect attention from InSITE as a producer of "border art," they readily acknowledge InSITE as a significant factor in effecting binational cultural collaboration. Their goal is to facilitate the creation of art projects that allow different aspects of the border to be brought into play—a process that is heavily dependent on negotiations between different political and cultural institutions. Thus to understand InSITE's art projects requires some familiarity with the complex binational arrangements that undergird them. Where previous border art arose out of situations of confrontation with authorities, InSITE seeks always to find some means to work with and within the law, to engage the authorities and transform them into collaborators. Although the roster of artists usually changes from InSITE to InSITE, the bureaucracies at the border remain constant and must be cultivated, for without their support InSITE cannot occur. Thus Border Patrol agents are given catalogues as gifts and invited to attend InSITE's gala opening events. They become friends rather than antagonists. Although InSITE's catalogues and publicly disseminated information do not reveal the complex strategizing and negotiating that subtend the art works, these are a crucial part of InSITE. Indeed, as Yudice has argued, they are as much its art as the completed works or events that the public, riding in buses rented by InSITE, their passage facilitated by InSITE, traverse the border to witness. Although some of these works (such as Wodiczko's and Jaar's) may be intended as gestures of provocation, InSITE itself is an agency of conciliation, an art project aimed at greater transborder understanding and collaboration. Indeed, it is InSITE's very success as an agency facilitating binational harmony that allows the staging of projects that highlight the region's harsh realities.

Notes

1. I borrow this phrase from James Meyer's "The Functional Site; or The Transformation of Site Specificity," in Erika Suderburg (ed.), *Space Site Intervention: Situating Installation Art* (Minneapolis: University of Minnesota Press, 2000).

2. According to Arturo Rosales, "elaborate etymologies" underlie the word Chicano. He writes, "To those who wished for the word to represent the movement, 'Chicano' derived from the ancient Nahuatl word 'mexicano' with the 'x' being pronounced as a 'shh' sound. Among the many versions that detractors used to disqualify the term was that it came from 'chicas patas,' an extremely pejorative reference used to denote new arrivals from Mexico." *Chicano! The History of the Mexican American Civil Rights Movement* (New York: Arte Publico Press, 1996), 261.

3. Activist Jose Gómez, cited in Philip Brookman, " El Centro Cultural de la Raza Fifteen Years," in Philip Brookman and Guillermo Gómez-Peña (eds.), *Made in Aztlán* (San Diego: Centro Cultural de la Raza, 1986), 19. My information on the history of Chicano Park is drawn from this text and from Raúl Homero Villa's *Barrio-Logos: Space and Place in Urban Chicano Literature and Culture* (University of Texas Press, Austin, Texas, 2000).

4. In addition to articles by scholars of the Chicano Movement and by local journalists, the Park was mentioned in an article on Mexican Americans in the June 1980 issue of *National Geographic*, which illustrated three of the murals. I am indebted for this information to Jane Ferree's *The Murals of Chicano Park, San Diego, California* (Master's thesis, San Diego State, 1994), 41. Ferree also mentions, but without citation, that "images of the murals had appeared in Rheims three years previously, and in Caen in 1980."

5. Villa, 6.

6. Douglas Crimp, "Photographs at the End of Modernism," in *On the Museum's Ruins* (Cambridge, MA: MIT Press, 1993), 17.

7. Meyer, "The Functional Site," 26.

8. My information here is from Philip Brookman's account, "El Centro Cultural de la Raza, Fifteen Years," in *Made In Aztlán*, a commemorative catalogue celebrating the Centro's fifteenth anniversary.

9. Ibid., 22.

10. Ibid., 14.

11. Ibid., 26.

12. All citations are from an interview with Torres in July 2001.

13. The Border Art Workshop (BAW/TAF) 1984.

14. Robert Sanchez, interview, June 1995.

15. This is the claim made by Philip Brookman in *Made in Aztlán*, 51.

16. First publlished by Gómez-Peña and Marco Vinicio. In 1987 when Marco Vinicio moved to New York, Gómez-Peña was joined, for different editions, by co-editors Emily Hicks, Harry Polkinhorn, César Espinosa, and Isaac Artenstein.

17. In "The Multicultural Paradigm" in *Warrior for Gringrostroika*, Gómez-Peña wrote: "In Latin America, the artist has multiple roles. He/she is not just an image-maker or a marginal genius, but a social thinker/educator/counterjournalist/civilian diplomat/human-rights observer. His/her activities take place in the center of society and not in specialized corners," 49.

18. Sanchez, interview, June 1995.

19. BAW/TAF member who requested not to be referenced by name, interviewed 1996.

20. *San Diego Tribune* March 1986.

21. My claims regarding Holley's attitudes come from an interview with him in 1995.

22. A loose association of international artists who shared a Dadaist sensibility, who worked across the borders among art, music, and literature and whose agenda was often political.

23. The reference is to the Capp Street Project, not covered in this chapter.

24. "The Spirit of Place: Border Art in San Diego," *Visions Art Quarterly*, Summer, 1989.

25. Meyer, 25.

26. Ibid. I have extrapolated from Meyer's argument, borrowing and adapting concepts that are useful to my own.

27. Ibid., 27.

28. Reasons for resignation were complex and involved many issues, this among them.

29. Interview, July 2000.

30. Ibid.

31. Ibid.

32. Interview, July 2000.

33. Ibid.

34. The first comments are by Harry Polkinhorn, cited in Shifra Goldman, "La Casa de Cambio," in *Dimensions of the Americas* (Chicago: University of Chicago Press, 1988). The second are by Goldman in the same article.

35. Ibid., Goldman.

36. Meyer, 25.

37. *High Performance*, Spring 1991. For a fuller discussion of the issues leading up to this article, see my "Conflict Over 'Border Art'": Whose Subject, Whose Border, Whose Show?" *Third Text*, Autumn 1997, 40.

38. *High Performance*, Summer 1991.

39. As stated in the catalogue for InSITE94.

40. Handout "InSITE2000: Landscape—Traffic—Syntax" given to participants to the residency for artists in the summer of 1999.

41. For further discussion on InSITE's relation to the border, see George Yudice, New York University "Producing the Cultural Economy: The Col*labor*ative Art of InSite," unpublished manuscript. Yudice also references cynical comments by artists and critics on InSITE's relationship to the border. I am indebted to this article for many illuminating insights about InSITE.

42. Olivier Debroise, "Private Time in Public Space: A dialogue with the curatorial team: Jessica Bradley, Olivier Debroise, Ivo Mesquita, Sally Yard," in Sally Yard (ed.), *Private Time in Public Space* (China: Palace Press International, San Diego, 1998), 57.

43. For a discussion of the artist as nomad and the artwork as deterritorialized, see Miwon Kwon.

44. *Non-Places: Introduction to an Anthropology of Supermodernity* (Verso, New York, 1995), 34.

45. Yudice, 23. By underscoring the "labor" component of "collaborative" Yudice seeks to redirect attention to the enormous contributions not only of the directors and their staff, but also of poor communities whose engagements provide "relatively uncompensated" value added to the art, 10.

46. Ibid., 16.

47. For the account of Wodiczko's project and the process that led up to it, I am heavily indebted to Garza, Ostrander, and Enríques, who generously shared their recollections with me. I interviewed them on separate occasions in July 2001. Garza and Enríques described Wodiczko's presentation in almost identical words.

48. From the interview with Garza.

49. Julia Kristeva, *Strangers to Ourselves*, Leon S. Roudiez (trans.) (New York: Columbia University Press, 1991), 7.

50. Yudice brought up the notion of the "obscene" in his "Presentation at Final 'Exploration Weekend,'" delivered at the Centro Cultural de Tijuana, February 25, 2001.

51. Ibid., 32.

52. And what of the women, his collaborators? What was the project's value for them? According to Enríques, Ostrander, and Garza, they "felt like stars, like celebrities and their self-confidence visibly grew." It offered them an opportunity to have time away from the routine of their lives and to effect a catharsis. They "were euphoric and happy because they were able to do it." It offered them, perhaps, a moment of empowerment.

53. Wodiczko, *Critical Vehicles: Writings, Projects, Interviews* (Cambridge, MA: MIT Press, 1999), xi.

54. Yudice, 13.

6

Border Representations
Border Cinema and Independent Video

NORMA IGLESIAS

Introduction

When we think of the United States–Mexico border, particularly between
Tijuana and San Diego, a variety of images come to mind. These images, as
social representations, are informed by direct experiences of the place, as
well as by the mass media. Many things are said about Tijuana–San Diego:
that it is the most frequently crossed border in the world; that the biggest
drug dealers operate there; that it is a violent, unsafe place; that almost every
day a person dies attempting to cross to "the other side," and that it is a place
of opportunities and dollars. Cities on "the Mexican side" are known as
places in which drink and entertainment are cheaply and freely available; a
paradise for underaged North Americans who can come as they please,
doing things they cannot do in their own country; home to donkeys painted
as zebras and good live music in bars. Everything is cheaper in these cities;
North American insurance covers medical services from cosmetic surgery to
cancer treatments and cheap medicines are available without prescriptions.
Fugitives hide there; it is a place fraught with "shopping malls," where technology can be accessed at much better prices than in the rest of Mexico and
where locals always carry dollars *and* pesos, and frequently carry passports
and United States visas "just in case." The border is like a third country because it is a mélange of the United States and Mexico, yet is unlike either.
The musical art of Santana, Julieta Venegas, and Nortec originated at the
border—a place full of dynamic artists and vibrant cultural projects, reflected

183

Figure 6.1 Tres camisetas on sale at the Tijuana-San Diego border. (Photo: Norma Iglesias.)

by the city of Tijuana itself, where we have cardboard houses alongside the grand facilities of the Tijuana Cultural Center (CECUT), and where creative artists work with few resources alongside cutting edge artistic projects such as InSITE. The border evokes so many images, as the illustrations throughout this book show.

This chapter examines the ways different people imagine, reconstruct, and represent this culturally complex and dynamic region through commercial films and independent videos. This requires us to consider the concept of social representation, and how images from these media form symbolic representations of the border. The United States–Mexico border, as the place where the first and third world come together, is recognized as exceptional and fascinating. Néstor García Canclini observed that it acts as a laboratory for the study of "postmodernity." However, the *nature* of the border's importance is significantly influenced by the observer's position within the asymmetrical north–south relationship. The Mexican gaze is constantly directed northward. It is impossible for us to forget our neighbors, and impossible to conceive of ourselves outside our relationship with the United States. The United States, meanwhile, can easily forget that Mexico is always by its side because it is confident that it does not rely upon it. The Mexican and Chicano populations in the United States, however, do not ignore Mexico because the country plays an important role in their identity, enabling them to identify as a group that shares common roots. Consequently, Los Angeles—with its important Mexican and Mexican-origin population—is more of a border city than San Diego, despite its more northerly location.

It is common to see images of the United States–Mexico border in films, television, and the press. The role of border cinema in the process of constructing representations of the region must be recognized. Its representations are the baggage from which young border artists have deconstructed and reconstructed their own cultural spaces.

The border has been represented in commercial film as a place of undocumented migration, prostitution, crime, and lost identity. Historically, these representations have been translated into normative criteria, shaping the Mexican central government's cultural policies in the region. They have also contributed to our own self-definition as border people. However, independently produced representations, such as video and other grassroots artistic enterprises, capture more profoundly the complexity and conflict experienced in this zone of encounter and divergence. This suggests that representational capacity is defined not only by the medium of expression, but also by levels of familiarity with, and commitment to, this place. These representations help us understand the symbolic structures and social meanings attributed to the United States–Mexico border.

Representation: Theory

Representations are interpretations of reality, ways of looking at the world. They attribute meaning to reality. Representations work not only to produce and communicate knowledge, but also to enable a sense of social reality. According to Moscovici, the objective of representation is to transform the unknown into something familiar.[1] Representations function as a system of codes, interpretative frameworks, values, classificatory logics, interpretative principles, and guides to action. As such, they define the collective consciousness, which functions as a normative force inasmuch as it sets the limits and possibilities of social action. The importance of representations rests upon their roles in communication and social interaction. We use them to classify, explain, and evaluate reality. Thus, representations have been defined as "a bundle of concepts, expressions, and explanations drawn from our everyday life, in the course of communications between individuals. In our society, they equate to the myths and belief systems that make up traditional societies and are the contemporary version of common sense."[2]

Representations have symbolic and interpretative relationships with objects. They render linguistic, behavioral, or material elements visible and legible. Consideration of representations leads us to question the origins of their social framing and function, and their relationship to other aspects of

our everyday lives. Representations are a symbolic version of the relationship between the object (in this case of the border and its cultural products)
and the subject who interprets it. As representations are constructed, perception and previous knowledge are fused together. Perception and knowledge are shaped by every subject's experience, as well as by their exposure to
information disseminated by the media. In other words, representations are
the product of constructive interaction between the subject and his or her
social environment and structure. Representations are internal models that
facilitate a conceptualization of reality. They are dynamic. They are constituted in social reality, and as such reality and representation produce and reproduce one another, and are collectively considered to be "real."

The border represents different things to different social groups. Each
groups' social, economic, political, and geographic positionality will determine what is, and what is not, perceived by its members. Thus, representations of the border vary between different groups, and accord different
meanings to border space. "Reality" cannot be considered in isolation from
representation. A representation is an indication of social consciousness.

To analyze representations of the border, the products of two very different media will be examined: (1) Mexican border cinema (as a cultural industry and as a film genre), and (2) border independent video (a form of
local cultural production). This chapter will focus upon representations
produced in the regions of Alta and Baja California. These regions have a
dynamic relationship, with the highest levels of interaction and interdepen-
dence. Yet, there is a high level of contrast between the two sides. I will provide an examination of Mexican commercial border cinema since 1936, and
of Tijuana's local video productions since the late 1980s. The analysis will
proceed by comparing the media of expression themselves, textual representational content, and the subjectivity of the producer. An important
distinction must be drawn between representations emerging from lived experience at the border, and those representations produced from afar, struc-
tured by categorizations and knowledge developed elsewhere. These two
categories of representation characterize independent local videographers
and Mexico City-based cinema industry, respectively.

In each case, an analysis is provided of the communicative context within
which the representation occurs. This foregrounds the notion that each
piece has been produced not only according to the characteristics of the
message it communicates in itself, but also to the relationship the producers
understand themselves to have with their audience.

Border Cinema

The United States–Mexico border has always featured in the cinematographic imagery of Mexican and North American film. Motion pictures

from *The Pony Express* (1907), through *Touch of Evil* (1958), to *Traffic* (2000) have forged an image of the border as a savage but appealing place, with few rules and much disorder; a generic place for outlaw narratives. Border towns and cities became spaces *par excellence* where one would flee justice. In Hollywood films, people arrived at the border from the north, and in Mexican cinema they arrived from the south. In both cases, the border was represented as a free, lawless place, open to all. Border cinema has played a significant role in creating and reinforcing such border stereotypes. Analysis of motion pictures and their audiences provides a basis for understanding the force and power of film and the role that film, as a sociocultural phenomenon, is playing in the daily life of its audiences.

Mexican commercial border cinema from 1938 to 2000 was artistically weak, highly centralized, socially uncritical, and limited to a restrictive set of conventions. Its motion pictures are generally produced in Mexico City. The stories told by border films either unfold in the space between Mexico and the United States, or focus on a character who comes from the border. They portray a Mexican population or, when set in the United States, a Mexican-origin population. A film's narrative typically revolves around the concept of the border, or around problems of national identity. Yet border cinema breaks traditional cinematic conventions. It ruptures genre and narrative limits,[3] establishing new production processes and audience relationships. As such, border cinema has distinguished itself from classical Mexican film.

Before the 1960s, border films were simplistic and infrequently produced. After the 1960s, however, the border was recognized by Mexican commercial film producers and filmmakers as a setting for interesting stories, as an accessible and cheap production location, and above all, as a market eager to see itself reflected on the big screen. Unfortunately, border cinema emerged just as Mexican cinema entered a period of general economic and political crisis. Consequently, border cinema became a repository for various, already overused, genre characters from Mexico City: the well-known "*Santo*" or "*Enmascarado de plata*" arrived at the border, along with actresses such as Lyn May and Isela Vega. Even westerns, bawdy comedies, and "*fichera*" (prostitute) films made their way to the border in a bid to postpone their demise.

The border theme and production formula proved commercially attractive, facilitating border cinema's consolidation. By the mid-1970s, border cinema production was concentrated in the hands of a limited number of companies from Mexico City. Films were produced on company-owned property in the United States, although technical staff and actors were paid in *pesos*. The producers thus avoided paying union dues and benefited by having one team to produce various films. Coproduction with a supposed North American company (usually a family business) allowed producers to retain the rights in Mexico and the United States. The U.S.-based Mexican

Figure 6.2 Advertising poster of the film *Deportados*.

population, with an income in dollars, was the industry's market priority. Topics such as migration, identity, and drug dealing were used to guarantee thematic interest for Mexicans in Mexico and the United States. They capitalized on the success of *corridos* and *norteño* musical groups by making film renditions of their more popular songs, as with *Camelia la Texana* ("Camelia the Texan.")

Border cinema production continues to be an important business. Although the production formula has changed in some ways, the content and the technical-narrative quality of these movies have improved little. There is a growing trend toward "straight-to-video" production, and toward film production by small companies located in northern Mexico, or by small Mexican-financed companies in Hollywood. The principal market continues to be Mexicans (and Guatemalans and Salvadorans) living in the United States, residents of northern Mexican cities, and central and southern Mexicans entertaining aspirations of crossing "to the other side."

Border cinema, viewed in terms of production, distribution, and markets, is quite the opposite from Chicano Cinema—a genre that also represents the border and identity issues. Border cinema has reinforced stereotypes about the border, simplifying border sociocultural life. Chicano Cinema, meanwhile, has been characterized by deconstruction and resis-

Figure 6.3 Advertising poster of the film *Santo en la frontera del terror.*

tance. For the Mexican film industry, the border has been a symbolic site of
excess, and thematic and generic transgressions. For Chicano Cinema, the
border has been a point of reference to the configuration of geopolitical
power, and this power's relationship to cultural processes.[4] Traditionally,
Chicano Cinema views the border as a space of cultural interaction *par excellence.* The value of the border from the perspective of Chicano film production is typically positive, culturally affirmative, and recuperative,
whereas in Mexican border cinema the border is viewed negatively, as a site
of cultural devaluation. Another substantial difference is that the border
cinema producer thinks of the audience primarily as a consumer. The audience for Chicano Cinema is a key element; the audience is inscribed in the
film from the project's inception. The producers of Chicano Cinema are
Chicanos, and the Chicano population is its principal audience.

Mexican border cinema is not popular because "the people" produced it,
nor because they demanded it. It is not even a product of a border empre-
sario. It is popular because its principal audience is the people of the border,
"*la raza fronteriza*," who appropriate border cinema and make it their own.
This is because, beyond aesthetic and social criticism, border cinema inadvertently manages to reproduce and recreate symbols, emblems, and

situations that are both everyday and extraordinary to the viewer. The relationship that the audience has forged with border cinema makes it interesting to study. Understanding border cinema requires more than just analysis of its texts and forms of production, exhibition, and distribution. It requires a detailed analysis of its reception, for it is here that we ultimately witness its communicative power.

Audiences are specific, historically situated, and above all, actively making sense of the film at the moment of viewing. The middle-class young man who goes to the movie theater with his friends in the city of Tijuana or Culiacán will not have the same interpretive experience, or appropriate the film in the same way, as an undocumented Mexican going alone to a movie theater in downtown Los Angeles. Both the spectator's life experiences and the context of exhibition produce different readings. Thus, producers of border cinema are obliged to consider their audiences, and the processes and relationships that cinema establishes with them.

Border cinema's representations can be categorized in terms of three important periods: 1938 to 1969, which saw an average of 2.7 border films produced per year; 1970 to 1979, with an average of 5 films per year; and 1980 to 2000, with an average of 14.7 border films per year. It was during the second period that border cinema consolidated itself. This consolidation was based upon three phenomena: public interest in migration, President Echeverría's efforts to revitalize the film industry, and the President's interest in the Chicano movement. President Echeverría's support of the film industry and his political and cultural interest in Chicanos were demonstrated when he invited Chicano director Jesús Treviño to produce *Raíces de sangre* (*Blood Roots*) in 1976, financed by Mexico via its production agency CONACINE. State participation in border cinema allowed the brief emergence of some quality work in the mid-1970s. However, private film companies also produced a large number of poor-quality films when they discovered a new market in the Mexican and Mexican-origin population of the United States. After the 1960s, the majority of border films premiered in the United States, generating profits in dollars. This attracted the attention of more producers, and thus fueled increased production.

The Border as a Place of Migration, Opportunities, and Suffering

One of the first representations produced by Mexican border cinema was that of gateway to the land of dollars. The place was introduced to public imagination through the dialogues of female characters left behind by men who traveled north, as opposed to any visual representation of the border itself. Although the border did not appear on the big screen, it was imagined as a place similar to the United States—as a place of opportunity, where money was readily available, but also danger. The theme of migration to the United States was border cinema's first obsession, and remains so to this day.

The earliest films were *La china Hilaria* (1938) and *Adiós mi chaparrita* (1939), dramas that begin when the head of the family leaves to seek work across the border. The stories revolve around the tragedy experienced by women who remain in the village. The call of the border, a wage in dollars, and other temptations of the northern lands made it unlikely that these workers would return, bequeathing a legacy of sadness for those left behind. In this way, the border and supposedly easy money were responsible for family disintegration.

A few years later, direct representations of the border location began to appear on film, although these scenes were shot in studios. They characterized the border as a dangerous no-man's-land. Images of extensive arid zones, cheap hotels for migrants, restaurants, and bars abounded. The focus moved to border cities and the suffering of migrant men. Such films include *Pito Pérez se va de bracero (Pito Pérez becomes a "bracero,"* 1947), *Espalda mojada (Wetback,* 1953), and *El fronterizo (The Border Man,* 1952). In these films, the protagonists are migrant men who feel guilty for abandoning their homeland. The north offers them the dollars they desire, but also promises hardship, beginning with the abuses of the migration process, including exploitation by employers in the United States. The masculine characters of these films are strong, tenacious men who become weakened by northern temptations embodied in northern women. Female characters appear as opposite extremes in these films: the abandoned heroines who experience the height of suffering, or personifications of the "bad influences of the north"; and *pochas* (Americanized Mexicans), dancehall girls, barmaids, thieves, or prostitutes, whose lives always end tragically. Northern women appear as "big girls," with well-formed bodies and slim morals.

The film that demonstrates this better than any other from the first period (1938–1969) was *El bracero del año (Bracero of the Year,* 1969), in which the well-known comic "Piporro" plays Natalio Reyes Colas (a Spanish rendering of Nat King Cole). Rather than meeting with the misfortunes that undocumented migrants typically encounter in the United States, he enters a strange and fantastic life when he is named "Bracero of the year." In addition to his honorary title, Natalio is awarded a new convertible and a Hollywood film contract, not to mention the devotion of a bevy of blondes.

During the second period (1970–1978), the prominence of the migration theme continued. The north was still represented as a place of opportunity and misfortune. Films of this period include *Deportados (Deportees,* 1975), *El llanto de los pobres (Cry of the Poor,* 1977), *Wetback—mojados* (1977), and *La noche del Ku Klux Klan (The Night of the Ku Klux Klan,* 1978). In these films, the border appears solely as a place of migrant workers' suffering. Central characters were no longer the classic figures of northern Mexico, but rather figures who brought the problems of the Mexican capital to the border, men who left their urban homes and arrived at the border in search of

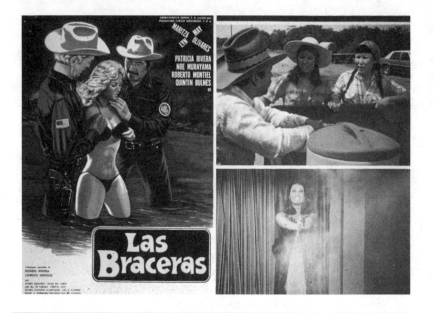

Figure 6.4   Advertising poster of the film *Las braceras.*

adventure, love, or English-language skills. One such character is Tomás, in the film *Soy Chicano y Mexicano (I'm Chicano and Mexican,* 1973), who is from Tepito (a large *barrio* in Mexico City), and who decides to migrate to the United States to learn English. Or the blind child of the film *El hijo de los pobres,* whose dream was to visit Disneyland. The father of the child goes to the "other side" to earn money, and to experience the fantastic world of Anaheim on behalf of his son.

The success of these films accelerated the growth of border cinema as it entered the third period (1979–2000). Existing border genres were updated, and new forms of production and distribution sought. The migration theme continued to dominate. In later migration films, bloodthirstiness and suffering reached their peak. Emphasis was placed on abuse against migrants. In this vein are such films as *Las braceras (Women Braceras,* 1981), *Contrabando humano (Human Contraband,* 1981), *Contrabando y mojados (Contraband and Wetbacks,* 1983), *Arizona- (Masacre Sangrienta) [Arizona- (Bloody Massacre),* 1985], *El carro de la muerte (The Car of Death,* 1985), *Mojado de corazón (Wetback by Heart,* 1986), *Muriendo a la mitad del río (Dying Crossing the River,* 1986), *La jaula de oro (The Golden Cage,* 1987), *Ni de aquí ni de allá (Not From Here nor From There,* 1987), *Ley Fuga (Escape Law,* 1988), and *Tres veces mojado (Three Times Wetback,* 1989).

Figure 6.5 Advertising poster of the film *Division narcoticos.*

In the film *Las braceras,* for example, Lyn May, Maritza Olivares, and Patricia Rivero develop a dark melodrama about prostitution at the border. This film was garishly advertised: "To cross the river is to fall into nets of brutality and ruination. These women suffer the same humiliations and exploitations as their men . . . and rape besides!" The incorporation of female protagonists in migration melodramas gave producers the opportunity to include sexual abuse in the catalogue of border tragedies. These films portrayed suffering, blood, and abuse, although they did not explore the historical, sociological, or political context of the border.

The Border as the Brothel, Bar, and (Later) the Drug Dealers' Empire

Another important characteristic of border representation, especially during its first period, was its portrayal as a great brothel and bar, in films about gangsters and prostitution. This characterization was first developed through the *melodrama de cabaret,* and after the 1980s as police action films. In the *melodrama de cabaret,* the border presented an ideal location for the conduct of illicit activities. The border cities of Ciudad Juárez and Tijuana were the preferred settings for these turbulent films, which were filled with stories of pimps, barmaids, dancers, drug smugglers, and detectives, all operating in an atmosphere of violence and vice. Such films include *Cruel destino (Cruel Destiny)* or *Allá en la frontera (There in the Border,* 1943), by Juan Orol—a true mélange of western, *melodrama de cabaret,* and *melodrama tropical,* where migration to the United States, the lustful passions and misadventures of a "*rumbera*" (rumba dancer) in a border cabaret, combined to make a surreal film. Other examples of border *cabaret melodramas* are *Los misteriosos del hampa (The Mysterious of the Underworld,* 1944) also by Juan Orol, *La herencia de la llorona (The Crying Woman's Inheritance,* 1946) by Mauricio Magdaleno, *Pecadora (Sinner Woman,* 1947) by José Díaz Morales, and *Frontera Norte (Northern Border,* 1953) by Vicente Orona. In the *cabaret melodrama,* men are rude and corrupt, whereas women remain polarized between the sweet, selfless wife and the evil seductress who proves to be the downfall of the protagonist. *Northern Border* (1953) is an example of a cabaret/gangster melodrama, in which characters are banished from the capital city and forced to seek refuge at the border. This film marked the transformation of the border into cinematography's badland. The films' stories unfold in bars, brothels, and homes. Plots focus on the evil and stupidity of female characters. One popular theme was the use of unsavory titles referring to females—a trend exemplified by titles such as *Mala hembra (Wicked Woman).*

These films were transformed during border cinema's second period into action movies about drug dealing, in which the border appears as a place controlled by drug cartels. It becomes a place free of police control, a mafia territory, a place of American life styles in which drugs and weapons are readily accessible. Films that contributed to this image of the border include *La banda del carro rojo (The Red Car Band,* 1976), *Mataron a Camelia la texana (They Killed Camelia the Texan,* 1976), *La muerte del soplón (The Death of a Stool Pigeon,* 1977) and *Contrabando por amor (Contraband for Love,* 1978). The combination of simple plots, lots of cars, helicopters, and sophisticated weaponry, all set against the supposedly "border" backdrop of central Mexico, provided one of the most successful production formulas. Scenes often included famous ballads about drug dealings, in which regional musical groups such as *Los Tigres del Norte* made their cinematographic debuts. In these films, the polarization of female characterizations continued. Characters are either a strong women like *Camelia la Texana,* who question male power, or simple sexual objects in the entourage of drug dealers.

The third period saw a fortification of the image of the border as a place of violence and outlaws. The success of this type of film is evidenced by the large number of movies produced: 43 between 1980 and 1990. These films feature all that is negative about the border, whether real or not. Examples include *Emilio Valera vs. Camelia la Texana (Emilio vs. Camelia the Texan,*

1979), *La mafia de la frontera (The Border's Mafia,* 1979), *El contrabando de El Paso (Contraband in El Paso,* 1980), *Gatilleron del Río Bravo (Trigger Men on the Rio Bravo,* 1981), *Contacto chicano (Chicano Contact,* 1981), *Asalto en Tijuana (Assault in Tijuana,* 1984), and the adventures of the famous Camelia with *El hijo de Camelia la Texana (The Son of Camelia the Texan,* 1989).

Mexicans on the Other Side

Border cinema has also been important in the creation of stereotypes formed around "folklore," nationalism, and the *pochos*. Film such as *Primero soy mexicano (I'm Mexican First and Foremost,* 1950), *Soy Mexicano de acá de este lado (I'm Mexican from This Side of the Border,* 1951), *La güera Xochilt (The Blonde Xochilt,* 1966), and *El pocho* (1969) are a few examples. These melodramatic and moralistic films characteristically ignore the issue of migration, presenting instead a complex, irrational nationalism, full of frustration and hatred for Americans. The pocho, despite appearing as a ridiculous, subversive figure barely able to speak Spanish, becomes the subject of envy.[5] The films portray the border as a place being absorbed into its neighbor's culture, a land of northern influences and dubious national identity. Their characters are Mexicans who live in the United States, or who have lived at the border for some time, and whose Mexican nationalism has weakened. The continuous struggle of these characters to demonstrate to "real" Mexicans (those from the central part of the country) that they have not lost their national identity, and to demonstrate that their love for, and loyalty to, Mexico has not been eroded by their contact with American life, form substantial themes in these films. A song on the soundtrack of *Primero soy Mexicano* illustrates this theme:

Si me gustan los hot cakes,	If I like hot cakes
digo hello sin dar la mano,	I say hello without shaking hands
y aunque pida ham and eggs,	And though I ask for ham and eggs
Primero soy mexicano.	I am Mexican first and foremost!

Men who long to return to their homeland are the usual protagonists of these films. When that return is made, their conflicted identities draw criticism from home communities. The display of northern influence, such as the wearing of American clothes, is seen as an indication of lost national identity. Female characters, always cast in supporting roles, would appear as dutiful sweethearts waiting for her pocho, traditionally "Mexican" in her selflessness, her cooking, her name (Lupe or María), her morality, her clothing, and her rural background and life style. Alternatively, they embody the pernicious influence of the north and its "modernity," as with Sara, "the city pocha," who preferred bars to kitchens. There are several common dimensions to border films of this genre: the difficulty experienced when trying to assimilate into an alien culture, the criticism of any cultural trait that could be construed as purely Mexican, and the comparison of different cultural values. Because of their role as reproducers of culture and values, identity conflicts were much more severe for female characters. Male characters, meanwhile, could more easily adopt both cultures without having to question their own cultural identity.

In the second period, border cinema also developed musicals, melodramas, and action films relating to the cultural identity of Mexican-American communities in the United States. The thematic discovery of Chicanos was the greatest innovation of this period. Chicanos were portrayed as "Latin lovers" suffering huge identity crises. The border was the ideal exotic setting for them to enjoy their love-and-action adventures. Chicanos had athletic bodies and a sexually active life style. Nine films were made using this theme, including *Soy Chicano y mexicano* (*I'm Chicano and Mexican*, 1973), *El Chicano justiciero* (*The Avenging Chicano*, 1974), *Chicano* (1975), *El Chicano karateca* (*The Karate Chicano*, 1977), and *Contacto Chicano* (*Chicano Connection*, 1977). *El Chicano karateca* (*The Karate Chicano*, 1977), in which Jaime Moreno plays a Chicano Kung Fu expert, was promoted with slogans like: "Karate is the weapon, justice is the goal!" "Lovable when he needs to be, but violent when provoked!" And "Strengthening the Chicano movement."

The female characters in these films, as with their male counterparts, enjoy noteworthy sexual freedom. These women are sexually "liberated," although they preserve certain Mexican customs. Exploitation of Chicanas and Chicanos through their casting as "Latin lovers" and sexual symbols was common. An illustrative case is the film *Johnny Chicano*, starring the well-known soap opera actors Verónica Castro and Fernando Allende. The sensuality of these young actors was accentuated in the advertising for the film: "Women call him a Latin macho, men just call him Johnny, but his sexual ferocity conquers all obstacles. Latin lover: Why do foreign women want this Latin man? His is the new face of an untamable race that is learning to turn the tables of discrimination on the gringos."

Chicanos were characterized as gallant, like Fernando Allende, and bold, like Verónica Castro. Both are recognizably untameable in sexual, if not political, terms, just as savage and exotic as the portrayals of the ancient cultures of Mexico presented in North American films. The Chicano character was presented cinematographically as different and distinct, just as Mexico's indigenous cultures appeared to the country's mestizo population, and was placed in opposition to rational, intelligent characters. Mexican film thus managed to reproduce an old stereotype that had been promoted by North American film since cinema's earliest days. These films offered two types of characters: good guys and bad guys, those guided by reason and those guided by passion. Although North American film would clearly identify the bad guy as Mexican, this identification was more subtle in Mexican filmmaking. Here, good guys and bad guys shared the same national origin. Mexican directors distinguished Chicano characters as exotic by focusing on their speech ("Spanglish"), their dress, and their sexual behavior.

The Border of Cowboys

In mid-1950s westerns, the border was presented as a lawless place that attracted foreigners and outlaws. The border town's image was a combination of action, love, and weapons, where fights and shootings were common. Between 1955 and 1966, 25 border films in the western genre were produced, including, *El terror de la frontera (Terror of the Border*, 1961), *La vieja California (The Old California*, 1962), *La frontera sin ley (Lawless Frontier*, 1964), *Los Sheriffs de la frontera (Border Sheriffs*, 1964), *Sangre en el Río Bravo (Blood in the Rio Bravo*, 1965), and five films about *El Texano (The Texan)* by Alfredo B. Crevenna.

The border western offered producers two advantages: the proximity of the United States allowed them to use a mixture of North American and Mexican characters and the location was appropriate for the use of several terms in English, which appealed to Mexican audiences. Border westerns questioned the cultural differences between Mexico and the United States. Some were set in nineteenth-century California, at the time when it was being integrated into the United States. The stereotypes of the North American western are reproduced in these films, where nationality and ethnicity distinguish the good guys from the bad. These films borrow a second theme established by the North American western: an ethnically defined sexual standard. This standard dictates that transracial sexual relationships are wrong. When they occur, they end in disaster.[6]

The Place for Blondes, Alcohol, Sex, Sarcasm, and Laughter

The production of the film *Entre gringas y la migra (Between Gringas and the Migra)* marked the beginning of a new phase in border film. Production was now carried out entirely in Hollywood, with some movies made for television. This new phase combined danger, women, and (yet again) migration. The producers of this new genre christened it "sexy comedy." Among films in this class are *Nos reimos de la migra* (Who's Afraid of the Border Patrol?), *Dos Chichi-mecas en Hollywood* (Two Chichimecas in Hollywood, 1988), *Tijuana caliente* (Hot Tijuana, 1982), *Mojado . . . pero caliente* (Wet . . . but Hot, 1988), and the strange adventures of *El taco loco está acá* (The Mad Taco Is Here, 1988). All involve the transfer of bawdy comedy to the border. In these films, the problem of national and regional identity is explored at the gastronomical level. Identity dilemmas revolve around characters' preference between Mexican and American foods.

Border Cinema, Audiences and Reception Process

Border cinema is not a loose collection of lost films among the hundreds of Mexican movies, but rather a large and complex communicative phenomenon that has influenced the film industry itself, as well as providing representations of the border and establishing particular relationships with its audience. The manner in which border cinema has simplified and decontextualized a complex border reality, and the migration process, has served to stifle border residents' critical engagement with their reality. Moreover, these films are the only cultural products available to Mexicans and Central Americans working in the United States. Despite the simplicity of its themes, the repetition of its plots, and its graphic and visual poverty, border cinema has succeeded in forging a deep relationship with its audiences because it is the only medium through which border and migrant audiences see themselves represented on the screen.

Movie theatres became spaces of socialization and escape, of relaxation, of dreams and fantasies, places where audiences experience the sensation of being a migrant and a border person. One such place was the Bay Theatre in National City, California, which for many years was the only place in San Diego County that showed Mexican and border cinema. In the early 1990s, this theatre became a Protestant church, yet the same audiences continued going there to talk about their personal situations. Commenting on the theater's importance to San Diego's Mexican community, the theater's owner, Mr. Juan J. Torres, stated:

> Mexican cinema is deteriorating. We think that in the near future Mexican films won't exist anymore, we'll have to show American films because our producers will be working for foreign countries. Those living in Mexico may feel they are not losing Mexico because in the end they are still there, in their country. But for those of us who are not in Mexico, where film is one way to keep in touch with Mexico, with our roots, what are we to do? Here, it's as if we were losing a part of ourselves.[7]

Border cinema audiences generally have lower levels of income and education, and are linked to the United States by migration. They prefer Mexican cinema over North American or other foreign films. Border cinema is usually shown in older theatres in the downtown of cities. In the case of the Tijuana–San Diego area, the border cinema audience is different from that of multiplex theaters located in malls. It tends to be made of mobile, non-English-speaking, single young men who attend the cinema regularly. A lack of English language skills is a common characteristic of the border cinema audience in the United States; it prevents them attending movie theatres showing American English-language films. For a largely undocumented population, going to the theatre constitutes a risk of exposure to official scrutiny. Their willingness to face this risk seems to demonstrate audiences' need for leisure, and for interaction with others who share their circumstances.

The narrative quality of border films draws audiences into the action. Pierre Sorlin argues that this obliges them to passively accept the films' rules.[8] The drama creates an artificial universe in which spectators are immersed, and which partially deprives them of their agency. Another characteristic of a border cinema narrative is the presentation of conflict between two opposing forces, usually embodied in two characters of different nationalities: American versus Mexican. The audience is always placed on the Mexican side. The elasticity and richness of border cinema make it an effective educational instrument. Its various potentialities as dream, illusion, reality, entertainment, and spectacle have contributed to the creation of a specific border cinema culture. The movie theatre is the place where audiences "go to find faces, scenes, attitudes, places, that move us, attract us, irritate us or seduce us[9]"; it displays and teaches specific codes of conduct that we may choose, or not, to imitate.

Some audience members watch border films to forget their troubles. Others identify with their past or their future, or sense a connection to their homeland. Border cinema in the United States is received in ways that are distinct from mainstream cinema. At one moment the audience surrenders itself to the narrative and lives as one or more characters. Then, outside the theater, it becomes an active subject, a character in the drama of real life, a drama experienced by all those present. The theater's physical space is a space of common dreams and fantasies, of shared stories and conditions. These spaces provide a dimension to the spectacle that permits constant transition between the fantastic and the concrete. The process of reading and appropriating border cinema is experienced both individually and collectively. The individual viewer is relating both to the movie and the other members of the audience. As such, the film's text is reconstructed on individual and collective levels.

Independent Film in Tijuana

Independent audiovisual production in Tijuana is a very recent phenomenon.[10] Before 1990, the only local productions were documentaries or materials distributed by educational institutions, including the Universidad Autónoma de Baja California (UABC) and the Colégio de la Frontera Norte (COLEF). The UABC in Mexicali started to produce documentary material in 1982. Its productions include *Palmas de Cantú* (The Palms of Cantú, 1983), *Tres mil kilometros al norte* (Three Thousand Kilometers North, 1984), and *Bajacalifornianos* (1988). COLEF's Communication Department was established in 1984. The department's first production was the television miniseries *Llegando a la frontera* (Arriving at the Border), and a series of five documentaries: *Malaquías Montoya* (1986), *Malaquías y Oakland* (1986) (Malaquías and Oakland), and *Aguas negras: problema o recurso?* (*Sewage Waters: Problem or Resource?*, 1988) by Eugenio Bermejillo; . . . *Y tan cerca de Estados Unidos* (. . . *And as Close to the United States*, 1986) by Norma Iglesias, and *El mundo del Cañón Zapata* (*The World of the Zapata Canyon*, 1986) by Gabriel Huerta. Later came *Detrás de la raya* (*Behind the Line*, 1988) by Guadalupe Rivemar and *Los que se van* (*Those That Leave*, 1991) by Adolfo Dávila and Helena Tamayo. Since 1988, influenced by the schools of communication in Mexicali and Tijuana,[11] the film and video fiction that emerged demonstrated a new familiarity with the community.

Young border videomakers[12] have transformed traditional representations of the border. Their new forms have deconstructed the images of border cinema, and have contributed original and more complex forms of exhibition that greatly enrich the stock of video and cinematographic portrayals of the region. Local video artists, using their own small cameras, began filming realities that were absent from commercial productions. They did not set out to create "border" video. Indeed, they sought to avoid being labeled as "border" in order to resist established stereotypes. Despite this, the border's inescapable presence served to inform and enrich their creations. The border featured in this work because their preoccupations, experiences, and spaces all alluded to it. They went out into the streets in search of what were, for them, everyday images, stories, and situations. Although these facets of border life were not new to those who experienced the place first-hand, they were an entirely novel contribution to the audiovisual history of Tijuana. In contrast to commercial border cinema, where fictional stories issue from writers' imaginations, the independent visual artists of the border construct stories using images directly from the city—images intimately entwined with their experiences as border residents. A range of subjects, from middle-class young people, *quinceañeras* (fifteen-year birthday celebrations), dance rooms, women factory workers, tourists, and theater managers featured on the screen for the first time. New situations also appeared, such as a family from Tijuana going to a San Ysidro laundromat; tourists using tourist spaces; genealogic trees and experiences of the border passage; the consumption and life style of the "other side"; local children's enthusiasm for Californian amusement parks; social life on the *calafias* (buses); domestic and private spaces of Tijuana's houses; swap meets,[13] thrift stores, and recycling economy.

Video artists not only sought to represent daily life on the border but also its condition as a transnational space, a place of encounter and divergence. They insisted on addressing intersections, mixtures, contrasts, interaction, and exchange. They addressed the issue of violence, going beyond simple physical definitions to uncover its social manifestations. They dealt with these issues without resorting to conventional moral discourses or proven formulas. As such, these videomakers[14] have been recovering their city, and in doing so have discovered new perspectives. In their experimental documentaries, urban spaces are used as an entrance or an exit to products, people, ideas, culture, art, and technology. As a fixed rupture, the border facilitates mixing, simultaneously permitting separation and recognition of what belongs.

The formation of production groups for scholarly enterprises was another important development that facilitated the growth of independent production. The first in Tijuana was "*Lente sucio*" ("Dirty Lens") formed by alumni and professors of UABC's communication major. The purpose of the group was to serve as a support network, enabling collective production of its members' projects, using members' own equipment and financial resources. In 1994, at the same university, the group "Bola 8" (8 Ball) was formed to encourage widespread participation in the production of independent films. It sought to stimulate production exploring Tijuana's issues from a variety of perspectives, in unrestricted formats:

> The super 8 cameras that we worked with were our own property; we bought them used at swap meets. Héctor had two. We got old cartridges, and with those resources, and the support of the rest of our colleagues and our families, we produced films.[15]

Two events played pioneering roles in the development of independent film and video production in Tijuana, opening important doors that would facilitate the future work of other artists in the city. Fran Ilich, who was linked to cyber culture and electronic music, and who made his debut in 1992 with the video *Arruinado en un día* (*Ruined in One Day*), created new spaces for exhibition of his art in cafés, bars, streets, or institutions. Alongside this work was the production of the film *Todos los viernes son santos* (*All Fridays Are Sacred*, 1966) by Héctor Villanueva. Villanueva invited significant local involvement in the film's production. Through this film and his work as the television workshop coordinator at the Humanities School of the UABC (Tijuana), he succeeded in stimulating local interest in production, and inspired a whole generation of new video artists. Independent production blossomed in Tijuana after 1996,[16] due to the formation of collective groups, the development of cinema technology, and a significant decrease in production and postproduction equipment costs. Further impetus came from the establishment of certain spaces in the city that could be used to exhibit the films, secured by the hard work of the artists themselves. Present-day Tijuana is witnessing an effervescence of independent film production, the destruction of conventional limits of the media, and a new freedom of artistic expression.

Todos los viernes son santos (All Fridays Are Sacred)

Todos los viernes son santos is a video made in documentary format for television, set in Torrecillas, a fictional city in Baja California that resembles Tijuana. There, ever since the celebration of Sacred Fridays in 1991, an assassination has occurred every Friday. The movie features a detective who, obsessed with the case, kills a person every Friday in the hope that he may eventually eliminate the killer.

Urban border logic, or more accurately, the illogicality, chaos, and absurdity of a border city is revealed in this film. It presents interviews, dramatizations, and diagrams that seek to explain the events, and the psychology of the story's characters. It portrays serious reporters who strive for objectivity, but who descend into sensationalism. Japanese factory managers exploit the city's circumstances to increase their profits; boosters take advantage of the situation to encourage tourism with the campaign slogan, "the only city with a fatal attraction." Residents live in fear of being assassinated, while police officers develop strategies to ensure the city's security. Tourists keep coming to Torrecillas in search of the thrill of cheating death by drinking in the city bars on Fridays. When news of a killing circulates, they, along with the city's remaining residents, celebrate their status as Torrecilla's survivors.

Todos los viernes son santos deploys a metadiscourse—television language—that speaks to the media's power and influence. It provides an astute social critique, demonstrating that communication technology can capture our minds and structure our thoughts. The video uses dark humor to explore the complex realities of the border. Made with virtually no economic support, it had a huge impact on the artistic community of Tijuana. It was shown in many local cultural and educational theaters in the city. It was even recognized in the Video Biennial of Mexico City. Many youngsters, through their participation in the project, were convinced that they too could make films.[17]

"Bola 8" and the Multimedia Artist Generation

Bola 8 is a good example of what a group of young artists committed to the visual image can do with few economic resources, some access to technology, team work, and a lot of imagination and creativity. The border dynamic is embedded in their work, and in the group members' lives. Group members are for the most part bilingual and bicultural, and operate in cultural circuits on both sides of the border. According to Salvador V. Ricalde:

> The region's filmmakers have a concern for the border, as a theme, but also as a resource for visual creation. On many occasions we have tended to look toward the north and not to the south, sometimes because the north is the only place we can exhibit our work. Several Tijuana artists have been trained over there. We

Figure 6.6   Image of *Salon de baile La Estrella.*

have networks with students and artists from "*el otro lado.*" We present our material in local theatres and university festivals, as well as in galleries and museums. It is evident that the local theatres are bigger in San Diego, Los Angeles and San Francisco than in Tijuana or Mexicali.[18]

Today's younger generation has been raised with electronics and digital manipulations of reality.[19] Tijuana, with its access to cutting-edge technologies and expertise in handling and appropriating new technologies, has opened many doors to creativity and expression. The Internet has proved an invaluable resource, keeping artists abreast of technological developments, enabling them to promote and expand their work, and putting them in contact with others. *Glicerina* ("Glicerine"), coordinated by Antonio Arango, was the first Mexican electronic video magazine, and has been an important vehicle for the dissemination of Bola 8's work.

Bola 8 members use their cameras as their primary tools, alongside their own computers and editing programs. They are transmedia and transnational artists. According to Octavio Castellanos:

I think that photography is the sister of cinema, and that cinema has a very extensive relationship with the video image, and at the same time the moving image requires sound—all of them are part of the image universe.[20]

Although their work as visual artists is primarily concentrated in short experimental pieces in video and films, a majority of them have also experimented in other media, such as photography, design, video installation, and video jockey ("V.J.") image manipulation. It is this latter medium that has presented the greatest opportunities for production and exhibition.

Disneylandia pa' mi (Disneyland for Me)

Universities and academic institutions in the United States have provided another important working space for Tijuana's independent filmmakers. Work produced in such cross-border enterprises include *Disneylandia pa'mi* (Disneyland for Me, 1999), *Doomsday* (1999), and *Baby Frost* (2000) by Giancarlo Ruíz. In *Doomsday,* Giancarlo faces himself and his camera when he finally decides that he wants to be a filmmaker. Appearing both in front of and behind the camera, he shows some of the spaces of Playas de Tijuana, portraying the concerns of a youngster who wants to be an artist. *Baby Frost* is set in the interior of a small government-owned house in Tijuana, where the presentation of a childless couple is used to explore relationships and gender roles. A woman is shown tied to her domestic routine, while the man works outside the home. They have a small dog and a mouse, which they treat as their child. One day the mouse disappears (apparently eaten by the dog), and the woman is consumed by despair because she no longer has anyone to take care of, and has failed as a mother. The man then buys a frozen child, which he puts into a microwave oven—a place where the child can develop and grow. A labor-saving appliance becomes a source of emotional and family stability, a substitute for the woman's womb.

Disneylandia pa' mi (1999) looks at the dream of visiting Disneyland from the perspective of a child. The protagonist is a boy who anxiously awaits his ninth birthday—the day his dad is to take him to Disneyland. The boy talks to the audience as if they were his imaginary friend. They keep him company from 4 o'clock in the morning, when he wakes up anxious with anticipation. We share his emotions as preparations are made for the big day. We keep him company as he crosses the city, and passes the border with its vendors, murals, and long lines. Finally, we arrive at his Disneyland—a small, 25-cent ride in the parking lot of a San Ysidro shop.

Coca-Cola en las venas (Coca-Cola in Our Veins)

Coca-Cola en las venas (1995/2000) by Ana Machado is an autoethnographic film in super-8 format inspired by, among other films, *La formula secreta o Coca-Cola en la sangre* (*The Secret Formula or Coca-Cola in Our Blood*) by Rubén Gamez. It is an examination of everyday transborder life at the time when debates about California's (antiimmigrant) Proposition 187 were raging. *Coca-cola in Our Veins* is a personal exploration of migration issues, more a visual than a discursive piece, and is concerned with the meaning of border crossing and bicultural sensibility.

Figure 6.7 From the film *Coca-Cola en las venas* by Ana Machado.

It presents an intimate portrait of Tijuana through the vision of a family photo album. Tijuana is represented as a dynamic city, illustrated by a multitude of feet walking from one place to another, with a variety of shoes denoting a diversity of cultures and social classes. Everyday rituals of border crossing are examined, such as trips to the laundromat, parks, or fast-food restaurants. These glimpses speak of the quality of life made possible by access to North American markets, and of ambitions to live the American dream. The film starts with the following lines:

> Right after I was born, the doctor asked my mother, "Mrs. Machado, would you like me to get you something to make you feel better?" And, she answered, "Yes, please. I'd like a glass of Coca-Cola."[21]

The film ends by stating: "Borders are made to be crossed." Ana Machado argues that cultural phenomena in border cities are symbolically manifested in the Coca-Cola that has been coursing through our veins for generations.[22]

Coca-Cola's symbolism alongside the economic power of the United States, as well as the influence of its advertising, led another artist from Tijuana to use it as a central element of border culture. In *Toma violencia, escucha violencia* (*Drink Violence, Hear Violence*, 1997), Octavio Castellano parodies Coca-Cola's global slogan "Drink Coca-Cola." In the first of two scenes that comprise this "advertisement," a young man wearing head-phones sits on a sofa, reading, and drinking Coca-Cola. Noises can be heard that suggest domestic violence. The camera pans the house looking for the source of the violence, but finds nothing. The bedroom is empty except for the young man happily reading and listening to the sounds of violence on his headphones.

Border Audiovisual Imagery

Some Bola 8 members, alongside their production jobs, are devoted to the organization of an important local film festival that provides a forum for the exhibition of independent productions. This festival started in 1997, and since 1999 has also been known as the *Imaginaría Audiovisual de la Frontera* (Border Audiovisual Imagery), or IAF. The festival has attracted recognition and audiences because of its ability to bring together work by both Mexican and foreign independent artists. It is a multidisciplinary effort that facili-tates art exhibitions, conferences, courses, and workshops, as well as experi-mental film projections with electronic musical events.[23]

The festival has, through the reappropriation of urban spaces, signifi-cantly contributed to the creation of alternative spaces and situations for in-dependent film exhibition. At the 2001 IAF, independent productions were shown in such spaces as Tijuana's Brewery, the Latin Cinema (an old theater that until a couple of years ago showed only pornographic films), the House of Culture, the parking lot of UABC, the Electronic Inn Don Loope, and "The Chicken Bar" in northern Tijuana.

Past Show Rooms, Future Projections:
Recovery of the City's Cinematographic Spaces

Past show rooms, future projections, by Julio Orozco, is an image production project concerned with forms of border representation, and with the overall recovery of the city's abandoned public spaces. Orozco began his work as a photo-journalist for a local newspaper, documenting the transformation and closures of big movie theaters. This grew into a huge collection of pho-tographs of the northern border cinemas of Mexico (especially those of Ti-juana), and of important events such as the burning of the Bujazán cinema, the transformation of Cinema 70 to a church, and the closure of many im-portant theaters in the city's downtown. His collection also features a variety of cinematographic exhibitions in the city, such as the presentation of films in prisons, cinema clubs, and elementary schools. Each picture tells the story of a medium (cinema) that appears to be losing ground in the city, provok-ing the recovery of the histories attached to each movie theater.

Orozco reclaims the language and format of the Mexican cinemato-graphic billboard, and has developed ten stories using his picture archive to create new narratives. These imaginary movie billboards come alive in the minds of those who read them. They have been exhibited in Paris, Mexico City, and Tijuana. These billboards are not exhibited in galleries or museums, but on walls, accompanied by commentary.

The imaginary movies narrated by Orozco's billboards employ meta-narratives, appropriations of the border cinema's style. They represent a deconstruction of Mexican cinema by disorganizing a narrative in order to reorganize it through the same media and style in which conventional stories are told.

The billboard for *El monumento (The Monument)*, for instance, is made from an image of the workers who demolished Tijuana's Roble Cinema, and tells the following story:

> On the verge of the demolition of the cinema, a group of Islamic workmen block the entrance to machines. A message from God had appeared on the last standing wall, which they call The Monument. Based on a true story.[24]

On the billboard of the ficticious film *Murió Calcinado (He Burned to Death)*, which uses an image of the remains of the projection room of Tijuana's Bujazán Cinema after the fire in 1994, the reader is asked the following question:

> Did the industry orchestrate a massive short circuit? Study and diagnosis of the economic forces that affect cinematographic exhibition.[25]

Murió Calcinado (He Burned to Death) "is the story of a projector that dies of desire because it is very old and because it has been showing pornographic films."[26] The film was projected onto the exterior of the planetary cinema of the Tijuana Cultural Center (CECUT), better known as "*la bola*" (the ball)—the site of many other artistic interventions (as discussed in Chapters 5 and 7 of this book). According to Orozco, the image projected onto the ball "is filled with significance, as it represents the essence and title of this project, *Past show rooms, future projections*, with two projection systems appearing from two different time periods." The burning projector seen in the film is the oldest still in operation at the Real Cinema of Tijuana, and we see it projecting onto the surface of the CECUT globe, which houses one of the most advanced projection systems available, the OMNIMAX system. *Murió Calcinado* was the first moving image projected onto this enormous building.[27]

Another billboard that is part of the Orozco series is *Las . . . alas quemadas (The . . . Burnt Wings)*, which uses an image from the burnt ruins of the Bujazán Cinema, questioning the cultural and artistic cost of losing exhibition spaces. The billboard *AHU! Almacén de Historias Universales (OUCH! Warehouse of Universal Stories)* narrates a story about a letter's rebellion against all kinds of advertising signs and publications. Four letters were published in the general information section of the *Frontera* newspaper in the days before the billboard's exhibition. One of these letter reads as follows:

> Letters from all over the city continue deserting. . . . They abandon their places in neon signs and diaries. Their march will not stop until they get to the old film house that appears to have become their billboard, . . .

The last letter stated that the photographer Julio Orozco, in spite of the attack by the letters, had returned to his neighborhood and found a videotape that contained part of the letters' manifesto, and that he was considering releasing it to the general public. Orozco added a further level of sophistication to his work by incorporating videomaking and multimedia exhibitions in five of his stories.

Following the same formula, the billboard and the clips *Bombazo taquillero (Box Office Explosion)* and *El monumento (The Monument)* were shown at the Festival of Cinema in Mexico City, in October 2000, with the support of four articles in *La Jornada.*[28] In March 2001, all the billboards were exhibited at a spectacular event in the ruined Cinema Bujazán of Tijuana. The cinema consists of a well-maintained lobby in which billboards were displayed and in which food and drink were available. In the box office, the clip *Bombazo taquillero* was shown repeatedly. On the huge wall of the end of the show room, where there had previously been a big screen topped by a ceiling, *El monumento* was projected. This made for an interesting cinematic experience. The audience had a sky filled with stars for a ceiling, and watched a film that told the story of a cinema's demolition. The video *Murió Calcinado* was shown in the abandoned projecting room. Spectators lived the experience of the four walls that had formed part of cinematographic life for generations of Tijuana's residents.

The appropriation, reactivation, and redefinition of significant abandoned places in the city, and of elements of popular and cinematographic culture, have defined Orozco's work. He has produced other important multimedia projects and video installations, including *La virgen llorona (The Crying Virgin,* 1997). After circulating a rumor about an apparition of the Virgin at a Tijuana cinema, he succeeded in making her appear using a lamp and a copper silhouette.

The Visual Recovery of the City

A fascinating musical, audiovisual, artistic, and cultural movement called Nortec has recently emerged in Tijuana. Nortec's music is characterized by its mixing of electronic music with rhythms from northern Mexico. Nortec has also innovatively mixed the city's sounds and cultural environment. Performers present their music at parties in large abandoned settings, appropriating urban spaces. Young people participate by dancing and interacting

Figure 6.8 NORTEC Live Poster.

with music, performances, lights, dance, ecstasy, and beer. From its inception, Nortec has incorporated a graphic component. Its artists create their
own album covers, t-shirts, tickets, flyers, posters, and internet sites that
reinvent popular country style through a mix of traditional and modern.

Soon after Nortec was founded, five filmmakers joined as video jockeys
(V.J.s) to add digital images to the musical mixes. Calling themselves the
"Nortec Visual Collective," and using the latest technology, V.J.s mixed live

Figure 6.9 NORTEC Visual Collective. (By Adriana Trujillo.)

images in manipulated segments or *loops*, creating new possibilities for artistic expression:

> We view this new interpretation as a cultural phenomenon. We regain the image of popular culture . . . to create something new. . . . All this is connected with a cultural globalization. The border has given us the images, the cultural baggage but also the capacity to buy the equipment, to have access to the technology that in other parts of the world is inaccessible. The border gives us themes, marks us with style as well as the access to other cultures, to cultural consumption and to technology. In general we are bicultural and bilingual, we know how to move on both sides, and we grew up going to concerts and movies in the "other side."[29]

By mixing images, V.J.s represent the culture enveloping Nortec. Images representing the musical culture of northern Mexico are displayed, including the guitar, accordion, and the *tololoche* (a large guitar-like instrument). Cultural objects connected to country/band music are also used: the *sombrero* (hat), boots, sideburns, a belt's big buckle, a necklace or gold medal, and the Virgin of Guadalupe. Images of the city's cultural spaces also feature: bars and their musicians, dancing salons, streets, parks, taverns, bus stops, and grocery stores.

> Thanks to our jobs, and our own independent artistic projects, we've been able to accumulate images of the city and its social life. And we use those images in events with Nortec. . . . Everything we do in digital manipulation is self-taught.[30]

Today, Nortec's V.J.s seek out places of intense movement and interaction, such as crowded railway crossings and public transportation. They have developed what they call "Anthropological Tours," where the goal is not only to capture images, but also to recognize and understand their own agency in the situations they encounter:

> We seek those elements that constitute us, that give us character. . . . We don't just want to be "outsiders," though we are conscious that our work is reality interpretation. . . . It gives us great pleasure to make fiction out of images that we've captured in the city. . . . Once we make the mix and project it, our interpretation leaves, disappears, is ephemeral. It remains in memories, or in the multiple readings from the public's part. Even if it's repeated and it's once again utilized as an image or a sequence, it is never the same.[31]

The goal of "Nortec-city," a Nortec celebration held in a semiabandoned setting, was to show everyday features of Tijuana that are usually ignored: people moving around the city, from their work to their house, and from their house to their work:

> We seek to show a fragment of the city that isn't commonly seen by the middle- and upper-class young people who go to a party. We show the culture and the music of the north, but with new elements as strategies to make the invisible world of this same city visible. To see what is probably in your daily routes and routines, but that you don't see anymore, things we deliberately or unintentionally forget. . . . Our images in a sort of way are the substitute to the absent lyrics of the music of Nortec.[32]

Another objective of Nortec's parties was to recover the city by using spaces that had been forgotten, such as buildings that form a substantial part of the urban and symbolic interior of Tijuana, or buildings located on Revolution Avenue that have been closed for years, as well as reuse material and elements that characterize the city.

At a party called "*Maquiladora de Sueño*" (Dream Factory), many visual artists sought to make visible another aspect of urban reality that is commonly overlooked: the factories and their workers, the production process, and the enormous plants located throughout the city. The repetitive work rhythms—represented by the loops of hand, arm, and feet movements of workers—alongside the musical rhythms of Nortec, produced images of young women who are frequently excluded from the city's representations.

Conclusion

Border cinema and independent video are two forms of expressions that are *very* different, in terms of format and production formula, and of the relationships they establish with the issues and characters they represent. In border cinema, topics and spaces tend to be limited by use of formulas and stereotypes. Border cinema tends to standardize forms of representation, thus avoiding the complex cultural, social, and political realities of the border region. To border cinema's producers, the border amounts to nothing more than a marketing device. Their films are a response to commercial interests. Their productions have few if any links to the daily experiences and dynamics of the border. This nonemotional, nonexperiential characteristic has proved the greatest obstacle to border cinema's creative development. On the other hand, the recent birth of independent video and cinema, characterized by creativity and deconstruction, is much more than a commercial product. Its projects stem from resistance to regulations and stereotypical molds, and strive to show everyday life at the border. It helps us understand the border on both intellectual and existential levels. Every independent production requires both artist and audience to explore the border's social and cultural environment.

Freedom of form and subject matter enable independent video and cinema to enrich cultural production by capturing the diversity of border realities. Independent artists' contributions go beyond the field of artistic production and aesthetics to include the appropriation of urban spaces. Artists have reclaimed old spaces and created alternative spaces for their exhibitions. They are creating new perspectives on their city that contrast with weaker, traditional cinematic formulas. Border cinema and independent film confront contrasting forms of border representation and offer different symbolic versions of the relationship between the object (the border and its cultural products) and the subject, whose interpretations are indicative of, and active in, producing social consciousness.

A new generation of filmmakers from Tijuana is engaged in a project of urban reclamation, searching for new ways of representing "the border" as something personal, and redefining this space through the involvement of filmmakers themselves. This generation seeks to represent the border in a way that is entirely different from that of commercial cinema. Their representations reveal the transnational character of their lives. Their familiarity with multimedia has swept aside conventional barriers. These artists do not require great resources to imagine, create, or produce their works. They have revived abandoned urban spaces for the benefit of the broader community. They have mined their own graphic memories to create new border narratives. They have used all the images at their disposal in their visual productions, and have developed new perspectives on the border's people and dynamics. Their lives are a good example of what Canclini has defined as a hybrid cultural experience, characteristic of this zone of cultural convergence and divergence. They are a generation of young artists absorbing influences from both sides of the border without losing sight of their most profound identity: their Tijuana-border experience, their local character, their place-specificity. They are global artists who fearlessly cross cultural and mass-media borders. They are constantly reinventing and rediscovering themselves. They possess enormous potential and fear neither assimilation nor experimentation.

Notes

1. S. Moscovici, "On Social Representation," in J.P. Forgas (Comp.), *Social Recognition. Perspectives in Everyday Life* (London: Academic Press. 1981), and S. Moscovici, "The Phenomenon of Social Representations," in R.M. Farr and S. Moscovici (eds.), *Social Representations* (Cambridge: Cambridge University Press, 1984).
2. S. Moscovici, *Social Recognition. Perspectives in Every Day Life* cited in José Luis Alvarado. "Social Representations," in the *Critical Dictionary of Social Science* (www.ucm.es/info/eurotheo/d-alvaro1.htm), 1.
3. They can be found in just one border film that mixes such genres as police action, drug dealer-bashing, and the sexy-comedy with a little melodrama.
4. Rosa Linda Fregoso, *The Bronze Screen. Chicana and Chicano Film Culture* (Minneapolis: University of Minnesota Press, 1995).
5. See Emilio García Riera, *Documental History of Mexican Cinema, Vol. 5* (Mexico: SEP, 1985).
6. Carlos E. Cortés, "Like Watching the Neighbor: The Book of Hollywood Text about Mexico," in *Images of Mexico* (Mexico: Base of Economic Culture, Future Commission over United States-Mexico relations, 1985), 122.
7. Interview with Mr. Juan J. Torres owner of the Bay Theatre in National City, CA, July 1989.
8. P. Sorlin, *Cinema Sociology. The Inauguration for Tomorrow's History* (Mexico: Base of Economic Culture, 1985).
9. Gabriel Careaga, *Cinema Stars. The XXth Century Myths.* (Mexico: Oceanic, 1984), 9.
10. I understand independent film as an alternative form of visual expression, produced without regulation and with limited economic resources, and unrestrained in terms of themes, aesthetics, and format.
11. At the Autonomous University of Baja California (UABC) and the Iberian-American University.
12. These video artists are focused primarily in the Tijuana–San Diego area.
13. These are ephemeral weekend supermarkets where all sorts of new and used articles are found. The practice of buying and selling at such places has constituted a whole new leisure activity concept for families in Tijuana, San Diego, and Los Angeles.
14. The great majority of the artists work in video because it is cheaper and more accessible.
15. Interview with Octavio Castellanos, Tijuana, September 2001.
16. Adriana Trujillo Méndez, "The Cinema and Independent Film in Tijuana from 1996 to 2000" (Tijuana: Thesis for Major, UABC, 2001), i.
17. For more information about the development and growth of cinema and independent film in Tijuana, I recommend the work of Adriana Trujillo Méndez, "The Cinema and Independent Film in Tijuana from 1996 to 2000."
18. Interview with Salvador V. Ricalde, Tijuana, October 2001.
19. Interview with Octavio Castellanos, Tijuana, September 2001.
20. Ibid.
21. Opening narrative in *Coca-Cola in Our Veins*.
22. Interview with Ana Machado, September 2001.
23. Adriana Trujillo Méndez, "The Cinema and Independent Film in Tijuana from 1996 to 2000."
24. From poster advertising *The Monument*.
25. From poster advertising *He Burned to Death*.
26. Interview with Julio Orozco, September 2001.
27. Ibid.
28. A Mexico City Daily Newspaper.
29. Interview with Sergio Brown, Tijuana, September 2001.
30. Ibid.
31. Ibid.
32. Ibid.

PART **III**

Regional Hybridities

7
"Where Am I at Home?"
The Interplay of National, Local, and Imaginative Space

RICHARD CÁNDIDA SMITH

Daniel Joseph Martínez is an American artist. Born in 1957 in Lennox, California, a multiracial, working-class town in Los Angeles County, his U.S. citizenship legally establishes him as an American. That his first language is English and that his family has lived in the United States for several generations should establish him culturally as an American as well. The unequal, colonized status of peoples of color within the United States, however, throws his cultural identification into question, following an old American custom of distinguishing "nationality" from citizenship.

Martínez is often described and discussed as a Chicano artist. He was a member of the Asco collective in East Los Angeles in the 1980s, which beyond his ethnicity makes him an important contributing figure to a new movement in American art history. However, Martínez largely avoids ethnic markers within his work identifying his own personal origins. He has highlighted questions of ethnic self-identification in photographs he has taken of adolescents, as well as in conceptual projects as at the 1993 Biennial at the Whitney Museum of Art, when he handed out admissions buttons to patrons that declared, "I can't imagine ever wanting to be white." His care for revealing how ethnic and racial classifications shape institutional spaces such as schools or museums speaks to a central issue of U.S. politics at the end of the twentieth century. That alone might affirm that cultural and political identity are not easily cut asunder.

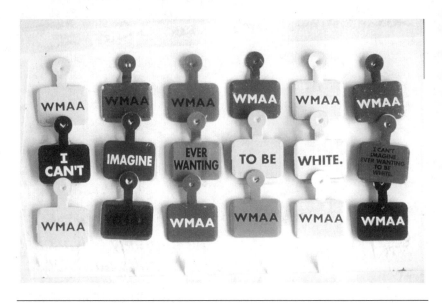

Figure 7.1   Daniel Joseph Martínez, *Museum Tags*, Second Movement, Aria Da Capo (Action with Hired Audience Members). Whitney Museum of American Art, 1993 Whitney Biennial, New York, Performance. Transposition/replacement of Whitney Museum of American Art (WMMA) for "I Can't Imagine Ever Wanting to be White." (Photograph courtesy of the artist.)

Ramón Tamayo, born in Ensenada, Baja California, in 1958, is by citizenship and culture a Mexican artist. He lives and works today in Mexicali, where he has a position at the Universidad Autónoma de Baja California. His family has lived in his home state for generations, and an important theme within his work has been connection to and responsibility for place. Tamayo is a writer, sculptor, theater director, actor, and performance artist who takes seriously the charge to think globally and act locally. Tamayo's pieces reconstruct an often ignored history of northwest Mexico and the U.S. southwest, a region in which Native Americans, Mexicans, Anglo-Americans, and many other nationalities have been in daily contact for more than 200 years.

Both Martínez and Tamayo are "Latino" artists, in this case a questionable category because it implies that people with Spanish surnames or Latin American heritage share a common culture defined through a colonial relationship to the United States. They are both "California" artists, immersed in the life of their native states. Art historians writing on California art, however, have so far referred only to work produced within the part of California annexed to the United States in 1848. Art from the rest of California has remained Mexican, Latin American, or perhaps most trivializing of all, "border" art.

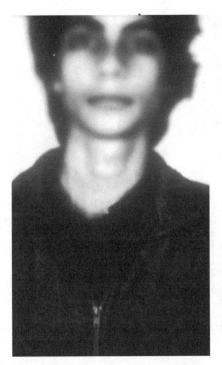

Figures 7.2 and 7.3 Daniel Joseph Martínez, *Kill Your Dogs and Cats.*
Mexican Museum, San Francisco, multimedia installation, 1994–1995. These
photographs are digitally reconstructed photographs of alleged terrorists. The
images were originally found via the internet in buried FBI files that were top
secret. The images were then morphed with images of people who looked
similar to the original images. These are both a constructed fiction and real
photographs at the same time. A simultaneous collision of realities and the
unseen. (Photographs courtesy of the artist.)

Categories of nation, region, and ethnicity are ostensibly external to the
formal features of the work that artists produce. Nonetheless, a belief in
their centrality has been important to the development of art history. They
reflect a nineteenth-century nation-building ideal that culture, language,
history, citizenship, and economic relations should form an organic unity.
Academic art history emerged as nation-states asserted their sovereignty
over territories and populations, and the discipline has typically organized
courses around efforts to define the characteristics over time of each nation's cultural production. A national history organized around a sequence
of writers, painters, and composers arose to complement a political history
centered on kings, generals, presidents, and statesmen. Concern for the
defining features of artwork produced within a region, race, or ethnicity is a
variation on the nation-building theme. In this case, the idea that nations

Figure 7.4 Ramón Tamayo (right) in *De Sabaida*, produced by Mexicali a Secas, 1998. (Photograph courtesy of Odette Barajas.)

developed around shared cultures is revealed to be an illusion, but the quest for an organic social experience that is the source of authentic art survives.

The modern arts movements that emerged at the end of the nineteenth century more typically stressed the universal, transnational aspects of creative process. The truth that art revealed about the human condition was valid everywhere. Art helped people translate across the dizzying variety of actual custom and convention to find what they shared as human beings. This faith has been a defining feature of elite art movements since at least the 1870s, even as it has been extensively criticized. It persists because it provides an effective rationale for the autonomy of art as a form of knowledge. The idea has permeated popular culture as well. It forms, for example, the active organizing principle of the vastly popular if sentimental photography exhibit of 1955, *The Family of Man*, reputed to be the most widely seen art exhibit ever mounted and toured. *The Family of Man* contributes an intriguing if cautionary variation to conceptions of hybridity: the more people seem to appear different, the more we strive to blend them into conceptually defined connections.[1]

As active professionals, both Daniel Joseph Martínez and Ramón Tamayo spend much of their time outside their respective national homes, touring primarily in Europe and Latin America, as well as locations in Africa and

Asia that are increasingly important places for showing work. Invitations from foreign arts and educational institutions are markers in the struggle to achieve recognition as an artist of stature within one's own country of citizenship. International connections help promote deeper consideration of an artist's work. That Martínez's work has found an enthusiastic response in Northern Ireland suggests how effectively he has pondered the violent legacy of conquest and colonialism.

International connections also provide alternative sources of funding that offer experimental artists a measure of independence from national cultural priorities. This is not in any way a recent phenomenon. Positive American and British reception of Mallarmé in the 1880s provoked French critics to reconsider their more negative evaluation of his poetry. During the same period, Americans and other foreigners were more receptive to impressionism and postimpressionism and provided the markets needed to sustain avant-garde painting in France. The constant international traffic of cultural work supports a continuing value that art unites what borders and politics keep apart and thus must reveal a deeper, more persistent layer of reality than the ephemeral world of current affairs.[2]

Because modern arts institutions have long been organized around both national and international axes, the proposition that borders are unique places promoting the formation of hybrid cultures must be modified when applied to the activities of galleries, museums, and other formal cultural organizations. Whether they are located physically on a national frontier or not, arts institutions seek international exhibitions because they serve the broader educational functions of galleries, museums, and schools defined on a national level. Such programs create images of distinct national cultures as apparent facts, chart an imaginary topography of universal similarities and historical differences, and define a place for the homeland within an imaginary global culture. Were the border between the United States and Mexico to be demilitarized and opened to the same degree as the U.S.– Canadian border already is or if even more radical reform were to result in elimination of border crossings and controls, U.S. and Mexican educational and cultural institutions would still have distinct histories, organizational structures, funding sources, and priorities for what they do. They would continue to serve different conceptions of nation and art, even as they engaged in collaborations.

This essay explores the practical implications of artists working within both a national and an international framework by focusing on what it means to state that Daniel Joseph Martínez is an American artist and Ramón Tamayo is a Mexican artist. I focus on the careers of Martínez and Tamayo because they are working artists whose personal backgrounds share a few broad similarities. Their work, however, is very different and not directly comparable either formally or intentionally. The stories they told struck me as relating to a narrative with a long and respected tradition: poor boy with exceptional talent makes good due to perseverance and an opportunity for education. It is a story line that could apply to Caravaggio as well as Jackson Pollock, to Raymond Williams or Jack Kerouac as well as Henry Louis Gates, Jr., or Richard Rodríguez. Roland Barthes spoke of such narrative mythologies as enabling a history of desire and subjectivity.[3] Recurrent life-story patterns suggest what the members of societies have been trained to want to see happen and thus make sure do happen through a variety of institutional mechanisms.

By focusing on homologous narrative motifs as expressed by two artists from adjacent nations, I hope to clarify processes by which many contemporary artists achieve professional status and recognition within specific national contexts that are also always internationalized. How artists like Martínez and Tamayo resolve the sometimes conflicting demands of national, local, and professional identities will contribute to establishing the parameters for a "postborder" culture still in emergence, as working artists respond to the pressures of the time by participating in the imagination of an expanding, inclusive world. Their work, as that of many artists, aims to create a new imaginary, in Martínez's words, "to temporarily transform the environment and alter perceptions."[4]

National Space: Education and Formation of Professional Artists

Lennox has long been a tough area that outsiders avoid. It is a poor town, and its streets are controlled by gangs. When Martínez grew up there, whites, Mexicans, and blacks lived close together but were constantly fighting. As a child of slight physique, Martínez was an easy victim, preyed on by bullies from all three groups. He could be beat up because his skin was too light or because it was not light enough, because he did not speak Spanish or because he was assumed to be Spanish-speaking. Drawing and painting provided an activity that kept him away from the everyday violence of his hometown, while allowing him to develop a sense of personal identity as a sort of neighborhood "Rembrandt." His father worked as a service employee in the nearby aerospace industry, where he wound up deeply embittered by the racism he faced every day at work. Martínez remembers his father as a brilliant problem solver who could fix anything with his hands, but his contributions to the Apollo space program could not be recognized, not even minimally, because of class and race biases. Martínez credits his long-standing interest in exploring the applicability of laser, video, and special effects technology to the example his father provided, though he also is clear that their personal relation was often turbulent.[5]

Martínez was a poor student in high school, but the quality of his art portfolio gained him a scholarship in 1975 to the California Institute for the

Arts. He moved directly from the barrio to one of the most prestigious art schools in the nation. Working, however uneasily, with John Baldessari, Michael Asher, and Jonathan Borofsky, he found himself in the center of conceptual art as the new movement burst upon the national art scene. Eager to get away from a privileged environment that had little understanding or apparent interest for who he was or where he came from, he graduated a year ahead of schedule in 1979. He left with a deep knowledge of and taste for European avant-garde traditions, where starting with Josef Beuys but moving back in time to the surrealists and their nineteenth-century predecessors, Martínez found inspiration for his own projects.

Like many other young men and women in the late 1970s, he moved to downtown Los Angeles, where abandoned warehouses and factories were being converted into loft space. He was immediately across the river from East Los Angeles, ground zero of the Chicano liberation movement. Rather than continue to try to function in a culture dominated by young white bohemians, he searched out other artists of Mexican descent. He became friends with Harry J. Gamboa, Jr., the founder of Asco, a Chicano guerrilla art group. Between approximately 1979 and 1985, Martínez was an active member, working on street projects that challenged the racism of the Los Angeles art scene with sophisticated humor. They deployed postmodern and conceptual art practices against museums, schools, and arts groups that without any hint of shame or self-examination set standards for excellence automatically excluding the majority of the region's population. Asco raised important questions about access to resources and exhibitions in a provocative manner that many in the L.A. arts scene found "interesting." Asco contributed to the consolidation of a renewed avant-garde art scene as extension of a new turbulent, multicultural Los Angeles. Attention, however, did not mean equal patronage, only occasional publicity.[6]

Martínez's work in the 1980s was divided between his participation in Asco and a more personal interest in exploring the possibilities for new technology. The 1984 Olympics Arts Festival commissioned Martínez to create a work for the art and technology exhibition. He conceived and produced *The Peoples of Los Angeles*, a nine-part film and holographic sound installation. After the Asco collective broke up in the middle 1980s, Martínez explored the possibilities of video art as a form of postmodern street theater. He rigged slow-scan video equipment to his body, which allowed him to record or broadcast events he witnessed. In 1990, the Los Angeles Arts Festival commissioned an opera, *Ignore the Dents*, which was performed at the Million Dollar Theater in downtown Los Angeles.

By 1990, Martínez had landed a tenure-line position in the art department at the University of California, Irvine, a program with a reputation for a strongly conceptual and theoretical approach to art. Teaching provides him with basic sustenance and contact with successive groups of students, many of whom have come to form what he calls his "family," the group of like-minded artists who provide emotional and practical support for his many projects. He has had a very busy career since joining the faculty at Irvine. Every year, he has produced at least one major show or project that has garnered him a considerable international reputation. Despite critical success, however, no gallery offered to represent him and his work, a situation that changed only in 1998 when Christian Haye, owner of The Project, a gallery in Harlem, picked him up.

Ramón Tamayo grew up near the beaches of Ensenada. His father was a trucker who delivered goods in Mexico and the western United States, much like Tamayo's grandfather before him had transported goods throughout the region on mule pack. Like Martínez, Tamayo grew up in a place in which there was extensive interaction between different racial and ethnic groups. But as a tourist center, Ensenada was more fun-oriented and less strife-ridden than Lennox. Tamayo grew up playing on the beach with foreign tourists, learning to surf alongside them, and later drinking with them in the local bars. There were also fights, but hostility was only one element in a broad gamut of relations. Most of the tourists in Ensenada were from the United States, but there were also many visitors from Europe and Japan.[7]

Tamayo was a good student in school, and his teachers worked to develop his intellectual curiosity. On graduating high school, he left Ensenada to enroll at the Universidad Autónoma de Baja California, located a hundred miles east in Mexicali. Like Martínez, he was the first person ever in his family to attend college. He entered as a sociology major, and he earned his degree in that subject. While at school, childhood interests in theater and puppetry blossomed into a passion for theater and the visual arts. He participated in arts groups in the Mexicali area. For fifteen years, he worked with Mexicali a Secas, an experimental theater group with a strong political bent. His training in theater consisted primarily of workshops he took in Guanajuato with Sigfrido Aguilar Trinidad, now on the faculty of the University of California, Santa Barbara.

Another important personal influence was the Mexicali painter, Carlos Coronado, whose murals adorn the university, the public library, as well as hotels and commercial buildings throughout the city. From Coronado, Tamayo gained confidence that one could survive as a creative person in a provincial town. For the past ten years, Tamayo has been employed full-time to teach both art and theater at the university, while he has developed projects that have gained him a measure of recognition both in Mexico and abroad.

Like Martínez, Tamayo speaks of his parents as problem solvers, able to use their hands to get almost anything done they could imagine.[8] This sense of a family inheritance provides a way for both Tamayo and Martínez as products of working families with little regular exposure to elite culture to negotiate the relation of their professional art activity to their family background. A motif of native family skill facilitates a refusal on the part of both Martínez and Tamayo to see themselves as having been rescued from under-privileged backgrounds. Their careers remain, at least affectively and to the degree possible practically, in connection with the communities from which they came. They were not simply talented scholarship boys plucked from unfortunate circumstances.[9] Their origins have been as important to the successes they have achieved as the professional training their respective societies provided.

That claim notwithstanding, the presence of well-developed educational infrastructures marked the historical moment of their entrance into professional careers. That was not accidental, as it developed as a result of policy decisions and significant investments in both Mexico and the United States accumulating over decades. The careers of Tamayo and Martínez have taken the form they did because modern democratic societies have made education a priority and over the long term have expanded access to schools and increased the length of time students spend acquiring advanced skills.

In Mexico, with its much more limited fiscal resources, government acts directly and nearly exclusively to ensure educational structures that can nurture the intellectual and creative potential of its citizenry. Tamayo is a success story and shows how well Mexico has done along these lines, but as he is well aware, there are many talented, bright men of his age for whom the system did not work. Crediting his family is not simply modesty if their guidance provides a credible explanation for why he succeeded while many others fell through the cracks.[10]

In the United States, despite immense wealth, the educational system fails many, perhaps most talented young people of color. Perhaps Martínez was successful because he is relatively light-skinned and thus was a likely candidate for assimilation as a slightly off-beat, off-color member of a white-defined middle class. Perhaps he survived because he was not as tough as his schoolmates and he withdrew enough from street life that the police and penal systems failed to ensnare him before *miraculus mirabili* he could serve as a poster boy for the vaunted saga of American "opportunity." In his case the starved resources of inner-city schools were more than compensated for by landing in a well-funded private school whose students largely though not exclusively came from wealthy backgrounds.

Persistent structures of poverty governing the lives of people of color in both Californias short-circuit stated goals of using schools to nurture talent, but in the cases of Tamayo and Martínez, the educational systems functioned well enough that they did leap across barriers of class and space to become professional artists. In both their situations, the university proved to be the central, the essential institution for resocialization. In (Alta) California, much richer and with a more fully developed civil society, private schools are as important as state institutions, but in both Californias, the state has made university-level education an on-going, long-term fiscal priority. Sizable investments by the citizens of the two states enabled both Tamayo and Martínez to secure employment and pursue art careers that would be much more difficult to sustain if they had to rely on sales of their work for survival.

University-level education has become an essential underpinning for contemporary practice of the fine arts. It provides structures for recognizing young talent, while developing and testing their skills. That modern societies put such priority on developing the potential of the young provides positions for mature artists whose careers then are defined in part by service to the educational functions of the nation-state.

However, higher education in the United States and Mexico are not identical, even if externals are remarkably similar. The flagship campus of the Universidad Autónoma de Baja California at Mexicali is as attractive as that of any U.S. state university. Campus buildings and grounds appear every bit as modern, well equipped, and maintained. The library, the student union, and the campus theater provide students with the same level of amenities that students north of the border would expect. It is the internal structures that reveal different priorities and a distinct conception of the relation of the educated citizen to society at large. The Mexican nation, with an annual per capita domestic production that is only one-sixth that of the United States, has focused more sharply on a few key goals for its educational institutions.

Unlike the U.S. university with its dozens of departments, institutes, and centers, the Universidad Autónoma de Baja California, founded in 1958, has a much simpler structure. There are only a handful of faculties—the equivalent of departments in the United States—at the Mexicali campus all specializing in technical subjects: accounting and business, architecture, agriculture, education, engineering, health, law, and the human, political, and social sciences. Resources have been directed to the most pressing practical needs of the state. Graduates are given skills that will facilitate their occupying posts in the many maquiladoras that have sprung up along the border or in public agencies providing basic services to the region. Graduates needing advanced training will go to Mexico City or, even more likely, to a foreign university in the United States, Canada, or western Europe.

Education has been shaped around a strategy of building wealth in the hopes of raising the standard of living. Everything else is secondary. The narrative that the Universidad Autónoma de Baja California provides its students stresses education as a way of serving the larger community, though at times that noble goal may seem to be diminished into technocratic service to the multinational corporations that increasingly dominate Mexico's northern border communities.

As Tamayo's position at the university indicates, arts and literature are not absent from campus life, but these courses are offered as electives for personal improvement or recreational diversion. They are organized in conjunction with a variety of student clubs that provide resources for exploring theater, video, painting, photography, and music, including access to equipment most students cannot afford. Arts classes are open as well to the broader community as part of the general service the university provides to the citizens of the state, services that include regular arts festivals, concerts, and theater productions. When I visited the campus in April 2001, the university was hosting an international dance festival presenting sophisticated and intellectually challenging work. The structure of the arts on campus conveys a straightforward message that they are vital aspects of personal enrichment and intellectual development, but they are to be a private rather than a professional interest.

The U.S. university developed around a dual set of goals: providing undergraduates with a broad liberal arts education and graduate students with professional training for positions in the law, medicine, business, or education. Studio art and theater programs grew slowly until the post-World War II period when they became universal in colleges and universities. The mark of maturity for any field is the development of graduate programs that provide advanced degrees. In most cases, the holders of those degrees will find jobs teaching at another school, helping to perpetuate the field as a subject of learning and participating in the reproduction of a leadership group whose expertise rests on a theorized understanding of the field's practice.[11]

Howard Singerman's recent study of art studio training in the United States argues that the development of the professional graduate degree in most universities led to a "privileging of overarching principles over specific technical competencies—the grounding and guiding of art practice in visual fundamentals and the fashioning of individual works as experiments, researches, proofs . . . the theorization and formalization of knowledge." The relation of aesthetic process to language became so central that an object must be read rather than simply viewed. Singerman suggests that for studio art to function as an equal on campus, art could no longer be considered a vocation or calling. Art became instead a field of research, in which critical and theoretical perspectives are more important than practical skills.[12]

Criticality has become a defining feature of contemporary art as a professional endeavor in the United States. A mature culture institutes for itself a defined zone for disengagement, self-reflection, and autocritique, which can be directed against aesthetic theory, the forms that art takes, the epistemology of vision and performance, the commodification of art objects or processes, or the structures of symbolic power that are proposed for defining a social entity such as a nation. Within a professionalized art discourse, the use of aesthetic rather than social science theory to discuss political or social phenomena carries no implications about the nature of the realities that theories describe. It merely locates the discussion as taking place within an established institutional framework that has narrowed the terms of reference so that insights particular to that field can be deepened.

Differences between university structures and the place of the arts in university education reflect disparities in social resources as well as the relatively younger history of higher education in Baja California. They also express different conceptions of the relation of the individual to the nation. Mexican education stresses raising collective technical capacities, whereas U.S. education puts higher priority on individual development. The goals are not foreign to each other. Indeed, they are so easily translatable that one could easily think that the nature of educational structures reflects only financial realities rather than distinctive goals. However, the structures that universities have taken channel activity and provide guidelines for evaluating outcomes. The importance of this for everyday practice in the arts can be tested in assessing the projects that Martínez and Tamayo have developed to engage local communities, in other words, the projects they have undertaken to critique the nations that have formed them.[13]

Local Space: Engaging the Community

The first theater production of Tamayo's I saw was a rehearsal for a shadow puppet rendition of *Pinocchio*. In Tamayo's script, the wooden puppet boy has no interest in becoming a "real" little boy. He wants to be a man instead, *un hombre varón*. When the Blue Fairy refuses this wish, Pinocchio runs off to Hollywood where he can be a movie star. The play is performed by three actors for an audience of children, but the script has its messages and jokes targeted at adults as well. The form of the production rests on simplicity and accessibility of materials. The actors are students. The stage is a simple one-meter square white screen stretched across aluminum poles and backlit by a single lamp; the score is provided by a tape cassette player. The characters are represented by shadow puppets, with the actors emerging twice from behind the screen as a storyteller and as Gepetto, the toy maker who created Pinocchio. The entire production can fit in the trunk of an automobile and can be mounted in any classroom or on the street. Tamayo's students and associates bring to Mexicali a mode of performance that is the antithesis of the spectacle available in movie theaters or on television. Everything in the production derives from local resources. The props are bought at the local flea market, and they all can be hand carried by the actors.

This is theater that exists for the interstices of everyday life. Two short pieces that I saw were done in the vestibule of the UABC theater while the audience waited for the auditorium to open for the dance festival. Tamayo's rendition of Pinocchio trying to escape the world of fairy tales in order to get to Hollywood was performed to a group of elementary school children in the children's room at the Mexicali main library. He and his students performed a piece telling the story of a hunter magically transformed into a deer on the streets of Mexicali as shoppers searched for Christmas presents. The story explored the cosmogony of the Native peoples who originally lived in the Mexicali Valley, but it syncretized a local story with classic Greek myths, a combination that struck him as entirely natural, since the name California derives from a Spanish novel set in the mythic realm of Queen Calafia and her retinue of women warriors.

The danger for anyone, artist or not, who lives in a provincial environment is an assumption that there are inadequate resources for activities, which to be done well must be done elsewhere. The challenge is to escape the self-censorship that accompanies provincialization. "We do theater," Tamayo said, "but we have no theater, no lights. We accept the conditions that we have." Shadow puppet theater or *teatro de mesa* (theater performed on a table top) allows performance in a variety of limited conditions, even if there is only one person available to present a play. The "actors" for his one-performer version of Antoine de Saint-Exupéry's *The Little Prince* are Leggo-like figures and plastic toy dolls that he bought at the flea market. The performer moves the figures on top of a portable table while shifting from voice to voice. As products of commercial culture, the characters are grounded in readily recognizable cultural icons that his audiences can easily identify—in this case Merlin, a Star Trek figure, and a Ninja warrior who served as the Aviator.

In the theater of what Tamayo calls "antispectacle," storytelling is more important than technical bravura. The goal is to refocus the theater experience onto the immediate presence of other human beings and what they can suggest with vocal and movement gestures: "Every person carries everything needed for theater in and on his own person."[14] If all the resources needed for creativity are always at hand, then "lack of resources" can never be a reason for not creating. The university subsidizes Tamayo's projects as part of its service to the people of the state, providing a relatively secure environment for his exploration of an innovative idea that bureaucratically can be readily understood as cultural recreation. The regular invitations Tamayo receives to bring his work to other parts of Mexico or to Europe pose a problem for university administrators. They fund his position because of the service he provides to the citizens of Baja California. When his work leaves the state, it is no longer part of his job, and the government, struggling with limited fiscal resources, is reluctant to subsidize personal career development.[15]

His sculpture likewise has served dual purposes that mix art and public service. Like any visual artist, he explores plastic form in a variety of media and then exhibits the completed work at museums and galleries. At the same time, these forms have been redesigned for an experiment conducted by the engineering and architecture faculties at UABC to create controlled microclimates in child care centers. Hooked up with water conduits and placed in relation to shade trees, his sculptures will provide space where children can

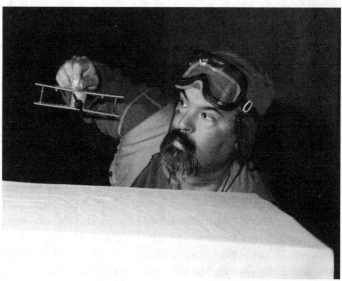

Figures 7.5 and 7.6 Scenes from *El Principito*, teatro de mesa adaptation by Ramón Tamayo from Antoine de Saint-Exupéry, performer: Ramón Tamayo, produced by La Bicicleta, 2001. (Photograph courtesy of Monica Gonzalez.) "Lo esencial es invisible para los ojos."

Figure 7.7 Ramón Tamayo, *Screaming World, or La Bufanda del Sufi*, 5 × 1.96 meters, paper, 1998. (Photograph courtesy of Monica Gonzalez.)

play and enjoy themselves outside during the summer, when the thermometer is usually above 40°Celsius. The project is not expensive, and the planners hope it will offer a prototype for providing schools in low desert areas throughout Mexico and the southwest United States with practical play space that is moist and cool.[16]

For Tamayo, his theater, sculpture, and architectural projects are equally important. Each reaches out to his fellow citizens to suggest that solutions to their problems may be close at hand and not as expensive as they want to believe. Although Tamayo has defined his project by a commitment to a city and a state, Martínez has typically created projects far from his home town of Los Angeles, where the ubiquity of art is such that even the most provocative piece will disappear into a plethora of stimulation provided in one of the true world cities, the very kind of metropolitan center that may be sucking the creative life out of countless cities such as Mexicali. His projects have taken a wide variety of forms: holographic films, satellite video transmissions from Europe, documentary and fine art photography, an opera production, and most recently a series of photographs that he has developed collaboratively with special effects masters from the motion picture industry to explore the design of intense, illusionary images that can sustain prolonged viewing. His best-known work has been a series of public art projects that took seriously the challenge of connecting art to immediate concerns of everyday life in particular locations. He could enter a local community as a relative outsider, listen to what people had to say, and then try to create a situation in which communication between opposed viewpoints would have to happen. For taking his role as a public intellectual seriously, he has gained a reputation as a difficult artist, paradoxically seeming to confirm the alienation of art from life, a central ideological tenet guaranteeing the privileged position of fine arts institutions.

Figure 7.8 Daniel Joseph Martínez, Quality of Life, public street banners, 1990–1991. Commissioned by the Seattle Arts Commission, Seattle, Washington. (Photograph courtesy of the artist.)

In 1990, the Seattle Arts Commission commissioned Martínez to prepare banners to be hung from poles along the streets of the downtown shopping district. The banners asked a series of simple questions that were in paired proximity: "Do you earn minimum wage" was adjacent to "Do you have a trust fund, savings account, or a credit card"; "Are you hungry" to "Are you a connoisseur with a refined palate. Do you have a wine cellar."[17] The Seattle Business Association and Seattle newspapers insisted that the banners insulted the majority of shoppers, though perhaps the real issue was undermining the thoughtlessness that accompanies shopping frenzies. After several weeks of debate, the banners were removed, but debate continued in Seattle over the nature of art and free speech long after the work had been suppressed.

Controversy dogged Martínez once again after he and two associates won a competition to design and build a major, million-dollar public art project for downtown San Francisco. Large signs were to arch over a busy street announcing in bright block lettering, "This Is a Nice Neighborhood," an ironic reference to the well-known fact that the project was part of a program to redevelop a "bad" neighborhood. Shortly after Martínez's team won the commission, politicians, developers, and even other artists began attacking the proposal so fiercely that the Redevelopment Agency reopened public hearings, and then used negative public opinion to justify canceling the already signed contract. This disappointment was followed by the controversy in New York City raised over his preparing and handing out museum tags at the 1993 Whitney Biennial stating, "I can't imagine ever wanting to be white." Mayor Koch wrote an open letter to the director of the museum charging the artist and the Whitney with fomenting racial tension and insulting white patrons.

The most dangerous but ultimately validating response to Martínez's work emerged at Cornell University in 1993, when he was commissioned to do a site-specific piece for an exhibition of Chicano art. He was reading in psychogeography at the time, particularly examining the writings of Guy Debord and the situationists on the May 1968 events in France. As he looked over the maps of how students and intellectuals set up barricades around the Sorbonne and effectively took over Paris and brought the whole nation to a halt, the paths around the Cornell campus reminded him of the streets surrounding the Sorbonne. He proposed erecting barriers to block movement around campus. This led to *The Castle Is Burning*, a title taken from graffiti in Paris in 1968, but to many at Cornell an obvious reference to the castle-like administration building overlooking the campus.

"Privilege is articulated through use of architecture and space," he told me as he described the project.

> So I thought I'm just going to mess it up a little bit. I'm going to overlay the exact pattern of barricades in Paris over the Cornell campus. Well, they wouldn't let

me do that. Health and safety reasons. So I took the arts quad and I created a wall across the whole thing. I made a barricade out of "black ice." It was as beautiful as a Reinhardt. But I created a line across the panels. When the snow hit the ground behind the wall, the light hit the snow and bounced up and created a luminescent line across the whole thing. It was my homage to California light and space. The real question is private/public. It was a way for me to create disorder. Maybe people misunderstood me. The panels that made words above started to be destroyed. A lot of negative press.[18]

After he returned to Los Angeles, a group of conservative students announced their intention to destroy it. Four hundred other students, mostly students of color, formed a human chain around the work to defend it. Following a battle between the student groups, there was a student occupation of the administration building. The university's passivity in the face of vandalism directed against a work by an artist of color was symptomatic of the administration's refusal to acknowledge, much less address, a long-standing pattern of intimidation against students and faculty of color. Access to higher education meant only being present on campus, but not being included. Students demanded hiring of more faculty of color, building library collections in ethnic studies, and changing the curriculum to address the interests and needs of students of color. Martínez recalled that the president blamed him for the situation rather than looking at how the university's policies created a hostile racial climate at Cornell: "'Individuals like Martínez will be the demise of western civilization.' Wow! Just one little person. It was like the servants taking over the house. You can't have that."[19]

In the end, student demands were met and the president resigned as a result of his failure to manage the confrontation. Since 1993, Chicano students at Cornell continue to celebrate the anniversary of the Day Hall takeover and honor the inspiration they or their antecedents received from *The Castle Is Burning*. "And what is it?" Daniel asked. "Just a little bit of art, a hope, an idea. I laid the plans out. They picked it up, read the plan, and enacted it. A sleeping giant lies at your feet and you don't even know it. An exceptional event, an exceptional moment."[20]

That Martínez's public art projects have so consistently generated intense public response suggests how well the work functions as research confronting the languages and subject-positions that the discursive regimes available have created for contemporary Americans to occupy. He begins with a proposition that whatever is said silences and his task as a poet is to return the absented, not for meaning to be overturned and replaced by nonsense, but precisely in order that the social relationships embedded in local, everyday language situations be revealed with crystalline clarity. He devalues the "real" as a shadow, which means that he must create an art that is "true" because it is not reducible to anything immediate.

It is hard to say that Tamayo has been isolated for choosing to work in a provincial city or that Martínez has been punished for the controversies surrounding much of his work. No doubt Tamayo has foregone opportunities for money and recognition that might otherwise have been available. No doubt the turmoil surrounding Martínez's projects has exacted a personal toll. Still, both have good jobs at major universities. Both lecture widely, and both continue to exhibit on an international basis. They are successful, working artists of interest to many precisely because they have succeeded in acting socially as artists.[21] Their reputations rest on their roles as public intellectuals who transform local spaces by a professional practice. The national context in each case shapes a distinctive conceptions of art as a profession. Tamayo engages the immediate locality served by his university in part because he works within a cultural framework organized around ideals of public service, personal enrichment, and cultural recreation. Martínez intervenes in local situations that are not his in part because the U.S. university gives priority to conceptions of art as research and thus supports autonomous professional development. Yet in both cases, art practice as sponsored within national university environments arrives at very similar results: work that reconstructs the immediate to allow the possibility for imagining alternatives.

Imaginative Space: Disciplines and the Politics of Meaning

Contemporary experimental art practice is defined by a goal of creating imaginative space that can transcend immediate social realities, be they national or local. The professional and disciplinary autonomy of arts practices and institutions has been a relative condition enabling artists to reveal to their fellow citizens alternative modes of perception. Autonomy is relative because, even if creative expression is universal, the organization and goals of cultural institutions are not. These are products of national histories differentially expressed in a variety of regional and local contexts. Innovative art practice that aims to provide alternative perceptions of social and political realities must simultaneously critique, negate, and transcend immediate structures for professional practice, be they of either a research or a public service model, if imaginative space that counters settled perceptual and cognitive habits is to materialize.

"I like the ephemeral and I like the transitory," Daniel told me shortly after we first sat down to talk. "Some of the most memorable things . . . are small conversations I have with other people."[22] The immediacy of face-to-face conversation invoked Walter Benjamin's conception of the storyteller whose narratives are accompanied by a gestural performance that circumscribes the special space within which narrator and audience become present to each other. What it all means is at the surface, for the storyteller's story conveys an evaluation that must be shared.[23] I like to think of this transitory, morally charged but imaginative connection as the model for what Daniel means when he speaks of the "third" or imaginatively freed space he hopes his art reveals.

As a person who has long done oral history interviewing for research purposes, I knew at first experientially but later more theoretically that no one can answer the questions interviews pose them unless they themselves grasp a point they want to convey. Answers grow out of morally charged evaluations placed on people, actions, and events. The conversation, with degrees of emphasis and indirection, yields clear, if often softly stated conclusions about how we in the present *should* act for the future. The ethical confrontation with the potential meaning of the past creates a situation in which the play of imagination becomes imperative.

For Daniel, working to reveal a "third" space in which the absented truths of national, local, and institutional structures become palpably present has ineluctably led him to what at first glance appears to be an iconoclastic or even nihilistic position: "In order to find the next space for us to consider our humanness, we have to smash the idols that preceded us. Smashing them in anticipation of something I don't understand and for something I can't *yet* imagine."[24] With a lineage extending back to Artaud, Jarry, and Lautréamont, Daniel invokes an escape from order precisely to escape the arbitrariness and cruelty congealed into a system of taste, logic, and authority.

The tradition Daniel invokes is made clear in the high regard he has for Friedrich Nietzsche's essay, *Twilight of the Idols*: "When I read that for the first time, I said that's it! This is imagination of a space that does not yet exist. What we do in our lives is that we exist in quantifiable spaces and we do not let our imaginations function. We're always trying only to recognize what we see and to deal with what is reality in a sort of Cartesian-based world, and why we are so boring is because that is where we situate ourselves."[25] The third space inserts "a discourse into a space where the discourse is not allowed." The gesture, bound to be misunderstood, puts fixed assumptions into play and allows for a resumption of "discussion" that struggles to resolve misunderstandings. A radical experience becomes possible, that if grasped will be understood as the purest form of beauty. Desire for the comfortable and known gives way to a need to confront the artificiality of the world as it is lived in an everyday sense and to transcend the limited imagination that habitual response allows. "If we give up our imagination, we give up our ability to discern," he says, "we give up our human rights. If we give up our human rights, we become something I can't even describe." Radical beauty invokes a space in which a person can discover the imagination of autonomy. Not individuality, but autonomy from all categories of identity, even those that one finds comforting and self-affirming.

The work flowing from an exploration of what such ideas might mean in practice has proven that Daniel's ideas touch on a tangible, actionable realm of contemporary reality. The response to his work has been such that he has developed a reputation as a "wild animal" whose ideas might be well-meaning but are suspect and possibly irresponsible.[26] By attempting to live up to the highest standards of the profession he joined virtually by accident, he crossed the fire lines that protect the autonomy of arts institutions in the United States as arenas for research. Publicly funded arts exhibitions need to satisfy two conflicting demands, "excellence" and "accessibility." Martínez satisfies the first demand, but the questions he raises challenge a comfortable relationship to art. He tried to export conversations that are relevant and serious among professionals and show why they were relevant to broader publics, including the communities from which he originally came. He showed that art can provoke discussion and debate, but in a way that questioned the need for professional control.[27]

The meaningful audience for Daniel's work, however, has been primarily professionals, who then mediate the ways in which the broader public hear of what Daniel has done. Even at Cornell, where students of color showed themselves to be the responsible ideal audience artists dream of reaching, an audience that knew how to respond and act upon the events that art made visible and understandable, they themselves were professionals in training, pondering in an alienating campus environment the existential meaning of the histories of communities of color within the United States. Higher education trains those who will become the leaders of the country (and hence putatively of the globe) in thirty years. To grasp that privilege, students of color have to learn how to convert apparent marginality into strategic assets. Daniel's work provided an important object lesson for the training of a new professional cadre who *may* bring into being a world where categories of race *begin* to be less decisive in determining individual fate. In this sense, Daniel has contributed to a on-going nation-building project that allows the U.S. state to endure and indeed expand because state and civil society become increasingly self-conscious and self-reflective about the conditions of their emergence and consolidation.

Martínez's work functions within a politics of subjectivity, directly addressing how subject-position is articulated in different discursive frameworks. His stated goal is negative, to offer a position to his audience by which they can disengage themselves from that which they occupy un-self-reflexively. Utopian aspects are part of the mechanism by which the important work of thinking about who the *I* is that one has been and that one can become. I say the utopian aspects are secondary because the possibility of leaving the institutional framework is not a given. One finds a "family" of similar-hearted comrades within the institution that one occupies. A reevaluation of subjective expectations takes place as a prelude to rethinking what the institution should be, what narratives it can offer, and if the resources of the *I* can be expanded and made more central to the enterprise.

In a variation on the concept of the "third" space, Daniel acknowledges that his work must be done for more than the immediate context: "One of the things I'm interested in is to create space bubbles where [exceptional people] can solidify into print, into production, a force that will have to be dealt with one hundred years from now looking back. Not the decoration, but what has force, who on the margins had the force to sustain themselves."[28] To this end, he and two other artists based in Los Angeles, Glenn Kaino and Tracey Shiffman, opened Deep River, a gallery space and a publishing venture in the Los Angeles artist district that allows him to connect with others by providing them with opportunities to be more adventuresome than they might in venues oriented toward sales and self-promotion. Artists who have exhibited at his space have often moved on to commercial galleries, and older artists have presented work that because of scope or novelty required some protection from the limelight before being shown in more conventional spaces. Deep River was a collaborative experiment to see how much exactly artists can do for themselves outside the parameters of commercial galleries and public museums. Perhaps Daniel's goal is to give his "family" courage to do more than they normally can imagine, for that will be the only way the discipline of art will stay alive and engaged. This requires a degree of accepting marginality within even one's own discipline as a strategy for contributing to its highest ideals.

The marginal, and therefore productive position that artists have found in modern social life brings to mind the seminal essay from 1928 by Robert E. Park, "Human Migration and the Marginal Man."[29] This is one of the first theoretical texts that posits hybridity and border-crossing as explanatory factors behind the political and economic power of the United States. Park, the principal figure in the sociology department at the University of Chicago, rebuffed fellow Anglo-Americans who naively believed that either religious or racial purity could have been the foundation of the greatness the United States enjoyed. Ten years later in a follow-up essay, he wrote, "Inevitably [the marginal man] becomes, relative to his cultural milieu, the individual with a wider horizon, the keener intelligence, the more detached and rational view-point. The marginal man is always relatively the more civilized human being."[30]

Innovation is the product of those who stand at the margins and are most easily able to move between cultures. In ancient days, Park reminded his readers, they were nomads like Abraham, Isaac, and Jacob. In the twentieth century, the innovators would move between races as well as cultures. They were mulattos and mestizos in the Americas and Eurasians in the old world. Given the racial and ethnic politics of the United States in the 1920s, his argument could have had little immediate practical effect, but he helped prepare the ground for changes decades later. His arguments found a more receptive readership in Latin America. Park's formulations, combined with Franz Boas's concepts of cultural relativism, provided intellectuals there with an inspiring rationale that challenged stereotypes that the primary impediment to progress in their countries had been the mass of impoverished

Indian or mixed-blood peasants. If Park were right, the primary force for modernization would be found in communities that appeared marginal. They needed access to a technical education that would provide skills for solving themselves their most basic problems.

In the Latin American situation, Park's concept of "marginal man" escaped its initial racial and ethnic setting to take into account differing levels of education and social mobility. The marginal man was the individual who could move between the value systems of his indigenous roots and the scientific and technological knowledge available from the broader world. His productivity rested in his becoming marginal to both and thus able to cobble together a creative understanding of the world. His imagination worked with the fragments of diverse cultural legacies, both within and without his homeland, to bricolage a picture of the world that was open to innovation and invention. The marginal man's example augmented the possibilities for others to dissent from the groups that insisted on social solidarity as the basis for either national or local progress.[31]

Ramón's strategies for creativity directly confront the limitations of being part of a nation that is relatively poor and that has long made concentration of wealth and talent the central strategy for national development. He builds on alternative traditions within Mexico that have focused instead on strengthening local talent. Following this strategy, the chief resource for progress lies within each human person, and Ramón's efforts contribute to national welfare to the degree that he succeeds in challenging students, colleagues, and audiences to think more deeply about their marginality as a potential rather than as a liability.

He has found a group of enthusiastic students. They understand that they must prepare themselves as amateurs, that is, in the literal sense of the word, as lovers of an activity. Ramón's students will likely be the agronomists, engineers, chemists, doctors, architects, and public officials of the state in the future. The process trains them to believe that the local must be valued and protected, that Mexicali can develop things of worth and take them to other parts of the world.[32] A few may redirect their careers as Ramón himself had done. Mexicali, with nearly one million residents, is home to more people than Athens, Florence, Venice, or Amsterdam had been during their golden ages. Unless we hold that the distribution of talent in the human race has shrunk radically in the past several centuries, Mexicali should be as vital an intellectual and aesthetic center as these cities have been. It would be but one of many, but its ambitious, talented citizens would no longer think automatically of migrating to Mexico City, or Los Angeles, or New York, or even to Tijuana, which has lately been developing into the metropolis of the Mexican Northwest. Cultural capitals are concentrations of mercantile opportunities. Culture in this sense is defined by the size of the market for consumption rather than by the potential for creativity.

Tamayo works in hope of a renaissance, a rebirth that involves a network of local sites, in exchange and interaction, with each developing the rich potential that the imaginations and talents of its populations already possess. Mexicali is provincialized when its leaders assume that the practical tasks of nation building require the city to develop, primarily, maquiladora production. "To include everybody is not a characteristic of contemporary culture," he believes.[33] That distribution of labor, which then drives the educational process, inevitably directs many residents away from their homes in order to find opportunity. As a nationalist, he says, "More than to protect Mexican culture, I want to share it, take it out, and let others enjoy it. . . . If the French know the history of Mexico as well as Mexicans know the history of France, there would be a recognition, a breaking of frontiers, and a shared history would develop. The same with the U.S."[34]

Neither the mounting of plays nor the exhibition of sculpture can, in and of itself, accomplish these goals. All Ramón can do is provide an example that insists on the universality of creativity and shows its presence in the most banal of circumstances. It is a model that has begun to attract students from other parts of Mexico and from other nations, who come to Mexicali to study with Ramón and work in his productions. Though he lives less than five miles from the U.S. border, which he crosses weekly to shop or to conduct other personal business, he has had little interest in seeking an audience in the United States. In part, he may simply be waiting for the right invitation. For the moment, there is interest in his approach to theater in Europe, but little response from community theater professionals in the United States. Underlying this is acceptance of how nationality shapes personal fortune. In Mexico, he is an intellectual working on a serious project. He can combine interests in modern art, classical Greek mythology, and the history of his region and see how his audiences respond to the ideas he dramatizes. In the United States, he would become a "Mexican," that is one of the millions who silently perform the manual labor necessary for the American standard of living or one of the handful of intellectuals who come north with messages arbitrarily limited to questions of borders and exclusion. For the metropolitan centers, whether Mexico City, Los Angeles, New York, or Washington, the frontier is a series of media problems associated with one-word, easy-to-remember tags—the Migra, cholos, narcotrafficking. "Here," asserting his sense of himself as a person rooted in a particular place with all the difficulties and rewards that offers, "if we who live here need to cross the border, we cross it."[35] The local environment, with all the limitations of a public service model, protects him from an institutional space built around the self-reproducing spectacle of empty discourse.

Tamayo has defined his work with theater form as a practice of antispectacle. The theater practitioner, be she performer or director, relearns the resources that she as an individual can master and deploy to a small, intimate audience. She relearns the power of direct personal contact and how that response can reshape what one presents. These are lessons appropriate for a theater of limited budget that fits within a bureaucratically defined goal of providing entertainment to children, senior citizens, and others in the community. It cannot compete with Hollywood or Mexican television. Those remain unchallenged staples of consumer culture. Small theater performances offer an alternative that remind audiences of the emotional power that *can* come with direct, one-on-one contact with another human being. It offers an experience that commercial media cannot. The public enjoying antispectacle theater learns to see itself anew. This is micropolitics with a vengeance, as the only way it can proceed is by a slow process of percolating through society while reminding people of who they could be and restimulating the pleasures and desires of direct human contact. The practice is sustainable because it conforms to the service mission of the Mexican university while providing an outlet for students seeking to participate in cultural life as creators rather than as consumers. To embrace the antispectacle is to accept the inevitability of limitations in any human situation and make one's marginality the basis for exploring what one's capacities might be in any real situation.

Art and the Experience of Borders

A tenet of modern arts movements was that everyone lives dual lives—one in the world, the other in the imagination. In the late nineteenth century, this imagined epistemological duality opened up the basis for a new politics of subjectivity, a politics still unfolding as artists and poets continue to explore what it means to be professional creators of experience. The subject and subject-positions revealed through works of imagination are, ideally, a stimulus to transform the world to conform to inner visions, even if the project is again and again chastened by the adamantine intractability of nature and society. Engaged art reveals transcendent visions of society—"correspondences," to use a word shared by Emerson and Baudelaire—but there are no *causal* links connecting culture with politics or economics. If there were, art would be instrumental and lose its status as a privileged site for freeing the imagination to produce alternatives to the actually existing.

The artwork, whether it is an object, a narrative, or a performance, presents a proposition about how to put aspects of the world in relation with each other. An effort to locate meaning creates the temporal world within which people have "experiences," that is a sense of action that remains meaningful and related logically to conclusions that have been understood and felt as "necessary" or, less strongly, "probable." Individual responses are experiments into the "as if" conditions posited in an aesthetic work to determine if the work has provided them a form of self-knowledge that they can use. The success of an artist presupposes that the work has provided a way of thinking about the self in its world that has proven meaningful to others.

Within this theoretical model, a work of art is a catalyst, serving as a presence linking disparate efforts to find categories that are workable but need not be perfect. By turning to practices of meaning formation, we shift away from individual discourse statements (the arguments and feelings of which are necessarily transitory responses to changes strongly felt but not yet comprehended) in order to give more attention to the social relations shaping a new imaginary finding fragmentary expression in any individual artist's projects.[36] The national, local, and professional experiences of Martínez and Tamayo continuously combine and recombine as each has reworked a project relevant to the worlds they have come to inhabit. New configurations of loyalties and subjectivities, reflecting contesting principles of governmentality, are being developed in their work, as in the work of other artists attempting to see the emerging world order more clearly.

During the 1990s the concepts of "borders" and "borderlands" entered U.S. intellectual life with a sense of tremendous urgency. The category has been fluidly applied to interaction of ethnicities, races, genders, and sexualities, but the border without equal has been the one between the United States and Mexico.[37] Given the growth of Mexican and Latino populations in nearly every region of the United States, it is fair to say that the entire United States has become a borderland where indigenous and immigrant understandings of nation, land, justice, and community are once again in forceful dialogue. The challenge of reincorporating the United States back into the Americas has prompted extensive symbolic investigation and creative activity.

Though artists and poets have little to say about the substantive details of international law and trade agreements, they have been among the first to explore the intellectual and affective aspects of the new world that politicians and corporations are busily constructing. Art has provided a place for audiences to experience what it *might* mean to live in a world with less restrictive boundaries. The impetus for this has been particularly strong along the United States–Mexico border where ideological and practical needs come into immediate conflict. For nearly a decade, arts and educational institutions in San Diego and Tijuana have collaborated to produce binational exhibitions of installation and site-specific art responding "to the potent and meaningful context" of "two major cities with distinctly different and historically disparate cultures [sharing] a common geography, yet . . . separated by a fiercely fenced international border."[38] The dozens of artists who participated, many not from the immediate region, often produced work that sought to unsettle conventional relations to place.

In designing *CYM 55296*, for example, installed in 1994 at the Athenaeum Music and Arts Library in San Diego, Hong Kong-born artist Ming Mur-Ray prepared seventy-two translucent panels inscribed with 768 completely invented characters (presenting the viewer with a total of 55,296

Figure 7.9   Marcos Ramírez ERRE's *Toy an Horse,* 30-feet tall, wood and steel, 1997. InSITE97, San Diego, California/Tijuana, Baja California border crossing. (Photograph courtesy of Iturralde Gallery, Los Angeles.)

unknown characters). Scattered through the library, Ming's free-standing units refigured a familiar environment with unreadable if presumably decipherable text. Occupation of space was transformed by a need to absorb and categorize the new context that the panels and their texts had created, much as many everyday practices are changing slowly under the pressure of new international conventions and regulations. If panels failed to yield any code to make their texts or presence comprehensible, they still had to be circumvented and avoided as library patrons moved from one part of the reading room to another.

A highlight of the 1997 InSITE exhibition was Marcos Ramírez ERRE's *Toy an Horse,* a thirty-foot tall, two-headed wooden horse straddling the border at San Ysidro, reputedly the most heavily trafficked international frontier crossing in the world. Effecting a clever English-language pun, ERRE called up nativist concerns in the United States that immigration had become a Trojan horse sapping national integrity. ERRE, however, visually reminded his audience of border-crossers, both U.S. and Mexican citizens, that the horse pointed in both directions. If the border symbolized danger, certainly Mexico was as vulnerable as the United States to unwanted changes, perhaps more so given its weaker economic condition and the relatively greater fragility of its political structures. The piece asked its viewers who else could be the secreted warriors threatening the future of Mexico and the United States but themselves, the 50,000 tourists, businessmen, shoppers, government officials, and workers who daily cross the border at San Ysidro. For those like ERRE who live and work on both sides of the national boundary, the frontier is lived with and around in the simple pursuits of everyday life. The procedures and protocols imposed on crossing the border into the United States have become increasingly complicated but nothing to stop the thousands of Mexican citizens who every day legally enter the United States at San Ysidro and places like it stretching 2,000 miles east.

ERRE's joke from 1997 provided a timely reminder that interchange between any two nations is a living process involving thousands of discrete acts by people with sundry motivations and intentions. Given that interpretation as a possible reading of the piece, it is necessary nonetheless to remember that the work was produced within a particular social structure that has its own relation to the border. If artists arrive at a telling formulation about borders, nations, and the mixtures they create, this is not because they have reproduced observable facts. Imagination has thrown forth an alternative way of seeing that stands in opposition to what can be observed, as much as ERRE's *Toy an Horse* stood over the actual business of crossing the international border. While it was installed, ERRE's piece in no way changed the process of passing between the United States and Mexico, though it may have sparked a variety of interior changes among the tens of thousands who passed it. We do not turn to artists or writers for policy recommendations but for relief, surcease, incitement, and provocation; we seek an alternative that can reduce complex, often intractable realities to images with the power to put ideas back into play.

The dilemma of artists speaking to public policy issues is that the internal logic of poetry as a materialization of a potential, of that which does not yet exist but which might, makes it impossible for them to make strategic, goal-oriented interventions. Others, like the students at Cornell who defended Martínez's *The Castle Is Burning*, must do that, and their engagement can turn the artist's imagination of hegemony overturned into an actuality. In most cases, this will not happen because the "public" that public intellectuals address is a notion rather than a situated group of people with interests to defend and advance. It may not have been chance that Martínez found his ideal audience at Cornell, but it was pure luck that the timing of his exhibition on campus allowed his concerns as an artist interrogating the discursive contradictions of U.S. society to coincide with the increasingly urgent need of students of color at one school to assert their own program for meaningful education.[39]

If there is no single public but only groups of people living and working in local situations, the visions of artists cannot be reducible to a common national experience. Nor can art about the border emerge spontaneously out of the borderlands or the immediate confrontation of two distinct national cultures. Formal expression requires the manipulation of discursive, institutional, and subjective traditions, each lodged in self-replicating organizations, which in professionalized disciplines claim the authority to determine what is and is not meaningful, what is and is not interesting, what is and is not innovative. To understand the imaginative space that artists from the United States, Mexico, and other nations offer as alternatives to a world of regulated borders, one needs to understand the institutional ethos enabling the practices of an artist. If a new "postborder" culture emerges in the Californias, it will require a synthesis of national expressive traditions facilitated through the emergence and consolidation of new arts and educational institutions that operate on both sides of the border.

In that now imaginary future, the citizenship of Daniel Joseph Martínez and Ramón Tamayo would be secondary to their participation in organizations dedicated primarily to creating a common cultural life transcending national borders. The epistemological claims of modern and contemporary art practice point strongly to that goal, but the organizational framework is largely fragmentary and ad hoc. For the time being the practices of artists and the imaginative revisionings they provide are still deeply embedded in national contexts or they remain invisible.

The imagination of a "postborder" world effected in the arts will be different from what will be worked out simultaneously in legal, regulatory, commercial, or political exchanges. The artist as a mediator of human experience falls into the logic of Robert Park's marginal man by providing through creative enterprise a possibility of moving between distinct ways of looking at the world. This new space does not alter the immediate facts of social relations, but by making present alternative ways of thinking, artists reveal social facts as actually unsettled, fluid, and ultimately suitable for renegotiation.

The political work effected by artists is and will likely remain a temporarily transformed framework for looking at the world. It does not require a specific set of behaviors, but opens up instead a possibility for critical relation to the normative and habitual. These unreflexive patterns of reproducible behavior are currently largely formed at the national level. What gives the work of both Daniel Joseph Martínez and Ramón Tamayo its particular power has been the ways in which each has brought to the surface fundamental assumptions governing personal identity and collective priorities of their respective nations. Cultural and political identity are indeed not easily cut asunder, for a critique of how societies provide for their members, develop loyalties and antipathies, and create hierarchies that determine personal destiny must target processes that remain largely national in origin and effect.

The visions artists bring today are likely to fade before the rechanneling of habit effected through infrastructure investment, business contracts, international treaty, and changes in laws made by national congresses and state legislatures of both nations—a rechanneling that may simultaneously transform the education of and support for artists, the distribution of their work, as well as the critical questions that will occupy artists in a future where national borders have become largely administrative boundaries connecting communities with many types of organized shared interests. For the moment, artists provide a way of responding critically to human needs and desires increasingly criss-crossing a border that emerged in order to impede interaction.

Notes

1. On "The Family of Man" exhibition see Eric J. Sandeen, *Picturing an Exhibition: The Family of Man and 1950s America* (Albuquerque: University of New Mexico Press, 1995). The exhibition catalogue is still in print; see Edward Steichen, *The Family of Man* (New York: Random House, 1955).
2. Richard Cándida Smith, *Mallarmé's Children: Symbolism and the Renewal of Experience* (Berkeley: University of California Press, 1999), 170–172, 187–190.
3. Roland Barthes, *Mythologies* (New York: Hill and Wang, 1972). See my essay, "Analytic Strategies for Oral History Interviews," in Jaber F. Gubrium and James A. Holstein (eds.) *Handbook of Interview Research: Context and Method* (Thousand Oaks: Sage Publications, 2001), 711–731, for a discussion of the use of paradigmatic and syntagmatic structures in the historical interpretation of life-story documents.
4. Artist statement in *Cola 2000: Individual Artist Fellowships* (City of Los Angeles Cultural Affairs Department, 2000), 38.
5. Information on Martínez's personal history and summaries of his perspectives drawn from my audiotaped interview with him, February 16 and 17, 2001, at his studio in Los Angeles, California. Six hours of interview were recorded; all remains untranscribed. This and the immediately following material are drawn from Tapes II, III, and IV.
6. On Asco, see Harry J. Gamboa, Jr., *Urban Exile: Collected Writings* (Minneapolis: University of Minnesota Press, 1998); Pascal Letellier, *Le Démon des anges: 16 artists "Chicanos" autour de "Los Angeles"* (Nantes: Centre de Recherche pour le Développement Culturel, 1989); Richard Griswold del Castillo et al., *Chicano Art: Resistance and Affirmation, 1965–1985* (Los Angeles: Wight Art Gallery, 1991).
7. Videotaped interview with Ramón Tamayo by the author, April 29 and 30, 2001, at various locations in Mexicali, Baja California, including his studio space at the Universidad Autónoma de Baja California. Seven hours of interview were recorded, all still is untranscribed. This material drawn from Tapes I and VI.
8. Interview with Tamayo, Tape I.
9. In the introduction to *Landscape for a Good Woman: A Story of Two Lives* (New Brunswick: Rutgers University Press, 1987), Carolyn Steedman notes that the figure of the scholarship boy was important to the mid-century generation of working-class scholars who were the first from their families to attend university. It created a way of thinking about democratic access to higher education that may have been appropriate for a period when class appeared unproblematically to be the primary contradiction of modern societies, but she notes as gender, racial, and colonial issues became more important and women and people of color entered the university, the narrative of the scholarship pupil failed to account for the many additional problems they faced in asserting their rights to full participation.
10. The role of universities in Mexican cultural policy is a topic in Hector Rosales Ayala, *Cultura, sociedad civil, y proyectos culturales en México* (México: Consejo Nacional para la Cultura y las Artes, 1994).
11. By "practice," I mean a set of regularized behaviors that includes explanatory categories but that are not necessarily or inherently analytical or theoretical. See Pierre Bourdieu, *The Logic*

of Practice (Cambridge: Polity Press, 1990), and *Language and Symbolic Power* (Cambridge: Harvard University Press, 1991). On the development of the U.S. research university, see Roger L. Geiger, *Research and Relevant Knowledge: American Research Universities Since World War II* (New York: Oxford University Press, 1993); Laurence R. Veysey, *The Emergence of the American University* (Chicago: University of Chicago Press, 1965); and Andrew Abbott, *The System of the Professions: An Essay on the Division of Expert Labor* (Chicago: University of Chicago Press, 1988).

12. Howard Singerman, *Art Subjects: Making Artists in the American University* (Berkeley: University of California Press, 1999), 8.

13. For a theorized discussion of the role of the nation in structuring life opportunities in distinct fields, see Gérard Noiriel, *La Tyrannie du national* (Paris: Calmann-Lévy, 1991).

14. Interview with Tamayo, Tape II.

15. Interview with Tamayo, Tape II.

16. Interview with Marco Antonio Vilchis, facultad de arquitectura, Universidad Autónoma de Baja California, April 30, 2001, 20 minutes untranscribed, on Tape V, interview with Tamayo.

17. Daniel Joseph Martínez, *The Things You See When You Don't Have a Grenade!* (Santa Monica: Smart Art Press, 1996), 96–8.

18. Interview with Martínez, Tape IV, Side 1.

19. Ibid.

20. Interview with Martínez, Tape IV, Side 1. See also Martínez, *The Things You See*, 54–6; Chon A. Noriega, "On Museum Row: Aesthetics and the Politics of Exhibition," *Daedalus*, 1999, 128, 57–81; Victor Zamudio-Taylor, "The Castle Is Burning," in Martínez, *The Things You See*, 105–7.

21. David Levi Strauss has noted how Josef Beuys provided Martínez with a model for acting socially as an artist rather than creating more discourse. See "Between Dog and Wolf," in *Between Dog and Wolf: Essays on Art and Politics* (Brooklyn: Autonomedia, 1999), 133–4.

22. Interview with Martínez, Tape I, Side 1.

23. See Walter Benjamin, "The Story-Teller," in *Illuminations* (New York: Schocken, 1969), 83–110, see especially sections V and VIII.

24. Interview with Martínez, Tape I, Side 1.

25. Ibid.

26. The response has not yet converted him into a *fauve* with all the privileges and honorifics that connection might carry in an art world resting proudly upon its avant-garde patrimony.

27. For a historical survey of this conflict in U.S. arts policy see Michael Kammen, "Culture and the State in America," *Journal of American History*, 1996, 791–814.

28. Interview with Martínez, Tape I, Side 2.

29. Robert E. Park, "Human Migration and the Marginal Man," *American Journal of Sociology*, 1928, 33, 881–93.

30. Robert E. Park, "Cultural Conflict and the Marginal Man," in Park, *Race and Culture* (Glencoe: Free Press, 1950), 376.

31. Manuel Gamio discussed these ideas in his proposal for reforming Mexican education advanced in 1926 while he was living in exile in the United States. See Gamio, *Aspects of Mexican Civilization: The Indian Basis of Mexican Civilization* (Chicago: University of Chicago Press, 1926), 129–54. After he returned home, Gamio served as one of the architects of the new educational system that the revolutionary government developed. See Ángeles González Gamio, *Manuel Gamio: Una Lucha sin final* (México: Universidad Nacional Autónoma de México, 1987), 79–159.

32. Interview with Tamayo, Tape V.

33. Interview with Tamayo, Tape IV.

34. Interview with Tamayo, Tape V.

35. Interview with Tamayo, Tape I.

36. See Paul Ricœur, *Time and Narrative*, Vol. 1 (Chicago: University of Chicago Press, 1984), Chapter 3, for a discussion of narratives as propositions about the parameters of meaning to be applied to particular situations and the role of performative reception in the reconstruction of ideology.

37. Important discussions of the borderlands concept in relation to the cultural politics of the United States–Mexico border can be found in Alfred Arteaga, ed., *An Other Tongue: Nation and Identity in the Linguistic Borderlands* (Durham: University of North Carolina Press, 1994); Héctor Calderón and José David Saldívar, eds., *Criticism in the Borderlands: Studies in*

Chicano Literature, Culture, and Ideology (Durham: University of North Carolina Press, 1991); Teddy Cruz and Anne Boddington, eds., *Architecture of the Borderlands* (London: Academy Editions, 1999); Philip J. Ethington, "Towards a 'Borderland School' for American Urban Ethnic Studies, *American Quarterly*, 1996, 48, 344–53; Claire F. Fox, "The Portable Border: Site-Specificity, Art, and the U.S-Mexico Frontier," *Social Text*, 1994, 41, 61–82; Guillermo Gómez-Peña, "Border Culture: A Process of Negotiation Toward Utopia," *La Línea Quebrada*, 1986, 1, 1–6; Guillermo Gómez-Peña, "Border Culture and Deterritorialization," *La Línea Quebrada*, 1987, 2/2, 1–10; Carl Gutiérrez-Jones, *Rethinking the Borderlands: Between Chicano Culture and Legal Discourse* (Berkeley: University of California Press, 1995); Lawrence A. Herzog, *Where North Meets South: Cities, Space, and Politics on the U.S.-Mexico Border* (Austin: University of Texas Press, 1990); Vicki Ruiz and Suan Tiano, eds., *Women on the U.S.-Mexico Border: Responses to Change* (Boston: Allen and Unwin, 1987); José David Saldívar, *Border Matters: Remapping American Cultural Studies* (Berkeley: University of California Press, 1997); Chela Sandoval, "U.S. Third World Feminism: The Theory and Method of Oppositional Consciousness in the Postmodern World," *Genders*, 1991, 10, 1–24. In *The Militarization of the U.S.-Mexico Border, 1978–1992: Low-Intensity Conflict Doctrine Comes Home* (Austin: Center for Mexican American Studies, 1996), Timothy J. Dunn presents an invaluable recent history of U.S. policy toward the border, examining its sources and influences as well as many of the practical effects.

38. Lynda Forsha, "Introduction," in Sally Yard (ed.), *in-Site 94: A Binational Exhibition of Installation and Site-Specific Art/Una Exposición binacional de arte-instalación en sitios específicos*, (San Diego: Installation Gallery, 1994), 8. For a history of the inSITE programs by Michael Krichman and Carmen Cuenca, see <http://www.insite2000.org>.

39. See Néstor García Canclini, *Hybrid Cultures: Strategies for Entering and Leaving Modernity* (Minneapolis: University of Minnesota Press, 1995), 100, for a discussion of the "public" as a concept.

8

Hybridities and Histories
Imaging the Rim

DAVID PALUMBO-LIU[1]

"Music, states of happiness, mythology, faces belabored by time, certain twilights and certain places try to tell us something, or have said something we should not have missed, or are about to say something; this imminence of a revelation which does not occur is, perhaps, the aesthetic phenomenon." (Borges)

In his short essay, "The Wall and the Books," Jorge Luis Borges puzzles out the significance of the fact that the emperor who ordered the construction of the Great Wall of China was the same ruler who ordered the burning of the books. What does it mean that the same person commanded that the empire be bounded by a huge barrier and that all prior history be destroyed? What common mentality (if any) anchors these two attempts to control space and the record of time? The answer to these questions is for Borges only imminent, not yet arrived. That imminence describes as well the as yet unsettled sense we have of our "postborder" condition; it is an imminence hinted at by the artwork displayed in *Mixed Feelings* (see the portfolio following the Introduction).

Looking at Larry Herzog's photograph of the U.S.–Mexico wall spilling over the soil and sand and running into the Pacific Ocean (Figure 4.6), we can imagine a similar dual purpose at work here—to extend the border into an infinite, invisible space, circumscribing a lateral boundary across the globe. In revising the historical understanding of borders and the spaces those borders seek at once to define and contain, the wall marks the desire, the will, to reinvent and control geopolitical space. But such inventions, although seeking to control and limit the flow of peoples, also have the effect of evoking, negatively, the possibility of transgression and reappropriation. Making art is one way of reappropriating the semiotics of the border and resignifying them, of expanding the possibilities of signification outside their "official" purpose, and thereby pointing as well to the human effects such actions cannot anticipate.

Borges surmises that the building of the wall and the burning of the books might have indeed been working at cross-purposes ("perhaps the burning of the libraries and the erection of the wall are operations which in some secret way cancel each other"); so too might we consider that the attempt to maintain the border is constantly under revision given the persistent historical revisions not only of "globalization," but of other, less broad and publicly heralded movements and intentions that seem to fly underneath the radar of our immediate historical sense.

The Great Wall of China as we imagine it exists in an entirely different historical epoch from ours; walls no longer aspire to, or even desire, such rigidity and permanence. The history of amnesties for and recriminalizations of migrant flows across the border tells us that. Those attempting to maintain the United States–Mexico border are persistently forced to revise their goals and methods—this "wall" must of necessity be made flexible to accommodate the shifting demands of transnational capital. The border thus marks a space open to negotiation, as nations themselves have yet to settle on policies that can ensure the proper control of such movements, given the imperatives of the moment. In our age, the border is not destroyed, but rather reimagined, and history itself continues to grapple with the problem of how to represent such a shifting and complex phenomenon. In art, we might take to heart Borges's notion that "this imminence of a revelation which does not occur is, perhaps, the aesthetic phenomenon," the puzzling out of these new formations of mixed feelings, the anticipation of a world under construction and revision, the struggle to represent the "new" without knowing exactly its entire nature, is concomitant with the production of new artistic forms, whose own contradictions and multiple meanings index that unsettled condition.

When speaking of the United States–Mexico border from the perspective of Asia Pacific American studies, there are numbers of points of contact.[2] William Randolph Hearst produced a film that depicted the invasion of the United States by hordes of Chinese. What is significant is that this prime exponent of Yellow Perilism (and Asian exclusion) did not have the Chinese come directly across the Pacific, but rather across the United States–Mexico border. Perhaps this was because it was not technically feasible to film such an oceanic invasion on a massive scale, but perhaps (also) this depiction served to convey the still-persistent fear of "invasion" (legal or illegal) by peoples of both "Latin" and "Asian" backgrounds. Although the histories of these two peoples are in Hearst's film only imaginatively linked, the film uncannily anticipates the revision of the United States that occurred after the 1965 Immigration Act, which lifted the quota system set by the 1924 National Origins Act and opened the door to immigration from Latin America and Asia, and hence prompted the fears of those troubled by the possibility that the border was now ungovernable, that the United States would never again look "the same." In many respects, they were right.

Another example of the historical convergence of Asian and Mexican immigration to the United States in the cinematic imaginary is that still remarkable, first and only "all Asian" Hollywood film, *Flower Drum Song* (1961). Here we have the resolution of conflict brought about by the main character's self-proclaimed identity as a "wetback," wherein the illegal immigrant from Hong Kong substitutes the Pacific for the "Rio Grande." One wonders how May-li comes to use the term? The night before her marriage, she wanders disconsolately into the living room and absentmindedly turns on the television (this automatic gesture implies her quick acclimatization to the modern American habitus). An image of a Mexican woman appears, dressed in a peasant frock, speaking to a white sheriff. She is distraught, "I cannot marry Rodriguez, I came across the Rio Grande illegally, I am a wetback!" To escape from her arranged marriage, May-li confesses and exhibits her illegality. She retools the woman's speech in her own confession: "I came across the *Pacific Ocean* illegally—I am a wetback!" In transposing an inter-American crossing to a trans-Pacific one, May-li inadvertently marks what will be the two most dramatic sites of new immigration in the second half of the twentieth century and unconsciously draws out their historical and problematic convergence.[3] What is most germane here is that this narrative already acknowledges, in whatever unconscious a manner, the historical occasion of the revision of "America" by legal and illegal means. The particular history of the Immigration and Naturalization Service's "Operation Wetback," which sought to control the United States–Mexico border under newly urgent conditions that demanded the control of new migrant labor from the south, takes on a larger, trans-Pacific, hemispheric significance.

In this essay I will approach the subject of the aesthetic representation of "mixed feelings" at the United States–Mexico border by arguing that the historical occasion for this new art incorporates Asia and Asian-American as well—"mixedness" at the United States–Mexico border should be understood to take place in the newly invented hemispherics of the Pacific Rim, a regional identity that stands in uneasy relation to national, racial, and cultural identities. I will thus engage the modern history of U.S./Asia/Pacific/Mexico/Latin America incorporation, and use this discussion to highlight some of the conceptual and critical problems such mixedness presents to our sense of art and its meaning. First, I discuss the issue of art and nations—how do our senses of mixedness relate to the idea of national identity, and how do our new senses of national and regional identity in a postborder condition produce different notions of art? Next I will outline some of the ways in which Asia and what I call Asian-America might appear in this project on postborder art; finally, I will make some theoretical comments on how we might, or might not, be able to ascertain "mixedness," and relate that problem to the issue of nations, regions, and borders.

Nations and Art

Even today, when we go to a museum and approach a work of art, we read it against a tiny white card affixed just outside its border. There is no telling whether we read the card first, before we view the painting (let us say it is a painting), or whether we are able to suppress our curiosity and attempt first to view the painting "naively," that is to say, without the benefit of the information displayed on the card. But if and when we do glance over to that card, we find the essentials: title of work, medium, artist's name, date of birth and possibly death, and nationality. Each of these bits of information makes different claim regarding the ownership, or proprietorship of the work a of art. These data forge alliances, linkages, affiliations to art history, familial history, national identity, regional and ethnic identity, and historical period itself.

Whereas the title and medium fix the painting within some aesthetic history, the name of the artist calls up the productive biography of the artist—that which is produced by and about her or him, in works of art, critical assessments, life stories, etc. The dates locate the artist in some historical time frame. But what does the national identity seek to convey to us? What sense of "culture" (continental, oceanic, "civilizational," spiritual, regional, national) is referenced? What continuity, even amid historical change, is evoked, if not a continuity that is named, precisely, "national culture"? Each of the pieces of information found on the card not only contributes to a reasonable and coherent explanation of the painting's own identity, at least as far as we can agree on essential information, but also lays out the possibilities for any and all of these affiliations to lay claim to the work of art as one of its own.

The situation of art today, at and across the borders of nations, calls for a questioning of those categories—do they make sense any more, or do they refer to a constellation of facts no longer as immediately and self-assuredly relevant as before? We can center our discussion on the following question: in this situation, does the "national" hold any semantic value in an age of art characterized by a radical revision of the contents of national identity (who belongs, what belongs, etc.), by increased hybridization of race, ethnicity, and nationalities; by increased migrancy and transmigrancy between and among different geopolitical spaces; by the proliferation of web-based art that would seem to ignore such groundedness and location; and, finally, by a newly intensive and extensive global economic system (and its accompanying neoliberal ideologies) that seems to cast the nation out as a point of reference, settling instead on the notion of unbridled freedom of the marketplace and constantly (re)invented forms of representation and mediation?[4] One key concern of the present inquiry is thus to understand the valence of "national culture."

The notion of "national art" is inseparable from the history of the institutions that collect, house, curate, and display it. In the modern age, these museums have been intimately linked to national projects. Art was to define national character, history, culture, imagination, and spirit. The Louvre itself was famously constructed as a national monument to the Revolution, a fact now buried under centuries of historical encrustation, the Louvre transformed into an icon of official high culture. In 1792, Jacques-Louis David remarks: "France must extend its glory through the ages and to all peoples: the national museum will embrace knowledge in all its manifold beauty and will be the admiration of the universe."[5] So too, did modern art in America become discussed in nationalistic terms. Emerging from a long period of tutelage under Europe and Great Britain, American art became analyzed in terms of its distinctive embodiment of an exceptional national character (as reflected in book titles such as *America As Art*). American art history can indeed be viewed as the site of a persistent struggle between "foreign" influence and mixing, American mastery thereof, and art movements that sought to elide or bypass entirely "nonnative" influence so as to disclose all the more clearly what was exceptional, and triumphant, about America itself.[6]

Now, however, we live in an age that many critics have declared to be "postnational," that is, an age characterized by the reputed weakening of the nation-state and the ascension of transnational, global modes of governance, finance, and telecommunications, as well as rapid and extensive transfers of cultural objects and images throughout the globe. As Saskia Sassen and others have pointed out, our socioeconomic, cultural, and political geographies are made all the more complex by the dense overlays of local and global, subnational, national, and transnational forms of embeddedness that frustrate any attempt to secure a sense of tradition in any simple or decisive fashion. We wonder not only if the integrity and stability of national distinctiveness are weakened (perhaps to the point of disappearance), but also if the ways we "read" art are not also compromised. How do we register and "process" new art phenomena and their attendant modes of representation? The way we "locate" art may be altered by the fact that traditional historical points of reference and framing now seem outmoded, inadequate to the task of locating as precisely as they may have done before the artist in *a*cultural tradition. Critics as different as Daniel Bell and Fredric Jameson have argued that the late twentieth century might be characterized by the rise of simultaneity, of the sound or visual "byte" in place of a grand narrative, of a great unanchoring of history, and its replacement by an intense and superficial fixation on a constantly changing, constantly produced, present. And under such conditions, what has happened to that venerable institution, the Museum? As Herbert I. Schiller has written, in the late twentieth century, more and more the production, packaging, exhibition, and circulation of "culture" are underwritten by corporate interests, many of them transnational conglomerates, whose patronage of the arts has infiltrated or replaced that of national ministries of culture.[7]

Asian-American literature has grappled with such effects on Asia Pacific. Karen Tei Yamashita's novels attempt to represent a new world of intensely revised localities and regional recombinations, as do the essays collected in Frank Chin's *Bullet-proof Buddhas*, and Russell Leong's collection of poetry, *The Country of Dreams and Dust*. Each of these authors, and many others, concentrates on the dense imbrications of various formations of "Asia" and multicultural America, and beyond. Under such historical conditions the descriptive term that seems the most relevant is that of "hybridity," made most current by critics such as Homi Bhabha and Néstor García Canclini.[8] This notion had a great effect on our sense of history and rootedness. But there is no consensus on the precise meaning or import of "hybridity"— hence, our "mixed feelings," our recognition of a state of hybridity, change and unsettledness, and our ambivalence as to its import and value.

One reaction to this condition would be to try to fix the relative value of such transformations: is the current condition of mixing, hybridizing, recontextualizing a betterment of culture or a testament to its decay? Is this progress or destruction? Are the social changes it references positive or negative? What is seen to be preserved, extended in art and national identity, or irretrievably lost? The task of answering these questions engages us in a myriad other concerns that demand to be addressed beforehand. How do we evaluate "progress"? Who are we to pronounce upon the effects of such historical change upon the lives of distant people? How can we isolate a particular national artistic feature that is incontestably "pure" and "original" (and is that in itself an absolute value, and if so, why)? In this essay, I will not attempt to answer these questions, rather I will try to understand more precisely *how* things have changed, how artistic forms have taken on the burden of representing such change, and how we are called upon to interpret such art in newly difficult manners. I will devote my discussion of these issues to the particular region of California, as an element of the U.S./Mexico/Pacific region, especially as it becomes incorporated into an even larger regional identity in a historical reformulation.

California as Pacific Rim Facet

Asia and Asian-American are most usefully understood here as both embedded within the restructuring of California as a Pacific Rim site, and as symbolic "others" whose "otherness" has to be reevaluated. That is, the formerly "foreign" (Asia) is brought within the sphere of the Americas in a particular fashion that is nonetheless consistent with its role in U.S. global development westward (and, as I have argued elsewhere, toward modernity) from the nineteenth century on. And this development took place in a context of even larger shifts in world history.

The image of California long ago was that of an exceptional, unique space and place. Early cartographic depictions make this literal. In R. W. Seale's "A Map of North America of the European Settlements and Whatever Else is Remarkable" (c. 1745), California appears as an island off the west coast of the continent (perhaps anticipating the predicted outcome of the earthquakes that will follow in a century and a half).

Although the Pacific Northwest is still "unknown," the cartographer seems to have a firm idea of the geographic particularity of California. Within a century, we will find California incorporated into the Pacific, as a mediating body between the "Far East" and the West. California's particularity is attached to a modern project that would define the nation as well in modernity.

California was to become the crucial link for the U.S.'s manifest destiny as a Pacific nation, proprietor of what became known as the United States's "Pacific Lake." In the unfolding of history, the early mapping of California as a huge Pacific-American island seems a prescient vision of the central role to which the state will ascend. The futurality of all this becomes clear at the turn of the century, when John Hay declares: "The Mediterranean is the ocean of the past, the Atlantic the ocean of the present, and the Pacific is the ocean of the future."[9] And Senator Albert Beveridge, speaking of the U.S. invasion of the Philippines, notes: "The Philippines are ours forever. . . . And just beyond the Philippines are China's illimitable markets. We will not retreat from either. . . . The Pacific is our ocean. . . . Where shall we turn for customers of our surplus? Geography answers the question. China is our natural customer."[10] Hence, we find California constructed in large part to mediate U.S.-Pacific capital—San Francisco is reconfigured as a Pacific port and the site of a stock exchange, clearinghouse, and a U.S. mint. This new

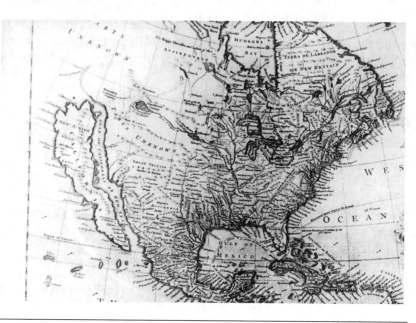

Figure 8.1 R. W. Seale, "A Map of the European Settlements and Whatever Else is Remarkable . . ." c. 1745. (Stanford University Libraries Special Collection.

trans-Pacific identity, which configures California not as the end point of continental development, but the real launching point for *modern* manifest destiny, is not merely a figment of the imagination, but an essential part of the U.S. economic plan.

Historical and economic change indeed transform the very nature of imaging this space. One may gaze upon the idyllic and picturesque"Coronado As Seen Through Japanese Eyes" (1910) and appreciate the integration of "oriental" motifs and techniques, but one might also wonder what prompted the question implied by the title: how *do* the Japanese see Coronado? How is this island, located a few meters off the shore of California, part of an oceanic identity shared with Japan?

What exactly has brought about this convergence of location and "foreign" perspective, and how does the latter affect the former? That is to say, we have to engage the question behind both the production of this graphic image and "our" reading of it. The title itself seems a response to an implicit question. The artist assumes an interest on the part of his anticipated viewer: Americans must wonder how "we" see their Pacific ocean vacation spot. And how does the anticipation of an American interest in a Japanese

Figure 8.2 Haruyo Matsui, "Coronado as Seen Through Japanese Eyes," c. 1910. Southwest Museum of Los Angeles.

perspective, and the imaginative construct itself of "Japanese Eyes," signal both a new cross-cultural interest and a concern over how one national landscape is apprehended by the Other? How does the "oriental" detailing reimagine Coronado as if through a Japanese visual tradition, and how does the very *discrete* yet strategic use of those motifs signal as well an attempt to leave the landscape itself "intact," but still delivered to us as a retitled, repackaged representation? In short, we must read this seemingly innocuous poster as a site of negotiation and discretion; how much will the artist impose his "eyes" upon the scene? How much is necessary to make good on the promise of the title—to offer the viewer a *different* view of Coronado? That is, how much is necessary for "Japan" to appear? This delicate balancing act is hard to appreciate fully without registering the significance of the date of the poster: 1910. For it is exactly 1910 when Japan colonizes Korea, and just after Japan's remarkable victory over Russia. In other words, from its mid-nineteenth-century "discovery" by "the West," Japan has quickly risen to become technologically advanced and capable of engaging the West on its own terms. This dramatic historical change has the effect of "mixing up" the usual categories of race, nation, and power that had previously been obtained.

For instance, in 1914, Kiyoshi Kawakami notes the suspicion with which some in the United States viewed the immigration of Japanese into Mexico and South America. He felt that the alarmist evocation of the Monroe Doctrine to stem this Japanese migration was uncalled for: in his view, this migration was attributed to the fact that the Japanese were merely following the "universal" trend toward modernity along with the rest of the western world:

> Japan clearly realizes the impossibility of casting her lot with the huge, inert mass of humanity that inhabits the Asian continent. She believes that her interest is more closely interwoven with that of the Occident than with that of the Oriental races, that in temperament and inclination she has much more in common with the Western peoples that with those of Asia.[11]

This passage distinguishes the enterprising, modernizing Japanese state from the "mass" of Asia, and articulates a new geopolitical imaginary that refuses to contain nations within racial categories.

My point in insisting that we pay due regard to the various historical occasions that have forced us to reimagine borders, and the representation of national spaces in art, is that those histories tell us much about how it is that the mixing of certain kinds of art is itself a reflection of a new set of cultural and national coordinates, in which old certainties give way to new recombinations and revisions of space, place, and identity. "American" art, like much art today, cannot but be affected by these radical changes in global history. The mid-twentieth century, especially the post-World War II period, presented the occasion for dramatic changes in California. The effects of the GI bill, the return of soldiers and their movement westward, the tremendous boom in housing and highway construction that accompanied it, all took place as the state retooled itself for the postwar economy.

Of particular relevance to this essay is the increased role the Pacific played in reforming California. Not only did the wars with Japan and Korea and Indochina speak of America's deepening involvement in East Asia, but as noted above, the 1965 Immigration Law, which removed the quota system for immigration set down in the 1924 National Origins Act, had the effect of dramatically increasing the immigration of people from Latin America, Mexico, and East Asia. Thus economic restructuring, geopolitical events (including Nixon's recognition of China), and immigration legislation all had a profound effect on California's Pacific aspect.

This in turn had a huge effect on the spatial and socioeconomic imaginary. Whereas the sixteenth-century map alluded to earlier had California set off from the continental United States as an island unto itself, floating somewhere between Nevada and Hawaii, the reimagining of the contours of the state and its precise location in a new Pacific economic order were gradually becoming more distinct. In 1970, Rudolph Peterson, president of the Bank of America (originally called the Bank of Italy), makes the inscription of California within the Pacific Rim perfectly clear in his redefinition of local and global spatial identities. This redefinition illustrates clearly my reasons for seeing this as the critical grounds for the mixing of the United States, Asia, and Mexico:

> When I speak of the Pacific Rim, I am putting the broadest possible construction on the term—the western coasts of South America, Central America, our own continent, and extending beyond Australia and the Far East to India. There is no more vast or rich area for resource development or trade in the world today than this immense region, and it is virtually *our own front yard*. . . . Were we California businessmen to play a more dynamic role in helping trade development in the Pacific Rim, we would have giant, hungry new markets for our products and vast new profit potentials for our firms. [emphasis added][12]

Not much has changed in spirit in the years since Beveridge. The domestication of the Pacific seems to have proceeded apace, with the late capitalist mode of production facilitating what monopoly capitalism could only hope for. As transnational capitalism hit its stride, the often burdensome apparatuses of monopoly capitalism gave way to a much more flexible, agile, transborder set of operations and protocols that integrated the region all the more effectively.

This redefinition of the local discloses the transfer of power to multi- and transnational interests. With a mixture of fear, fascination, and hungry anticipation, Viviano and Chinn write in 1982:

> The simple truth is that San Francisco's economy is no longer unfolding in the boardrooms of New York, the committee rooms of Washington, or the back rooms of Sacramento. . . . The Bay Area is slowly being drawn into a second great frontier of new possibilities: a transpacific urban community that will be the globe's most formidable economic powerhouse by the end of the decade. . . . In short, the cities of the Far East [Singapore, Seoul, Kuala Lumpur, Hong Kong, Taipei, Tokyo, Bangkok, Jakarta] are emerging as the nodal points of the twenty-first century—and no other western city is in a better position to join them than San Francisco.[13]

Capital investment in the Pacific included the proliferation of off-shore operations, export-processing zones that, under the North American Free Trade Agreement, produced a particular link between East Asian and Mexican export-processing zones, and the creation in China of "special economic zones" to facilitate the integration of China into the Asia Pacific economy. The new "open ports" of China, the export-processing zones of East Asia and Mexico, are all extraterritorial spaces that create a particular porousness and heighten the rate of influx and reflux of global capital.

We find the formalization and facilitation of this new "rim" as a special economic zone in 1989, when Australia's Prime Minister, Bob Hawke, formally proposed an intergovernment organization, the Asia-Pacific Economic Cooperation (APEC) including Australia, Brunei, Canada, Chile, China, Hong Kong, Indonesia, Japan, Malaysia, Mexico, New Zealand, Papua New Guinea, the Philippines, Singapore, South Korea, Taiwan, Thailand, and the United States. Originally it was assumed that the Russian Republic, which inherits virtually all of the old Soviet Union's Pacific real estate, would also enter. In sum, the "mixedness" of postborder California has everything to do with the ways the invention of the modern Pacific Rim has drawn together particular national and subnational economic and cultural spaces, in dense and overlaid ways that make it nearly impossible to disaggregate them.

The larger and deeply imbricated issues of national and transnational Asian-American identities are well-captured in Alice Yang's essay, "Siting China: On Migration and Displacement in Contemporary Art." Here Yang historicizes the shifting signifier, "China," across and between China, Taiwan, Hong Kong, and other diasporic locations in which China takes root as a hyphenated term. She ponders the varied historical referents that are too neatly subsumed under that name, and explains how Chinese-American contemporary art wrestles with that unsettledness.[14] In other essays from the same volume, Yang focuses on the particular economies of sexuality and gender as found in the works of artists such as Genara Banzon and Hung Liu, whose works explore the traffic in "Asian women" across the Pacific and whose mixed art articulates the contact zones and intermingled histories of Asia and America. Social science works by Paul Ong, Edna Bonacich, and Lucie Cheng and others have alerted us to the particular economies of labor, gender, and commodity production that are enabled by the invention of this Asian-American network.[15] All of which is to say that any consideration of "mixed art" has to account for the historical forces that enable, drive, and sustain the mingling and traffic between various national sites. Once set in motion, such mixing both calls into question previous modes of organizing social, cultural, and national worlds, and produces new modalities, not simply as mental constructs, but as concrete reformulations of material practices. I argue that the connection between "culture" and material history has to be acknowledged and wrestled with if we are to begin to make sense of either separately.

One of the most startling instances of the hybridization of local space and its cultural and material effects is found in Monterey Park, California. Monterey Park occupies some 7.7 square miles eight miles east of Los Angeles; it is one of eighty-four cities incorporated within Los Angeles County. It has the particular distinction of being the only city in the continental United States with a majority Asian population: some 56% of its 60,000 inhabitants are of Asian origin. Between World War II and the 1960s, the city grew in the aftereffects of the wartime economy, with new housing developments and GI loans. By the 1960s, it had become a modest middle-class suburb, attracting Latinos from East Los Angeles and Japanese-Americans from West Los Angeles, as well as Chinese-American professionals moving out of downtown Los Angeles Chinatown.

This produced a critical problematic in Monterey Park, for by the late 1970s, the city was suffering from a seriously weakened economy, its inactive commercial district decimated by the flight of capital to areas receptive to large-scale developments such as malls. The preservation of the suburban community was at a crisis point when there appeared what seemed to be a godsend. On one hand, more and more Los Angelenos were attracted to Monterey Park. But, far more significantly, large numbers of affluent, well-educated Chinese from abroad began coming to Monterey Park and investing their money. We have then the convergence of assimilated, upwardly mobile migrants from the Los Angeles urban area, and Asian immigration from overseas. It was the latter whose arrival was the most conspicuous. Instead of locating in traditional niches such as restaurants, groceries, and garment work, these new immigrants were involved in banking, real estate, health services, computer technology, and international trade in Los Angeles and, crucially, were connected to Pacific Rim economies as well. Monterey Park entered the circuit of transnational economy under the sponsorship and management of Chinese, who owned between two-thirds and three-fourths of all businesses.

Not only did the locals see their economy taken over by these investments, but, more visibly and startlingly, the built environment became a sign of this transformation, as former shoe stores, tire stores, veterinary hospitals, even doughnut shops, became converted into banks that had conspicuously posted Chinese business signs and advertising. Thus, the "appearance" of the third world in Monterey Park (cramped, high-density, foreign-language "cubicle" storefronts) is directly tied to the logic of capitalist innovation and its "creative destruction" of prior forms for the sake of greater accumulation. Here, that accumulation is attached to the particularities of transnational capital's penetration of national space, and the effects of such penetration on the quotidian landscape.

In such representations of lived space, we have a dramatic departure from the depiction of Coronado as seen through "Japanese eyes" in 1910. In the space of a little more than a half century, Asia has become an integral (and therefore for some disturbing) element in the American landscape—not as an occasional imaginative projection, but as a quotidian reality. The ornamental Oriental—as expressed both in the painting techniques used to signal an "Asian" perspective, and in the graphic lettering style pointing to the hybridization of English language and "Asian" orthography—is displaced.

Figure 8.3 Monterey Park, c. 1994. (Photo by Timothy Fong.)

What we find instead is the actual intrusion of those writing systems into the "American" city-space, crucially indexing the embeddedness of the economic activities that link Asia to America.

The impact of this image (Figure 8.3) relies precisely on accessing a prior, normative world in which such writing systems would not be found outside a museum or textbook. The invasion of "oriental" characters and their rough and seeming haphazard (and therefore unpredictable) mingling with other foreign and domestic languages are remarkable only when juxtaposed in the imagination with a world in which such mixings were not likely, or perhaps even possible. Figure 8.4 picks up the theme of the density of this overlayering and the compression of spaces together.

Here again we find a sense of collusion, claustrophobia, and inevitability. Note how the individual houses are indistinct, subordinated as simply part of a mass of repetitions of details all condensed together. The title of the photo itself seems too broad, as it collects this heterogeneous mix into one spatial designation. In short, the title can neither depict nor name particulars, but rather a condition of mixedness. This, I would argue, is the logical response to a world newly fabricated (although one might well argue that the mixing had begun long long ago, and that it is rather only the most visible manifestations of that process that capture our attention now, when, one might say, it is "too late" to do much more than remark upon it). Both these

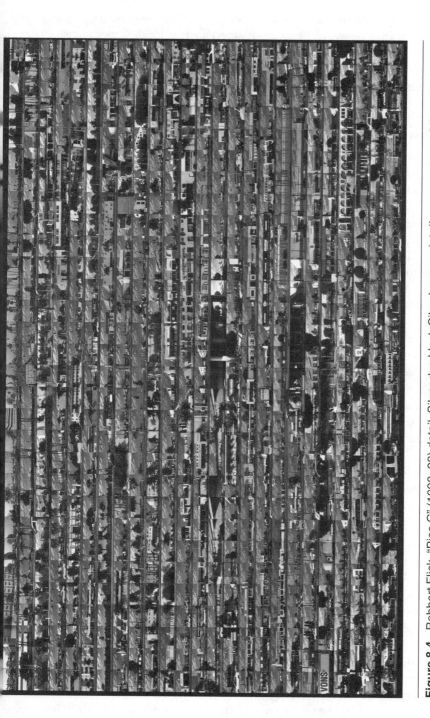

Figure 8.4 Robbert Flick. "Pico C" (1998–99) detail. Silver dye black Cibachrome print. (Image courtesy of the artist.)

images also share a sense of proliferation, the invasion and collusion of formerly separate worlds. This holds especially true for the latter image, which, like the Herzog photograph alluded to earlier, seems to spread out indefinitely across the horizon, perhaps implicating the space far outside the frame of the picture itself.

Intimating the "Postborder"

Mixed forms have always existed in art. Dozens of modern examples of cross-cultural "influence," or the integration of "foreign" elements into domestic art production, are available to us. Think of Monet's paintings at Giverny (indeed, the entire staging of "The Orient" in that space). What distinguishes contemporary allusions to, or use of the formerly foreign? The almost-universal starting point for such meditations is the permeability of national spaces in the twentieth century. This, again, is not entirely new. I think immediately of Americo Paredes's novel of the Texas-Mexico borderland, *George Washington Gomez*, which takes place between the 1920s and 1950s. In one of the earliest moments of that narrative, we find an allusion to a bar called "The Blue Danube," and someone called "Sara Juevo." What then is new about finding the unexpected traces of another nation in one's own backyard? Rather than claim that something absolutely new now gives us a set of unprecedented "mixtures," it is better to understand these phenomena as pointing to different set of historical coordinates and interpretive possibilities.

Jameson's notion of postmodern "pastiche" notes the passing of historical sense, the unanchoring of objects from history:

> In our time, it is technology and the media which are the true bearers of the epistemological function: whence a mutation in cultural production in which traditional forms give way to mixed-media experiments, and photography, film and television all begin to seep into the visual work of art (and the other arts as well) and to colonize it, generating high-tech hybrids of all kinds, from installations to computer art. . . . This is the true moment of image society, in which human subjects henceforth exposed to bombardments of up to a thousand images a day . . . begin to live a very different relationship to space and time, to existential experience as well as cultural consumption.[16]

Although this view seems most compelling, and fits well with much of what I am discussing here, I will be trying to see if all forms are equal in this regard, or whether specific graphic strategies and compositions point to a more complex and multifaceted expression of a postborder condition.[17] Again, when I speak of something called a "postborder condition," I am not asserting the demise of borders, but rather a condition within which the functions of borders have been revised significantly, their fields of contain-

Figure 8.5 Komar and Melamid, "Series Bayonne, 1990." Chromogenic prints.

ment shifted, their applications uneven, and their effects difficult to predict as the revision of national and global spaces continues. Under such conditions, Jameson's well-known critique of postmodern "hyperspace," in which the disappearance of historical sense results in a flattening out of the perceptual landscape, where nothing exists to anchor a sense of place, where time itself is contained in ephemeral instances that seem to emanate from nowhere and lead to nowhere—seems exaggerated, or at least only partially effective. Rather, I will argue that we find instead extremely uneven moments that *do* reference the historical and the real.

As we move through the next set of images, my questions will be: how have art forms responded to this historical condition? And how do the differences between artistic expressions or representations of this condition index a set of conceptual problems with which we must deal if we are to understand the complexity of the issues at hand (rather than reduce them back into our former modes of apprehending what we call "mixed" forms)? I have selected the images for their attempts to draw together formerly separate spaces, how they consciously or unconsciously depict the problematics of mixing and recombining national spaces. Figure 8.5 is from a series taken in the 1990s by Komar and Melamid, two Russian émigrés, to Bayonne, New Jersey.

The ostensible purpose of these transplantations of "foreign" elements onto "American" soil (New Jersey, no less) is to illustrate the artists's appreciation of the fact that America is home to many cultures. The juxtaposition of the American "ordinary" with the monuments of the foreign in the series is particularly interesting to me. Other photographs in the series place the Pyramids, the Kremlin, and other national landmarks in the midst of New Jersey. Here we have Mount Fuji. This juxtaposition seems arbitrary; there is a sense of *substitutability* here that makes it a matter of indifference as to whether the transposed object is an Egyptian pyramid, a Russian state building, or a Japanese mountain. Because of this substitutability, there seems nothing particular about any one of these juxtapositions; they refer only weakly to their national semiotic, and the meaning of the resulting image could be seen as easily paraphrased, as the artists's own statement attests.

A different dynamic from this mixing together is atomization and reconstruction, suggesting the disaggregation and remixture of indigenous elements of what might constitute national identity, and showing the analytical disaggregation and remixture of indigenous elements. Here is a photograph of a work by the Cuban artist, Antonio Fernandez, who describes his works in these words:

> I gathered hundreds of these objects to make the map of Cuba on the wall, to represent the "desired country" of many of my fellow Cubans. I'm trying to say that the things, the stuff that we produce and place in our surroundings, that we like and in some cases adore, is a reflection of our own image, of how we perceive ourselves and how we want others to perceive us. In the process of creating that image of ourselves, the origins and the points of departure for any symbol, icon or image that will be used are deleted, overviewed, considered of less importance. The accumulation of images, rituals, things, and ideas that results is nothing but what we truly want to be, the mirror where we look at our own desire. That Cuba (a very eclectic, mixed, even contradictory aggregate) would be, therefore, the "Desired Country." [Another piece], "Dream World," is in a way about nationalism: a world made out of little Cubas is the ideal world for those that, from the island, measure the world according to how much it resembles or differs from their national, even local "cultural model."[18]

Fernandez's works differ from the photos by Komar and Melamid in that, instead of taking as ready-made the established icons of national identity and juxtaposing them into/onto American space, Fernandez queries the very constitution of national identity, its building materials, and the imagined relation of the people to those materials. Here, each individual item becomes transformed into a symbol of a collective national vision, and the artistic process is tantamount to the recollection of national identity, gathering seemingly disparate acts of creation into the collective identity that each piece references separately. As Fernandez says, the "particular origins and the points of departure" for any symbol are of less importance than their shared sense of the nation. The "mixing," the aggregation of images, is thus held together by a common sense of national imagination. In the second work, "Dream World," Fernandez projects that desired image globally. The "Cuba" constructed out of disparate works of cultural production is

Figure 8.6 Antonio Fernandez, "Pais deseado (Desired Country)" 1994. (Slide from artist.)

placed into relation with the rest of the world; the "dream" here is the meditation on national difference projected upon the global stage. In both cases, the point of contact and interpenetration is distinctly located on the field of artistic representation, and produced as a collective national process.

Like those of Fernandez, the ceramics of Esterio Segura, another Cuban artist, comment upon the locatedness of Cuba, but Segura's representation of Cuba references the historical appearance of Leninism, Sovietism, and Asia on Cuban soil. If Fernandez's work locates the production of Cuba both physically and psychically within the hands and minds of the Cuban people, Segura fashions a representation of the interpenetration of the domestic and foreign.[19]

Segura's use of "Asia" here (referencing "Red China's" struggle with the USSR for socialist hegemony?)—and in another piece from the series entitled "Karl Marx Foundation," which casts Marx as a scowling white ceramic figure flanked by the female Cuban figures we see here, and ornamented with Oriental details—might be contrasted with the uses of Asian iconography in what Mexican artist and critic Reuben Gallo calls "Orientalism" in recent Mexican art. Gallo sees a trend in the 1990s of incorporating the "Orient" into Mexican art as a response to the neo-Mexicanism of the 1980s, which, he argues, puts forward a nationalist agenda of "purity." He sees the Mexican evocation of the Orient as a random gesture showing the utter arbitrariness of national identity: "If Neo-Mexicanism sought to be the main

Figure 8.7 Esterio Segura, "Paseo de carnaval" (1995).

expression of a cultural essence, Orientalism considers identity a game of masks in which there are no essences, only appearances." This is done through citations of what he calls Mexico's absolute opposite. Gallo writes, "in Japan, everything is orderly; in Mexico, everything is chaotic."[20]If we accept this view, then we can take the works viewed thus far and reinterpret them according to the different ways they handle this question of the reputed "arbitrariness" of identity versus "national essence." In this case, the Russian photographs would point to the randomness of national identity— any combination of national monuments could be transposed onto the American landscape. In contrast, Fernandez's pieces could be read as typically evoking national essence.

But this seems to me to be too simple an interpretive strategy. For, in point of fact, the Russians did not pick just any country for their statement. They chose the United States, and chose to articulate in particular its ideology of inclusiveness, an ideology that could function only in conjunction with America's geopolitical power. The folding of the historical density of the pyramids, of the Kremlin, of Mt. Fuji, into the bland temporal flatness of Baronne cannot be taken as anything less than a confirmation of the global reach of American ideology. The series, after all, is set in exactly the period just after the collapse of the USSR, after the tearing down of the Berlin wall. If we adopt the rhetoric of Francis Fukuyama, we find here the triumph of liberal democratic ideology, and the transposability of all other national spaces onto the United States—the end of ideological borders. Thus, in even what appears to be a fanciful slapping together of icons, the artworks reference an historical context whose genesis and consequences are hardly arbitrary. And Fernandez's works, although admittedly "nationalistic," are complicated by both the specific nature of their nationalist utopianism and the fact that utopianism in its global aspirations is countermanded forcefully by the reality of Cuba's position in the current world order, the persistent recognition of the gap between national vision and international realities. Finally, Segura's porcelains do not seem either particularly arbitrary or nationalistic—rather than being attached to such questions, Segura's works instead seem involved in tracing these historical conjunctions of the "foreign" and the "domestic." Thus, Gallo's linking the "mixing" of Asia and Mexico to the postmodern, the "random," and "arbitrary" may work in certain cases, but is far from universally applicable. Different artists explicitly deploy such techniques to articulate a sense of the nation as produced not arbitrarily, but historically.

Asian-American: Imbricated Histories

Turning now to Asian-American art, we find these same issues addressed by a Japanese American who goes by the ironic acronym "I.T.O." (International Trade Organization?). Like the works just discussed, this piece, entitled "Ethnocentrism II: The Revenge of the Sushi," juxtaposes different national and ideological symbols. The meaning of the work might seem elusive, but not if one puzzles through the title. The sushi's "revenge" seems to be indicated simply by its dominant presence in the foreground, which sets in relief the huge photograph of the whale's eye in the background.[21] The question becomes, against what is the "sushi" taking its revenge? And what does sushi, after all, stand for? Perhaps it is because of my background as a literary scholar, but the reference to that most famous of whales, Moby Dick, and its place in American national symbolism, seems hard to miss.

It is in *Moby Dick* that we find this poetic and historical description of the Pacific:

> To any Magian rover, this serene Pacific, once beheld, must ever after be the sea of his adoption. It rolls the midmost waters of the world, the Indian ocean and Atlantic being but its arms. The same waves wash the moles of the new-built Californian towns, but yesterday planted by the recentest race of men, and lave the

faded but still gorgeous skirts of Asiatic lands, older than Abraham; while all between float milky-ways of coral isles, and low-lying, endless, unknown Archipel-
agoes, and impenetrable Japans. Thus this mysterious, divine Pacific zones the
world's whole bulk about; makes all coasts one bay to it; seems the tide-beating
heart of earth. (Chapter 111, p. 490)

It is precisely into these waters that Ahab will pursue the whale. Here
Melville depicts the Pacific as the great ocean in which vast geographic distances are brought together—the "new-built Californian towns," whose
builders, those "recentest race of men," are contrasted with the "Asiatic" race,
"older than Abraham." Japan seems particularly elusive, however, and is cast
within a different, divine space of "milky-ways of coral isles," which is nonetheless folded back into the arms of the great Pacific, as is "the world's whole
bulk." In its subordination of "all coasts," its diminution of everything to the
status of one of its attributes, the Pacific reigns supreme not only in space,
but in time. Indeed, the life rhythms of the New World are set to the beating
of its heart, the Pacific.[22]

What is most germane about I.T.O.'s evocation of this great American
novel is the novel's own meditation of its own historical moment, caught in
America's shift of gravity, from the old world of the Atlantic to the new
world of the Pacific, a shift I noted at the beginning of this essay. This shift
has a particular effect in making California the most prominent state (the
only distinct part of American geography mentioned in Melville's passage,
for example), and calling attention to the problem of this arena of mixings,
convergences, and regional identities. In short, Melville's novel is laden with
oceanic figures, motifs, and images, which work together with his commentaries on human kind in the modern age, and specifically the link between
that new historical condition and the project of Americanism.[23]

I.T.O. juxtaposes that grand project of nineteenth-century American
oceanic empire-building and national imagining with the late twentieth-
century invasion of Japanese sushi into American haute cuisine. Which itself
indexes the well-known boom in the Japanese economy of the 1970s, and
the huge trade deficit between the United States and Japan, both of which
had a deep effect on America's self-image and confidence in its superiority
and independence. In this juxtaposition, the great whale seems to gaze in
wonder at the centrality of the tiny bit of fish set before it. Like the images
discussed above, I.T.O.'s juxtaposition of national symbols casts them
within a particular historical frame, without which we cannot understand
the motive behind their particular combination.

Finally, let me end this survey of artworks with "Self Portrait 15," by the
Vietnamese artist Dinh Q Le. In Le's montage, we have a different sort of
mixing, which goes beyond juxtaposition, using technology to show the
dense interweaving, coconstructedness of *mestizo* identity. Crucially, if the
figures that flank the central figure are seen as contributing to its identity, we

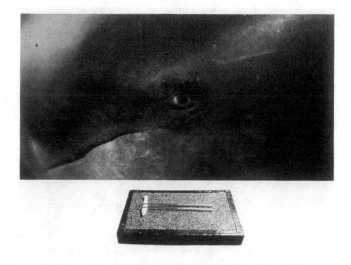

Figure 8.8 I.T.O. "Ethnocentrism II: The Revenge of the Sushi."

cannot ignore the fact that they are not only necessarily *unmixed,* that is, half of their image stands outside the interpixelated conglomerate, but also altered in their figuration in the dynamic of identity production. This is a fitting figure with which to end, for, unlike the previous examples, Le's artwork captures both the theme of mixedness in a profound manner, beyond the relatively simple operations of juxtaposition, and the necessity of using prior forms as points of historical reference. The interweaving of pixels, colors, and images represents the emergent, unimpedible progression of historical change, which is set nonetheless alongside the residual imagery of "unmixed" spaces.

Dinh Q uses the technologies that have played such a crucial role in linking local and global spaces to create the image of his own biographic data. A mix of different cultures brought to bear on Vietnam, the photograph combines the two elements and asserts their inseparable roles in constructing the artist's identity. But it is also crucial to note that to do so, each of those elements must be identifiable; they both stand inside the composite image *and* outside it. As such, this image allegories the situation of mixed art—though I hasten to add, mixed art at *this* stage of history. The question then becomes: how long will it be before that point of reference is lost? Certainly, others have noted that any idea of hybridity relies on the "prehybrid." What I have tried to argue is that the point of reference should not simply be read as an empty, outdated signifier, but as a still-productive force in shaping our understanding of the present. Furthermore, there is no guarantee that mixed forms cannot and will not be disaggregated, reencoded, and remobilized.

Figure 8.9 Dinh Q Le. "Self-portrait 15" from series "Portraying a White God" (1989).

Conclusion

My commentaries should be taken as tentative attempts to read and interpret examples of art that tries to depict a "postborder condition." As I have insisted throughout, there remain huge problems of interpretation. How are we to *read* such images, not only in art, but urban and rural spaces? The border itself might well be read as a sort of processing zone, operating in profound ways not only on the mentalities and imaginations of its inhabitants (think of the border movies that Norma Iglesias discusses in this volume), but also on all who participate or are implicated in the postborder world. Although it is clear that nation-states no longer operate in the ways they did in earlier, "classical" periods, there is simply no way to state with any certainty that the nation has "disappeared." Although its ways of doing business may have changed, its interests nonetheless can still be promoted and safeguarded. The term "postnational" would be better understood to mark a modification of national effects and activities upon a different set of terrains; it is crucial to note that there is no necessary *telos* implied—things can switch back and the nation can certainly recuperate some of its prior functions. The nation is therefore not so much replaced as it is *dis*placed; or, better yet, both the national and global are in constant dialectical modification. It is precisely because the traditional coordinates for identifying and laying claims of ownership to art have been shaken, and because in that destabilization we find ourselves in the midst of a particularly new historical situation, that it is now extremely difficult to decode art of the kind considered in this volume.

One way of thinking of this new historical formation is to argue that "mixed feelings" have very much to do with what Raymond Williams famously called "structures of feelings." Williams describes the gap between experiencing a new historical condition and trying to understand it via newly outmoded interpretive methods:

> There is frequent tension between the received interpretation and practical experience. . . . This tension is often an unease, a stress, a displacement, a latency: the moment of conscious comparison not yet come, often not even coming. . . . There are the experiences to which the fixed forms do not speak at all, which indeed they do not recognize.[24]

Williams goes on to specify artistic and literary forms as those media through which these new structures of feeling are most likely to find expression. He notes "the unmistakable presence of certain elements in art which are not covered by other formal systems is the true source of the specializing categories of 'the aesthetic,' 'the arts,' and 'imaginative literature;'" and argues that

> We need, on the one hand, to acknowledge (and welcome) the specificity of these elements . . . and yet to find ways of recognizing their specific kinds of sociality. . . . The idea of structure of feeling can be specifically related to the evidence of forms and conventions—semantic figures—which, in art and literature, are often among the first indications that such a new structure is forming.[25]

Thus, it is not only in the interpretation or decoding of art that we have difficulty, but also in the encoding, or creating of art about our contemporary age. Williams's notion of "structures of feeling" thus acknowledges the ways art and literature, in their imaginative worlds, can capture an as-yet indistinct intimation of a new historical moment, one that has yet to be fully recognized and set into social discourse. Although we speak all the time of globalization and its effects, only art in its various forms can suggest the multiple, unsettled, and unsettling effects of that historical process upon human beings. And here we should recall Borges's epigraph, which speaks of a different, but I think related "imminence of a revelation which does not occur;" and imagines that this imminence might, perhaps, describe precisely "the aesthetic phenomenon." Borges thus points to both an intuition of meaning and significance (an anticipation of revelation in which that intuition will bear fruit), and to its obdurate resistance to disclose itself. Art is thus itself placed at a sort of border—and mixed feelings thus dwell in that liminal, unsettled, anticipatory state. This unsettledness is well captured in Karen Tei-Yamashita's novel *Tropic of Orange*, in which she describes the appearance of a "New World *Border.*" She acknowledges at once the beginning of a new historical period, but also of the persistence of power, locatedness, and containment.[26] Under this condition, the writer is compelled to write, but the "order" and logic of storytelling are as yet being formed. The following pronouncement from a journalist in the novel could well stand in for the artist:

> I no longer looked for a resolution to the loose threads hanging off my story-lines. If I had begun to understand anything, I now knew they were simply the warp and woof of a fraying net of conspiracies in an expanding universe where the holes only seemed to get larger and larger. . . . I would follow a story or I could abandon it, but I could not stop.[27]

This compulsion to represent a historical reality that can only be intuited, mapped only incompletely, characterizes much of contemporary culture.

In these facets of artistic production and reception, I have argued that any consideration of "mixedness" must take into account the status of the contents that preexist that mixing. What have we (previously) imagined our world to be? What tidy compartments and categories have been used to describe it, and why and how are they no longer there? We must resist the purely celebratory reception of mere surface effects, and attempt rather to understand the historical forces that have brought together these formerly separate spaces, languages, and peoples. We might consider what newly constructed neighborhoods, communities, and regional identities now call upon us to locate ourselves in the present and imagine our futures. In sum, whatever else it might designate, "mixed feelings" most aptly describes a liminal sense of historical time, one which is still able to recall (or, perhaps, simply still strongly imagine) an age of discrete and stable national identities, *and* at once register their *imminent* eclipse. Perhaps that "revelation" of which Borges speaks will some day be known to us as our past history of knowing something new.[28]

Notes

1. I wish to thank Roshni Rustomji, Vanessa Kam, and Antonio Fernandez for all their help and friendship—this article could not have been written without them. I am also very grateful to Michael Dear, Héctor Lucero, and Gustavo Leclerc, Richard Cándida Smith, and all my other coparticipants in this project for their guidance and conversation.
2. For a discussion of my designation, "Asian/American," see my *Asian/American: Historical Crossings of a Racial Frontier* (Stanford: Stanford University Press, 1999).
3. See my discussion of this film in *Asian/American: Historical Crossings of a Racial Frontier.*
4. In a forthcoming essay, "Narrative, Affect and Ethics in an Age of Globalization," I address the issue of media, traditional literary forms, and ethics.

5. Quoted in Andrew McClellan, *Inventing the Louvre: Art, Politics, and the Origins of the Modern Museum in the Eighteenth Century* (Cambridge: Cambridge University Press, 1994), 91. McClellan also notes that in 1791, Armand Kersant stated that the new museum would "affirm at one of the same time the will of the nation" (93).

6. See Joshua C. Taylor, *American as Art* (New York: Harper & Row, 1976). For an excellent study of the subject, see Wanda Corn, "Coming of Age: Historical Scholarship in American Art," *Art Bulletin*, June 1988, LXX.2, 188–207. I thank my colleagues in the Art History department at Stanford, Michael Marrinan and Wanda Corn, for these references on national identity and art.

7. See Herbert I. Schiller, *Culture, Inc: The Corporate Takeover of Public Expression* (Oxford: Oxford University Press, 1989).

8. For a general study of the subject, see Avtar Brah and Annie C. Coombes (eds.), *Hybridity and Its Discontents: Politics, Science, Culture* (London and New York: Routledge, 2000).

9. Quoted in Arrell Morgan Gibson, *Yankees in Paradise: The Pacific Basin Frontier* (Albuquerque, NM: University of New Mexico Press, 1993).

10. Quoted in Howard Zinn, *A People's History of the United States* (New York: Harper, 1980; revised ed. 1995), 306.

11. Kawakami, *Asia at the Door: A Study of the Japanese Question in Continental United States, Hawaii, and Canada* (London and Edinburgh: Fleming H. Revell Co., 1914), 39.

12. Quoted in Hartman, *The Transformation of San Francisco* (Totowa, NJ: Rowman and Allen, 1984), 3.

13. See Frank Vivian and Alton Chinn, "The Hong Kong Connection." *San Francisco Magazine*, February 1982, 54–60.

14. Collected in Alice Yang, *Why Asia: Contemporary Asian and Asian American Art* (New York: New York University Press), 99–103.

15. See, for example, Paul Ong, Edna Bonacich, and Lucie Cheng (eds.), *The New Asian Immigration in Los Angeles and Global Restructuring* (Philadelphia: Temple University Press, 1994).

16. In Fredric Jameson, "Transformations of the Image," in *The Cultural Turn: Selected Writings on the Postmodern, 1983–1998* (New York: Verso, 1998), 110.

17. See, for example, my argument in David Palumbo-Liu and Hans Ulrich Gumbrecht (eds.), *Streams of Cultural Capital: Transnational Cultural Studies* (Stanford, CA: Stanford University Press, 1997).

18. Personal communication.

19. Of course, one should not assume the homogeneity, the unmixedness of "domestic" and "foreign" in the ethnic and racial and cultural identities of Cuba—what I wish to underscore here are the different articulations of mixedness. In Fernandez, difference is positively expressed in the composition of a collective vision that incorporates such differences into a national project; in Segura, we find the representation of foreign ideological intrusions and influences onto precisely that national vision.

20. Reuben Gallo, "L'orientalisme dans l'art mexicain" *Art Press*, no. 243, 19–22.

21. For a treatment of this particular facet of the whale, which plays off Melville's own, see Dick Russell, *The Eye of the Whale.*

22. If one wished to push the theme of "mixing" here, one could attend to Melville's reference to the whale's eyes. Here Melville contemplates whether the whale can mentally process two such distinct images as come from two entirely different sides of his head: "is his brain so much more comprehensive, combining, and subtle than man's, that he can at the same moment of time attentively examine two distinct prospects, one on one side of him, and the other in an exactly opposite direction? If he can, then is it as marvelous a thing in him, as if a man were able simultaneously to go through the demonstrations of two distinct problems in Euclid." Melville, *Moby Dick, or The Whale* (Berkeley and Los Angeles: University of California Press, 1983, reprint of 1979 Arion edition), 340.

23. See Rob Wilson, *Reimaging the American Pacific: From South Pacific to Bamboo Ridge and Beyond* (Durham, NC: Duke University Press, 2000).

24. Raymond Williams, *Marxism and Literature* (Oxford: Oxford University Press, 1977), 133.

25. Ibid.

26. See also Guillermo Gómez-Pena, *The New World Border: Prophecies, Poems and Loqueras for the End of the Century* (San Francisco: City Lights, 1996).

27. Karen Tei-Yamashita, *Tropic of Orange* (Minneapolis: Coffee House Press, 1997), 250.

28. For a discussion of the remapping of national borders and cultures after 9/11, see my essay, "Multiculturalism Now: Civilization, National Identity, and Difference Before and After September 11th," *Boundary*, Summer 2002, 2 29:2, 109–128.

9
Rewriting Cultural Studies in the Borderlands

NÉSTOR GARCÍA CANCLINI

To write the final section of a book about borders may be an impossible task, given that it should offer conclusions and some kind of order to a vague and arbitrary field. Even though we focus on the United States–Mexico border, we do not tread in a securely and clearly defined theoretical space.

Just as Jorge Luis Borges ascribed an animal taxonomy to a Chinese encyclopedia, the preceding essays (and other studies) lead us to classify borders as (1) a boundary that separates two countries; (2) an area to cross over; (3) an area that is impossible to cross; (4) a territory in which each adjacent country risks losing its identity; (5) a territory that allows each country to rediscover the importance of its identity; and (6) the place where Mexico loses millions of workers, many of whom are highly qualified (a 2001 study by the Mexican National Council on Population indicates that of the seven million Mexicans over 15 years old based in the United States, 255,000 are university graduates and postgraduates). The border also represents, however, the route by which large sums of money find their way back to Mexico by way of remittances from immigrants (US$9,213 million in 2001, according to an IDB report), thus contributing to the survival of thousands of Mexican towns.

In his commentary on the aforementioned text by Borges [*El idioma analítico de John Wilkins* (The analytical language of John Wilkins)],[1]

Michel Foucault explains that this wavering between classifications has prevailed for millennia, because of the difficulty in thinking about the Same
and the Other, "the dangerous mixes," and the malaise this provokes.[2] In
connection with the enumeration just proposed, I would add that borders
fail in trying to set limits on the sudden proximity of the dissimilar, and in
resulting attempts to objectify the exotic charm of what is different. The
present book increases that unease by problematizing the border metropolis, partly because the city is, among other things, one of the means used to
organize the heterogeneous.

In these urban/frontier comings-and-goings, we are encouraged to rethink several key themes in cultural studies. Here I will tackle three: the ba-
sics of hybridizing, metropolis and border, and different ways to study these
processes.

Hybridities

Although borders have emphasized hybridities, thereby destabilizing many
certainties in the study of culture, they also suggest a certain ordering of the
multiple processes that intermingle the material and symbolic aspects of
proximate nations.

Intercultural mixes are as old as the differences and encounters between
societies. They became more pronounced as social complexities generated
distinct cultural formations that interacted within each country, especially
as transnational contact was intensified in modernity by travel, economic
exchange, media innovations, and migration.

These processes have been given different names: miscegenation or cross-
breeding, syncretism, creolization, and hybridization. Their meanings overlap to some degree, but they need to be understood in conjunction with
different historical processes and intercultural places in which one term or
another prevails.

The concept of *miscegenation* is used, especially in Romance languages, to
designate interethnic mixing. It identifies the combining of races, i.e., the production of phenotypes through genetic fusion, as well as the joining of customs
and ways of thinking. Miscegenation applies, particularly in anthropological,
historical, and literary texts,[3] to the mixing of Spaniards and Portuguese with
Native Americans during colonial times, and to the multiethnic formation of
national societies during the nineteenth and twentieth centuries. The importance of biological miscegenation has diminished in recent years insofar as skin
color and physical features have lost some significance in social conflicts. Although such features persist in the processes of discrimination and self-rejec-
tion, scientific and political discourse is today more concerned with the
cultural dimension of merging identities. Use of the concept has expanded notably in the study of intercultural processes of the borderlands.

It is customary to speak of *syncretism* when belief systems are being mixed. Historically, this term was used in anthropology and the philosophy of religion to refer to a combination of icons, rites, and practices, e.g., of Catholic saints with African or American deities. Massive migration and the wide circulation of ancient and modern forms of spirituality have generated new syncretic forms beyond the orthodoxy of traditional cults. Chicano and Mexican iconography, along the border and elsewhere, combines (for example) national leaders of an independence movement with prominent media figures, images of Aztlán and devotees to the Virgin of Guadalupe with modern rituals. Presently, the form of syncretism called *New Age* incorporates the simultaneous adherence to beliefs (not only from religions) taken from many lands, and molded as fluid cultural phenomena, less institutionalized than in churches. To cure certain diseases or remove anxiety and stress, the same people turn to allopathic or herbal medicine, or Catholic, Afro-American, and indigenous rituals. The most eloquent cultural expression of these movements is today found in *World Music*.

Countries that experienced the slave trade produced a special kind of intercultural mixing. *Creolization* is the term used in linguistic and anthropological studies to designate the cultural variations and mixings generated from a base language in conjunction with other languages. Examples include the French in America and the Caribbean (Louisiana, Haiti, Guadeloupe, Martinique), and the Indian Ocean (Reunion and Mauritius island); or the Portuguese in Africa (Guinea, Cape Verde), in the Caribbean (Curaçao), and Asia (India, Sri Lanka).

Of all these concepts, miscegenation is favored in studies on race or ethic groups; syncretism, when discussing traditional religious or symbolic mixes; and creolization, to refer to well-defined contact areas. It is interesting to note the varying preferences in some languages for these words, together with the absence of an English term for *mestizo*. In this latter case, specialized books tend to adopt the Spanish word when discussing other societies, and they use, primarily for the United States, the terms *miscegenation, half-breed, mixed-blood*, and, more recently, *hybridity*.

The term *hybridity* has become established in the past two decades, mainly in Spanish, English, and Portuguese, to encompass *all the processes that combine discrete social structures or practices, which already existed in distinctly separate forms, to create new structures, objects, and practices in which the antecedents merge.* We should bear in mind that the so-called discrete structures were themselves the result of hybridizations and therefore cannot be considered as pure sources. The resulting hybrid often adopts paradoxical forms: "Every process of hybridization has the property of making equal what is different, and different what is equal, but in a way in which the equal is not always the same, or the different simply different."[4]

Literary and art critics, as well as social scientists of various disciplines, turn to the hybridity concept to name the vast variety of interbreeding among the cultural inventories of contemporary societies. Hybrids refer to traditional processes that would fall under the labels mixed-race or syncretic, as well as to truly modern fusions in which the highbrow combines with the traditional, e.g., crafts and ethnic music intermingled with contemporary artistic products. Such hybridties also occur when literature incorporates stylistic media devices or messages, or when mixing takes place between artistic disciplines of various origins (jazz with rock, painting with performance), or gastronomies of different countries (Tex-Mex, for instance), and even technologies of diverse traditions (as in the cases of the fantastical alterations of cars by Rubén Oritz Torres and by low-riders; for an example of Ortiz Torres' works, see the portfolio immediately following the Introduction of this volume).

Studies on communicative transnationalization and media reception reveal that film and television circuits (which foster the blending of the learned and the popular, of heterogeneous languages and styles) at the same time cultivate Manichean polarizations between what is national and foreign, Anglo and Latin. Norma Iglesias' excellent text (Chapter 6 in this volume) extensively documents, through border film imagery, the fact that intercultural oppositions and conflicts proliferate along with disparate hybridizations. Moreover, the most successful hybridization does not create only positive processes; as we know, as migrants integrate into a new country, there is usually an enrichment, but also a loss or uprooting from the original society.

An increase in transnational, intercultural mixing generates new hybridities that are sometimes perceived as destabilizing the racial mix that defines what we call national identity. Ignored by simplistic labels such as "American" or "Mexican," the subtleties of mixing these mixtures feel threatening, generating fundamentalist reactions, including a longing to take refuge in one's own identity, or to close national, ethnic, or religious borders. Such malaises may be justified in cases in which the inequality of exchange brings in its wake the extinction of languages, a weakening of cultures, or unequal access to globalized goods and messages. Nevertheless, recent studies on the symbolic effects of globalization[5] show that, in fact, hybridization broadens the range of cultural offerings, complicates the options, and often creates new contradictions. There are no data that foresee a homogenized hybridity as a fatal consequence of globalization.

On the other hand, intensified exchanges and mutual dependencies among countries lead to new challenges: e.g., constructing theoretical/methodological systems for comparative studies of linguistic systems, intermingling communication and artistic processes, as well as mediation of emergent conflicts. From a political point of view, the challenge is to move forward in regulating the increasing exchanges resulting from free trade, and to curb the takeover and monopolization of indigenous cultural industries. This last is perhaps the largest homogenizing threat, due to the control that a very few companies exert on print, music, and film production. Because they usually allow a certain degree of diversity in order to sell more in niche markets, the greatest risk does not lie in absolute homogenization, but in the reduction of cultural production to what is internationally lucrative, and in the stifling of diversity and experimentation.

In short, studies on hybridization are helping to reformulate old subjects addressed by art, the humanities, and social sciences, including identity, difference, cultural pluralism, cultural authenticity, and racism. It has become a useful principle when contemplating the spread of intercultural mixing, both within a society and in transnational movements. However, beyond this first stage, in which the term was used to overcome essentialism by acknowledging the positive aspects of cultural heterogeneity, the *hybridization processes*—not the hybrid as an object—are now understood more fully, making it necessary to distinguish between unconscious and deliberate hybridizations,[6] among hegemonic, resistant, and negotiational ones.[7] Furthermore, this concept is being constructed in a more complex manner in the study of hybrid literary and artistic works,[8] and to further the cultural understanding of a globalizing, regional integration, segregation, and border reproduction.[9]

In contrast to the early sociology of culture, where a tendency prevailed to interpret cultural processes within their national context and noting local antagonisms (among classes or ethnic groups), contemporary research on hybridization has paid more attention to interaction between societies and to border exchanges. We may now ask to what extent intercultural mixes help weaken borders, or inspire forces of resistance to reaffirm what separates us.

Metropolises

Our choice of certain cities as metropolises reveals the different ways in which we develop our relationships with the Other and others. Territorial borders establish close referents: for those who live in Ensenada and Tijuana, San Diego and Los Angeles serve, in some ways, as *their* metropolis. But through migration and the media, links are also established between metropolises and nonneighboring urban centers. The points of reference considered as cultural may even not be large cities.

Such is the case with Mexican and Latin American college students, whose metropolises have been New York, Paris, London, and, more recently, Duke, Iowa, or Stanford, i.e, campuses without a city. Urban fantasies are formed around Disneyland or Disneyworld, or shopping centers that, although they are located within cities, offer nonurban experiences when compared with the typical European city—which has exact parallels in only a few North American cities, such as New York or San Francisco.

What I am saying may be related, to some extent, to the disintegration of the megacity and of many large Latin American cities such as Mexico City,

São Paulo, or Caracas. The transformations occurring in these places are due to numerous endogenous and exogenous factors derived from unequal development: massive migrations, and contractions of the job market; urban politics, housing, and human service policies that are inadequate to effectively deal with population growth and urban expansion; interethnic conflicts, decline in the quality of life, and an alarming increase in insecurity. It is worth noting the contrast between the images of urban development from the 1940s to the 1970s that envisioned cities as the outposts of modernization, and recent images of the city as a chaotic arena for informal markets, for the "ecology of fear,"[10] and places where boundaries multiply through the proliferation of "cities of walls."[11]

Besides being laboratories for an often-degraded cultural plurality, first world cities as well as many in Latin America develop as strategic globalization nodes through financial, computer, and business innovations that invigorate local markets by incorporating them into transnational circuits. Los Angeles, Mexico City, and São Paulo become extreme experiences of borders: between people of many countries, between the global and the local, between deterritorialization and reterritorialization movements.

Undoubtedly, the geographic border between the United States and Mexico offers one of the most novel manifestations of these experiences of transnational bonding: i.e., the various cross-border cities, which are complex binational conurbations that defy most of what classic urbanism teaches us. Lawrence Herzog's essay (Chapter 4) explains the principal dynamics of such cities: the creation of industrial parks that transcend national urban settlements, spaces for transnational consumption and globalized tourism, areas of cross-border residence and slums, shared conflict zones, and invented or imagined connections between different kinds of urbanization. Despite the fluid convergence of urban spaces in both countries, despite everyday cultural exchanges—exemplified by the artwork and urban narratives documented in this book—the convergence of peoples is not supported by legislation that would guarantee their rights. The similarity between "city" and "citizenship" does not yet imply any real proximity between what those words represent. *Living* in a cross-border city does not necessarily mean *being* part of its many dimensions.

I doubt that we are in, or will be able to attain in a few years, a postborder condition. I find, rather, that persistent experiences of divisiveness, persecution, and the multiplication and reinforcement of walls are bringing with them a "postpostmodern" era, if we consider that one core of urban postmodern cultural studies was the dynamic of migration/nomadism.

Borders

From recent studies about borders, and the work of numerous artists who elaborated on the ambivalences they generated, we can deduce that borders can be geographic or symbolic, material or invisible, places of loss or recovery of identity. The hybridities produced by border displacements cannot be confined by fixed categories. Their uncertainties may be captured in scientific studies that are sufficiently flexible and attentive to qualitative differences. But these usually appear, with greater frequency, in the metaphors of artists and writers.

Unlike maps and cultural documents in history museums, which offer stable views of travel and the cultural transitions occuring at borders, many studies today explore hybrid languages and formal solutions that, by their very instability, make it possible to question intercultural confrontations. Travel and borders need metaphors that contain multiple and flexible representations. For such works and performances, documentation does not stop the process and ritualizing does not mean creating a conflict; nor can artistic metaphors and ironies be interpreted in only one way. In my opinion, the most thought-provoking artwork does not simply stop with the postmodern celebration of nomadism, or with a global connectivity in which differences and spaces between societies would dissolve (as was the case in the celebrated work by Yukinori Yanagi, *America*, where flag-boxes that held national colors dissolved because ants moved the colors around).

We now feel a need to avoid the concept of "hotel migration," infused by a postmodern idealization of nomadism. Following authors such as James Clifford, we must distinguish between travel due to work, to persecution, or to "a search for novelties and pleasure."[12] As a matter of fact, ethnographic studies on borders, and the work of artists who investigate them, show that at borders, horizons expand, but that barriers to trade, migration, and identity persist. In Pablo Vila's words, "border crossers" and "border reinforcers" operate in tandem.[13]

Ethnographic research on border crossings—even, as in the case of Tijuana–San Diego, when traversed 70 million times every year—shows that travelers carry with them an openness to difference, but they also report frustrated encounters, that the search for a better (or different) life runs up against fences, police and dogs, death and suspicion, and confusion about conventions governed by different rules. Border-crossers demonstrate their share of discovery and indifference, unrest and transgression, joint borrowings and discriminations of every kind. These ambiguities can be documented, to a degree, in social science studies (especially anthropology), but literary and aesthetic studies and even the language of everyday life better convey the metaphorical weight of artistic media.[14]

Occasionally, artistic events succeed in marking sites, fixing meanings or recreating them in the midst of a world transformed over and over again by travel, or dissolved in passing media events. In other cases, accepting the uncertain meaning of our lives, and the vicissitudes of travel, requires that we concede the instability of referents at geographic borders. At a time without stable maps, artists cannot function as monumentalizing cartographers. In my judgment, the selections in this book, as with other polyphonic programs (the most successful being, perhaps, InSITE), have, among other merits, the effect of convening artists as witnesses who see the world without a definite atlas or cartography, who adopt several points of view simultaneously, and show how they can be interchanged. (Joanne Berelowitz discusses some of these ideas at the end of Chapter 5.)

Perhaps an innovation of this turn of century might be that we will not have to choose between different meanings of artistic work. Nor will we be forced to select a single metaphor to represent travel and multiple borders. Social science studies have passed though that phase that insists on theorizing with a general "border model" in mind; on the contrary, they now encourage the idea that there is neither *one* U.S. vision of the border nor *one* Mexican vision.[15] Far from the certainties of border fundamentalism, and the opposite illusions of nomadism, today we poeticize and understand space with all its paradoxes: as horses facing both ways, so that one does not know if they are coming or going (Ramirez ERRE's *Toy and Horse;* see Chapter 7), or as indecisive balloons that freely violate borders (Alfredo Jaar's *La nube,* see Chapter 5).

In addition to exploring what artists can do with borders and crossings, this kind of work makes us rethink the way art must discover what to do with itself. At a time when many artists feel dissatisfied and constrained by institutions or markets, we wonder whether they will be able to find a vocation in the uncertain territories of the borderlands, reformulating the icons of history (such as the Trojan horse), and even exploring the communication potential of technological resources such as video and the Internet.

Contemporary art, having so often recycled traditional and modern popular cultures, systems of ancient and non-Western cultures, spaces and circuits created for nonartistic purposes, is now trying to decide whether it can recycle itself. If indeed there is still time to recycle the idea of art. Borders and cities, as stages where others' objects and messages are constantly being remade and reused, are auspicious places to formulate this question.

The border as a stage continues to seduce artists, because what remains undecided there serves as a context for art's uncertainties, its indistinct boundaries. Hybridization is not synonymous with reconciliation, in the same way that artistic fusions cannot eradicate contradiction. So-called "postborder cities" are only partially so, because they do not put an end to borders or segregation. It is difficult to imagine globalization as the unlimited circulation of goods and messages, much less of people. Rather than suppressing borders, globalization reorganizes and disorganizes, even as it opens up new horizons for struggle between the Same and the Other.

Notes

1.   Jorge Luis Borges, "El idioma analítico de John Wilkins," in *Jorge Luis Borges. Obras completas* (São Paulo: Emecé Editores, 1994).

2. Michel Foucault, *Las palabras y las cosas* (Mexico City: Siglo XXI, 1978).

3. See Carmen Bernand, "Altérités et métissages hispano-américains," in Christian Descamps (ed.), *Amériques latines: une altérité* (Paris: Editions du Centre Pompidou, 1993); and Serge Gruzinski, *La pensée métisse* (Paris, Fayard, 1999).

4. Eduardo P. Archetti, "Hibridación, pertenencia y localidad en la construcción de una cocina nacional," in Carlos Altamirano (ed.), *La Argentina en el siglo XX* (Buenos Aires: Ariel and University of Quilmes, 1999), 223.

5. Ulrich Beck, *¿Qué es la globalización?: Falacias del globalismo, respuestas a la globalización* (Barcelona: Paidós, 1998); Anthony Giddens; Ulf Hannerz, *Transnational connections* (London: Routledge, 1996); Gustavo Lins Ribeiro, *Cultura e política no mundo contemporaneo* (Brasilia: University of Brasilia, Department of Anthropology, 2000).

6. Ulf Hannerz, *Transnational Connections* (London: Routledge, 1996).

7. Stuart Hall, "Une perspective européenne sur l'hybridation: éléments de réflexion," in *Hermès Cognition, Communication, Politique*, no. 28 (Paris: CNRS Editions, 2000), 99–102.

8. Homi K. Bhabha, *The Location of Culture* (London-New York: Routledge, 1994); John Kraniauskas, "Hybridity in Transnational Frame: Latinamericanist and Postcolonial Perspectives on Cultural Studies," in Avtar Brh and Annie E Coombes (eds.), *From Miscegenation to Hybridity?: Rethinking the Syncretic, the Cross-cultural and the Cosmopolitan in Culture, Science and Politics* (London: Routledge, 1998).

9. Néstor García Canclini, *Culturas híbridas. Estrategia para entrar y salir de la modernidad* (Mexico City: Grijalbo, and Buenos Aires-Barcelona: Paidós, 2001); David Harvey and George Yúdice, "La industria de la música en la integración América Latina-Estados Unidos," in Néstor García Canclini and Juan Carlos Moneta (Coordinators), *Las industrias culturales en la integración latinoamericana* (Mexico City: Grijalbo, UNESCO and SELA, 1999), 181–243.

10. Mike Davis, *Ecology of Fear. Los Angeles and the Imagination of Disaster* (New York: Metropolitan Books, Henry Holt and Company Inc., 1998).

11. Teresa P.R. Caldeira, *City of Walls. Crime, Segregation, and Citizenship in São Paulo* (Berkeley: University of California Press, 2000).

12. James Clifford, *Routes: Travel and Translation in the Late Twentieth Century* (Cambridge, MA: Harvard University Press, 1997), 237.

13. Pablo Vila, "La teoría de frontera versión norteamericana: una crítica desde la etnografía," presented in the International Seminar "Fronteras, Naciones e Identidades" (Buenos Aires, May 26–28, 1999).

14. Scott Michaelson and David E. Johnson (eds.), *Border Theory. The Limits of Cultural Politics* (Minneapolis: University of Minnesota Press, 1997). Pablo Vila, "La teoría de frontera versión norteamericana: una crítica desde la etnografía," presented in the International Seminar "Fronteras, Naciones e Identidades" (Buenos Aires, May 26–28, 1999).

15. Pablo Vila, "La teoría de frontera versión norteamericana: una crítica desde la etnografía," presented in the International Seminar "Fronteras, Naciones e Identidades" (Buenos Aires, May 26–28, 1999).

Translated by Chelo Alvarez

About the Writers

Jo-Anne Berelowitz. Associate Professor of Art History, San Diego State University. Her recent work focuses on representations of the United States–Mexico border. She is particularly interested in the shifting meanings that the concept "border art" has undergone in the past 25 years—from something with a specific denotative meaning to something more connotative, metaphorical, and subjective.

Richard Cándida Smith. Professor of History and Director of the Regional Oral History Office, University of California, Berkeley. He specializes in nineteenth- and twentieth-Century U.S. and European intellectual life, aesthetics and subjectivity, oral history, art, and architecture. He is the author of *Utopia and Dissent: Art, Poetry, and Politics in California* (University of California Press, 1995) and *Mallarmé's Children: Symbolism and the Renewal of Experience* (University of California Press, 1999).

Michael Dear. Professor of Geography and Director of the Southern California Studies Center at the University of Southern California. He was recently a Fellow at the Center for Advanced Study in the Behavioral Sciences at Stanford, and held a Guggenheim Fellowship in 1989. He received Honors from the Association of American Geographers in 1995. He is the author/editor of twelve books including *The Postmodern Urban Condition* (Blackwell Publishers, 2000), which was selected by *CHOICE Magazine* as an "outstanding academic title" for 2000.

Néstor García Canclini. Professor of Anthropology at the Universidad Autónoma Metropolitana-Iztapalapa in Mexico City. He has recently published *La globalización imaginada* (Paidos, 2000), and the Spanish-language edition of his *Hybrid Cultures* (University of Minnesota Press, 1995) won the 1992 Premio Iberoamericana.

Lawrence A. Herzog. Professor in the School of Public Administration and Urban Studies, San Diego State University. He specializes in urban/environmental design and planning with an emphasis on public space, community planning, downtown redevelopment, and comparative urbanization in the Mexico–United States border, as well as Latin America. Awards include Fellowships from the U.S. Fulbright Commission, the Graham Foundation for Advanced Studies in the Fine Arts, and the Center for U.S.-Mexican Studies. He is the author of *Where North Meets South*, University of Texas Press, 1990) and *From Aztec to High Tech* (Johns Hopkins University Press, 1999).

Selma Holo. Director of the University of Southern California's Fisher Gallery and the graduate Master's degree program in Art History and Museum Studies. She has been at the University of Southern California since the summer of 1981. She is the author of *Beyond the Prado: Museums and Identity in Democratic Spain* (Smithsonian Press, 1999). Her newest research will lead to a book on Mexico's political and museological changes.

Norma Iglesias. Assistant Professor of Film Studies, San Diego State University, and Senior Researcher at COLEF. Her areas of interest are border culture, gender studies, social identity, and film. She has a B.A. from the Universidad Autónoma Metropolitana, a Master in Communications from the Universidad Iberoamericana, and a Ph.D. in Communication Theory from the Universidad Computense de Madrid. She is the author of various books, including *The Most Beautiful Flower of the Maquiladora; Entre Yerba, Polvo y Plomo: Lo Fronterizo visto por el cine Mexicano; Medios de Comunicación en la Frontera;* and *Miradas de Mujer: Cineastas y Videastas Mexicanas y Chicanas.*

Phoebe S. Kropp. A Southern Californian by birth, she now resides in Philadelphia where she teaches in the Department of History at the University of Pennsylvania. She is currently completing a book based on her University of California San Diego doctoral thesis, "'All Our Yesterdays': The Spanish Fantasy Past and the Politics of Public Memory in Southern California, 1884–1939."

Gustavo Leclerc. Partner and founding member of ADOBE LA (Artists, Architects and Designers Opening the Border Edge of Los Angeles) since 1992. He was a fellow at Harvard University in the prestigious Loeb Fellowship program during the 1998–1999 academic year. With ADOBE LA, he was involved in the *Revelatory Landscapes* exhibit at the 2001 San Francisco Museum of Modern Art. He co-edited the book *Urban Latino Cultures: La vida latina en LA* (Sage Publications, 1999). Currently he is a research consultant for the Southern California Studies Center at the University of Southern California. Exhibitions include *Urban Revisions*, MOCA Los Angeles, 1994. *Facades: Architecture, Urban Space and the Moving Image*, Long Beach Museum of Art, 1998.

Héctor Manuel Lucero. Born in Mexico City, he is a graduate of the School of Architecture of the Universidad Autónoma de Baja California in Mexicali. In 1998 he was awarded a CONACYT scholarship to pursue a Master of Architecture Degree at the University of Southern California. Since January 2000, he has been directing the Border Cultures Project of the Southern California Studies Center at the University of Southern California. He has recently completed a book on Mexicali's first 100 years of architecture and urbanism (*Mexicali Cien Años*, Editorial Patria, 2002).

Carlos Monsiváis. Based in Mexico City, Carlos Monsiváis is one of Latin America's most insightful and prolific commentators. He is the author of *Mexican Postcards* (1997), and in Spanish, *Amor Perdido* (Lost Love), *Escenas de Pudor y Liviandad* (Scenes of Frivolity and Shame), *Entrada Libre* (Free Entry), and *Rituales del Caos* (The Rituals of Chaos).

David Palumbo-Liu. Professor of Comparative Literature, and Director of the Program in Modern Thought and Literature, at Stanford University. He is the author of *The Poetics of Appropriation: The Literary Theory and Practice of Huang Tingjian (1045–1105)* and *Asian/American: Historical Crossings of a Racial Frontier* (Stanford University Press, 1993, 1999).

About the Artists Represented in the Folio

Laura Alvarez. Born in Southern California in 1969, Laura Alvarez earned her M.F.A. from the San Francisco Art Institute in 1996 and her B.A. from the University of California Santa Cruz. Alvarez is a recording artist, children's book illustrator, as well as an art educator. Presently, she lives in Santa Monica with her husband and two young sons, and commutes to her studio in Huntington Beach where she grew up. As a child, Alvarez spent her summers in Tamaulipas, Mexico, and continues to visit as an adult. The combination of these specific environments and culture, in addition to her time in San Francisco and Los Angeles, informs much of the work she does today.

Mariana Botey. Mariana Botey was born in Mexico City in 1969. She worked in experimental theatre and studied film at the National Autonomous University of Mexico (UNAM) between 1985 and 1991. In 1991 she moved to London to study at Central Saint Martin's School of the Arts. She lived in London for several years, working on many different live arts, installation projects, and exhibitions. In 1998 she returned to Mexico for thesis research, while living and working in the rural community La Garrucha, Chiapas. Botey earned an M.F.A. in 2000 from the studio art department at the University of California, Irvine. Her work in film and video installation experiments with ritual, coded, and subcultural languages as tools for critical resistance.

Mark Bradford. Mark Bradford earned both his B.F.A. and M.F.A. from the California Institute of the Arts. His work draws from art theory and the space where new trajectories of black popular culture are performed—that place being the city. The materials he uses are often recognizable, especially

291

those associated with a presumed class or cultural aesthetic. He often uses style and/or art history as a point of departure to initiate a dialogue that negotiates both cultural hybridity and the location of meaning without an assumed or imposed hierarchy.

Einar and Jamex de la Torre. Einar and Jamex de la Torre were born in Guadalajara, Mexico, in 1963 and 1960, respectively. They currently live and work in Ensenada, Mexico, and San Diego, California. Combining the ancient and sophisticated art of blown glass with disparate materials such as barbecue grills, metal racks, leather, and other found objects, the brothers create works that defy notions of high art and good taste. Using irony, *double entendre*, and embellished iconography, the artists invite viewers to reconsider their preconceptions of what supposedly constitutes "authentic" Mexican art and culture. Drawing from such varied sources as art history, religious iconography, contemporary popular culture, and even the display practices of swap meets and flea markets, the de la Torres's work is driven by a logic of *horror vacuii*, in which every void must be filled, if not crammed, with texture, color, and symbol. The artists' aesthetic directness provokes both humor and discomfort, engaging viewers by catching them culturally off-guard.

Rita Gonzalez. Rita Gonzalez is a video maker, independent curator, and writer living in Los Angeles. Her video work has been shown at the Canal Isabel II (Spain), the Armand Hammer Museum, the Bronx Museum (New York), the Center on Contemporary Art (Seattle), and festivals internationally. Together with Norma Iglesias, she curated a film and video series for *InSITE 2000*, the binational art festival in San Diego and Tijuana. Currently, Gonzalez is the Coordinator of Arts Projects for the Chicano Studies Research Center, UCLA. She is also working on her doctoral dissertation "In transito: Journeys, Itineraries and Historical U-Turns in Contemporary Mexican and Latino Media Art" in the Critical Studies program, Department of Film, Television and Digital Media at UCLA.

Jesse Lerner. Jesse Lerner is a documentary film and video maker based in Los Angeles. His work has screened at the Museum of Modern Art in New York, the National Anthropology Museum in Mexico City, the Reina Sofía museum in Madrid, the Sundance Film Festival, the Guggenheim Museums in New York and Bilbao, and other festivals and museums internationally. His films *Natives* (1991, with Scott Sterling), *Frontierland/Fronterilándia* (1995, with Rubén Ortiz-Torres), *Ruins* (1999), and *The American Egypt* (2001) have won numerous prizes at film festivals in the United States, Latin America, and Japan. In addition to his work as a filmmaker, his critical essays on photography, film, and video have appeared in *Afterimage, History of*

Photography, Visual Anthropology Review, and other media arts journals. He has taught at the University of California San Diego, Bennington College, California Institute of the Arts, and the Centro de la Imagen in Mexico City, and is currently the MacArthur Chair of Media Studies at Pitzer College in Claremont, California. In 1999 he was a Fulbright fellow at the Universidad Autónoma de Yucatán in Mérida.

Barbara Jones. Barbara Jones is a Los Angeles-based visual artist, curator, and member of ADOBE LA since 1998. She received her double B.A. degree from the University of California, Berkeley in Native American studies and Art Practice in 1997. Her multimedia artwork explores representations of domestic space, power relations, and imagined landscapes. She has exhibited her artwork in venues such as the Long Beach Museum of Art in *FACADES: Architecture, Urban Space and the Moving Image* in 1998, and at the San Francisco Museum of Modern Art in *Revelatory Landscapes* in 2001. In 2001 she curated the exhibit *A Symmetrical Aesthetic* at Scripps College's Clark Museum, based on work from their permanent Native American art collection, and is currently the associate curator for the contemporary art exhibit, *Salon: an exhibit about hair.* Jones taught at Otis College of Art and Design in a workshop on vernacular architecture and social space in the Tijuana region in 2000.

Joe Lewis. Joe Lewis was born in New York City in 1953. He earned a B.A. in Art from Hamilton College and an M.F.A. from the Maryland Institute, College of Art. His professional experience includes Printmaker in Residence at the State University of New York, Potsdam, Exhibition Coordinator for the Jackie Robinson Foundation, and Assistant Professor at Carnegie Mellon University. He currently is Dean of the School of Art and Design at the Fashion Institute of Technology in New York, and he serves as the President of the Board of Directors for the Noah Purifoy Foundation.

Daniel Joseph Martínez. Daniel Joseph Martínez was born in Los Angeles in 1957. He is associate professor of art at the University of California, Irvine, where he teaches in the new media and new genres departments of the graduate studies program. He is one of the co-founders of Deep River Gallery. For the past two decades Martínez has engaged in artistic and social practices derived from radical aesthetic discourse, public interventions, identity conscious politics, and his progressive social awareness. He is often noted as the standout at the 1993 Whitney Biennial where his entry figured prominently in the "cultural wars" of the 1990s. Martínez's work, particularly his interventions, interrogate assumptions of public and personal space and cultural hierarchy through audience participation. He is engaged with the idea of radical beauty, and the breakdown of boundaries between two systems of agency and how transformation affects the play of power within a field of social action. His newest series of photographic works and animatronic sculptures created in his exact likeness explore ideas of cloning, simulacra, reality and its virtual, artificial, and subjective manifestations, as well as the dynamics between technological and human development.

Amalia Mesa-Bains. Amalia Mesa-Bains is a sculptor whose altar installations incorporate Mexican historical figures in the arts, religion, and cinema. She uses symbols in her work such as skulls, hearts, crosses, and images of the Virgin. One of her major works, *Altar for Sor Juana Inés de la Cruz* (1982), is a mixed media of wood, paper, and cloth. She has exhibited at the Galería, and also at the Museum of Art in San Francisco. She received her Ph.D. in clinical psychology with a dissertation on Chicana women artists. She has depicted women such as the Virgin of Guadalupe, Catholic nuns, fertility goddesses, Mexican actress Dolores del Río, and Frida Kahlo in drawings and altars. Her altars have transformed from the political Chicano movement to personal cultural exploration.

Milena Muzquiz. Milena Muzquiz is an alumna of California College of Arts and Crafts, Oakland. After living and working in Mexico City, she currently lives in Los Angeles. A multidisciplinary artist, Muzquiz has worked collaboratively on three extensive projects: C.C.S.I.S., Los GORDOS, and Los Super Elegantes, a rock band that combines traditional Mexican music forms and punk. Muzquiz is co-founder of the art space Mamacita Fashion, in Mexico City.

Rubén Ortiz Torres. Rubén Ortiz Torres was born in Mexico City in 1964. He currently lives and works in Los Angeles and Mexico City. Employing a diverse array of artistic practices including photography, video, film, installation, and painting, Ortiz Torres explores areas of cultural intersection and interrelations between Mexico and the United States and resulting hybrid aesthetics. Dissolving distinctions between "high" and "low" art, Ortiz Torres employs icons and emblems from popular culture and manipulates them to address the many levels of exchange among art, society, politics, economics, and culture between these two countries. Ortiz Torres' work draws on numerous visual sources from both countries including sports imagery, pictures of popular Mexican nationalist heroes such as Zapata, Disney cartoon characters, "low-rider" culture, extraterrestrials, and religious images.

Marcos Ramirez ERRE. Marcos Ramirez ERRE was born in Tijuana, Mexico in 1961. He currently lives and works in Tijuana and San Diego. He studied law at the Universidad Autónoma de Baja California and has exhibited throughout Mexico and the United States since 1989. Ramirez immigrated to California in 1983 and worked in wood house framing as a subcontractor. As a relatively unknown artist he was invited to create a project for *In-SITE94*. His work, entitled *Century 21*, was a one-room shanty placed on the plaza of Tijuana's Centro Cultural. The contrast this project explored, of officially sanctioned culture and actual life, was critically well received. His selection for the Whitney 2000 Biennial was a work seen previously in Monterrey, Mexico, called *Stripes and Fence Forever (Homage to Jasper Johns)*. It employs the shape of a flag while evoking the fence separating Tijuana and San Diego.

Norman Yonemoto. Norman Yonemoto was born in 1946. He studied film at Santa Clara University, the University of California at Berkeley, the University of California at Los Angeles, and the American Film Institute. He has been a contributing writer for *Artweek* magazine, and is the author of the commercial films *Chatterbox* (1976) and *Savage Streets* (1983). His work deconstructs and rewrites the hyperbolic vernacular with which the mass media constructs cultural mythologies. Ironically employing the image-language and narrative syntax of popular forms such as soap opera, Hollywood melodrama, and television advertising, Yonemoto works from "the inside out" to expose the media's pervasive manipulation of contemporary reality and fantasy and individual and collective identity. In recent years Yonemoto has produced a series of multimedia installations, many of which address issues of Japanese-American identity in the context of popular media representation, history, and autobiography. In these installations, as in his narrative fictions, Yonemoto locates meaning in the interstices between myth and memory.

Index